PURPOSEFUL INTENT
MOTIVATING YOUR MIND FROM WITHIN

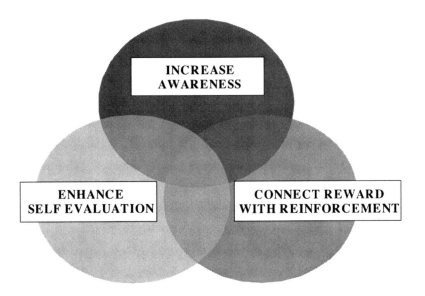

INCREASE
AWARENESS

ENHANCE
SELF EVALUATION

CONNECT REWARD
WITH REINFORCEMENT

THE TRIAD

Dr. Pete Andersen

TRIUS
PUBLISHING, INC.

Published and distributed in the United States jointly by:

Trius Publishing, Inc., P.O. Box 571, Wayne City, IL 62895 • Office 618-898-1300 or 618-599-4804 • www.drpeteandersen.com
BookSurge Publishing, 7290-B Investment Drive, Charleston, SC 29418 • Office 866-308-6235 or 843-789-5000 • Fax 843-577-7506 • www.booksurge.com

The author of this book does not dispense medical advice or prescribe the use of any technique as a form of treatment for physical or medical problems without the advice of a physician, either directly or indirectly. The intent of the author is only to offer information of a general nature to help you in your quest for performance improvement. In the event you use any of the information in this book for yourself or to help others is your constitutional right, the author and the publisher(s) assume no responsibility for your actions.

Library of Congress Control Number: 2009900725

Purposeful Intent: Motivating Your Mind From Within
Pete Andersen, Ph.D.

Paperback ISBN-13: 978-0-9820248-0-5

First Edition printing February 2009
Printed in the United States of America

CONTENTS

Acknowledgments   i

Dedications   iii

Preface   v

1 Science of Purposeful Intent   1

Part One: INCREASE AWARENESS

2 Mind-Body Connection (structure)   49

3 Growing Antennae (ability)   87

4 It's YOUR Job (accountability)   132

Part Two: ENHANCE SELF EVALUATION

5 Pre Performance Evaluation   197

6 During Performance Evaluation   233

7 Post Performance Evaluation   258

Part Three: CONNECT REWARD WITH REINFORCEMENT

8 Principles of Reward-Reinforcement   289

9 Leading Purposeful Intent for Success   323

Appendix   347

Glossary of Terms   402

Index of Names   411

Key Phrases   413

List of Illustrations   418

References   420

ACKNOWLEDGMENTS

I want to thank my wife Marcy for helping to proof manuscripts and listen to concepts that probably made no sense to her until the end product was achieved. I credit my coaches, Dobbie Burton at Evanston Township High School, Evanston, Illinois for instilling a focused work ethic on quality and how to adapt, learn, and outwork a competitor, and, "Doc" and Marge Counsilman who made every swimmer a special member of their family and encouraged us with a scientific "can-do" attitude. A special thanks to John Terhune who taught me how to teach anyone to swim without asking for their IQ, socio-economic background, or ethnicity, and for promoting our swim school phrase, "A pat on the back is better than a kick in the pants." Dr. John Drowatzky, my doctoral advisor, who taught me to question why people are driven to behave the way they do, and the choices they make to understand people and give them a chance. His last words to me on campus were, "Pass it on."

To my children Christian, triplets Doug, Matt, and Brett, born three months into my doctoral program, Brian, and Kate who have the purposeful intent within them to be successful. They all have college degrees and grew up in three different environments to show how this model works! I also thank my American born Norwegian parents, Albert and Elaine, for providing a foundational purpose for learning in the home despite not being able to attend college after the depression.

I need to thank Dr. Tony Victor, a practicing clinical psychologist, for being a good listener that I could bounce my theories and ideas off of, and for providing valuable feedback about the concepts of this work.

I want to thank all the people I have taught and been associated with who have taught me more to gain the knowledge needed over time to write this kind of work.

I also want to recognize two Masters swimming buddies who have set world records, and are like brothers contributing in these special ways: Michael Freshley is a certified financial planner in La Jolla, California, and stated the qualities of top performers who learn to use their abilities in chapter three, Growing Antennae; Vinus van Baalen, Edmonton, Alberta, Canada, formerly of the 1964 Dutch Olympic team, is my main graphic artist and modern art painter with his original works on my website www.drpeteandersen.com

I give special thanks to my editor, Rebecca Jensen, a fine freelance writer and editor, wife and mother – who just happens to love swimming, too. Her suggestions for outline revision and editing of the manuscript have significantly improved this work over these last four years. The folks at Book Surge, division of Amazon, have put these words into eye-pleasing print. The cover and interior design are their creations.

Pete Andersen, Ph.D.

DEDICATIONS

This book is dedicated to my parents, Elaine and Al, my coaches Dobbie Burton, John Terhune, Robert Elliott, Doc and Marge Counsilman, Hobie Billingsley, my Ph.D. advisor Dr. John Drowatzky, and all the performers I have taught, coached and led. My work was also made possible by the help of my wife Marcy and six successful kids, Christian, Doug, Matt, Brett, Brian, and Kate. They are living proof The Triad works, and tolerating my obsessions with the study of successful performers.

PREFACE

Most of us are conditioned to think of motivation as something someone does to us or someone else, or as a pep talk from a top performer that seldom motivates personal performance improvement beyond 72 hours. Both are extrinsic and less valuable. This book is about how leaders and managers can learn and teach intrinsic self motivation principles and skills to consistently improve performance without micromanagement. A simple TRIAD of three primary overlapping and interrelated skills as if three balls were joined together is introduced to facilitate learning this highly complex task in three parts: Increase Awareness, Enhance Self Evaluation, and Connect Reward With Reinforcement. Once you learn The Triad, it is like riding a bicycle – you never forget how to apply the skills to motivate improving your performance for a lifetime.

Besides the interrelated skills of The Triad, I have applied 14 common themes throughout the book: Leadership, Needs, Value, Extrinsic-Intrinsic Dichotomy, Personality, Goal Setting, At-Will-On-Demand, Purpose-Intent, Focus, Task Familiarity, Systemic Change, Planer Thinking, and Drives-Motives- Motivation. I also introduce 18 new concept strategies to learn to apply intrinsic motivation skills, 16 Behavioral Rules, and 3 new personality types: Group, Verbal, and Self. How to use natural human drives or intrinsic motivations are also explained.

The trick in teaching and learning intrinsic motivation is to make the new knowledge and skills meaningful and relevant in the mind of the learner who must make that conscious decision to create *value*. This affects how the information will be stored as knowledge to be readily accessible, and *value* is the hypothesis of Purposeful Intent. Parents, teachers, and managers of all kinds can stress how valuable new knowledge and quality performance may be until they are blue in the face and have little effect on motivating performance improvement. Goals and objectives set by others are all extrinsic to meet the needs of those who set them. However, when the learner makes a conscious paradigm shift to make the new knowledge or activity and work valuable, they will be intrinsically motivated to improve their performance as they will equate quality of effort with quality of reward. Any kind of personal performance improvement is purposefully self rewarded, and the desire or motivation to improve the next performance will be slightly greater. The greatest drive motivation comes from setting a personal goal only one point higher than your own immediate past performance or average. You have no excuse if you apply a little more purposeful intent to your effort. The question to answer is whether motivation is a function of intelligence, or is intelligence a function of intrinsic motivation?

To my knowledge, no one has ever attempted to teach intrinsic motivation as a learned skill. Several authors have described the difference between extrinsic and intrinsic motivation. As a complex skill it is easier to learn when broken down into component parts as I have using The Triad. Each part is its own skill to master over time. However, think of the strategies and cues you use to learn any skill as atoms or molecules. When you begin to become familiar and understand each skill, the cues or molecules heat up and bounce around into the other two parts of The Triad and a light bulb goes on for them, too.

Learning intrinsic motivation skills can have huge positive results. More performers will be able to identify and meet their own needs and be less dependent on others or government social services that are extrinsic, costly, and unrewarding. School systems would reduce drop out rates and classroom disruptions that have climbed with extrinsic methods because the personal motivation to improve has been taken away. Corporations could increase their net profits by reducing the need for middle management to coerce and extrinsically motivate front line performers with vacation trips and cash bonuses. With less micromanagement when your performers in the home or at work know their purpose, you also gain personal accountability. You cannot build accountability in a micromanagement system.

The sad fact of extrinsic motivation is that you have to keep increasing the value of the reward to motivate the performer to do the same amount of work. With intrinsic motivation, the value is created in the mind of the performer. Once the purposeful intent is defined, low positive improvement goals are consistently selected by the performer to create the value. Then any kind of improvement better than their own immediate past performance can be valued and reinforced to motivate slightly more purposeful effort to ensure achieving the next goal and so on. Top performers do not wait for the approval of others because they already know how they feel inside about each new performance and whether they improved. They have learned and developed a personal feedback system that reflects on their immediate performance output to judge its improvement value compared to the previous input. Are you improving? If not, why not?

I have been interested in what motivates behavior for over fifty years. I think of my work as a behaviorist in the tradition of B.F. Skinner and Robert Gagné. All behavior is motivated by satisfaction of a personal need. Your personal needs help you identify your purposeful intent. When you have a purpose in mind for any activity or performance, even if you did not win the contest or ace the test, 95-99% of the time, you could walk away with something of value to be proud of and reinforce your effort. On the other hand, when you have no purpose, you may as well flip a coin because your odds on being successful to create value are at best 50-50. This lack of purpose will not consistently motivate you to improve, and the quality of your life will suffer.

The goal of this book is to motivate consistent performance improvement over time so you can become a top performer. Corporations spend billions of dollars to micromanage employees they fear are unable to motivate their personal performance improvement because their managers do not understand principles of human behavior and intrinsic motivation. The failure to properly motivate performers creates an accountability problem that causes the uninformed to create harsher rules, more regulations and micromanagement to control their behaviors. But at some point you realize that you cannot control the world and all the people in it. Top performers and corporations single out best practices and mobilization of energy to focus on what to do right and increase their probability for improvement.

The more you engage in control rather than empower a people, they will become dependent upon a socialized system of care to have their needs met by others rather than be motivated to meet their own personal needs and help others. The strength of any society is in its people who work to improve their personal performance. Unfortunately, the more affluent a society becomes, it also becomes more literal. The ability to organize and plan and be self motivated to meet one's personal needs for the future is lost when the government creates social programs to enable a dependent system to meet those needs for them by taxing the producer and giving benefits to the unproductive worker who expects the extrinsic reward. This practice causes democracies and civilizations to fail as more people become unmotivated to provide for their own needs and are extrinsically rewarded to be a victim and accept free aid. This overwhelms and breaks the system. When a people are overly taxed and suppressed with more rules and regulations, they are conditioned to expect a personal handout or reward for their efforts, too. This is a natural behavioral consequence, and exactly what we have been experiencing with the collapse of financial markets world wide. Whole societies and cultures will collapse faster than green house gases will turn the earth into toast. We simply must apply the principles found in Purposeful

Intent so that we can teach people how to fish and they can feed themselves for a lifetime.

To teach intrinsic motivation principles is not a simple task. There are perhaps well over 400 personality variables that contribute to one's motivation. There are also great varieties of environments that have produced top performers. My first approach was to pare down 400 to 14 top personality variables that I thought were descriptive of intrinsically motivated top performers. However, to write about all the interaction effects would create a table of 14 to the 13th power, and proved to be overwhelming. The problem was in simplifying the process so that the average person could learn how to apply and master these interrelated behavioral skills over time. I was too frustrated to keep writing the book in that first approach, but still believed that intrinsic motivation could be taught as a skill.

Inventor Thomas Edison was famous for his "cat naps," and Albert Einstein would relax in his chair for several hours keeping notable physicists waiting. I believe they were waiting for a divine answer. At 4:30 p.m. I pushed away from my desk, and asked, "God, I need your help. I need a simple way to teach this skill of intrinsic motivation so that anyone aged 12-80 can understand." My answer came in 11 hours! I awoke out of a deep sleep at 3:30 a.m. to these very clear words that created The Triad: Increase Awareness, Enhance Self-Evaluation, and Connect Reward with Reinforcement. Now I am the author and the messenger.

My experience started in the third grade by reading the biographies of a variety of great Americans. I noted they had a lot in common. In college I began to study the personality patterns and performance motivation of great coaches, then athletes and leaders. I have learned that top performers have similar personality traits, needs, and motives, which helped produce quality performances over their lifetimes. None were or are overnight wonders. I began to reflect on how I have applied the skills in The Triad in my personal life just as you will when you read this book.

As a behaviorist, I have had to use observation and a multiple regression approach to predict which variables would account for the most variance to write about. Behavior is unpredictable, but top performers have personality patterns that we can use to describe how they perform their specific tasks well and stay motivated. This book is meant to empower you to learn and use The Triad to become successful in what you choose to perform.

The Triad encourages performers to hold themselves accountable for their performances to produce quality and not take shortcuts. Technology has increased our ability to instantly communicate world-wide so that we can better understand

and appreciate the diversity of cultures. Now is the time for all nations to enter into a spirit of cooperation to help motivate all peoples to improve their personal performance skills to do good and not bring harm to others. Using Purposeful Intent and The Triad, each performer only has to take accountability for improving their own immediate past performance. If every citizen of every country were to learn to do this, then we would have outstanding growth and quality of life. This will make the world a safer place of equal opportunity for all. Then those who are motivated to work and gain success will share more with others less fortunate without having to regulate and force taxation upon the worker. This will naturally create jobs and increase the self respect of any people. Then everyone shall succeed, and reduce the need for power and authority over the people. My hope is that what you learn from this book you will pass on to others.

Science of Purposeful Intent

"Your education and personality identify you for a lifetime."

Andrew Christian

Objective: To understand how successful performers apply intrinsic motivation as a skill to mobilize and focus all their abilities and skills at will on demand to achieve consistent results over time.

Introduction

Purposeful Intent and The Triad are the foundation for all motivation. The Triad is a unique leadership approach for any company, organization, or school system that needs to improve. If you would like to have 100 little engines that can rather than 100 little engines that cannot without middle management or your help, then purposeful intent may be a solution to your needs. Billionaire J. Paul Getty once said, "I would rather have 1% of the proceeds from 100 performers than 100% of the proceeds of my personal effort."

Motivation is a universal concern. It is irrespective of ethnic origin, religion, and politics. This is about the study of intrinsic motivation as a learned skill or motivating your mind from within that you can learn to improve your performance and teach the skill to others. Intrinsic or internal motivation means you apply personal skills to improve your performance by how you think, act, and do to meet your needs and values. Extrinsic or external motivation means that others apply tangible rewards like money to induce you into improving your performance to meet their needs and values. Once you learn these fundamental skills in The Triad, they are like riding a bicycle – you never forget how. These Triad skills you can never perfect but will constantly be learning how to apply and improve your performance for the rest of your life. It does not matter what age you start, but obviously the sooner the better because learning to be intrinsically motivated to direct and improve your performance takes time. This is not a locker room pep talk that lasts for 72 hours. These skills create permanent changes in your thinking and personality patterns and ultimately the environment you create to be successful over time.

For almost every skill, a study has been made to learn how to learn that skill faster and perform with more efficiency to improve performance. Learning intrinsic motivation as a skill is no different, and The Triad helps you improve learning this skill. While motivation has been linked to learning and performance of skills, the concept of intrinsic motivation has not generally been viewed as a skill that can be taught. Motivation has been viewed by most people as something you acquire from experience in your environment, and the idea is to provide the correct or conducive environment for motivation to take place. Historically, motivation has been viewed more as an outcome-carrot on a stick- than a process skill. The use of extrinsic means to motivate people is easily applied, but they are not long lasting: Once the performer decides the value of the reward is not worth the effort, you have to increase the reward. The study of intrinsic motivation is hindered by experimental research design that requires interdependent variables be held constant when the experimental variable is changed to determine its effect on motivation and performance. However, it is next to impossible to hold all interdependent variables constant that are based on a performer's perception. You cannot easily control what a performer is thinking at the time you introduce the experimental variable. Human beings are complex organisms that are constantly adapting to change within their organism and environment. The body is growing and developing mentally and physically, and the environment changes daily and even more so when a move or job change takes place. Therefore, it is easier to let the organism adapt and manipulate the variables you would hold constant to observe positive changes in performance improvement over time. Longitudinal research offers the best solution to the study of behavior. The researcher can observe behavior over a longer period of time to determine the effect of introducing new information or a variable in the form of better cues and strategies on performance improvement.

Motivation is highly complex, and easier to learn as a skill by being broken down into three separate but overlapping and interconnected skills that I call The Triad.

Overview

The science of <u>purposeful intent</u> is an overview of The Triad used to teach intrinsic motivation as a leadership-management skill to improve personal performance. Throughout this work, the term **PI** will be used interchangeably to mean purposeful intent. In business circles, PI has also been interpreted to mean performance improvement, and a positive association for both terms.

Theory and Hypothesis

In theory, your Purposeful intent is the conscious cognitive motive you have to satisfy personal needs or goals. The hypothesis is that <u>valued</u> information is more readily stored and retrieved in the brain through the development of cognitive associational neurons that connect positive, pleasurable, and successful stimulus-response activities at will on demand.

As with any complex skill, it becomes easier to learn when broken down into manageable parts. The Triad is three separate manageable parts: Increase Awareness, Enhance Self-Evaluation, and Connect Reward with Reinforcement. Each of these three components will be broken down further into several chapters to explain strategies for learning that skill. Part I will explain relationships between your *structure, abilities,* and *accountability* to Increase Awareness. Part II will explain relationships between *pre-, during-,* and *post- performance* to Enhance Self-Evaluation. Part III will explain the relationship between *principles of reward-reinforcement behavior,* and *leading purposeful intent for success* to Connect Reward with Reinforcement.

The Triad

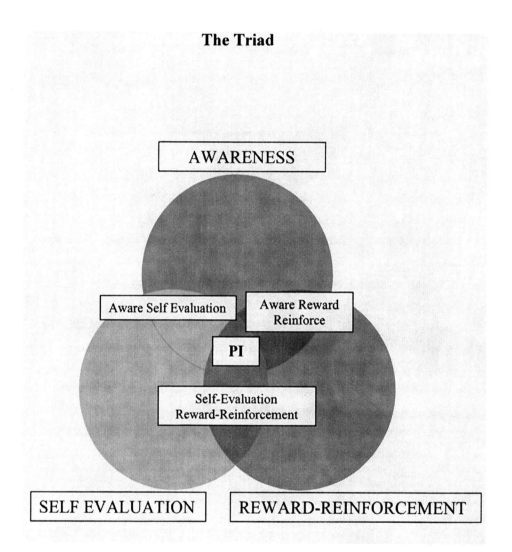

The three main skills of The Triad are the foundation for all motivation. Think of three balls or spheres that are interconnected so that they overlap each other by one-third of their size. Each sphere has a particular loaded with all kinds of strategies and cues like atoms to assist your skill development. The pictured atomic particles figure shown was taken from Dr. Craig Freudenrich, http://science. howstuffworks.com/atom.htm, 2003. The more you learn each strategic skill, the atomic particles heat up, become very active, and bounce around to bump into

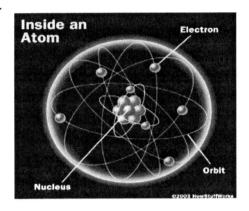

the other two spheres. The next sphere gets agitated and its atoms heat up or strategies start to make sense; a light bulb goes on that turns on the value for understanding how that specific knowledge and practice can improve your personal performance. Once you learn these foundations, they are like riding a bicycle; you never forget how. As you continually improve these three interrelated skills, your personal performance will consistently improve over time.

The first sphere is **Increase Awareness**. *In order to appreciably increase intelligence you must learn how to increase your awareness at will on demand.* Top performers do not operate at 110% all of the time, but are conditioned to sense when to increase their awareness to focus on mobilizing their energy and recognizing essential cues to raise their level of performance when it counts to be successful. The four key words are: AT WILL ON DEMAND. Increasing your awareness also creates value to organize, store, and retrieve differentiated information you find meaningful and relevant to successful performance from past experience. You perceive value from new experiences by associational neurons comparing them to stored, familiar past experiences. Behind the forehead the frontal lobe does the thinking, predicting, and reasoning. The pre-frontal cortex immediately in front of the frontal lobe acts like the cache ram memory in your computer. As you acquire more knowledge and experience with specific tasks, you create an array of associational neurons that link the information stored in various parts of your brain. When you learn to value information, you tend to store that information differently than non-valued information and with more associational neurons to facilitate retrieval at will on demand to help you perform at higher optimum levels. Top performers use the pre-frontal cortex to retrieve valued information and hold in short term memory. Then they modify and correct past performance mistakes by reviewing the sub routines or specific parts of the whole skill using mental practice and visualization strategies. These strategies create slow motion mental movie videos to fully rehearse the stimulus cues and response connections about to be performed in each part. After the corrections have been made, the pre-frontal cortex executes the connected sub routines without having to think and interrupt the whole performance. Non valued information is not as readily retrievable. It would be like storing an un-named file on your computer in a documents folder, within a folder, within a folder instead of labeling and storing it directly on your desktop. A long retrieval sequence hinders learning and performance, and is harder to associate pleasurable past experiences to self-evaluate past performance and improve your motivation to strive for a goal and connect to a reward.

The second sphere is **Enhance Self-Evaluation.** *No top performer ever waits for the approval of another.* Creative performers and leaders value their self evaluation criteria and feedback more than to wait on their critic's opinion who is less familiar with the work. Can you imagine the great modern painter Picasso, waiting for the critic's opinion to decide what to paint? Great leaders and performers will consult with others, but they will not wait for the approval of a critic with less talent or skill to proceed. Our schools, organizational, and business systems condition and reinforce exactly the opposite. We explain to students, trainees, and performers what is meaningful, relevant, and valuable instead of showing and teaching them a self-evaluation system or rubric to objectively score their performance. Learn how to fish for the answers to learn how to learn and be self-sufficient. We all know quality when we see it, but we cannot always describe it or the reward we feel. Performance evaluations are often vague or non-existent because no feedback system has been taught to the performer. In the end, though, it is not the extrinsic evaluation that the teacher or evaluator thinks, but how the performer intrinsically evaluates him/herself that matters the most.

The third sphere is **Connecting Reward with Reinforcement.** Routine performances and familial relationships are subconsciously automated to be unaware of a connection between reward and reinforcement to improve that performance. The key, however, is to bring these performances to a more conscious awareness level and attach significant value to our involvement. We are not motivated to improve mundane tasks because we are bored and not consciously aware of small improvements to value enough to feel any reward. You cannot reinforce a reward you do not feel or value from exerting a conscious effort. By increasing awareness of your innate drives and working with them, you immediately enhance self evaluation and self reward. This connection reinforces and increases your motivation to improve skilled performances with more purposeful training and effort. Your ability to properly recognize, receive, organize, store, and retrieve information or perform (RROSR) will help you to value your efforts to improve any task, and seek greater rewards to condition positive intent to succeed. To begin this process, imagine your reward feelings in doing a task well. Now, imagine a task or event you didn't do well. No one likes to fail; no one says, "Boy that was fun! Let's do it again!" The oldest behavioral notion is that we tend to repeat satisfying performances, and avoid those that are painful. In order to override routine subconscious behaviors and condition positive conscious behavioral responses, it's necessary to selectively focus on the correct cues to associate with correct responses with a purposeful intent. When your personal feedback system learns to associate quality of effort with quality of reward, you will build value and a stronger personal reward system, which will help you overcome occasional failures. This is the only way to build your confidence and self-esteem. No one can convince you with words. It must occur by your own actions and intrinsic motivation.

"I kept repeating to myself over and over. 'This is what you want. Now here is your chance'," Annika Sorenstam after winning the 2006 U.S. Women's Open Golf Championship. Her comment indicated how she could have used The Triad to deal with the pressures; stays focused, and mobilize her energy to succeed.

As you read these chapters stay focused on learning and applying these skills over time to put yourself in position to succeed. No great performance was ever created with a few trials. If you apply these principles and make them a part of your daily routine, you will see measurable consistent improvements in your performances and relationships over time. Without knowing your purpose you will only be able to experience haphazard inconsistent success that will require you to be extremely lucky to be successful. Those odds hardly seem very motivating to want to work hard to improve your performance. If you also subscribe to being a servant, then as you learn you will also be a messenger to others, and I thank you for spreading the word.

Introduction of New Concept Strategies

To apply purposeful intent leadership skills to improve performance, I have introduced several new concept strategies that will be described in greater detail throughout this book:

1. Purposeful Intent theorizes that it is the conscious cognitive motive to satisfy a personal need or goal that improves performance.

2. Purposeful Intent hypothesizes that valued information is more readily stored and retrieved in the brain through the development of cognitive associational neurons that connect positive, pleasurable, and successful activities.

3. The Triad is the interrelationship of three knowledge skills represented as spheres that are the foundation for all motivation: Increase Awareness, Enhance Self-Evaluation, and Connect Reward with Reinforcement.

4. Purposeful Intent is to become skilled at taking unconscious sensations to conscious perceptions that increase your awareness of meaningful and relevant value associations to enhance self-evaluation, and connect reward to reinforce activities that improve performance.

5. Value is central to the hypothesis of the theory of Purposeful Intent. Valued information is associated to prior knowledge and connected by neuronal pathways to readily retrieve it. This is why Albert Einstein had more associational neurons than any human being, and a reason to learn purposeful intent skills using The Triad to build intrinsic value in learning.

6. RROSR is the anachronism for processing information Recognizing, Receiving, Organizing, Storing, and Retrieving valuable knowledge to improve skilled performance.

7. *At Will On Demand* is knowing how and when to mobilize all of one's abilities and skills for a given moment in time to be successful when it counts the most.

8. Congruence is when the goal expectation and actual performance more closely approximate each other to affect the personality trait of Realism. Similarly, a performer's self-evaluation has more intrinsic motivational value when it approximates the manager's performance evaluation.

9. Task familiarity is when your personality patterns are modified as you become increasingly familiar with a task. With any new and unfamiliar task you are more likely to feel insecure, apprehensive, and lack levels of confidence. But as you become more familiar with a task, you will feel more secure, confident, and less apprehensive about making new trials or attempts. Be patient with new performers.

10. Planer Thinking is when you become more highly familiar with specialized tasks to think on higher and higher planes of thought processes that incorporate more knowledge from the specific previous experience.

11. *Multiple regression task analysis* for performance and personality patterns is a prediction equation that subjectively selects and weights by relative importance specific variables in the form of cues or strategies, patterns or traits to more efficiently learn and perform a criterion skill. For any specific skilled performance the equation might look like:

$$V_1 + V_2 + V_3 + V_4 + V_5 = C$$

12. <u>*M a S > M a F*</u> *means your motive to achieve success must be greater than your motive to avoid failure.*

13. *Group, Verbal, and Self* are personality types like Type A and Type B used to describe how a performer prefers to set goals to motivate their behavior and performance. Each type shows a preference for using performance data to form a perceptual anchoring point about which to judge the worth of each new personal performance goal.

14. *Receptacles of Knowledge to Facilitators of Knowledge* means the model for education has changed. The Internet is a major vehicle to facilitate knowledge. No one has a lock on the door, and you cannot increase your intelligence without learning how to facilitate knowledge acquisition. According to W. Edwards Demming, knowledge is the key to all performance improvement.

15. *You cannot build accountability in a micromanagement system* when the people performing the work are not empowered or feel accountable for their performance to be intrinsically motivated.

16. *Affluent cultures produce literal societies* as performers become less aware of their needs and abilities to be motivated to meet or improve them when those needs are met by others.

17. <u>Trick your brain</u>. As a complex micro processor, the brain does not know right from wrong. As easily as you can focus on a negative thought, image, or pattern, you can also suggest and visualize how to perform correctly, and build self-confidence with familiar tasks.

18. *Set low positive goals only one point or slightly better than your own immediate past performance or average.* This increases your probability for success and conditions your reward which connects motivation to reinforce more

purposeful effort to continue improvement. This concept strategy contradicts what others have told you to set high goals to be successful that are rewarded less frequently. Over time frequent reward conditions your motivation to work to improve to feel successful.

Definition and Use of Terms

Edward Murray in <u>Motivation and Emotion</u> defines a motive as "an internal factor that arouses, directs, and integrates a person's behavior." (1964) He further suggests that, "Motivation is distinguished from other factors that also influence behavior, such as the past experience of the person, his physical capabilities, and the environmental situation in which he finds himself, ..." (1964) He breaks down motivation into two components: <u>drive</u> and <u>motive</u>. A drive, according to Murray, is the internal process that empowers the person to act. You experience a variety of sensory triggers in your daily environment such as temperature and food that influence your behavior or motivation to act. Stimulating sensations and associations are absorbed and reinforced in the brain by these kinds of external triggers, but the drive to satisfy the need that they create is still internal. In our literal society we are reinforced to expect instant rewards. I am hungry, feed me, and you get a cheap immediate fast-food in ten minutes. I am cold, and you get a free sweatshirt out of the lost and found bin or local church mission. If you complain loud and long enough about anything, someone or something else will always meet your immediate needs. You do not have to think how to meet your future needs to acquire knowledge, be independent, and hold yourself accountable for your performance. Your motive is diminished or even terminated when the goal or reward is obtained. This implies a satiating effect that psychologist Clark Hull (1943) explains as <u>drive reduction</u>. Motivation becomes the *conscious* desire for something you want to meet a <u>need</u> or <u>value</u> that you cannot immediately obtain. By learning to acquire, improve, and value new knowledge and skills with a purposeful intent, you increase your intrinsic motivation. The internal desire and the value you attach to obtaining what you want that you cannot immediately have creates your drive level to be satisfied. This becomes the goal-seeking/selecting function of motives. To acquire a strong purposeful intent, you must learn to identify your personal needs and goals in life. Then you need to attach meaningful and relevant value to your personal work effort to achieve those needs and goals. This planning and perceptual reflection reinforces the connection to reward to want to repeat all kinds of successful behaviors. You learn to personalize your education. In schools and society in general, you become conditioned by others in a system that teaches you to meet other's needs before your own. However, the needs, goals, and values of others are external and less motivational than the values, needs, and goals you learn to apply for yourself.

The motives that cause your behavior and performance improvement are tied to your needs. To better understand this relationship, I will define these psychological terms and progressive relationships:

Needs – these are a personal call to action stimulus to satisfy the acquisition of an object, or with goals, to demonstrate a skill with a reasonable degree of proficiency. Examples are the need to improve where the conditioned response is to satisfy a positive feeling and want to repeat that behavior. Needs and goals are often used interchangeably in psychology.

Goals – there are intermediate short-term and ultimate long-term goals defined as an objective unit of measure to achieve a pre-set personal standard. Goals are greatly influenced by a perceptual anchoring point or PAP about which the objective measure or goal is shifted to positive or negative depending on the perceived value of the effort divided by the reward. The greatest motivation is when the goal is set only slightly higher than the performer's own immediate past performance or average.

Drives – are a persistent and dominant subconscious behavior until the desired need is sufficiently satisfied to reduce the drive stimulus and behavior. When there is a conscious awareness of the behavior and need being satisfied, the drive stimulus is converted to be a motive and there is increased motivation. Drives are associated with intent and personality traits that are not as readily changed except over time. Starting in early childhood, you can condition children to be more consciously aware of their consistent improvement by comparison to their immediate past performance to let them self evaluate and develop a personal feedback system. By teaching the strategy to set low positive goals only one point higher than their own immediate past performance or average, you increase their probability for improvement. They will experience success and reward more frequently to enjoy learning and take accountability for their improvement. Then it is unlikely that this conditioned drive stimulus will be reduced very easily as they progress through the later grades and into an adult life. In everything you purposefully choose to do with a positive intent, you will be driven to improve upon your performance.

Motives – are the conscious awareness of a drive stimulus to purposefully satisfy a personal need or goal. Motives are associated with purposeful behavioral patterns. A strategy to increase your motive strength would be to first create your need, second try to understand your purpose, and third holding yourself accountable to achieve it.

Motivation – is the specific purposeful strategy you use to satisfy a personal need or goal. Two performers can have the same personal need or goal, but the stronger motivation will come from the performer who uses a purposeful strategy to achieve that need or goal. The strength of your motivation is hard to improve when you have no satisfaction of an underlying personal need or goal.

Intrinsic motivation is the performer's internal desire to satisfy a personal need or goal.

Extrinsic motivation is another person's need or goal imposed on the individual or group.

Bias is the unreasonable personal judgment or prejudice of an expected outcome prior to the performance.

Value as The Concept

Value is the cornerstone of Purposeful Intent and The Triad. There is a big difference between what someone tells you to value, and what you consciously decide to value. The former is extrinsic; the latter intrinsic. A leader, like a teacher or coach, can tell you the value of a bit of knowledge by creating a need to learn and making that information meaningful and relevant to your current level of understanding based on your prior knowledge and familiarity with each task.

Thinking takes place in the frontal lobe of the brain behind your forehead. Immediately in front of the frontal lobe is the pre-frontal cortex (PFC) believed to function as a value, organization, and planning center. This area acts like the cache ram memory on a computer that allows you to open multiple programs. You can use visualization and mental rehearsal techniques to create and perfect parts of complex skills called sub routines. The PFC filters incoming sensory information to decide what is meaningful and relevant to be organized in short-term memory and routed to selected parts of your brain for long term memory. Associational neurons are interconnected brain cells that act like the electrical wiring in your house to connect and readily route information in high speed pathways. Neurons allow you to recognize and associate new cues using learned cognitive awareness skills to retrieve and associate previously stored meaningful and relevant information. This stored information you assigned a relative value with mental rehearsal and visualization strategies to perfect a skill prior to performance. You learned to connect or associate a specific stimulus cue with a correct response. This is called conditioning. The more you increase your awareness skills for using specific practice cues and strategies that predict successful learning and performance you will be able to perform at a higher level to consistently succeed more often than fail. Purposeful intent is a learned skill-based leadership program that teaches you how to improve personal performance with intrinsic motivation over time by developing the three primary skills found in The Triad.

When you do not intrinsically value new information, hypothetically you store these data in less retrievable parts of your brain. This is like creating a word document on your computer and placing it in a file folder that is in a folder of another folder. By the time you perform those three iterations to retrieve the document in the file, the timing of the performance to be successful may be lost. You can learn to organize and store valued information in a more readily retrievable structure via associational neurons and specific access parts of your brain at will on demand. When a student states out loud or silently thinks "I hate school," picture an imaginary switch at the base of their brain that moves into the "off" position. The value of learning is low. Very little new information is going to get past the switch to be stored in that brain. You can also imagine how less valued, hated, prejudicial, or negative information is stored in obscure file drawers compared to valued information kept on your "desk top" for easier retrieval. The strategy, then, is to learn to teach yourself and others a purposeful intent to develop intrinsic motivation based on a conscious value system.

RROSR

Hypothetically, I believe your brain can more readily recognize, receive, organize, store, and retrieve knowledge that is valued and what I call RROSR. Non-valued information may be stored, but it is not readily retrievable because it lacks the positive intrinsic associations to other pleasurable successful activities. When you just go through the motions without a clear purpose, your success is haphazard and 50% probable at best. You'd be lucky if you succeeded, but you cannot attribute your success to your skills. Purposeful Intent leadership training will develop your intrinsic motivational skills to a conscious cognitive level to understand your motives. Through the acquisition of this knowledge you will be able to consistently improve your performance and help other performers. Many people use intrinsic motivation occasionally by chance, and successful performers identify, create, and use their **PI** skills every day to consistently improve their performance in small increments. By becoming aware of your intrinsic motivational skills, it is possible to create long-term success. Your ability to create your own learning process is known as meta cognition. To make meaning of all the sensations you receive is your perception or construction of your knowledge also known as the "constructivist model." Students, employees, athletes, professionals, families, and individuals all benefit from PI skills training to improve their performance.

I will frequently ask people if they know how to ride a bicycle. After they respond yes, I will ask if they think they will ever forget how. No one has said yes, which implies that once you learn the Triad, you will never forget how to apply and improve upon these skills for the rest of your life. It would be wrong to think that a highly complex skill can be learned over night. As with any skill, knowing how and what to practice are key to improving your performance. You cannot be a champion swimmer by swimming one lap, but you can apply what you learn to continuously motivate your improvement so that over time you can look back and see your success. Always remember that the truest measure of success is the continuous improvement of your personal performance over time.

What follows is a verbal schematic diagram of what happens to create consistently motivated and successful performance. If you expect to lead, you must empower others to succeed more often than fail. This requires appealing to the personal needs of individuals that are intrinsic as opposed to group management needs that are extrinsic. You will learn how to identify and frequently acquire those needs and hold yourself accountable for achieving an increasingly higher standard of performance. You will learn that what matters the most is not what others think of your performance, but what you learn to value from the standards you hold yourself accountable for achieving.

Value of Intrinsic Motivation

Purposeful Intent skills adapt to all your needs as they change over time. For example, my neighbor told me his story about quitting smoking. He said when he was a young man, if someone had told him smoking was bad for his health he would have ushered the person out the door. His health needs were invincible then. However, later on when his <u>need</u> to preserve the quality of his life increased his awareness, he quit. Unfortunately, we all have a hard time projecting our future needs, and wait until it is too late to see greater benefits from changing our behavior because without the skills to know how, we are not motivated to do so. As you develop, PI skills can help you to project future personal needs to a higher relevant value to control this notion. You can also use these skills to be a better consumer and apply more critical thinking skills. Advertising works against PI skills; it seeks to lure you into being part of a bigger more accepted group behavior instead of thinking through the best value for you.

When you focus on identifying and meeting your personal needs through purposeful intent, you can achieve above average results. If you become part of the masses that resist changing their behaviors because of the unfamiliar stress it will bring to their personality, then little will change in your life. You are extrinsically motivated to meet the needs of others when you are manipulated by a need for acceptance, and will do what everyone else does. In Part II, Pre Performance Evaluation, you will learn why the best goal setting strategy to increase your motivation is to set a goal only one point higher than your immediate past performance or average. How you establish perceptual anchoring points to set goals that intrinsically motivate your performance are also linked to your personality. I have identified three new personality types; *Group, Verbal, and Self* create different perceptual anchoring points: Group types prefer an awareness of the team's performance; Verbal types prefer to use what they say they will do; and, Self types prefer to use the measure of their own immediate past performance or average. The Group types are the least effective intrinsic motivators of performance improvement. The strongest motivation for performance improvement comes from the Self types who know their immediate past performance or average and often keep daily journals or logs. Recording and recognizing past performance efforts is a PI skill to improve your conscious awareness for the amount of effort and value you create. To perform better some changes may be required.

The Extrinsic-Intrinsic Controversy

Leaders must understand the difference between intrinsic and extrinsic motivation. An extrinsic motive is provided by someone else in the form of a tangible product with the expectation that the one providing the extrinsic motive will gain something in return. Examples are money, paid vacations, candy, gifts, jewelry, clothing, praise, special recognition, grades, plaques, bonuses, and so forth in return for more productive work, affection, better behavior, and leadership conformity. An extrinsic motivator is another person's need or goal imposed on the individual or group. On the other hand, an intrinsic motivator is the performer's internal desire to satisfy a personal need or goal. An intrinsic motive is one that comes from within yourself by understanding your personal abilities, skills, and strengths to meet your personal needs. It is fueled by your internal *feelings* of success, self-worth, image or identity exhibited by your passion or need to produce quality work that you value. Caring for others, and heart of a champion are examples how ideas form to create your predisposition or expectation for feeling good about your performance. You are responsible for how you feel, but you must also be conditioned to be accountable for your behaviors. You gain stronger feelings toward self-reward, relationships, and contentment to relieve stress providing for primary needs if you condition the internal need to hold yourself accountable for your behaviors and outcomes. When others hold you accountable, the conditioned responses are external and less powerful. Discriminating between extrinsic and intrinsic motives can be difficult at times because you use many extrinsic means to motivate (manipulate) others to improve their performance. Extrinsic rewards are easier to provide and more common because they are more quantifiable. The danger is that when extrinsic rewards are used, performers learn to under perform until the extrinsic reward is perceived as a higher value to make it worthy of their effort. Learning how to create intrinsic motives within the performer is harder, but not difficult with a little knowledge and understanding. You are conditioned by common extrinsic rewards like a paycheck, and they are short-term motivators even when given randomly or intermittently. Intrinsic motives are long-term, and are a stronger motivation over time than any extrinsic motive. An intrinsic motive, once learned and understood as a need to fulfill a purpose, will continually motivate your behavior until your personal need or goal is satisfied and requires less supervision and monitoring. A goal created by a set of criteria with any kind of evaluation by someone else is always extrinsic. Remember this rule: A goal created by a set of criteria with any kind of performance evaluation by someone else is always extrinsic.

Natural Drives

No one strategy to increase awareness and improve motivation is more important than understanding and working in concert with natural drives. The best strategy is to learn what your natural drives are by understanding how they motivate your behavior in the short and long term, and use them to motivate your future performance. There are numerous natural drives that motivate your performance every day. Leaders do not know about or understand how to effectively use natural drives to improve intrinsic motivation and performance. The most basic of all drives is quality of life. Performers do not get out of bed planning to fail but to improve their life and the lives dear to them. You have a natural drive to improve your performance. It is built in, but you must learn awareness skills to recognize your small improvements to feel rewarded and sustain your drive motivation to improve. As children mature, they are driven to be independent. But many parents love to micromanage their children to avoid personal embarrassment to their egos for their child's mistakes. Vicariously reliving your life through your children is a huge mistake. Children or performers you lead do not learn to be accountable for their performances in a micromanagement system to perform exactly as you would.

Your nervous system also has a natural drive to automate your responses to routine sensations. William D. Cannon (1929) referred to this biological drive as *homeostatic equilibrium* to regulate your hormones, respiration, heart rate, and all your sensations. As you become familiar with tasks, you also need to continually increase your conscious awareness of specific performance and biological feedback cues to help you continuously improve your performance over time. To fulfill your basic instinctual needs for food, clothing, and shelter are natural drives. Also included are self preservation and procreation to maintain our species. Being naturally curious to learn and create are drives, too. As with all natural drives, their strength is reduced by other conditioned behaviors that do not reinforce their use.

As a parent, use your child's natural drive to be independent and accountable and avoid conflicts over independence. You can mean well to micromanage your child's work to help prevent their early mistakes. But a child learns to gain feedback from mistakes to correct as input in their brain. This process transforms a negative thinking pattern such as focusing on the wrong stimulus cue or incorrect response and replacing it with a positive response output to the correct stimulus cue. If you take that process away, they will not learn how to hold themselves accountable for their behaviors or process their personal performance feedback to self evaluate and improve their performance. More house rules will cause more conflicts than independence and accountability. Keep your rules simple and pertinent to the growth and development of your child, and then enforce them so that they will focus on the higher order thinking skills they will need to be adults. Conflicts arise in the home as your child matures and is naturally driven or motivated to become more independent by making responsible decisions. Give your child opportunities to be responsible and know the consequences of poor decisions up front to build a sense of trust; and not to belie that trust. Empower your child to make their own decisions without excessive fear of failure or criticism. They need age appropriate opportunities to take risks and learn to develop their personal feedback system for performance self evaluation. Children are naturally curious and want to explore, take risks, and seek rewards. Providing a dichotomy to clearly indicate the correct choice without choosing the decision for them is a parenting skill. Help them to reflect on their positive behaviors that produce performance results so they can self-evaluate and reinforce their positive performance feedback and learn to grow physically and mentally. The best strategy to use is to answer a question with a question. Always remember the cardinal rule of evaluation: If you evaluate, it automatically changes to an extrinsic motivation. Whereas, when asked something like, "How did I do?" Your answer would be, "OK. What did you have to do to learn that?" Your child cannot grow mentally or learn to hold themselves accountable for their performance if you protect them by making all their decisions for them. They will make mistakes and learn from them. This is how you learn valuable feedback to evaluate your past performance and know what to improve. You cannot protect your child from every thing forever. They have a right to their own life eventually, and your job as the parent is to teach them values to be self-reliant and independent in thought and decisions or suffer the consequences. Thus, teach your children moral values early and pray they do not make brutal life-changing mistakes. Your child wants to have limits and have reasonably fair discipline apply to their behaviors in the home, society, at school, and even with their friends. Socialization can be cruel, and the withdrawal of friends, family, teammates, or significant others can be powerful motives to change good or bad behaviors.

How Needs Drive Behavior

In affluent societies, the higher needs of children are met more frequently by others. These children are not conditioned to project for the personal satisfaction of their future needs, and they do not waste their time thinking about how to acquire the skills to meet those needs – a term often interchangeable with a goal. By the time these needs are realized to have to learn to think, act, and do for oneself, free and public education is over, and students do not have the acquired skills to continuously improve their performance or begin to hold themselves accountable for performance improvement. With a conscious purposeful effort, you can instill value for an education and learn how to make new information meaningful and relevant. Maslow's (1943) Need

Hierarchy, demonstrates the relationship between purposeful intent, drives, motives, and need satisfaction.

At the bottom of the pyramid are lower-order survival needs such as food, clothing, and shelter. At the top is self actualization which drives many successful people to fulfill their internal needs by purposefully helping others. At this highest level, your needs are personal and what others say or do to motivate a change in your behavior is less important than what you need for yourself. In a sense, once lower-order needs are consistently met, you shift your desire to meet higher-order needs.

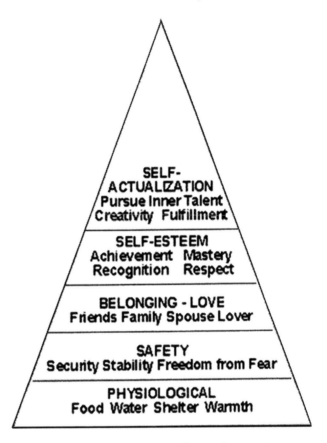

Maslow's Hierarchy of Needs

SELF-ACTUALIZATION
Pursue Inner Talent
Creativity Fulfillment

SELF-ESTEEM
Achievement Mastery
Recognition Respect

BELONGING - LOVE
Friends Family Spouse Lover

SAFETY
Security Stability Freedom from Fear

PHYSIOLOGICAL
Food Water Shelter Warmth

PI consciously builds value by tapping into your natural drives and motives. Extrinsic motives selected by others to meet organizational or management needs or goals, and used by traditional motivational speakers, only briefly modify your behavior. The more powerful intrinsic or self-motivation requires you to create new ways of approaching tasks and to make a paradigm shift to equate quality of effort with quality of reward. This paradigm shift enhances your self-reward system; that is, when you consciously reflect on your performance to self-evaluate and acquire valued rewards you intrinsically reinforce your efforts. The psychology of reward and reinforcement is a simple process. People desire to repeat those activities they find satisfying, and avoid those activities that are not valued due to excessive difficulty, minimal reward, are unfamiliar, stressful or painful. These principles of reward and reinforcement are the third part of The Triad, and the weakest link for most top performers as they have not brought this skill up to a conscious level. When you continuously improve your performance through conscious awareness, knowing and observing feedback from self-evaluation to reward your behavior, you increase your desire to continue learning and improving.

In the following chapters you will learn how to:

(1) Identify and prioritize your personal needs and abilities, and the essential drives that strengthen your purposeful intent.

(2) Create personal realistic goals that are frequently achievable to enhance your personal reward system.

(3) Self-evaluate your performance as you become more consciously aware of personal feedback to create meaningful and relevant value.

(4) Reinforce the connection between your purpose and value to build stronger motives to achieve.

(5) Mobilize your energy to perform at a higher level at will on demand when it counts.

The Greatest Motive

With intrinsic motivation, the greatest motive to improve your current performance is to set a goal only slightly better than your own immediate past performance. *To be highly motivated to achieve and value a new goal, you must be aware of your past performance.* Great performers perceive the relation of the performances of others far less important and use their own past performance as benchmarks to improve. Set goals only slightly better than your own immediate past performance like successful performers have been doing. As the leader, instill in your performers the importance of how to use their performance feedback to improve and hold them accountable. Then focus every practice or training session on an individualized purposeful intent to improve the quality of the next performance. Your performers must know why they are practicing. Former Dallas Cowboys coach Tom Landry said it best. "A coach gets his men to do what they don't want to do to get what they want." This is a value-based system of learning. It must be intrinsic.

The Second Greatest Motive: M a S > M a F

Your motive (M) to achieve (a) success (S) must be greater than your motive (M) to avoid (a) failure (F). This sounds complex but is the heart of purposeful intent. By converting to a positive focus strategy, you will have an affinity for positive and fortunate events. As a leader you must look for the positive good to reinforce in your performers to keep them motivated from within teaching them how to use their own feedback to self evaluate their performances for improvement. Reinforcing a performer's faults does not reward them to want to repeat good behaviors. They will create avoidance behaviors and motives to avoid failure more than focus on how to achieve success. You fear failure only because it was conditioned in you by external forces. You were taught an external system to meet the needs of others instead of learning how to identify and meet your own needs in a successful strategy that will be detailed in the accountability chapter, *It's Your Job.*

Personal Value System

Leaders always place emphasis on a personal value system they know is a feeling inside of every performer. Good leaders have a pulse on their performers to know their needs they value often better than they do. The hiring process of companies and schools condition their performers and students with managers and teachers and their set of expectations. Everyone in your organization will not understand, buy in, or value the importance of learning purposeful intent leadership skills. Your values will be faulty when you lack a purposeful intent. To continually improve your performance you must focus on the specific positive elements you need to perform to value them, and let the total product or outcome take care of itself. Your critics or evaluators may want to change your focus if they do not understand the leadership principles of purposeful intent or have personally performed those skills you are being taught at a high skill level. You have to reflect to self-evaluate your performance to gain positive feedback and self-confidence about the rate and progress of your learning.

Purpose Versus Intent: Strategies for Change

Awareness levels focus on learning how to move from a natural, automated, unconscious sensory state, to a more conscious purposeful perceptual level in your capacity to think, learn, and make choices. Typical responses to stimulus cues result in a behavioral pattern that gives you some idea of your purpose. Your responses can be observed to follow a similar response sequence to a stimulus. Behavioral patterns, however, can be changed easier by understanding and changing your purpose and conditioning a correct performance response to a trigger stimulus cue (S-CR). Your intent is not something you can easily question or change in an individual. Purpose and intent are similar to personality patterns and traits. Intent is your early conditioned desire to improve and be curious. Intent and traits are mostly fixed by the age of three to five. Intent, like a personality trait, is an unconscious general disposition of personal conditioned behavior. You learn to ask questions to get answers to satisfy your curiosity, or by lack of response or negative response, you are conditioned not to ask questions. If early in life your intent is conditioned negatively by others, it can take years to overcome and have a positive purpose to approach new skills. Your personal success is reinforced with correct behaviors that build your confidence to perform specific tasks.

Your positive intent does not always transfer to all other kinds of tasks. However, a nurturing environment will more often have a positive effect on children that is displayed in adulthood to condition a greater expectation of success. If you want your children to enjoy reading, you must read to them as if you enjoy reading to make it fun. If an infant is not securely held, cuddled, and given affection, or a child is constantly belittled or shamed by his/her parents, they will be more likely trait insecure and less confident to attempt new tasks. As an adult he/she might be a highly erratic performer, unable to mentally concentrate to process performance feedback in a timely manner, and be conditioned to have their needs met by others that reinforces micromanagement. He/she may also have a highly developed sensory awareness system to protect him/herself from others, but a poor self-evaluation feedback system for providing essential personal reward and reinforcement of positive behaviors. When your personality traits are unstable, it is more likely that your positive intent will be unstable. Unstable intent contributes to inconsistent, haphazard, and conflicting purposes without focused thinking capacity. You focus on the wrong things at the wrong time, and you learn wrong things. You may have learned that the approval or disapproval of your performance to feel rewarded comes from external sources like parents, siblings, and significant others. In this way, the strength of your purposeful intent to do well is proportional to your feelings of security: if you are insecure, you are more likely to have a weak strength of intent and vice versa; if you are secure you are more likely to have a strong strength of intent. Because intent and traits are tied to your personality, it is necessary to focus on how they developed and how you can change your personality over time to increase your consistent intent. The best strategy to motivate this kind of personality change is to identify and create a high personal need to improve one or two areas in which you have some talent or ability and begin calling those better abilities your passion. The word passion becomes your personal trigger word to do well and can help establish positive intent to increase your intrinsic motivation. Once you've chosen something to call your passion you can follow all the strategic steps for learning PI, and your performances will improve over time and with experience.

The best strategy to change your purposeful intent is to increase your conscious focus on personal leadership to hold yourself accountable for your performance and behaviors and not blame others for your shortcomings:

First, create your personal need to look for the good in others and yourself, and reinforce those qualities by calling attention to them. Bring conscious attention to your purpose and the idea that whatever negative feelings or prejudice you have toward others in your frontal lobe for thinking will be spoken in your body language. Therefore, displace negative thoughts and replace them with positive thoughts. When negative behaviors occur, rate them. If insignificant, why bother to condition a response in a minor negative behavior that can make it a major behavioral problem later? You can correct bad behaviors like a coach would point out the error in thinking that causes the performance and replace the trigger or stimulus with a positive one that is conditioned to lead to a better response. The more often a similar consistent pattern of behavior emerges that can be observed, you can become more consciously aware of the changes in your personality.

Second, take the approach that you are not perfect either. Before you can be overly critical, first think about getting your own house in order. You could be an unbelievable model in a negative way. What may work for you and your personality may not work for another's personality and experience.

Third, love people and develop relationships by caring to help your performers succeed instead of looking to take all the credit.

Fourth, teach others how to help themselves instead of enabling their bad behaviors that condition "learned helplessness" when you perform the tasks for them. If you are asked a question how to perform a task, simply answer with another question: What are you going to do if you can't do that _____ task or skill? Teach a man how to fish and you feed him for a lifetime. Teach a man how to learn, to think, act, and do for themselves, and they will be successful to eventually help and lead others.

Meaningful and Relevant Bias Debate

Educators have experienced an explosion in the use of technology and communication as innovations in learning to motivate performance improvement. But is technology a biased aid or hindrance?   I see more people with headsets in their ears or watching TV instead of participating in activities that can increase their sensory awareness with the environment they create. Increasing your sensory awareness can create a greater number of associational neurons that have been linked to intelligence. Artificial intelligence is unmotivated. Technology is at best an aid, but not a replacement for sensory awareness. In all organizations and systems, few demonstrate a skill for teaching their workers how to evaluate their own meaningful performance to improve. This includes teachers and schools that mass produce education as one size fits all. There is always a boss to explain the level of performance expected and achieved or not achieved. Even the most successful performers fail to be more conscious of their day to day efforts and intermediate successes to self-reward their work and reinforce their work ethic. When you are taught how to evaluate your own feedback to judge the personal worth or value of your work you gain a positive intent to steadily improve your motivation. Learning how to set low positive realistic goals to increase the frequency of your success will enhance your reward system to condition or reinforce like behaviors. However, the bias has been to tell everyone to set high goals that are not what top performers actually do. Unless you choose to make the company expected outcome your goal, when the goals are set by an external source they automatically become biased extrinsic goals and less powerful motivators than personally meaningful and relevant intrinsic goals or motives based on your need to achieve.

Information is occurring at exponential rates and certainly much faster than we can keep up. Educators define what is the most meaningful and relevant material to learn, and the sequence. College professors did research and taught the teachers who taught you what they believed was most meaningful and relevant. Your professors applied the *receptacles of knowledge* model. They were also filters who decided what and how you would learn. With the rapid advances in Internet technology and communication, it has become more critical to be intrinsically motivated to acquire knowledge in a meaningful and relevant way with a purposeful intent using The Triad.

Desirable Paradigm Shifts

Desirable performance paradigm shifts can happen when you learn how to use The Triad. These important shifts relate to moving from:

1) extrinsic motives to more powerful intrinsic motives,
2) unconscious sensory awareness to conscious perceptual awareness,

3) non-valued to valued knowledge acquisition, and

4) from being outer directed by others to being inner directed and holding yourself accountable for your personal behaviors and performance.

The most realistic performer knows the bottom line truth, and can choose to change their behavior to perform better over time.

Practicing your PI skills creates two major shifts:

1) You learn to equate your *quality of effort with quality of reward.* You learn to get out of life what you put into it by becoming less dependent on others to meet your personal needs. This realization ultimately leads to a higher quality of life.

2) Your model for education has shifted from "*receptacles of knowledge*" to "*facilitators of knowledge.*" This is being driven by the vast amounts of knowledge readily available through the Internet. As the performer acquiring the knowledge, you decide what is meaningful and relevant by a PI choice, and then readily recognize, receive, organize, store, and retrieve (RROSR) this multi-sensory information in your pre-frontal cortex (PFC). The PFC is immediately in front of your frontal lobe behind your forehead. The PFC plans, sorts, and sends information to the appropriate lobes of your brain for storage by connecting associational neurons for faster retrieval.

Educational Paradigm Shift

A paradigm shift is taking place in education. Educators are no longer the *receptacles of knowledge* to pass on to the next learner what they regard as most meaningful and relevant. Educators are the *facilitators of knowledge.* Each learner constructs their knowledge by choosing what is meaningful and relevant from their experiences with the help of their parents and teachers. With this responsibility comes an even greater task of teaching students how to learn to apply perceptual skills that make meaning out of the sensations they get bombarded with every day. This increases their awareness to take in more information, and self-evaluate for meaning and relevance. Students must learn to think critically, and judge the value of material they are reading as well as the environments they are learning from. With perceptual awareness skills, you can learn to apply inductive and deductive reasoning and personal feedback skills to compute probabilities and potential outcomes necessary to increase your motivation. All of these skills rely heavily on intrinsic motives that must be skillfully created by the teacher and learner. Educators must create the need and performance expectation that embraces the learner's thought process and natural drives to improve their performance. This will increase the personal motivation to satisfy that need or goal using structured principles, methods, and strategies for learning found in purposeful intent. The teacher-facilitated learner will construct and discover the answer for themselves, having worked to achieve a sense of value and level of confidence in understanding what they know.

Success Comparison

Successful performers use PI strategies and skills daily without knowing how or why they do them. They perform them unconsciously through trial and error because they have found that they work to motivate performance improvements. You can learn to employ these observed techniques to consistently improve your performances. When I began to study psychology over forty years ago, I became fascinated with how successful leaders and performers stayed motivated and continued to improve. The first athletic icon that came to my mind was watching the development of Michael Jordan. When I speak to groups, I will ask a show of hands for those who think Michael knew he would be THE Michael Jordan when he was in high school? Not one hand will go up. Then I ask about Abraham Lincoln, Henry Ford, Thomas Edison, Eleanor Roosevelt, Babe Ruth, and Martin Luther King, and still no hands go up. I mention that Ray Kroc founded the McDonalds restaurant chain when he was 54, and popularized "fast food" into culture. I suggest to you that with PI skills training, you can still achieve more in your lifetime no matter what age or level of success you start from. High achievers are not focused on their date next weekend. They increase their awareness to focus on acquiring the specific knowledge to live their passion! They acquire a purposeful intent for what they want to do with their lives, as do all highly successful people. When you learn how to use PI, you will consistently perform above average. You do not have to display extreme star performances to be highly successful over time. A successful performer is someone who is generally average, but consistently performs above average by increasing their awareness skills with a purposeful intent *at will on demand* when it counts the most.

Looking Glass

When I read the sports pages, I pay special attention to those average athletes who become stars because the article mentions their strong work ethic. It is much easier to work at something if you have a purposeful intent. PI is the looking glass that brings your life into focus to help you mobilize all your energy at any given moment in a positive preplanned process. You use your prefrontal cortex to assign meaningful and relevant value to new information and hold it in short-term memory until it can be organized and stored properly. Your prefrontal cortex can also set up a planned executable program drawing stored experiences from all parts of your brain to start with a trigger word or sound you select. Without PI, your personal plan for success, you can lose your direction to fragment your performances. Imagine yourself in a maze confused with every turn. Everything you try turns out the wrong way from what you intended. This is what happens with confused performers without PI strength. Great leaders create the need to achieve and help performers focus on selected cues to respond to and realize their full potential. In an assembly plant, they call this retooling. From a psychological point of view, purposeful intent is retooling how you think to make the correct choices to cues you learn to recognize with better awareness skills that will consistently improve your performance over time. Everyone is happy when the improved performances start happening. Subconsciously, without knowing PI principles, the rookie-laden 2004-5 Chicago Bulls turned their season around. The Boston Red Sox also won the 2004 World Series after being down 0-3 to the powerful New York Yankees in the ALCS. Both applied PI principles without knowing it to increase their motivation and change the momentum. When you understand how PI strategies work, you can see how these teams could have applied these principles to produce winning performances.

Add Purpose to Focus Success

To teach purposeful intent leadership skills to be motivated from within you have to feel rewarded enough to want to repeat your behavior. Extrinsic or outside motivators provided by others are selected to satisfy their needs. You need to be more aware of your personal needs to create and select your intrinsic motives to focus on your purpose. The best goal-setting strategy is what champion athletes use. You set low positive goals only one point higher than your immediate past performance or performance average to increase your probability for success. This increases your drive motivation the most as you have no excuse for not improving with a little more focused purposeful effort. Your intrinsic motives are value centered in frames of reference from your specific past experience that is unique only to you. The value you connect is a perceived amount of effort divided by the perceived amount of expected reward and represented by $V = R/E$ where value is the reward divided by effort. This is your specific value expectation, and will vary for the same activity with different trials or performance of sub skills, and from less experienced ability performers.

Activity Value Index

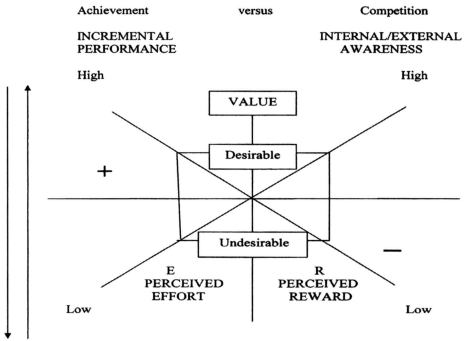

Optimal value comes from those performance activities that will contribute the most to reinforce consistent incremental improvements.

Desirable + - Optimal low positive realistic effort and reward in the rectangle

These performances increase your probability for success to enhance your personal reward system.

Undesirable -
- Maximum effort; Minimal reward
- Minimal effort; Maximum reward
- Maximum effort; Maximum reward
- Minimal effort; Minimal reward

To increase your purposeful intent:

The <u>first step</u> is to identify your intrinsic motives based upon your personal short-term and long-term needs. Personal need satisfaction is intrinsic to enhance your personal reward system and reinforce your positive work ethic behaviors.

The <u>second step</u> is to learn to be consciously aware of any performance improvement from your immediate past performance or average to feel rewarded. You can feel more reward when you are taught the performance cues to recognize (cue recognition skills). When you recognize a stimulus cue and correctly respond to be successful, you have developed a conditioned response represented as S – R to S – CR using the same stimulus or: S $\longleftrightarrow$ R
$$\searrow CR$$

Imagine having antennae or a satellite dish on your head to take in more information. Otherwise you go through the motions to recognize, receive, organize, store, and retrieve meaningful and relevant data.

The <u>third step</u> is to analyze all your past experiences. Use a sheet of paper and draw a line down the middle of the page. On the right side record as many positive experiences as you can recall for a given activity. On the left side record as many negative experiences as you can recall. You naturally rationalize the world the way you are conditioned to see it through a camera lens into your past experiences. If your experiences have been good, you are probably rewarded enough to want to repeat similar behaviors. The pain of an electric shock or any negative behavior reinforces your opposite avoidance behaviors. Modification of behavior is to reward and reinforce positive behaviors and extinct negative behaviors by not calling attention to them. The question is, can you learn to perform this process for yourself by self-evaluating the quality of your continuous performance with a feedback model? At some point in your life you must learn to become your own teacher. At some point you must become the patriarch or matriarch of your family to make good decisions when the advice of your elders no longer applies. Cleveland Cavaliers NBA star LaBron James recently commented before the first championship game of his career in 2007 that he had to mature early. In a single parent household with his mom, he had to step up to be the man of the house at age 10. These example steps help to explain how life changes to create your purpose whether you want it to or not. You may be put into a servant leadership role that you do not choose. Plan to be ready. Usually you take these maturity changes in stride and do not focus on them as purpose driven. But God has a purpose for you, and change, although unpleasant at times, happens for a greater reason that you will know later. Accept and trust in your purpose.

Leadership Philosophy

All good leaders have a foundation that is their philosophy. If you want to be a successful performer, you would improve your chances with a good philosophy that builds your character and integrity. Purposeful Intent is also a philosophical approach to teaching others to learn how to learn, to think, act, and do for themselves and eventually others. Purposeful Intent blends the elements of a strong philosophy to know why you personally perform or intend to perform the way you do, and a self-evaluation system that compares what you have actually performed in your experience to your positive goal intent. This process improves your talent whether you live in the urban, suburban, or rural environment. A sound philosophy provides the foundation of need to create quality standards that are adhered to by your performers. Philosophy provides the basis for understanding how and why you must create criteria to judge the worth of your personal performance. *Lifelong success is determined by learning the value of your quality performances and associating your quality of effort with your quality of reward.* You must learn to set your own intrinsic standards to excel, and persevere in a passion when critics may disapprove of a single performance. Philosophically reflect on the body of your work and how you are improving. You must learn that one performance does not identify your life's work, or that one mistake makes or breaks you. Neither can you assume by watching role models, who have already spent considerable time practicing for their success, expect to achieve what they have achieved without paying the same dues. You must learn to be your own person and not be a copy of someone else. I like to think that I have a hard enough time thinking of what I plan to do that I can hardly imagine what goes on in the mind of someone else. I was taught to get my own house in order before I could find time to criticize other performers. You have a purpose, and you are not going to find what that purpose is by copying other performers. The fifteenth century English play writer, William Shakespeare, also said, "To thine own self be true." This is but one more factor to take into account in your pre-performance evaluation. Dr. Wayne Dyer (2004) in his book <u>The Power of Intention</u> suggests that you only regret the things you did not try to accomplish. It is not your failures, but your awareness and ability to act with a purpose that will define your life's work. Philosophically, I try not to take life too seriously because we do not get out of it alive. We are only on this earth a hundred years at most. Why can't we be motivated to help each other improve and achieve the gifts God has given us in a spirit of cooperation instead of competition to see who is best in religion and politics. Instead we are mislead by radicals who want to control us and will resort to killing us if they cannot achieve their aims. Are not all religions motivated by a belief in a higher power? I will never believe that a loving higher power intended for all of us to die at the hands of each other. That supreme motive is in the higher power's hands. Personally, I have always tried to believe that I am an average performer who tries to do a better than average job. Trying to improve your personal best is all that I can ask of anyone, and all that you can ask of yourself.

Cognitive Leadership

Leaders are made not born. Using their cognitive thinking skills, leaders quickly learn to assign relative value to all incoming information as if they had antennae or a satellite dish sitting on top of their head to take in more information. Cognitive implies a purposeful thought process brought to a conscious level to be learned. Leaders are highly observant to continuously learn by sampling new incoming information compared to what they know from their experience to observe trends and project vision to guide their current behaviors to achieve future events. Leaders continuously self-evaluate their performance and hold themselves accountable for their learning and application of knowledge to succeed. A cognitive leader "sees" the big picture to have vision based on successful performance of a learned skill. That learned leadership skill can be taught and is called purposeful intent. Successful leaders are also top performers and will be used interchangeably in this work concept. Unconscious data are also learned and stored in the brain, but are not always readily available. We are still a human animal with built-in survival skills. When you act unconsciously without thoughtful purpose to plan and learn from your performance, your performance is impulsive, inconsistent, and also necessary to preserve life such as the use of the "flight or fight" mechanism that automates behavior and is responsible for us still being a species and not extinct.

With Purposeful Intent, you must learn to override these built-in innate survival skills and other physical limitations that will always operate. PI skills can help you to overcome the natural physio-biological limitations of the flight or fight mechanism, a natural response that limits sensory information that can overload the brain in life-threatening situations so that the body's response can take over. Another mechanism, sensory satiation, also shuts down neuro-receptors from repeated sensory stimuli to prevent system overload. Our drive to automation makes higher order thinking and reasoning skills almost non-existent unless you learn PI skills to override these mechanisms. Biological theories, like W. D. Cannon's (1929) theory of *'homeostatic equilibrium'* explain why the body's processes, such as heart rate, respiration, hormones, and adrenalin production are automated, thus decreasing sensory awareness. Think about which arm or leg you insert into your shirt or pants first, what you ate for dinner yesterday, or focus on the rhythm of your heart rate and breathing for an extended period. Only half the people can tell you with any certainty which pant leg they put on first. And practically everyone who drives a car has experienced this notion – I think that light was green. Our bodies are biological organisms designed to self-regulate to easily process learning simple or mundane tasks for self-preservation, but this decreases the <u>value</u> and <u>purpose</u> for learning those tasks and performance skills that can enhance your memory and performance.

Top performers increase their awareness by focusing on the specific cues that contribute the most to their success. Their ability to identify specific cues that predict faster valued learning and applying them to correct their skills performance with personal feedback to self-evaluate over time is what defines their career. The purpose is to breakdown generalized intent to specifically mobilize and focus personal energy, abilities, and skills to enhance a selected goal performance at will on demand. A top performer senses when to raise their level of performance at critical points to be successful. NBA star, Michael Jordan, did not play at 100% of every minute of every game. Thomas Edison, famous for his cat-naps, wanted to achieve divine intervention more than the rest. When you have a clear purpose for performing an activity coupled with a positive intent to improve or be successful, chances are good that 95–99% of the time you'll have a positive outcome that you can value.

Establishing PI

To establish purposeful intent there must be a personal need or goal to be satisfied. The problem is that most people do not have the skills to identify their personal needs apart from their desires or wants. More confusing than how your personal drives and motives operate is how you were behaviorally conditioned from the time of birth through the present. You behave in the way you are rewarded and conditioned to behave. Everyone has a different need to achieve (N-ach) motive. You can lack direction, a focus, or purpose until you are told what to do and how to do it. This would determine if you are inner or outer directed.

A simple illustration makes the idea of purposeful intent clearer to understand. The first time you travel to a destination your unfamiliar task uncertainty slows you down. The second trip is much smoother because you recognize signs as cues and become more familiar with the route in your selective attention or task sequence strategy. Task familiarity is related to your personality. To acquire purposeful intent skills you need to change your awareness and focus on your personality patterns along with the learned skills to make permanent performance behavior changes. Your personality plays a greater role than you may realize when learning any skill well; just observe the top performers of that skill.

To refer back to the identification of your personal needs, what has changed the most is our affluence. Several hundred years ago, food, clothing, and shelter were dominant needs that had to be met on a daily basis. In an affluent society these basic needs are largely taken for granted especially by youth with fast-food restaurants everywhere. We need to understand that our most basic needs are met by others. This enables other sorts of behaviors – some good, some bad.

The #1 behavioral rule is:

The more you do for people, the less they will learn to do for themselves.

As a former public school superintendent dealing with many children and their parents in families, I saw this happening more and more. The more we want to do for our kids, the less they are learning to do for themselves to meet their basic needs. Some kids dress and groom themselves very differently to express themselves not realizing that if they had to provide for their own basic needs, they would have extreme difficulty and not be able to focus on their other activities to satisfy less important needs. By increasing government and social programs we violate this #1 behavioral rule. Society becomes conditioned to expect "Big Brother" will take care of them. Instead, why not teach every performer to learn how to meet and be held accountable for their own needs. Enabling this kind of expectation is dangerous to the development of the people and their resourcefulness. Whatever happened to the biblical adage of teaching a man how to fish?

The two most important needs I try to teach young people are: 1) The need to become educated. Your education and personality identify you for a lifetime. These two basic life skills no one can take away from you – EVER! The job or need of every student is to work at becoming educated. Parents have a job to supply the basic needs for shelter and food by putting a roof over their heads and bread on the table. 2) The need to work on their character development. A quality character begins with integrity to oneself and others. You may get away with lying to others, but not to yourself. Your word must be a commitment that has meaning and value to hold yourself accountable. A quality character cares about helping others, and shares their knowledge and skills. They learn to strengthen their self-concept and feel good to reward and reinforce these valued behaviors. People learn and are reinforced by an awareness of a personal good feeling to do good deeds, and can help build stronger organizations, systems, and communities to make a difference by their positive outlook and example.

Applying Purposeful Intent

In all cultures, millions of dollars are spent micromanaging the efforts of others. Rather than develop training programs to intrinsically motivate individual performance improvement for the long term gain, it has been easier to use extrinsic means to motivate personnel for short term gains.

Keep these thoughts in mind also:

- You cannot appreciably increase intelligence until you increase awareness [The Triad – Part One – Sphere I]
- No top performer has ever waited for the approval of another person, they will enhance their own self-evaluation system [The Triad – Part Two - Sphere II]; and,
- It is natural behavior to repeat successful activities that reinforces the connection between reward and reinforcement [The Triad – Part Three - Sphere III].

Several years ago when my daughter was a junior inducted into her high school National Honor Society, I asked 18 of the 256 students some simple questions about their purpose and achievements related to their goals. They all reported a preference for looking at their own past performance to strive to improve, and set lower goals to feel rewarded more often and stay motivated. When I asked them where they learned that strategy 16 immediately said at home and 2 said from a coach. Being an educator and behaviorist interested in personal motivation, I thought it was odd that not one successful student in this random sample reported they learned this important strategy from a teacher.

Olympic swimmers I tested in 1972 also taught me that the greatest drive motivation comes from setting goals only slightly better than your own immediate past performance.

In my personal life, all six of my children will have earned college degrees by using this purposeful intent model of intrinsic motivation despite growing up in three separate environments caused by divorces and remarrying. All have continued to use this model to be successful in their personal lives and avocations.

All throughout your life you have probably been told to set high goals to challenge yourself. Actually, the most important goal you can have that will increase your intrinsic motivation the most is to set your goal only one point higher than your own immediate past performance or past performance average. The effect of this rule is to increase your probability for success and reinforce your personal reward system. A low positive goal coupled with a purposeful intent to improve with a little more focused effort will cause you to value and retain more information. This occurs because you have no excuse for not improving such a small increase when you create a positive focus on your efforts. When you personally sacrifice and pay the price for your success, you value the effort to increase your motivation.

You cannot control what others think or tell you to perform, or how they will perform. You can control your thinking to create a positive purposeful intent to improve your performance every chance you get. The more frequently you succeed, you become conditioned to repeat those strategies that helped you improve and you build upon your success. Hence the term, success breeds success. In the long run, a top performer becomes less concerned with what others think of their performance than what they personally have learned to self evaluate and think of their performance. This is why they do not wait for the approval of others. You must also make this conscious shift in how you view your performance to take personal accountability for learning the skills that will advance you to a higher and higher level of performance.

Take a moment to reflect on your past performances. Include performances you were successful and a few that you were not so successful. Your intent for both was probably positive. It is rare that anyone gets out of bed and thinks how they can mess up their day. We all start out trying to be positive and desire to succeed. This is a natural drive, and an innate need to improve. The difference between being successful 95% of the time lies in your purpose. When you know why you are participating to understand the underlying personal need you are trying to satisfy to increase your awareness of purpose, you create a perceived value from your efforts to project a similar reward. When you simply go through the motions of performing and do not have a purpose or goal to achieve, your results are inconsistent and haphazard perhaps more than half the time. If you are unable to connect reward with reinforcement, your motivation to want to repeat and improve upon those kinds of behaviors will be less.

Throughout this book, I will apply comparisons such as the typical performance outcome for having a purpose or not having a purpose. There are dichotomies, a division of two usually opposed parts, like right or wrong, that I will use to compare and contrast many ideas and thoughts. My purpose is to challenge your thinking for how you will learn to motivate your mind from within to improve your performance. Here are a few other examples: extrinsic vs. intrinsic; purpose vs. intent; sensation vs. perception; inner vs. outer directed; personality patterns vs. traits; and lower order thinking skills vs. higher order thinking skills.

PI and Learning to Compete

Several notions operate for any learned purposeful intent strategy. Athletes learn to compete against unequal skills and abilities displayed by other competitors. They learn to overcome their skill deficiencies with specific hard work selectively attending to cues taught by coaches that help speed up the learning process. Top performance athletes learn to equate *quality of effort with quality of reward* and also learn to delay the onset of their rewards until the championship season ending contests to display their learned skills at will on demand. In athletics, no one creates a level playing field for individual performers. The rules and regulations apply equally to all. If you are less talented, you become motivated to outwork your competition to overcome your deficiencies. In athletics it is illegal and demeaning to the sport and performer to fix a competition so a performer will win. In school systems, we have created the notion that if a student is deficient in their learning skills, we will change the playing field to accommodate their deficiencies and inabilities without having them make any sacrifices or extra effort to adapt personal skills. The individual educational placement or IEP is supposed to be designed to help students learn how to adapt to overcome their deficiencies. Instead, many IEP's have simply provided less than desirable extrinsic rewards to motivate a work ethic to learn and overcome early mistakes. Laws of use and disuse apply to learning and using purposeful intent skills. Without a purpose and intent to do well, students or performers do not do as well maintaining their focus. Special education students are micromanaged to control their behaviors until they can learn to function on their own, but the teaching methods used seldom condition that process for an outcome. This detracts from learning accountability with a purposeful intent. The IEP student is generally unable to identify and project their personal needs because these basic needs are enabled by external sources. This further reduces the need for achievement. As a consequence, IEP students are not able to mobilize all of their energy to perform given tasks like homework at will on demand. They often select non specific goals or are completely aimless and confused about what to perform. PI skills must be learned and constantly applied or through disuse they will be forgotten and performance quality will diminish. The body will adapt to stress. A man will develop upper body strength if confined to a wheelchair. A sightless person acquires a keener sense of hearing. A deaf person will learn to read lips. Whatever the disability there is an adaptation mechanism to overcome some of the deficiency. These principles also apply to purposeful intent strategies that can be adapted to meet the personal needs of any performer.

All performers can learn from top athletes who quickly learn to compete from within because they know that they cannot control the performance of another athlete. They can, however, control their own performances by competing from within against their own personal standard known as immediate past performance or average. This becomes their perceptual anchoring point or PAP. By increasing the probability for success, you also increase your frequency of success to create a positive reinforcement schedule to motivate future performances. This same idea can easily be applied to business management, school systems, or any kind of training program designed to improve personnel performance.

Your ability to learn and apply specific skills gets stronger with more use and weaker with less use. Leaders, like coaches, can learn to use trigger words to elicit a correct response pattern to a recognized stimulus or host of behaviors that immediately recall knowledge gathered with a purposeful intent. For example, if a performer has a specific personal goal or need, the purposeful intent and trigger words need to bring these intrinsic variables into a stronger focus from time to time. An athlete on a team may want to do well for the team, but has a specific goal performance to meet by a certain deadline with the intent to perform well to catch the attention of scouts who will be in attendance. The focus will be on specific skill sets that can display personal abilities. In business, the sales group is usually given quotas based on forecasts and previous production numbers. However, each representative has specific personal needs that good managers must appeal to intrinsically motivate each rep with a purposeful intent mutually exclusive of the team and the company net profits. Trigger words keep the focus on purposeful intent, and can be conditioned and reinforced for each performer to increase their conscious awareness.

Conditioning Purposeful Intent
In Homes and Schools

A serious problem that is rapidly growing in our school systems are the number of children diagnosed with ADD Attention Deficit Disorder or ADHD Attention Deficit Hyperactivity Disorder. These children display learning disabilities because they cannot focus on their work for extended time periods. They lack the discipline to stay on task, move from one task to another without completion, and are unaware of the intrinsic reward benefits. Heavily relied upon extrinsic rewards fail to create a long term effect on positive behaviors. When children misbehave, observe what well-meaning adults do to stop the intrusion in their lives. Adults enable and condition bad behaviors by providing unnecessary extrinsic rewards for being good that are short lived. Children quickly learn to be disruptive to get a reward for the promise of future good behavior. They temporarily stop misbehaving while savoring the extrinsic reward (candy or attention), and then resume their misbehavior. These behavior cycles become conditioned responses. For all learners, purposeful intent strategies break the negative behavior-reward cycle by providing more conscious awareness of other positive personal needs to be satisfied and rewarded to stay on task. This process is called displace-replace operant conditioning. The rewards are changed from extrinsic (candy) to intrinsic (reflection), "How do you feel about your performance?" Intrinsic strategies build value and respect for prior knowledge to create the need to acquire new knowledge in smaller, personally rewarded successes, and knowing and being in control of their learning. The focus is modified to meet the needs of the learner in smaller increments to be consciously self-rewarded and reinforced with greater frequency than to concentrate on single whole performances. This builds confidence, self-discipline, and self-esteem with more frequent success. The intrinsic process takes longer to condition, but will last a lifetime learning self-evaluation and self-reward skills. You want to get the learner to reflect on and care about their own immediate past performance to learn how to self-evaluate and improve that performance on the next trial. If the improper needs are withdrawn and proper needs are slowly reintroduced, specific behaviors can be reconditioned and satisfied by the performer. To correct failure cycles, leaders need to identify performance breakdowns and go back to re master the basic performance skills. To begin mastery learning every task there is a learned sequence that can be broken down into smaller measurable and rewarded subroutines or parts. This increases opportunity and probability for reward to condition a work ethic. This also re builds success and confidence in smaller incremental steps to condition personal self-reward and self-esteem. In the current American public school system, too much emphasis is placed on SEL – Social Emotional Learning, and more effort is spent on keeping a student with their social grade level peers than on mastering fundamental benchmark learning skills first. Modular based computer assisted instructional units could remove learning deficiencies, and advance learners at their ability to master skills.

In China, the educational system is not overly concerned with a child's self-esteem or social level. Student talents, abilities, and skills are identified early, and selected for specialized education and training to place more emphasis on mastery. A student performs at designated levels and moves on to be provided with government supported opportunities. Consequently, there are more Chinese students in gifted programs than the entire American public school population. There should be no doubt that changes are immediately necessary in our educational system. How we choose to intrinsically motivate our students to want to learn more with a purposeful intent would be a good start.

PI Skills Development Model

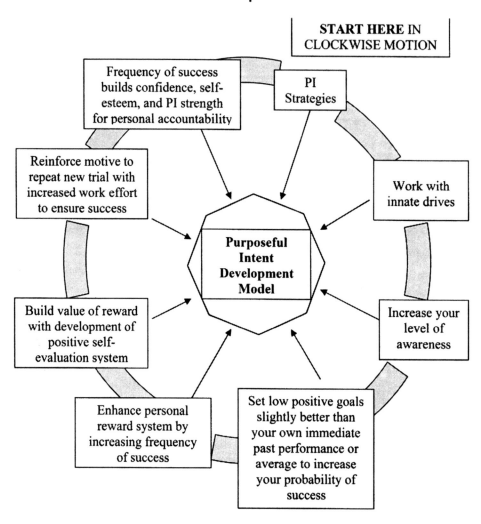

START HERE IN CLOCKWISE MOTION

Frequency of success builds confidence, self-esteem, and PI strength for personal accountability

PI Strategies

Reinforce motive to repeat new trial with increased work effort to ensure success

Work with innate drives

Purposeful Intent Development Model

Build value of reward with development of positive self-evaluation system

Increase your level of awareness

Enhance personal reward system by increasing frequency of success

Set low positive goals slightly better than your own immediate past performance or average to increase your probability of success

The PI Skills Development Model shows the organic nature of these skills, and how one leads into the next to develop your purposeful intent. The first step is PI strategies. You identify all the component skills for any activity or task and the personal need that is motivating you to achieve performance improvement. The second step is to identify and work with your natural innate drives. Maslow's Hierarchy provides a good start. The third step is to increase your levels of awareness using RROSR by learning to attend to selected predictable cues that are most important to aid your performance. The fourth step is to set low positive goals to increase your probability of success. This process enhances the fifth step to develop your personal reward system by increasing your frequency of success. In the sixth step the value of your perceived reward serves to develop a positive self-evaluation system. By the seventh step, your motives are reinforced by your success to increase your work effort to ensure your continued success. Finally, the eighth step leads to the development of your confidence, self-esteem, PI strength, and personal accountability. As the cycle is repeated your PI skills improve, get stronger, and your personal success continuously motivates you to greater achievements.

Psychology of Intrinsic Motivation

As you have read thus far, the psychology of intrinsic motivation is a complex issue. There are perhaps well over 15 interrelated variables operating within the individual at the same time. You cannot partial out the bad variables, but you can narrow your performer's focus or conscious awareness level using selected cues that predict the best on performance improvement for that performer or job skill. There are numerous articles about intrinsic motivation, but I have not seen a work that details a training program that teaches you personal skills to be intrinsically motivated. I have simplified this skills training for you using a three part approach known as The Triad. Most successful performers consistently perform in an automated subconscious mode without knowing how or why they do what they do. The Triad teaches you skills to increase your awareness from unconscious to conscious. This process creates value and stronger associations through use of RROSR.

As a former school superintendent, I heard educators complain how most students do not have a good support network or motivation in the home, and that there is nothing we can do in educational systems to change that. If we can eliminate curriculum gaps and provide formative assessment, we can also learn to teach PI strategies that will intrinsically motivate every student. Teachers must be a coach in the classroom and *facilitators of knowledge*. I cannot imagine a freshman Algebra teacher thinking that they cannot teach one of their students because they believe the parents are incapable of solving a quadratic equation. I cannot imagine a coach thinking they cannot improve the skills of one of their athletes because they believe the parents are incapable of performing that skill. Then why do educators feel they cannot intrinsically motivate one or several of their students because they do not have parents who are motivated, set a good example, or try to motivate their children in the home? These teachers and parents resort to extrinsic bribes to get students to learn. It is counter-productive to extrinsically reward students to learn. They will not learn to value their education. By the time they get to junior high school, the extrinsic reward is never large enough. Each unique performer is what matters most. Teachers and managers are leaders to teach PI to those who need it, and reinforce successful performers so they can understand why they are successful. Stephen Covey (1989) used the same process in his book, The Seven Habits of Effective People to summarize observations of successful performers. Every performer brings to the table something positive that they are doing correctly. Leaders must look for those positives to reinforce and condition instead of the negative fault finding that conditions bad behaviors. When leading create the right environment and needs with PI skills training. The rest is up to your performers. The 19th century German poet, Goethe, said it best, "If you treat an individual as if they were what they ought to be and could be, they will become what they ought to be and could be." You cannot be a boss leader and assume your personnel are incapable of intrinsic motivation to improve their performance. If you lead properly, they will perform properly.

How To Improve Your PI Skills Using The Triad

How to improve your PI skills will be explained using the three parts of The Triad: Increase Awareness, Enhance Self-evaluation, and Connect Reward with Reinforcement. Occasionally remind yourself with a mental image of The Triad to trigger your motivation to practice the skills. Think of those three interconnected spheres with molecules. As you heat up one sphere the molecules bombard and excite the molecules to get the other two spheres working. Be patient with the changes you will be suggesting to your personality patterns. Some personality adjustments will take time to condition and self-reinforce to make them a habit. You will notice these changes more readily when you begin to master the awareness skills taught in Part I. As you read, learn to apply these skills to yourself and those you lead. As with any unfamiliar task, your learning process will seem confusing until you become more familiar with each task. The PI concepts and skills that you will acquire will make more sense when The Triad comes together in your life. You will become more aware of your subtle performance improvements to feel your success and enrich the quality of your life and those around you. Thus, purposeful intent is:

#1 A learned skill that must be practiced over time to achieve consistent results. Use it or lose it.

#2 Formed by the sum total use of your personality, education, past performance, experiences, values, beliefs, conditioned responses or biased beliefs and prejudice, abilities, skills, attitudes, goals, needs, and motives.

#3 Not hard to learn, but is neither a quick fix nor opportune motivational system that lasts for 72 hours from a motivational speaker telling you their uplifting experiences. Permanent changes take time and are motivated by knowledge and understanding of how intrinsic motivation works and taught through The Triad.

#4 Intrinsic motivation based on proven psychological principles and observed behaviors. The skills learning process can seem complex because there are many interrelated variables that are difficult to control. Once you become conscious of the specific variable interactions, you can control their effect with more purposeful effort to improve your performance. You will see performance improvement when you learn and teach purposeful intent to meet specific identifiable needs.

These common behaviors are used by successful performers often without their knowing it because they have been subconsciously conditioned. Think of how much faster and greater learning could take place when performers understand a conscious purpose for what they are learning and performing. Learning how to mobilize your energy, talent, ability, and skill for a given moment in time at will on demand is the key to your success over time. But first you must learn what your needs and abilities are. Take the personal survey found in the appendix. Create your purposeful intent and motivate your mind from within. You will achieve more consistent and positive results that will define you. Once you learn these skills, I hope you will <u>pass them on</u> to those whom you will lead or try to help.

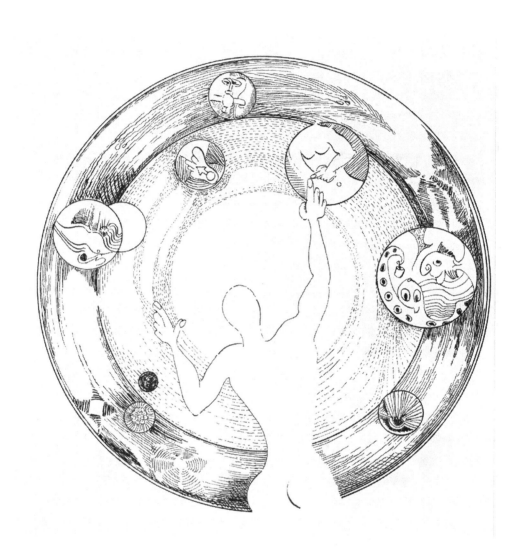

PART ONE

INCREASE AWARENESS

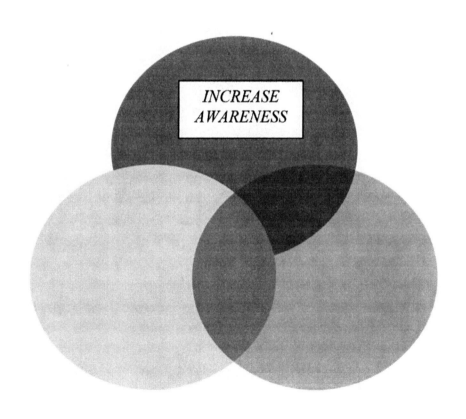

You cannot appreciably increase your intelligence until you learn how to increase your awareness to recognize, receive, organize, store, and retrieve (RROSR) meaningful and relevant information you decide is valuable to your learning. Parents, teachers, managers, coaches, and leaders can tell you what is meaningful and relevant to speed up the learning process, but you ultimately have to decide how new information has value in your performance system. You create the value to make that knowledge acquisition intrinsic. Based on that value system you create with your own set of personal standards is what makes or breaks you as a top performer over time from the choices you will make.

Part One helps you learn three main ideas:

Mind-Body Connection. Your mind and body have <u>structures</u> that help you perform better once you understand how they function together. This chapter will be broken into three parts: Structure, Awareness, and Learning. Your brain directs your body and all your behavior. You can get in touch with your body through your mind and vice versa. This involves both physical and mental activities. Your body carries your brain around like an ever-present personal computer that needs no plug in for electric power. Your brain has its own generator when you learn how to turn it on and focus your performance at any given moment in time. This is to motivate your mind from within.

Growing Antennae. When you understand your structures, you can focus your awareness on learning your <u>abilities</u>. This chapter is broken into three sections: Discover to identify, reflect, assess, and plan; Define your need, drives, and motives, abilities, value, personality, goals, focus, mobilization of energy, and reward with conditioning; and Realize your purpose and potential using The Triad and RROSR. Everyone is good at something, but even a butterfly cannot survive without its antennae and neither can you. When you understand your abilities, you will try new activities to find the one you can excel in performing. Try creating a word document on your computer with your monitor off. Not much is going to go on your hard drive. Think of your head with a satellite dish mounted to receive signals of information from a variety of sources. The more information you can take in, assign a purpose, and store properly by associating new knowledge to what you have already learned, your retrieval process to help you perform at a higher level must be improved over time. The key to consistent top performance is your ability to retrieve valuable information necessary to perform a given task well at will on demand. You create value by making what you learn meaningful and relevant. A teacher can tell you the new knowledge you are being taught is valuable, meaningful, and relevant, but this is not the same as you telling your brain that it is all those things. You will also perform better with a well defined purposeful intent. Champions create their will to win by how they value what they do; and like leaders, they are made, not born.

It's YOUR Job. When you understand your structures and abilities, it will be time to learn <u>accountability</u> for your performance. This chapter is broken into two large sections: Education and Learning to understand what school systems, teachers, and parents can do to a traditional system to include Purposeful Intent that conditions meaningful and relevant learning in a value based curriculum; and Management to understand how management can be refocused on purposeful strategies to improve personnel performance. No one can make you learn or do anything with quality until you see the personal value in performing. Top performers accept personal accountability for their performance and do not blame others for their lack of effort or poor performance.

Mind-Body Connection

"Virtuous man sees depth of character."

Andrew Christian

Objective: Understanding the structure of your mind and body to coordinate your mental and physical responses.

Introduction

Make a list of your successful performances. What was your mind-set when you began and ended? Chances are you had a positive purposeful intent and you clearly understood why you were working on a task. Conversely, list several times when you were just going through the motions in a job or task. What was your mind-set? What were the outcomes? Your mind and body must work together to motivate performance improvement.

STRUCTURE

The Brain as a Microprocessor

The brain is an awesome organ made up of billions of cells linked by associational neurons. The central nervous system connects the body to the brain with nerve cells. Practicing skills helps create nervous pathways and speeds up transmission through the nervous system network. The brain is a micro processor that responds to a continual barrage of stimuli by the second and minute. We have built in synapse filters to prevent our brain from being overloaded with non-essential details, or we would have been an extinct species a long time ago. A built in sensory flight or fight mechanism does not require thinking to delay action.

When programmed properly, the brain is a highly organized storage and retrieval system of feedback loops, comparator operations, predictive capabilities, projection, and vision skills connected by associational neurons. Without programmed skills, your brain is also highly inefficient to send conflicting signals for the body to perform in speech and motor activities. The brain has long and short term memory to learn and make sense out of complex sensations to make perceptions about the value and projection of that information on future performance.

Albert Einstein was believed to be the most intelligent of any man. It was estimated that he used 7–8% of his brain capacity; the normal average is 3–4%. Upon his death, his brain was illegally taken and studied. Researchers found that he had extremely high numbers of associational neurons that linked all parts of his brain. Einstein practiced multi-sensory learning that you can also learn to do. After observation, he would imagine what an object might feel, taste, sound, or smell like that created numerous associations to help organize and retrieve stored information.

Specific information is stored as compressed data known as bit maps in specific areas or lobes noted for those skills by blood flow studies from brain scans. Each lobe has a specific function. For example, visual bit maps tend to be stored in the occipital lobe at the back of your head. Performers who fall hard on the back of their head can also experience vision problems. The frontal lobe is behind your forehead and where your thinking takes place. Immediately in front of the frontal lobe is your pre frontal cortex or PFC.

In the early 1900's, Korbinian Brodmann defined specific structures and functions of the cerebral cortex or human brain. Brodmann area 11 is defined as the prefrontal cortex, and is involved in planning, reasoning, and decision making. Persons who have had brain injuries to this area are not able to use these skills.

Theoretically the prefrontal cortex acts like the cache short term memory on your computer. This short-term memory space is where you assign value, meaning and relevance to any information, add it to prior knowledge, and plan where to store the new information. This calculative valuation process establishes the quality of your personal need to be satisfied that develops your motivation. More importantly, this part of the brain can be used to preplan a correct sequence to perform a complex skill at will on demand by recalling prior experiences specific to the program you want to create; then you set up a trigger cue like a race starting gun or pre-shot routine. U.S. Olympic gold medalist Michael Phelps is a swimmer who has set numerous world records in a variety of events. He has a pre planned and mentally rehearsed to perfect a subroutine for eight events whether it is the 200 meter butterfly or a 400 meter individual medley. Phelps has practiced for and performed these events countless times and stored a greater source of information that he can draw upon when he needs to execute a skill.

As a performer you can set up similar executable files using mental imagery or visualization to see yourself performing a skill as if you were video taping your performance. Through practice you program the correct stimulus-response connections to perform in the proper sequence and set up a trigger to start your program. Then you must trust your experience and prior stored knowledge to execute the plan to the best of your ability. To achieve the best results, learn the best strategies and cues that can predict success. When the information you used in your stored files is more accurate to start with, and you have practiced and conditioned yourself for the task, you're more likely to be successful. However, there are leaders who believe success is governed by natural intelligence. The behaviorist believes environment plays a more significant role as learned behavior can be conditioned to perform successfully. Even though you may live in a very poor physical environment without models to extrinsically motivate you, you can condition your brain, as a defense mechanism, to take you to a private place. In your quiet place, motivate your mind from within with positive self talk and a "can do" attitude using The Triad and intrinsic motivation skills. Motivation is more than what you do to someone that is extrinsic. Intrinsic motivation is what you skillfully learn to do for yourself by creating personal needs, values, and a purposeful intent. We are not all born intelligent, and many strong performers do very little to enhance their intelligence by decreasing their sensory awareness skills. The process for increasing your awareness, enhancing your self evaluation, and connecting reward with reinforcement to repeat successful activities to learn more and continuously improve your performance is a teachable leadership skill. This is your purposeful intent and the foundation for all motivation to improve your performance.

The synapse is the bridge between two adjacent neurons and requires a strong enough sensory impulse to create the chemical acetylcholine to bridge the gap between one nerve ending and another. The synapse filters unwanted sensory stimuli from over loading the nervous system. The figures shown are taken from Neuroscience For Kids http://faculty.washington.edu/chudler/synapse.html (2007). In mille seconds after the impulse, acetylcholine esterase is secreted to erase the acetylcholine. If the impulses are continuous and strong enough to repeatedly bridge the synapse, the brain can also shut down the input with a process called sensory satiation. It is why you no longer smell the odor working in a cheese factory after an initial period of time. Similarly,

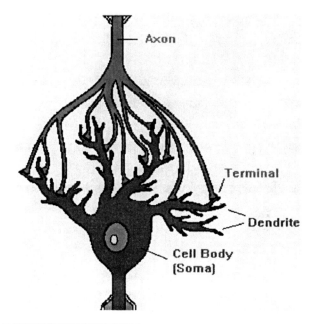

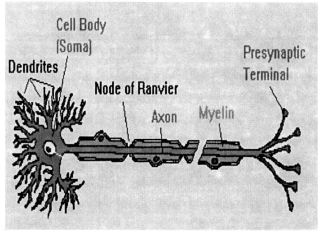

severely injured burn victims shut down pain receptors. Sensory deprivation works in the opposite mode. Your mind is constantly gathering data. You must move to learn. When sensory data are taken away, the brain loses all sense of function to result in confusion. An example is hypothermia. The body cannot maintain normal temperature to operate. Hallucinations have also been produced by putting blindfolded people in a wetsuit floating in a secluded lukewarm tank of water to remove the effects of vision, hearing, gravity, and skin sensation.

A common mistake all leaders make by not understanding how the brain functions as a microprocessor is to focus the performer's attention to negative cues and outcomes you wish to avoid, but conditions the association to make the event more likely to happen. I once overheard a gymnastics coach yell out instructions for the entire team to avoid mistakes today to prevent injuries. A sport psychologist tells the story about a pitching coach who came out to the mound with the bases loaded to tell his pitcher how to pitch to the next batter. "Whatever you do, don't pitch him anything low and inside. That's his wheelhouse." You know the image this pitcher made. Your imagery creates an automated response and reinforces the behavioral connection. The pitcher's behavior was to replicate that image and the batter pounded a grand slam. The 2008 U.S. women's Olympic gymnasts made a huge blunder by watching the performances and mistakes of the Chinese gymnasts immediately before their performance. Several made similar mistakes because this was what was last programmed in their mental movie subroutine. Tiger Woods never looks at another golfer's swing, and only programs his personal short visualization in his pre performance routine. If I yell a negative instruction loud enough to bridge the synapse for you NOT to think about oranges, you immediately create an image of 2–3 brightly colored oranges that demonstrates your brain is a microprocessor that does not know right from wrong. This supports why positive self-talk, mental rehearsal and conscious PI can improve your awareness and performance.

The brain and nervous system is structured to process sensory information, and make it meaningful and relevant to increase its value which implies a transition to perception and learning. The prefrontal cortex coordinates the mind and body activities so that we can learn to perform routine skills efficiently. When you have a purpose, you can use your brain to focus on the essential cues to improve performance. A pair of binoculars will not work until they are focused. Without a purpose and focus neither will you perform as well as you could.

AWARENESS

"Houston, we have a problem."

I have often thought about how to reach kids who are failing in school to learn why they are not self-motivated. I keep thinking that failure is a painful feeling, and these students must not know what or how to meet their personal needs. Because of the initial failures, everyone thinks they are helping this student by doing the work for them to show them how. The exact opposite effect occurs to enable more of the failing behaviors by not doing homework assignments or taking notes in class. No one likes to feel pain. So you block it out. You don't want to remember your immediate past performance. The idea of improvement is also remote because no one has taught a strategy for teaching intrinsic motivation. Getting failing students to want to increase their awareness is a huge task because it may provide painful feelings. The trick is to get the performer to hold themselves accountable for their performance instead of an evaluator like a teacher or parent holding them accountable and threatening punishment in the form of poor grades, time outs, or being grounded. The process is not unlike getting someone, who is in denial, to recognize that they have a problem. The punch line is, "Houston, we have a problem." This line was spoken by the crew of Apollo 13 returning from the moon. Now that was a problem. The fact is everyone experiences problems in life, but none are impossible. The biggest problem is death. We all are faced with it as an inevitable conclusion to our life, but we still live a life. First we live, and then we die. What about the time in between? Each performer is blessed with abilities and a purpose. There is so much to do and so little time, yet many performers are easily bored simply because they have not been taught how to increase their awareness to look for their purpose and discover what their needs and abilities are. Increasing awareness is an essential Part One of The Triad for teaching the skills to be intrinsically motivated and improve performance.

No one is perfect, but trying to improve is perfect. Keep your expectations in line with reality and you will not be frustrated. Our schools need teachers who understand more about human behavioral psychology and how to intrinsically motivate students to explore and find their talents to create a passion for learning. Our schools need teachers who are patient and understanding to not penalize students for taking risks or making early mistakes they cannot recover adequately from or for not doing their homework when they already get A's on all the tests. The easiest to change would be to set up a grading system that rewards improvement. Students are performers. They are easily rewarded by seeing their own improvements through learning skills that teach purposeful intent in The Triad. They don't need an extrinsic motive like a candy bar or $ 5.00 for every A grade. You cannot buy the feeling you get when you know you can read a chapter and understand what you've learned to produce that knowledge on an assessment. The performer that does the work needs to get all the credit to improve their intrinsic motivation.

You can fool yourself into thinking you know more than you really do, but this behavior will not build your self-confidence. Eventually your behavior falls into the trap of don't think, don't ask. If you think about the results of even your immediate past performance, you find your success is not what you want it to be. You can block past performance out of your mind as you would any painful experience by choosing not to think about them. You are ashamed to lower your standards or false belief that you are not as good as you think you are, and so you do not ask questions or seek help. You continue to show off trying to build up your ego when there is not much evidence to support your claim. The sad part is that your inner brain knows the truth. There is never a greater time to be honest with yourself and become aware of your inner truths. You need to commit to making this one change in your life, and to understand your purpose by growing your awareness antennae. Then you will have the opportunity to consistently improve your performance over time to be a better than average performer. All behavior is motivated by the desire to satisfy a personal need or goal. All performers have personal needs, but they are not usually brought to a conscious level. Even if you become aware of your needs, you still must learn how to best meet those needs. You cannot rob others to get the money to feed yourself. If you allow your mind to work in the subconscious level, your behaviors will be impulsive, spur-of-the-moment-quick-fix, and inconsistent with less value. This will decrease your opportunity to feel success and reward or store knowledge in a meaningful way to readily retrieve when you need it. Without a conscious purposeful intent, you will create hit or miss chance opportunities, and do not produce consistent successful results. Impulsive behavior is like trying to hit a moving target blindfolded. Chance behaviors require no work or preparation to expend energy. They also have limited value which makes the reward temporarily seem greater and more reinforcing to chance again. An example would be a compulsive gambler. You falsely believe that you can make up for your losses on the next trial. If gambling is so successful, then why aren't there more winners than losers? If you want to be a top performer, you do not gamble with your life's experiences. You acquire purposeful behaviors that require learning to focus on specific cues that produce consistently better responses. This process takes time to practice and learn the skills over a lifetime. To be purposeful, you have to bring subconscious behaviors to a conscious level by learning awareness skills. **Your PI skills are always improving but never mastered.** There are no shortcuts.

Nervous pathways must be developed to speed up your response time to select stimuli as you reinforce the most efficient S-R connections to perform skills. Over several trials you condition a more efficient direct route for your trip to work at a new job. Thinking about the proper cues will make your responses happen faster only if you connect and reinforce them in practice. However, once you are familiar with a task there is some evidence that mental rehearsal can aid learning, but we are not sure how or why. PI skills bring the selected cues to attend to into a more powerful focus to speed up learning, creating associational neuron links (S-R connections), nerve conduction pathways, and response time. Your prefrontal cortex functions as the temporary program server. With visualization you can create and perfect a specific subroutine or part of a performance in your mind prior to performing. Then mentally rehearse the fine points of your performance to improve the execution of the actual performance without having to think about it during the performance, as if to automate it. Learning with a purposeful intent to improve your performance is also aided by understanding these concepts: selective attention, cueing in response, task familiarity, personality patterns, positive self-talk, goal-setting, and stacking or thinking through a process in steps to a conclusion using a specific sequence or serial learning. All of these concepts and skills can be taught in our schools.

The essence of purposeful intent is to become skilled at taking unconscious sensations to conscious perceptions that increase your awareness through meaningful and relevant value associations. Thinking modifies the sensation into a perception of right and wrong, also known as your conscience. If you are improving, it is right; if you are not improving, something is wrong. The approval of others like teachers in schools is inherently conditioned in your daily life and a powerful social motivator, but it's an external motivation and a trap. How you feel about yourself is what must really matter the most. This self-awareness comes from within and no one can give it to you; you have to earn your confidence by learning the PI strategies. When you consistently improve your performance in smaller more manageable segments, you can control and increase your probability for success. Knowing your purpose increases your motivation to improve your performance *at will on demand*. This learned awareness skill drives your intrinsic motivation. Learning how to be self-directed and not externally directed is the goal. Leaders cannot expect to externally motivate every performer every day in every setting. If parents fall into this trap, when their children get older, they seldom do anything that is not connected to a conditioned external reward. If external rewards are not great enough in value, performers do not act to improve, and their behaviors are meaningless and irrelevant. Many wealthy people are unhappy because the extrinsic rewards are not great enough to satisfy their needs. They have never learned that the giving of oneself to others is greater than money as a wealth. To know that one life has improved because of your personal efforts is to have succeeded.

Intrinsically motivated performers use PI skills to focus more on the process and sequence with smaller incremental rewards to reinforce their work ethic behaviors and let the outcome take care of itself. With a purpose you condition a successful result that can consistently help you perform good outcomes over time and define your success or career. Ultimately, high performers search for satisfaction from intrinsic rewards that involve giving back to others as Maslow (1943) described in the highest need of self actualization.

Stimulus-Response Conditioning

A stimulus is any agent or action that causes an activity in an organism. A cue is an agent or action, however, the activity that occurs is generally associated through a practice set to increase the recognition of the cue with the desired response. This is called conditioning and the symbols used are S-R, but to get the desired conditioned response it becomes S-CR. The stimulus remains constant, but the response changes as performance improves. To perform a complex task there may be a huge number of stimulus-response connections that are chained together. In this manner, the response for the first link in the chain then becomes the stimulus for the next response. When these connections are rapidly performed they appear to be fluid in motion. With practice the cue is readily recognized, and the synapse is bridged more efficiently to increase neural transmission speed and decrease response time.

Great leader/coaches will teach using a displace-replace refocus strategy to condition correct responses to selected cues. They replace the incorrect with the correct cue, and verbally explain or visually demonstrate an image that will increase the performer's awareness to improve the response. This selective stimulus cue recognition is a learned awareness skill which displaces the incorrect stimulus and replaces it with the correct stimulus to improve the desired response. Using this strategy helps performers refocus on a smaller more manageable specific positive outcome with a purposeful intent that will increase their probability for success and build confidence. **Increased intelligence is directly proportional to increased awareness.**

Paired-Associate Conditioning

Sequential learning increases the number of associational neurons and is essential for conditioning the correct stimulus-response connections in your brain to process information more efficiently for storage and retrieval. The way it works is information is stored and retrieved in your brain as bits of information. Two different stimuli are paired up or associated with the same response. For example, when teaching a skill, your instructor may provide a visual demonstration and use verbal cues to describe how the action will feel in the muscles providing the movement. This actually pairs up visual, verbal, and kinesthetic stimuli to provide a specific cue for every kind of learning preference. They call this differentiated instruction. It is also more resistant to forgetting what to do as these kinds of associations are very powerful motives. Similarly, the performer learns to associate pleasure with conscious feelings of success in an activity. The reinforcement comes from increasing the motivation to continue that same feeling in continued activity by putting forth more effort or PI. How the smartest man, Albert Einstein, learned to create more associational neurons with multi sensory learning is a clear message. We need to create more associations that we can learn to transfer similar or identical elements to provide more highly probable solutions to problems. This means you have learned skills to increase your awareness or focus on specific sensory stimuli to acquire experience and task familiarity that comes from practice. Diverse skills are also important to transfer to new tasks.

Complex visual patterns sequence large amounts of generalized stimulus information compressed into a single bit of information. This process speeds up storage and retrieval to give the impression of faster nerve transmission. It is why you can learn to perform complex routines and tasks by first visualizing them in person or on tape for your imagination in the form of mental rehearsal. With more correct practice using the highest predictable cues by observing experienced successful performers, you learn to "associate" specific cues to condition specific responses and make them familiar. Over time that sequence becomes generalized to automate the task. Skilled performers learn to associate visual, verbal, and kinesthetic stimuli with the same response that becomes resistant to forgetting and helps retrieve this stored information. Taking good notes provides the kinesthetic feeling cues to associate and pair up with the visual and verbal cues presented by the teacher. This increases your awareness to condition learning and help make the information more meaningful and relevant and resistant to forgetting.

Awareness, Intelligence and RROSR

The Increasing Awareness flow chart on the following pages creates a visual flow for how to increase your awareness. You cannot appreciably increase your intelligence to be a top performer until you learn how to increase your awareness. Intelligent top performers develop and use their sensory and perceptual awareness skills to learn how to efficiently recognize, receive, organize, store, and retrieve more information when they assign personal meaningful and relevant value. I call this RROSR. Top performers increase their awareness to routinely access a greater variety of information. The ultimate goal is to increase your ability to RROSR - recognize, receive, organize, store, and retrieve information. During your lifetime you must learn how to increase the storage and retrieval efficiency of the associational neurons connected in your brain's "hard drive." Good coaches and teachers provide more specific cues to selectively attend to (recognition) that improve the response. As the task becomes more familiar, the complex pattern with its host of cues (receive) is compressed (organized) into a "bit map" for faster (storage) and (retrieval) that anyone can learn (RROSR). When you increase your sensory awareness to consciously value any input, you will be able to link the new information by increasing your associational neurons using RROSR – recognize, receive, organize, store and retrieve information faster at will on demand. Increasing awareness and the value of activities enhances our ability to RROSR more quality information, solve new problems, or learn new skills.

Abuse of drugs, inhalants, smoking, or alcohol deadens your senses to decrease your awareness levels. Your mind will not learn how to direct your body. The quality of your life will not improve, and your problems will not go away. These self medicated solutions are not the answer to finding your purpose in life.

Increasing Awareness Flow Chart

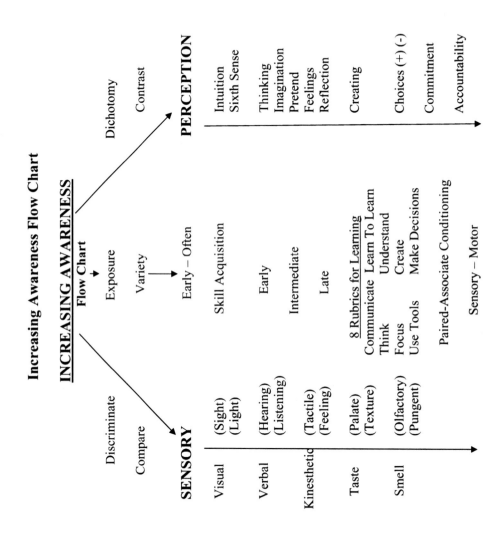

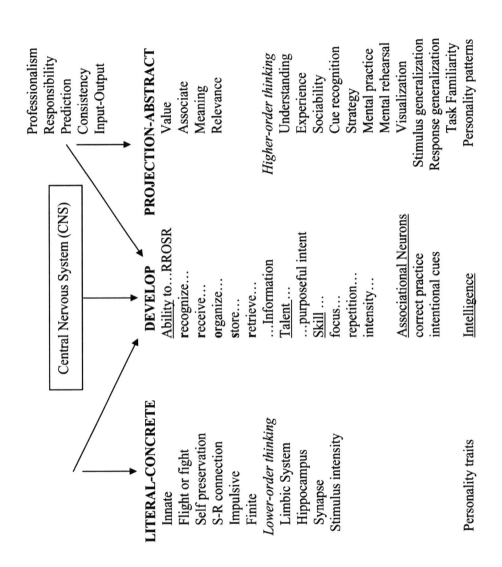

Automated Routines: The Biological Autopilot

When our activities become too routine, our brain switches to autopilot and the value of the activity is decreased. Routine automated experiences become less meaningful and valuable, and hypothetically are stored in slower retrievable sequences. Typical sensory responses are routinely automated to reduce conflicting messages to the brain in potential life-threatening flight or fight situations. The brain would be quickly overloaded and unable to attend to specific cues, avoid confusion, and perform poorly when life depended on a correct response. Otherwise, we would have been an extinct species a long time ago. However, increase your awareness of your routines to consciously override them occasionally to achieve greater value that motivates learning and improvement. Experienced airline pilots practice their skills in flight simulator refresher courses after flying 1200-2000 hours to reduce pilot error. Automation does reduce stress which partly explains why change is difficult and no improvement occurs. Not all routines are bad, but you must be aware of them to guard against errors, stagnation, and boredom. W.D. Cannon (1964) presented a biological theory of homeostatic equilibrium in 1943 that explains how heart rate, respiration, hormones, and other physiological functions are automated to achieve balance or equilibrium.

The brain can override automated impulses to increase awareness or block pain to attend to more important cues and perform purposeful tasks *at will on demand*. Great marathon runners and other athletes routinely block pain when they "hit the wall" to go beyond normal performance. Similarly, unconscious environmental conditioning shows how poverty affects social and emotional learning and acquiring knowledge with a purpose to motivate changing your environment, learn a value system, and seek hope to improve the quality of life. The best hope for impoverished communities or individuals is to rely on a faith based system to empower a purposeful intent for every member to contribute and make the necessary changes in their life. Alcoholics Anonymous is a perfect example for using faith to inspire a purpose that can intrinsically motivate an individual.

Mundane Tasks, Emotion, and Learning

Highly familiar tasks become routine to have only mundane value and are automated to a subconscious level. As you learn routine behaviors you also lose conscious control of your needs and abilities to meet them. You must learn to override this built in response.

To effect a change in this learning pattern requires greater emotion such as shouting new instructions or information to be retained. Simply bringing new information to a higher awareness or conscious state by using a strategy like positive self-talk also works. Tell your brain that this new stuff is important and you can do it. Or, you can review the old stuff – what was and was not working, set some kind of value for a low positive goal improvement, and tell your brain to remember it. Your brain is a microprocessor to process information from your senses that does not know right from wrong. A mental image is created and reinforced from a negative statement the same as if you had stated it in the positive. To extinct behaviors you cannot talk about them unless you connect the correct response to the same stimulus. Effective leaders are positive thinkers looking for the good in others, and wisely spend time on the positive reinforcements to teach their performers how to think about satisfying their personal needs and goals to accomplish tasks. You achieve what you focus your efforts on by bringing your thinking to a conscious level, and like that pair of binoculars they only work when you focus them.

Awareness As A Learned Skill

Top performers are not unique: they eat, sweat, sleep, bathe, breathe, and brush their teeth like you do. The hallmark of top performers is that they are aware of when to increase their level of performance (LOP) at critical times. Their increased awareness helps them keep a pace or readily mobilize their energy. Average performers, however, have fewer awareness skills to create value and miss meaningful and relevant cues. You could be motivated and not know how depending on your subconscious needs. However, by identifying your needs now and for the future in five year increments, this PI strategy will help you bring your intrinsic motivation to a conscious level. This will consciously increase both your PI and motivation to improve your performance. Then, as a parent, you will not have to ask your teenager, "What were you thinking?" Unconscious behaviors need to be brought to a conscious purposeful level in the mind of the performer more than the mind of the evaluator. To visualize this process refer to the Increase Awareness Flow Chart.

Energy Mobilization

PI skills training helps achieve the same kind of energy mobilization as flight or fight at will on demand. The only difference is that PI skills rely on conscious perception and flight or fight is an unconscious automated sensory mechanism. Automation does not enhance sensory awareness to accommodate and assimilate more selective information. Conscious learning, also known as meta-cognition, reinforces the connection between pleasurable feelings, from reflecting on your performance feedback, and reward. The pre-frontal cortex associates a relative value to any successful activity that increases your motivation to improve your future performances and maintain those pleasurable feelings. You are motivated to try harder to improve your performance in events and activities that you value.

Biofeedback Awareness

To increase awareness you have to turn your sensations into perceptions. Biofeedback is the feedback you learn from the interaction of your environment with your biological senses. You can only develop your senses by using all of them. This is what multi sensory learning attempts to achieve. You associate pain coming from your senses when you touch something hot, or your muscles are sore from excessive activity, then your perception takes over. Using your vision and projection skills – if I touch that stove, it will hurt. Using your touch and feeling resistance – if I lift these weights too much, it will hurt. You can have the perception of pain when you feel the anguish of losing valued efforts. You sense when something is wrong with your biological system when a specific function is not working correctly. Or, you can raise your conscious awareness for your heart rate and check it during and after a bout of strenuous exercise. Athletes who use physical skills learn to frequently apply biofeedback to judge the worth of their next performance or practice based on how they feel while getting ready or performing. You gain an expectation or value by how easy or hard the activity is to perform with your current skills and knowledge. If you allow your expectations to exceed reality, you will be frustrated, be negatively motivated, and more likely perform poorly. You've heard this phrase before: Get Real! Every performer has a valuing system, and this will be discussed in more detail later.

Spatial awareness is a biofeedback feeling for how each body part performs in space in relation to the whole body. Great athletes test higher than regular athletes in spatial awareness. Think about how aware you are of the needs of your mind and body, and transfer your personal example to academic feedback for equal importance. Do you value your education? Do you value your relationships? Do you value your spouse or significant other? With a purposeful intent, you value your performances more and process the necessary feedback to develop and improve your mind and body by conscious control. To increase your awareness skills, you must bring more sensory and perceptual information and knowledge to a conscious level to perform with a stronger motivation to continuously improve all your life.

Technology and Awareness

Is technology increasing our awareness or reducing sensations from the environment we create? I see people "tuning out" the very sensations that can increase their knowledge. People jog in parks wearing music players in their ears and tune out nature. Kids on car trips watch movies in the back seat instead of seeing the beauty of the countryside, mountains, meadows, lakes, rivers, sunsets, and fields waving in the breeze. Boredom and lack of motivation occurs when you suppress your multi sensory experiences, and do not increase your awareness and readiness to take in more relevant information. This would not seem to help increase your motivation or intelligence to rely on sensory information that you can process to improve your skills. Technology can threaten your ability to personally learn processing skills such as computation when you always use your calculator or cash register. The brain is designed to develop and use predictive data, but the more technology we produce the more we become dependent on its use. Technology must be viewed as an aid and not a replacement for our thinking ability.

The electronic age has not appreciably increased our intelligence or our awareness any more than letting others do your thinking for you to be micromanaged due to your lack of intelligence for self-directed behavior. Knowledge and awareness skills are proportional: The more you have, the more you expand your curiosity to want more. You get out of life what you put into it. The electronic age has simplified our lives, but not in a good way: kids are bored despite having cell phones, direct TV, I-Pods, computers, video games, Game Boy, and portable DVD movie players. Bored performers become less motivated and prefer to let the technology create the sensations for them. They don't increase their sensory awareness beyond the made up sensations of a screen. I was in Las Vegas and recall an animated woman gesturing and talking loudly as she walked by herself down the "strip." Her mannerisms suggested she was crazy, and needed a hospital. Then I saw her "Bluetooth" cell phone ear piece. I see lots of kids playing video games, or instant messaging with cell phones instead of taking notes. These kinds of technology greatly increase your sensations but block your perceptual awareness skills to project your future needs or current abilities to develop and improve. Parents as leaders should be wary of electronic games replacing real life sensory activities. Games may keep your children occupied so they won't bother you, but down the road they may not have all the awareness skills a variety of real life sensations can provide their memory bank of experience.

Task Familiarity

As you acquire experience and skill in any task, you also learn task familiarity. While testing our 1972 Men's Olympic swimming team, I found that task familiarity is related to your personality (Andersen, 1973). As you become more familiar with a task your personality patterns change from being less confident and insecure to being more confident and secure. By increasing your sensory and perceptual awareness, you enhance all the specific cues you will need to learn how to be more familiar with any task. As you become more familiar with a task, you build your confidence that increases your motivation to perform more consistently over time.

Great leaders and coaches employ better strategies and cues to communicate knowledge that familiarizes task performance to inexperienced performers so they will have more realistic expectations. Conversely, poor teachers and inexperienced leaders have either false and misleading, or lower expectations for others to apply a significant bias that holds back the development of better performers. Top performers create unique strategies to compare expectations with past experiences to increase their task familiarity and learn more. The more you increase your awareness to become familiar with a variety of tasks to find your abilities and understand their relationship to personality patterns, you will adapt to change and motivate your performance improvement with less stress.

The effect of RROSR training is to build your task familiarity. Familiar details using as many possible sensory cues are introduced in practice prior to the actual performance. This applied psychology stabilizes personality patterns like confidence and anxiety. The great leaders and teachers, even veteran teammates, who have been there and done that before, have acquired familiar experiences to communicate the selected cues and roles to other performers. They focus on the positive cues and strategies that predict expected outcomes. You cannot be a great teacher without having first been a good student with the awareness skills to observe what the great performers have learned. The cues and strategies are what provide the most familiar and predictable process to improve learning and performance. Experience is still the best teacher, and specific experiences in selected job content skills are essential. If you lead performers and impose your will on them to perform or process unfamiliar skills to satisfy extrinsic group needs, the unfamiliarity will cause undo stress to the personality to temporarily hinder the outcome. In other words, top performers will be motivated to leave your company or organization as fast as they can. To best learn PI, practice the skills in RROSR to connect the valued correct responses to the weighted cues in the predictive equation you set up performing specific jobs.

Predictive Equations

The beauty of the human mind is that it can make predictions that are essential to learning how to increase your awareness and improve your intrinsic motivation. Successful performers rely heavily on their past experience to make predictions about their future success, and set realistic goals. The kinds of goals you set are also related to your personality patterns. Learning to predict success or failure or the amount of reward or effort you expect to feel for a given task plays a key role in your goal setting and motivation. The whole process assigns a relative value to make information more meaningful and relevant that will more readily organize, store, and retrieve information at will on demand to motivate your performance. To make accurate predictions you need to be familiar with a host of variables that are interrelated and based on your past experiences. These interrelationships and weighted strength of each variable is represented by a multiple regression equation to predict performance. The equation will look like this:

$$V_1 + V_2 + V_3 + V_4 + V_5 = C$$

All predictive equations use a host of variables (V) to predict a criterion (C). Variance is the degree that a single variable will vary from a mean value that if added together with other variables and their mean values would equal 100% of the prediction of a criterion. Variance explains how each variable accounts for its portion of the total 100% prediction. It is rare to determine all the variables that account for 100% of the variance. Variables overlap and are not mutually exclusive of each other as shown in the figure which further compounds the total variance accounted for in the equation. Variables that account for more variance in the predictive equation are assigned Beta weights multiplied by the variable raw score. For 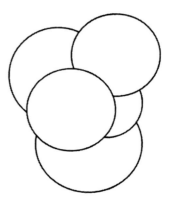 example, if you decided to use ten cues to teach a novice how to shoot a basketball free throw, you could get some idea which cues worked better than others by how the learner acquires and performs the skill. Through your observation, if you find that, by your guess, five variable cues account for 80% of the variance, you would want to spend all your time working with only those selected cues. You may also find that one or two cues in particular stand out as being the most meaningful and relevant based on the past experiences of the age group you are teaching. Therefore, as a point of emphasis, increase the learner's awareness for those cues and connect them to the proper response which provides immediate feedback – did the ball go in the basket? If not, refocus attention and restate the specific cue or two. This simple analogy using a multiple regression equation is what it means to increase awareness, the first sphere in The Triad, to improve performance motivation. Along with those already mentioned, here are a few other suggested strategies to increase your awareness:

First, assess, define, and prioritize your abilities and skills demonstrated in your experiences to determine the key variables you are looking for to account for the most variance that predict your success on a future performance for each specific skill. A detailed abilities assessment exercise in the appendix can help you learn this process.

Second, imagine and select only three to five top variables or qualities you feel are the best keys to your successful performance. Your brain cannot focus on more than five variables at one time in your short term memory to execute the program.

Third, go back and subjectively assign a percent weight to each key quality variable so the total weight will not exceed 100%. The idea is to predict potential success. You want to place more practice and competitive emphasis learning those selected variables or cues. The first R in RROSR is your ability to recognize the most meaningful and relevant cues to learn and perform a skilled response.

Fourth, reflect and sort through your personal memory bank to pick out variables that have demonstrated your success history to predict performing your future performance. A complex task may require numerous skills variables to perform well. To focus on learning a new skill faster, you want to spend your energy practicing the few variables that account for the most combined variance.

Great leaders, teachers, and coaches who understand and communicate this process to intrinsically motivate performers with PI skills training pre select only the key variables that predict the highest to efficiently learn new skills or perform given tasks. This conscious strategy to pre select key identified variables is called selective attention and cue recognition. If a skill requires ten variables to account for 90% of the variance in the predictive equation, you would be more confused trying to focus on and practice each sub skill or sub routine. Consciously using the subjective predictive equation, the leader pre determines from past experiences four variables that can predict as much as 70% of the outcome. You want to spend most of your time teaching and learning those key variables to speed up your learning.

The predictive question to answer is what percent probability do you predict to be successful on your future performance? Your probability will predict high, low, or in between success. Your predictive probability skills affect the goals you set, how strongly you hold yourself accountable to achieve your goals, and your frequency of success to build your confidence and reinforce your motivation to achieve continued success on future performances. Successful performers subconsciously plug in these mental equations all the time. You need to perform this process on a higher conscious level until you are skilled in your predictive ability. As your predictive ability improves, your actual performance will be more closely aligned to the goal you set. You bet on yourself to improve upon your own immediate past performance as the benchmark for your next or future performance. You set a conscious awareness skill in motion that will increase your purposeful intent. You cannot control the performance behavior or work ethic of another performer. All you can do is focus on what you can control knowing your past performance history. Keep a performance log to help you remember and chart your rate of progress.

Prediction Transfer

The same conscious positive awareness prediction skills can be transferred to subjective feelings that become associated with a variety of events, concepts, or thinking processes such as emotions and choices you can make. You can subjectively raise your conscious awareness to predict more than objective performance success. You can predict and choose to be happy. You can choose to look for the good qualities in others to develop your performance, form healthy relationships, and lasting partnerships. You can create in your mind a positive image of how you want to perform by formulating a statement or question. For example, you can state, "I expect the probability for my success on the next test or in the next game – (you define the specific task) - will be_?_%." Key words that you can use to trigger your conscious thinking process are: predict, reward, effort, value, skill level, ability, intelligence, problem solving, decision making, reflective relationship, mate selection, shopping, working, studying, social skills, emotion, success, failure, etc.

Selective Attention

Selective attention is your ability to focus on specific cues that predict the best to learn or process a skilled pattern. This is another conditioning process that cannot happen unless you learn how to override your unconscious sensory system. Create a conscious cognitive perceptual awareness to take in more valued meaningful and relevant information at will on demand. PI skills increase your sensory awareness for recognizing selected cues that are effective for improving your performance. This increases your conscious perceptual awareness of their value to your success to feel reward. When you begin to connect your success to valued work and preparation, you increase your intrinsic motivation. You can increase your awareness to recognize these performance success cues by keeping diaries, logs, or portfolios of your work in order to reinforce your personal accountability and recall of immediate past performance.

Response Generalization for Success

Tiger Woods creates masterful golf shots that he could not have practiced all those kinds on the course. He has practiced a variety of swings addressing the ball, or holding the club faced differently to get the desired ball flight, and then transfers those skills to each unique situation on the course. This is called response generalization. It is practicing and learning a variety of cues to use in a generalized situation that cannot be practiced normally. For any practiced skill you must use purposeful intent to increase your awareness and focus on a greater variety of stimuli to get one positive generalized response. To create a temporary executable file in your pre-frontal cortex you visualize your shot in your mind by retrieving all your past practice stored in your memory like on your computer when you open up a program. Then you execute the performance. You increase your awareness of stimuli that create positive responses and condition these stimulus-response (S-R) connections with practice. If you approach each day or practice session with a negative attitude, your mind will automate tasks to a subconscious level and reduced their value. Later, it will be more difficult to retrieve this information to perform a skill because your brain sees this information differently and compresses it so that you can only retrieve it with more effort. By the time you locate the stored information in your brain, the opportunity to perform well may be lost. Learning without a purposeful intent is inefficient learning. Purposeful practice increases your awareness of greater varieties of stimuli that become reduced or compressed for storage and retrieval value. As you initiate your generalized response, you are better able to retrieve more specific stimulus-response connections to perform.

LEARNING

To apply motivation to learning it is important to know where we have been, where we are now, and where we need to go. Education has many variations of the same theme. Time honored practices have been replaced by new ideas that essentially communicate the same message under a new name. Consequently, not much has really changed in the educational system. It has been said that the answers for what we need to perform are already here and known. There are many experienced educational theorists that are telling us what we need to do, but these ideas are not being linked together in a database. Knowledge is like a puzzle that keeps getting put together piece by piece, and if we could construct an educational database we could move forward instead of retrying what we already know in a different form. The educational system has been slow to uniformly perform those fundamental skills that research has confirmed work the best, a.k.a. best practices. The real problem for most educators lies with how to teach the teachers what is most meaningful and relevant with the current times. The focus has been on creating national standards and benchmarks that students need to know by a certain age. Very little attention has been given for how to intrinsically motivate students.

Compounding the national movement for uniform standards as advocated by the No Child Left Behind Act of congress in 2002 is the enforcement of compliance. If school systems do not meet AYP or acceptable yearly progress in their student test scores, the Federal funded Title monies administered through the states may be withdrawn. In some regions, the poverty stricken school systems are threatened with having to provide vouchers for students to pay their tuition to other area school systems. However, the view held by the adjacent school systems is to refuse those students with tuition vouchers because they fear those low test scores will pull down their population of students and cause the same effect. The concept of AYP seems hardly enforceable as it is a negative motivator. AYP would work better if schools were given incentives to obtain more funding instead of fearing withdrawal of critical funding they have depended on. Also, if more students were taught and conditioned with purposeful intent skills starting in pre-school, then more students would be intrinsically motivated to learn despite what their environment may be like at home. If a school or school system is failing to meet AYP, it makes no sense to withdraw needed Federal funds from students who need this support.

The problems of American public education are created by a flawed system of local control that dates back to the late 1800's, and an unequal financial support system based on local property taxes to fund schools. How do you advance education in a system when the local control is largely in the hands of uneducated people? America is the land of opportunity, but how do you provide opportunity when smaller school systems will not consolidate? School board members face community pressure to keep their identity with their schools or face living in a ghost town. Friday night lights are the only entertainment provided by the local high school football or basketball game. There are some parents who, if you consolidate schools to provide more academic opportunities, would have to watch their child sit on the bench instead of get to start on a mediocre team with little talent to learn from each other. Our priorities are wrong. Since most of our needs are met by others and public education is free, we no longer value having to work to become educated. School administrators and teachers are not as respected overall as they used to be up to about 1960 when all the social ills of society moved into our school systems. Then schools could have elected to be the "beacon of society" but instead chose to be the "reflection of society." With our affluence and increase in social programs like welfare we have lost our individual need to improve. During the Great Depression, my dad was turning 16 and he knew what the family and his needs were to survive. He quit high school to go to work, and four years later earned his diploma. Today, the majority of Americans do not know what their needs are or how to figure them out today and for tomorrow. Schools would do well to have planning activities that develop blood flow to the pre-frontal cortex, and to learn how to plan for future needs. No one plans well enough for retirement because those needs are too distant. We love to live in the present for all the pleasure it can bring, and let someone else take care of us later if we can't by ourselves. People are conditioned to think, "If I mess up, the government will bail me out." We have not conditioned accountability, but instead have enabled these kinds of behaviors with a flawed welfare system. All this goes back to violating behavioral Rule # 1: The more you do for people, the less they learn to do for themselves.

When are we going to teach men how to fish so they can feed themselves?

State financial support is dependent upon how well state government is run. If a business were run as poorly as most states and over a third of the school systems in America, they would be out of business in two years of operation. School and state administrators are not adequately educated in business practices like budget and finance, and there are many businesses that are not adequately trained in educational best practices. There are more lawyers in state legislatures passing the bills than there are businessmen, and worse they know nothing about human behavioral psychology and what motivates people. They continually enact laws and under funded social programs that enable unmotivated behaviors from the very people you wish to help. This is a grave injustice to humankind. God did not put man on earth to be taken care of, or to be his brother's keeper, but to have dominion. This starts with personal accountability from intrinsic motivation to improve one's performance, and ultimately give back the knowledge to others.

Common to both business and education is inadequate training in the motivation of personnel and students in the learning system to go to college, a trade school, become a CEO, or department head to manage an army of people. Richer areas where the per capita income and median house price is very high spend almost twice the average per student to educate their students, and get much less state and federal assistance. So how do you balance out the financial system to ensure equal educational opportunity? The only way to provide equity is to have a uniform state sales tax on consumable goods so that through these tax dollars, every student is given the same funded amount. Then, in local areas, there could be justified property tax relief that would still allow local communities to add to their school funding.

Another documented problem is the effect teachers' unions have had on public education to maintain a flawed tenure system to protect their poorest incompetent performers from being fired by school administrations who produce documented evidence. Labor laws apply to all employees. Every teacher has a right to the same due process afforded any other kind of worker in America. However, it is almost impossible to fire a teacher for incompetent teaching or to provide merit pay increases to reward teaching excellence. Every teacher is motivated in the same way which is why intrinsic motivation needs to be taught to the teacher-leaders to apply to their work and professional growth that can improve their teaching. I would be pleased to know that more than half the teachers in America can discriminate an extrinsic from intrinsic motivator because extrinsic motivators in the form of grades and good behavior check marks are more frequently used than rubrics to motivate students to learn how to self evaluate their work. I would also be pleased to know that more than half the teachers can create a rubric. An example of a rubric for writing is in the appendix.

The key to good schools and good business is to identify potential talent early and develop each performer's personal skills. What I have been advocating is this system of Purposeful Intent that is designed to intrinsically motivate performers to want to improve their performance. This starts by conditioning motivation fundamentals found in The Triad starting in pre-school, and not waiting until high school. Sadly, our schools have become more social institutions with bullying problems than academic institutions with merit scholars. In our literal affluent society, we have allowed all the same social ills of society to creep into our schools. For some teens, the focus is on being like Brittany Spears or some other social icon instead of the academic icons like Albert Einstein or Thomas Edison of the science or math world. Many students live in an unrealistic dream world. High school football players think they will play in the NFL when the odds are greatly stacked against them; and they do not study dreaming they will be a professional athlete making millions. Consistent success does not come easy. There is an old phrase – easy come; easy go. With a solid educational foundation to understand principles of behavior and motivation, you can build a business, a talent, a relationship, or a life to sustain the normal ups and downs.

At some point in your life, you must recognize that your God-given talents are closely aligned with your purposeful intent. You are here to fulfill a purpose in life. Every performer is valuable. By trial and error, you may have found that you were better at some activities than others. You may have motor skills to be a talented athlete; the excellent verbal skills to communicate with and lead other performers; the finite skills to crunch numbers as an accountant, or ability to recognize patterns and sequences to be an engineer. When you approach a new task with a positive attitude, it is possible to transfer your previous familiar experiences in order to perform the new unfamiliar task successfully with less stress. This requires awareness skills to process feedback and learn how to perform at a higher level by gradually improving your immediate past performance. Your probability for successfully completing a new task increases in relationship to your purposeful intent, which is related to your task familiarity and awareness of the specific cues and strategies you have learned. This is purely an intrinsic motive to achieve success.

As you become more aware of your needs, you focus on achieving the component skills that are imbedded in your talents. Your level of skills and talents is based upon your abilities to perform. Improving your skills requires more awareness of the cues and strategies on which to focus your energy. For example, athletes that are unfocused go all out at the beginning of competition, do terribly at the end, and more often lose. You do not have to be an athlete to experience the same affect. Practicing PI will increase your conscious awareness of cues that heighten the meaning and relevance of information for later retrieval.

To get more out of life, you have to put more into it as a basic intrinsic motive. When you are mentally engaged, you can fully appreciate your work, feel rewarded, enjoy a quality of life, and be happy meeting your specific needs. No self-satisfaction and pride is ever achieved when you allow others to continually meet your personal needs. Tracking your progress with a performance log or portfolio system that includes performance improvement graphs or even a daily diary can reveal initial patterns in your performance to provide positive feedback to self-evaluate.

Great performers consistently use logs to set positive goals slightly better than their immediate past performances in order to increase their drive motivation. Setting low positive improvement goals increases your probability for success and your self-reward system with more frequent success; *success breeds success*. The more you feel rewarded, the more reinforced you will want to repeat those kinds of positive work behaviors to ensure your success on succeeding attempts. By tracking your consistent improvement, you also create the need to improve. Inconsistent performers are not focused on their immediate past performance to create a need to improve. Performance inconsistency encourages micromanagement by others, and the more people are micromanaged the less they learn to do for themselves. This will not build good leadership or personal accountability.

Curiosity-Frustration-Knowledge-Understanding-Wisdom

My college swimming coach, Doc Counsilman, taught us lessons about life while driving to competitions. He explained that the learning process was curiosity – frustration – knowledge. He was right and I would also add understanding and wisdom. Curiosity is a natural drive. If you don't have it, it is because curiosity was conditioned out of you. Conditioning can increase or decrease your intrinsic motivation. The idea is to be in control with valued knowledge and understanding about how motivation works. You already know that when you have a purpose you achieve better outcomes. Then, do not let others have to motivate you to act using all those extrinsic means. Learn the principles to motivate yourself and achieve what you choose. For example, a child is naturally curious and will ask more questions. If this bothered the parents, the child received fewer answers until none were given. To redirect questions parents cannot answer they provide a chore that seems like punishment instead. If you were misdirected, you would apply your curiosity in another less bothersome way. This would condition you not to ask so many questions. If you bother people, why not learn how to learn on your own to satisfy your curiosity and be less dependent on others? You need to create curiosity that will define your purposeful intent for learning. Better teachers and better students pose better questions than answers. In Gagné's Hierarchy of Learning (1985), discovery learning is the peak of the pyramid. This lends support to the meta-cognitive constructivist model for teaching and learning. In this kind of interactive learning the learner, not the educator, chooses and constructs what knowledge is meaningful and relevant in value to fulfill purposeful needs. You must know that when your curiosity is not satisfied; you do not master learning or understanding new material. It is natural to become frustrated because you are not familiar with every new task or can immediately master every new skill. However, you must also keep your expectations in line with reality, or you will be frustrated by your performance. It is better to get real and do what top performers do and set low positive goals only slightly better than their immediate past performance. Top performers know they can control their frustration, and turn more attempts into positive improvements that over time make them a top performer. Use this approach to increase your motivation and learn to overcome your frustration. It is highly unrealistic to believe that you will be a one-hit wonder or hit the jackpot on your first attempt. Great performers have paid their dues and learned from their mistakes.

However, this initial frustration phase of learning declines with practice and experiencing success. As your personality becomes more familiar with tasks, you reduce stress and produce knowledge that can be stored and retrieved efficiently. It is important to create understanding by how and why you increase your awareness to value what you are learning enough to effect changes that will improve your performance. Your wisdom is to know the difference between what you understand and don't understand. Understanding extrinsic from intrinsic motives facilitate the process of learning for others to perform up to their potential when you are not there to help. Top performers find a way to make positive performance outcomes happen. You want to perform well to connect stronger feelings of reward to reinforce your positive behaviors. Ultimately you acquire the wisdom to pass on what you know to other performers by your teaching and leadership. This would be the self-actualization peak of Maslow's Need Hierarchy.

Literal Society Affect on Needs

We have become a very literal society with many automated unconscious routine behaviors. These routines confuse our ability to consciously identify current and future needs. I am hungry – feed me. Fast food is everywhere from your microwave oven to street corner food vendors. Poor folks have footwear and food is so abundant we have problems with obesity despite trashing one-third of what was prepared. However, when others do not provide for your basic needs, your higher order needs to belong or for safety are quickly dropped, and you are driven to provide for your more basic needs for food, clothing, and shelter in Maslow's hierarchy. Refer to Abraham Maslow's Hierarchy of Needs shown in Chapter One.

Role models for youth that grab headlines in the news are not reality. All human beings follow this behavioral rule #5: The principle of the path of least resistance. Aristotle wrote 384–322 B.C. that young people want the most and to do the least to get it. With increased awareness for activities that serve a purpose, early learners are better able to identify and create personal higher order needs for knowledge, meaning, and relevance. You need to understand how you subconsciously automate your thinking about meeting your lower order needs for food, clothing and shelter because they are provided by others when you are growing up. Consequently, you are not aware to make the inference or know how to project for your current and future needs.

Value

Nothing affects your motivation more than value. You learn value by having to exceed your expectations. If something is too hard or too easy to acquire or understand, you do not value it as much because you did not have the expectation. Your expectation is your subjective assignment of probability for attainment. When you understand what your needs are, you prioritize them for value. Different needs have different motivational values which are based on a subconsciously assigned positive or negative feeling about your previous experience. Those needs that are harder to come by, you tend to value more. This approximate overall value (V) is computed by dividing the amount of perceived effort (E) into the perceived quality of reward (R) expressed as $V = R/E$.

Motives

Motives are less powerful than drives that are associated with intent to meet primary needs for items like food, clothing, and shelter, and rarely diminish in strength because you always need them. When deprived of primary needs, the drive level or intent to get those needs is very high to preserve life, but once satisfied the drive is temporarily reduced. By comparison, a motive is a conscious perception that has a foundation in a drive. If you are hungry, your drive is to obtain and eat food until you are no longer hungry or fear a loss of your next meal which may drive you to overeat to store fat as needed future fuel. Your motive is in consciously thinking how to perform specific skills to keep providing the means to obtain and prepare the food. The need to be loved and wanted has driven people to meet those needs by practicing crazy behaviors like stalking. You cannot easily question what drives an individual or their intent. You can question their motives and purposes that require perception and thinking skills.

Motives, once satisfied, dissipate in strength until the need slowly increases in strength again. By learning to understand your needs and motives on a conscious level, you are better able to control and motivate your behaviors to continuously improve your performance and hold yourself accountable. By increasing your understanding of the interrelationship of your drives and intent and your motives and purpose, you can condition your awareness of whether you are improving or wasting your time going through the motions. Successful performers can override their feelings of satisfaction or failure to immediately refocus and increase their motive strength rapidly at-will-on-demand. They know they cannot operate at full throttle every play, every game, every performance, but they can improve the quality of the key performances at-will-on-demand when they matter the most to affect the outcome. Professional athletes provide numerous examples. An NBA player can miss 9 of 12 shots early in a game, but with the game on the line can mobilize the energy at-will to get in the "zone" where the hoop appears larger and time goes into slow motion. In this zone of increased awareness, all the senses are working in concert. A few seconds seem like twenty seconds to provide you time to get your body secured or prepared to perform.

Planer Thinking

Howard Gardner, (1999), a Harvard psychology professor, writes about multiple intelligences in his book, <u>Intelligence Reframed</u>. My personal view is that intelligence is the execution of small specific stimulus-response (S-R) connections that create awareness for higher acquisition of knowledge in task familiar planes. I call this Planer Thinking. Intelligence, then, is specific. Intelligent learners increase their specific awareness level to another plane with activities they are passionate about and value. This allows them to RROSR more meaningful and relevant information to increase their knowledge. As they become more familiar with their tasks, they are able to retrieve stored associated knowledge and skills to readily accommodate and assimilate by more numerous associational neurons, as did Albert Einstein, new information that adds to their body of knowledge and makes them intelligent. Individual intelligence is to know more about your subject than anyone else. How you acquire that knowledge requires intrinsic motivation skills that can be taught using The Triad.

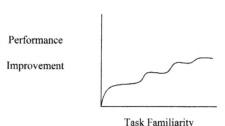

Planer Thinking Curve

Performance Improvement

Task Familiarity

As performers learn to create value for information they process in their pre frontal cortex, that specific information becomes more meaningful and relevant to meet their personal needs. When you are consciously driven with a PI to identify, acquire, and fulfill specific needs, this will allow you to select even higher order needs to increase your motivation and PI strength. You will think on different planes, or 'think outside the box' as some would prefer the term.

Sequences and Patterns

In a figurative way, to create the need to increase your awareness to RROSR -recognize, receive, organize, store, and retrieve important cues with a purposeful intent, you can imagine growing antennae like a butterfly. Any complex task can be broken down into a logical progressive sequence in parts called subroutines that increase the opportunities for reward and reinforcement that strength RROSR. A subroutine is the connections of specific sets of predictable cues (S) with correct

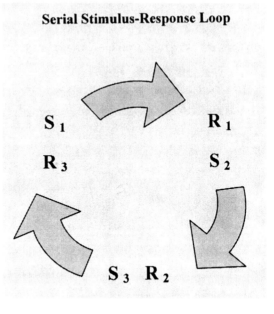

Serial Stimulus-Response Loop

S_1 R_1

R_3 S_2

S_3 R_2

responses (R) that are known for learning a skill faster. After each subroutine part is practiced, improved and rewarded, you chain them all back together again. To learn the more important cues for a given task, you have to observe and ask the highly skilled people performing those skills and their coaches who create the specific cues, what their thinking perceptions are to link with a response. All learners have a variety of learning preferences for visual, verbal, and sometimes kinesthetic or feeling cues. Great coaches and teachers are able to discern learning styles and accomplish faster learning rates by adjusting the cues they use. They explain and demonstrate the appropriate cues matched to the learning style and condition a better stimulus-response connection. The Serial Stimulus-Response Loop gives you an idea of how S-R chains work. The immediate response becomes the new stimulus for the next response. These links are conditioned so that after a specific cue is perceived, the brain center processes it by associating the most reinforced connection. In most physical skills, these processes happen faster than you can think of all of them. Therefore, you only selectively attend to one or two cues at most at a time while practicing to reinforce those specific connections. Eventually after enough practice, those responses will appear fluid or automated as the associational neurons create the nerve pathways. This learning process is called instinct and muscle memory by those who do not understand the details.

As you become familiar with each performance task or subroutine, you process information or cues faster by compressing the data into smaller retrievable bit maps and think in planes. You begin to recognize and receive more data to process and organize into your system than the average beginner that contributes to your motivation to learn. Sequential learning focuses on selective cues or stimuli to increase awareness and decrease response time. For example, the brain learns ordinal position as a sequence with ease. Children first learn a simple number sequence 1, 2, 3, 4 ... 10, then to 100, and an alphabet sequence A, B, C, and D ... Z. Colors and shapes have similar progressions as the brain forms bit maps to compress these kinds of data. A repetitive motion pattern with practice develops a series of hundreds of specific stimulus-response (S-R) connections as associations. Each connection rapidly stored and retrieved separately would produce terrible performer response times sorting through each connection. With specific practice this large number of connections that comprise the pattern is stored in a single compressed bit map like a computer video file. When demonstration models are correct there is a strong likelihood the visually stored bit maps will be correct. By compressing large amounts of data from a pattern into a bit map that is a series of specific S-R connections where the response becomes the stimulus for the next response, the brain simplifies or automates the storage-retrieval process.

Higher IQ performers more readily identify a pattern or sequence that produces early cue recognition and a faster response time to aid performance. Average IQ performers can learn large amounts of data in sequence to perform specific skills with a high degree of skill if they are taught the proper sequence for the content to perform. Experienced leaders can translate large amounts of meaningful and relevant streams of data into simple appropriate cues and strategies that speed up learning tasks and enhance performance outcomes.

Multi Sensory Awareness and Learning

Your nervous system provides you with the structure to respond to sensory information. By learning to choose a purpose to use that sensory information, you can develop your awareness to apply that information in a valued manner called perception. B.F. Skinner, the behaviorist, refers to mental perception and thinking capacity of a performer as a "black box." Multi-sensory learning is more resistant to forgetting because of the associations you can create. If you learn something new in one sense modality like vision, try to imagine what that process or object might be like in the other four sense modalities. What would it taste, smell, feel, or sound like? Albert Einstein did this as he learned, and so can you. As you mature you tend to use several sensory processes less and depend more on the dominant senses of vision and feeling when you should enhance all of your senses. Great teachers do not tell performers what to think, but how to think with all their senses to create more associational neuron links. Leadership means having a congruent evaluation system where the performer begins to think like the leader to equal their standards and expectations. Great leaders create the need to learn using all the senses and perform in personal terms. Growing antennae to evaluate and value meaningful and relevant performance feedback sensations creates information is critical to your learning success, and ability to lead your personal development for a lifetime. Eventually teachers go away and you have to know how to evaluate your performance and learn to improve on your own. You associate known information to the feedback you receive from a new performance to compare for improvement. More often average performers lack sensory awareness, and they:

1)   do not know their personal needs,

2)   have no clue about what they are good at or even like to do for activity,

3)   seldom select group activities if they are not already organized,

4)   spend inordinate amount of time plugging up their senses, and

5)   do not understand the importance of basic learning skills to learn and transfer to acquire more knowledge.

Unless these performers are led through a step by step approach sequence, by a great leader or coach, they become underachievers for failure to project their knowledge and skills to solve new problems. This problem is getting worse because of the mindless activities marketers are encouraging, and because we have not taught critical thinking skills for increased awareness and self-evaluation. From infancy little is left to the imagination. Television programs and electronic technologies have increased our dominance on visual cues. Kids need to crawl on the floor to explore, project, and grow all their senses and imagination. Then progress to experiencing a variety of multi sensory learning activities to activate greater numbers of associational neurons to enhance their thinking capacity. Increasing sensory systems through sensations increases the capacity for perceptions and higher order thinking that will affect later learning. They are absolutely essential for learning how to read and comprehend, and need more emphasis in the primary grades.

If you want to increase your awareness, go to the appendix and select a sensory awareness exercise you feel comfortable and safe trying to perform. For example, determine how your touch and hearing improve when you darken a room and blindfold yourself to recover an object across a room you are already familiar with the layout. Then go to another room being led blindfolded where the layout has been changed and perform the same task. Hopefully, the object you need to recover has an odor or sound or something to identify its location. This will increase your appreciation for your senses enough to want to use them more in a conscious way whenever you have the opportunity. Einstein tried to learn things in every sense modality possible to create numerous free associations and develop millions of interconnected associational neurons that became superhighways for sensory nerve transmission and thinking capacity. This greatly affects your microprocessor speed to retrieve information. Not only will value help you store information in a more readily retrievable manner, but if you add multiple sensations to your stored data you will be able to associate to the file you want faster if at first you cannot locate in the imaginary drawer of the filing cabinet in your head. You do not have to be a genius like Einstein to use the technique to acquire this skill. All you need is a purposeful intent. You will be guaranteed a higher awareness to solve problems with effective solutions, or improve your relationships with others to understand their needs, and teach them how to meet them.

Mastery Learning

Mastery learning is learning how to perform one segment or subroutine of a whole skilled performance well before attempting to learn the next segment. It can also be viewed as mastery of the reinforced connection between a specific cue and response before learning another cue. Eventually all the segments are tied together in one complete performance. When you have a concept of the whole performance or "Gestalt," and know the purpose for how each learned segment plays a role in the final performance of that skill, then your intrinsic motivation to learn and attach significant value to the new information will be improved. This is a learning to learn skill that is more important than making your brain into a storage receptacle of meaningless facts that are not associated to anything significant to retrieve. When you have a purpose for learning, your brain recognizes and receives sensory information and then organizes it with perception to project and predict stored knowledge to retrieve and apply to future performance. This is RROSR and forms an essential and recognizable sequence or pattern that helps performers transfer familiar or identical elements to learn new sequences and patterns retrieved as bit maps. In the haste to teach new information, learning has become fragmented facts and difficult to make inferences from connections between stored and new information. Prior learning is the most effective way to consciously identify similar elements to associate and improve new learning and recall. There are also best sequences and strategies to enhance learning what I call the Big Five fundamental learning skills - reading, reading comprehension, writing, organization and study skills, and motivation and goal setting. Each performer can be taught the awareness skills to learn strategies and sequential patterns that can increase their intelligence in a specific task. RROSR teaches performers how information should be learned and mastered.

An extension of mastery learning is "do-overs." You keep doing the project over or correcting your English theme until you get it right to earn an A or B to value your performance and condition your reward. Failure is not an option. In fact, some school systems will not accept D's. I attended one conference where the speaker-consultant remarked that he overheard one high school junior boy saying, "If I can't get a D, I may as well get a B." If every teacher enforced this rule, then more students would try harder to get it right on their first attempt to avoid the additional work. This would cause them to increase their awareness in class to take better notes and get the assignment correct. Compare this example from education to the adult world. Students generally get one chance to get it right. Those who don't on their first attempt are made to feel stupid. This hardly reinforces the motivation to study harder to learn more. The experience was painful, and avoidance behaviors kick in. In the adult world you have multiple chances to get it right. If you produce a sales brochure, perhaps no less than 3-4 people will review the copy and make suggestions for change 2-3 times each for a total review of 6-12 times that of a student's work.

Differentiated Instruction

Performers learn a variety of subjects at different rates. Teachers and trainers can improve instruction by: explaining the purpose for learning the new information, how the new information can be applied in the life of the performers or associated to what they already know, breaking the whole performance into smaller segments that provide positive opportunities for success, and creating value connecting quality of effort with quality of reward. When leaders encourage differentiated instruction to allow performers to pace their learning, it forces the teacher to redefine content and sequence to focus on the performance improvement outcomes that accommodate all performers. It is almost impossible to make all performers conform to one set content and sequence. Intelligent performers learn similar material differently because they model their past learning experiences. Trainers who are aware of the same purposeful intent strategies bring common needs and goals together to produce uniform outcomes. This training process allows the performers the freedom to do the job according to their personality, personal needs, and innate drives that lead to job satisfaction and control over their work environment. In turn, this leads to worker satisfaction meeting personal goals on the job, and loyal company employees to reduce turnover.

A whole field has emerged known as *brain based learning* to define how the brain learns, and try to differentiate the instruction to meet the learning styles of the performers. This study is difficult because you cannot remove a brain and put it back in place. You can only observe behavior patterns of those who have experienced brain injury to report what functions have been lost by damage to specific areas. Because there is so much to learn, educators must decide what is the most meaningful and relevant information to gain knowledge and record in a curriculum guide for each course. This poses serious bias questions in that those who would provide the information base that knowledge on their personal set of experiences which in a changing world may no longer apply. A more serious question to answer is why do we teach learning to learn as a lifelong skill without teaching intrinsic motivation skills? Formal learning stops after high school or college, yet performers must continue to learn how to motivate themselves to master new job skills as their lives and environments change. As each new skill or level of learning is accommodated and assimilated, identical elements of the learned skills are transferred to learn new skills. What makes purposeful intent significant is the hypothesis that for learning to take place you must attach value to the information. You do this by creating a purpose for learning the new information. The prefrontal cortex holds new information in short-term memory to define its value, meaning, and relevance through association to previously stored information; knowledge.

Learned Helplessness

Children with low awareness skills behave what I call "learned helplessness." They learn to condition others to provide for their every need including learning knowledge acquisition and awareness skills. Adult leaders, mostly parents, condition this effect by enabling maladaptive behaviors with extrinsic rewards, and then complain their youthful performers are irresponsible, immature, ungrateful, and unaccountable for their behaviors. Some parents have been known to do their child's homework to ensure they get good grades. Other parents do most of the work to avoid personal embarrassment from their child's performance. This does not teach accountability. Early learners who are not conditioned to manage their personal affairs condition leaders responsible for their performance to "manage" and control their behaviors. More control means more micromanagement that decreases learning personal accountability to provide for one's needs that violates the # 1 behavioral rule: The more you do for people, the less they will learn to do for themselves.

Summary

These examples demonstrate the complex structure of the connection between the mind and body. The body provides the structures to respond and move to perform while the brain provides the thinking or meta-cognitive ability for increasing the awareness to evaluate current with past performance, assign meaningful and relevant value, and learn to improve performance over time.

Growing Antennae

"Learning is a treasure no thief can touch."

Chinese Proverb

Objective: Learn how to discover your sensory and perceptual awareness to define your needs and abilities through observation and performance feedback to realize your purpose and potential.

God put you on this earth for a purpose and your job is to find that purpose. God helps all those who try to help themselves. You are not designed to fail, but to succeed. For all your abilities that you have been blessed with, your gift back is to find and develop your abilities and pass them on to others. In doing so, you will learn to fulfill your own needs instead of expecting others to always provide for you. Learn to focus on what matters most to make that your passion, and create your personal needs to motivate your mind from within to find your abilities. You can use positive self-talk and be your own best friend to think of realistic goals you can achieve. This is your purposeful intent to realize your potential.

Introduction

This chapter is divided into three sections: Discover – to identify, reflect, assess, and plan; Define – your needs, drives, and motives, abilities, value, personality, goals, focus, mobilization of energy, and reward with conditioning; and Realize – your purpose and potential using The Triad and RROSR. Discovering your needs and abilities and defining how they are created and formed is the key to realizing your purpose and potential. Otherwise, your aimless direction is trial and error wasting valuable time, and more like trying to hit a moving target blindfolded.

Periodically assessing what your needs and abilities are provides you with a road map for your life. Otherwise, it is hard to motivate yourself when you are not aware of your needs and abilities. They will change as you mature, and you will have to think about how to fulfill your needs with your abilities. Very early I learned that I had poor depth perception that reduces the potential for success in a number of sports like basketball. I was also a late bloomer, and did not get a big growth spurt until my first year of college. I also needed physical activity that sports could provide. So I chose competitive swimming and using this system made it my passion. This eventually led to coaching All-Americans, a doctorate in perceptual-motor learning and sport psychology, and knowledge of behavior.

In China, children are assessed early. Those who meet the early predictors are given the opportunity to learn skills and train in government paid schools. How to develop predictors in a multiple regression equation was discussed in the last chapter. Contrast this system to the United States and other countries where children self-select their activity preferences by chance. A child could have perfect pitch and never sing a note or play a musical instrument because music and art are the first programs to be cut to conserve finances at struggling schools. My guess is that better than half the students who graduate from high school do not have a clue what all their needs and abilities are. These are unmotivated students who complain of their boredom. Perhaps two-thirds of public school students are underachievers; they do the least to get by with only a passing grade to focus on their social skills. As adults, we are routinely caught up in our jobs and do not take time to ponder our needs or consider other abilities to try and improve.

DISCOVER

To discover your needs and abilities think about growing antennae like a butterfly or picture a satellite dish mounted on top of your head to take in more information from all your senses you can make meaningful and relevant to value. What is most important? What do you prioritize? What do you already know? Take time to discover your personality; your traits and patterns can be altered to define you and affect how you perform. The personality traits of persistence and realism are conditioned by success after repeated trial efforts where the actual performance more closely approximates the goal. You can change your personality to improve your performance.

Michael Freshley is a Masters swimming world record holder buddy of mine and a certified financial planner in La Jolla, California. A few years ago he got my attention in a conversation about what drives performers to succeed. He had these four points I want to share with you with his permission. To be successful — at least financially and a physical skill — he has observed these four steps:

1. Decide what you want. You cannot be confused about your needs and ability to work to get what you want.
2. Make a plan. Decide how to get what you want. This establishes your purpose and intent.
3. Decide what you are going to give up. Many performers want lots of things but are not willing to make the necessary sacrifices in their time and relationships to focus on achieving their goals.
4. Never give up. Persistence is the key. Worthwhile activities take time to produce a return on your investment.

Mike also remarked that 25% of the performers drop off at each step which is why 3% of the people own 90% of the world. To clarify this discussion you must realize that in a free market performers are able to purchase what pleases them, and discard what they perceive no longer has value. One man's junk is another man's treasure. What may be stressful to someone is joy to another. Perhaps Shakespeare said it best. "Nothing is either good or bad, but thinking makes it so." "If you think you are beaten…." - you know the rest of this prose. You have a choice to think positive or negative, be happy or sad, smart or dumb, but chances are that without a purposeful intent not as much good will result in your lifetime unless you assess and plan. History is loaded with creative works once thought by critics as inappropriate for their time that later became precious works of art. When Picasso led the modern art revolution, there were legions of people who thought this new work was extremely distasteful. Today his works sell for millions of dollars. This is the real value of learning how to assess your past performance feedback. Not one top performer has ever waited for the approval of another person. If you have a passion and talent that God gave to you, you must use it to the best of your ability and share with others when appropriate to pass it on. This is the circle of life; your meaning and purpose. Read The Purpose Driven Life by Rick Warren (2002) to understand how purposeful intent skills will help you get where you need to go in life. You have a purpose to fulfill in your life, and knowing purposeful intent skills can make it happen. Reflect on your accomplishments. When you knew your purposeful intent, you experienced a greater number of successes over your average performer going through the automated motions.

To identify your current needs and abilities, compare to reflect what they were in prior five-year increments. Make a list. Use Maslow's Need Hierarchy, and break abilities into physical, mental, social, and emotional categories. As you compare and contrast your past with the present, look for trends or patterns in your personality, too. Are you changing for the better or worse? What incidents changed you the most or least?

Assess your list objectively to be certain that items are real needs separate from desires or wants. For example, you may think you need a car when you turn 16, but you can get to your job and school using the bus or getting a ride to eliminate the expense and increase your net income. Now the car is a want or desired item for the convenience.

> An example exercise of a need and ability survey is in the appendix.

After you have taken time to reflect your past with your present needs and abilities, start to project and plan for your future needs also in five year incremental periods to note the changes you expect. Use the multiple regression analysis to plug in specific variables your needs and abilities define to predict the criterion of where you want to be and what you want to do. This will help you to define your purpose. A plan is nothing more than a long range goal based on your past performance history. In order to assess and plan, you need to learn how to use your own performance feedback that will be presented in the next section of this chapter. Keep in mind that you were given unique needs and abilities to fulfill your purpose, and you do not have to copy some of the ridiculous role models that young people choose today. You are a unique individual; act and perform like it. Be yourself. Learn and do what you can do best and keep improving in as many abilities as you discover who you are. Do not be troubled by early failures. Treat them as opportunities to learn. Thomas Edison learned there were 1119 ways how not to build a battery before discovering the answer on the 1120th try. If at first you don't succeed, try, try again. How many people do you know are that patient or persistent? You must plan for success with a purpose and not leave your performance to chance. What are you willing to sacrifice? Persistence is a learned personality trait; so is realism. You cannot be somebody you are not designed to be. Look at your physical abilities. If your parents are both short and compact, you probably are not going to play basketball or volleyball but could swim, play golf, tennis, or baseball with some power. What emphasis have you placed on your mental abilities? Learning to learn is a skill that can be improved. Can you focus on any task for a period of time? How do you make new information meaningful and relevant to what you already know or want to know to motivate your memory? All this relates to your personality and planning to set realistic goals that achieve some purpose. You were given a brain, and if you condition it properly you can use it for all kinds of ways to improve upon your abilities and accomplish your needs.

DEFINE

Before you can define who you are, your needs, abilities, personality, and values, you must learn B.F. Skinner's 'Black Box' feedback model. You really cannot control what other performers do, but you can control how you learn, plan, and have a purpose to improve your performance. This feedback model is essential to your personal evaluation, and will be used extensively in Part II of The Triad, Enhance Self-Evaluation.

B.F. Skinner's Black Box

INPUT	**BLACK BOX** (Mental Perception)	**OUTPUT**
	FEEDBACK LOOP	

Performance Feedback

B.F. Skinner, a noted psychologist/behaviorist, referred to the thought process or mental perception of a learner as a "black box" and introduced this model in 1953. He did not concern himself with the performer's thinking process. The primary concern was how to change behavior through learning feedback to condition a response.

Feedback is what allows performers to learn to judge the value of their performances against a personal standard and set new goals for improvement.

Performers learn to process their own immediate feedback and self evaluate the worth of their performances against their immediate past performance or average, top performers, a state standard, benchmark, or teacher expectation. The primary objective is to improve. When you learn to form congruent evaluations of the worth of your performances approximating a standard, you also reinforce your motivation to achieve success and perform above your immediate past performance that is your standard. This is why it is important to get off to a good start to set your personal standard to improve rather than start at the bottom and have to work harder to make up for early mistakes. Benchmark learning standards for a course that are posted or in a syllabus can become your goals. By using a rubric or other self assessment to gain valuable feedback, you learn to evaluate your performance. Consider using a graph to visually quantify your improvement progress. An example form is in the Appendix. However, the strongest motivation is created by focusing on improving your own immediate past performance that you can control by working harder.

The perception or feeling of success resides with the performer. You can lead and tell performers they are successful over and over to build their self-esteem, but if they do not feel successful properly judging the value of their performance in their own mind, nothing else matters. This is why self-esteem psychology does not work. You have an innate drive to want to learn and improve that leaders must know and use. You do not need to offer an extrinsic reward to bribe their performance. You would do better to get your performers to refocus on their own immediate past performance and set a goal to slightly improve upon that performance frequently. Portfolios are one way to provide a reflective comparison of actual past performance to expected future performance to increase value. Graphs also help visualize improvements by tracking performance results that can form the basis for setting new realistic goals. For students, homework is another essential feedback tool that can have a positive effect on learning by equating quality of effort with quality of reward.

In this next series, you will be given suggestions for how to define and increase a variety of concepts that help you realize your purpose and potential:

Needs, Drives, and Motives

Needs are different from drives in that they can be subconsciously motivated by drives to cause you to perform poorly without a purpose. Siblings can grow up in the same environment and all have different needs. Your motivation in the unconscious state is a drive, but when brought to a conscious purposeful level becomes a motive. By bringing your needs to a conscious level, you can satisfy them with motives that can be planned and self-directed behaviors to improve performance. Maslow's Need Hierarchy shown in chapter one describes food, clothing, and shelter as primary needs. The need for food is normally motivated by the drive for self-preservation. A baby spontaneously cries when it feels hunger pains (S), and a conditioned response occurs when given food (CR). The need for food is temporarily satisfied, and the drive level decreases.

The problem in affluent societies is that:

1) Primary needs such as food, clothing, and shelter are always met by others in a support system.
2) Most performers are not consciously aware of their needs, and
3) We do not normally relate our needs to drives that create the motives to achieve. Purposeful intent attempts to teach you with The Triad how to discover unconscious needs and drives and define them on a conscious level to motivate your mind from within. This directs your performance in a variety of ways until conditioned to stay with you, like riding a bicycle, for the rest of your life. This is how you realize your purpose and potential.

In systems or home environments that micromanage your performance, you are conditioned to fulfill the needs of your manager or parent. You must learn to recognize your personal needs with awareness skills. Your decision making skills to plan ahead to meet your projected needs are never learned because micromanagers control the decisions for you. Neither will you learn accountability when you can blame your poor performance decisions on management. Egos are the reason why others feel an intense need to direct or control your performance. When the ego of the micromanager is connected to and reinforced by your performance, they have an increased drive or motive in their need to control you to avoid embarrassment. This boss micro-management style never proves effective for the long term. As the leader you cannot live your life vicariously through the lives of others or your successful performers and achieve long term happiness or quality of life. Only through your own learned purposeful intent for need satisfaction will you acquire any kind of quality of life. By learning purposeful intent leadership skills, all your relationships will improve as you condition your performers to learn how to meet their own needs and be less dependent on you and others. This is a great skill and gift to teach others like teaching a man how to fish to feed him for a lifetime. When you learn to become aware of your personal leadership skills and abilities, you can acquire a realistic motivational growth pattern. <u>By defining your purpose you achieve intrinsic motivation, and consistent performance.</u> If you have no purpose, you wander aimlessly only occasionally reaching performance goals by chance. You may as well flip a coin to get a 50% probability of being successful.

It is less likely that you can consistently improve to be a top performer until you can increase your awareness of the relationship between your personal needs and drives that intrinsically motivates your performance improvements. The #1 key is to find your abilities and keep improving them. The best strategy you will find repeatedly in this work is to set goals only one point better than your own immediate past performance or average. This increases your probability for success to enhance your personal reward system. You no longer have to wait for the approval of others when you can consistently demonstrate you are improving by what you are purposefully thinking and doing. Frequent reward reinforces your intrinsic motivation to continue the good feelings by working harder to keep improving. In life, it does not matter where you start, but that you try to improve. What matters most is where you end up.

Value

Value was defined in the last chapter as the perceived amount of Reward divided by the perceived amount of Effort usually expressed as a per cent. The equation is $V=R/E$. Value like beauty is in the eye of the beholder. You assign meaningful and relevant value based on prior knowledge and past performance. Hypothetically, the assignment of value determines the strength of your purposeful intent and motivation to achieve success.

Two suggested steps to take that will increase your motivation are:

The <u>first step</u> is to create awareness improving your performance. This is an ability you can improve through conscious awareness for understanding your purpose.

The <u>second step</u> is to increase the conscious value of your performance skills. Setting a value and purpose for your performances will increase reward opportunities.

Value, though, is a relative term. Easy performance outcomes are not valuable. Giving money to a beggar will not increase their personal value because the money was not earned by some effort and is an external reward. As a leader, try to understand the root cause of the bad behavior or poor performance to learn if it is intrinsically or extrinsically motivated. When you create a personal connection for the value of the work accomplished and the quality of the reward you motivate your intrinsic desire to continuously improve performance.

In order to raise the conscious value of your performance skills, the best strategy is to articulate your Intent – write this down clearly and briefly. Your Intent is your drive motivation that comes from your larger vision of successful experiences in any performance activity. Learning the proper awareness cues can evaluate any performance with positive feedback and help you adjust mentally and physically, in order to increase your chances for improving in the next situation. Adjusting is learning, and you learn more by working to correct your mistakes and failures to build your <u>character</u> because you value the effort you put into your work. Increasing your conscious awareness to value improving your performances with a purposeful intent will produce many more quality positive outcomes and build your confidence. Every great leader has had their share of failures and set backs that they had to learn to overcome, and improve their awareness skills.

Steps to increase value:

1. make new information meaningful and relevant by associating it to what you know
2. choose slightly more challenging tasks
3. decide how you would like to feel after accomplishing a goal
4. be more aware of your rewards for completing average tasks
5. always try to perform better than your immediate past performance
6. be more consistent
7. say what you mean and mean what you say
8. use more of your senses to accomplish tasks
9. think positive
10. look for the good in others and every thing you do

Personality

Personality is described by traits and patterns that define your needs and abilities. Your personality traits are largely formed by the age of five; some psychologists suggest by the age of two. The 16 PF, 5th Edition, (2008), is a personality factor questionnaire developed by The Institute for Personality and Ability Testing. There are 16 primary personality traits measured. Top performers for a specific skill may have the same personality trait scores to indicate a pattern. If you want to be a top performer in that skill, then look to improve your personality traits to replicate their pattern. However, understand that traits are harder to change except over time or a great emotional shock to the system. Patterns are easier to modify in the way you typically respond in a habit or can be the strength of specific traits similar to a group of performers to model. Persistence and Realism are also traits. The perceptual anchoring points you use to set goals are also linked to personality. Significantly, top performers report early discipline in the home typically learned more from the mother that enables them to focus on higher order thinking skills later.

Conscious purposeful motives over time create personality patterns that can be observed and changed with awareness counseling over time. A personality pattern is a similar behavioral response to a generalized group of stimuli. For example, when stress of any kind occurs, you personality behaves the same way. Conversely, understanding your natural drives and working with them can help shape your positive personality patterns. The desires to be independent, see performance improvements, and improve the quality of your life are natural drives. Changing your drives into positive intent motives for example, by choosing to be happy rather than sad, think positive instead of negative, and reflect on your more frequent successes in smaller incremental improvements condition rewards that motivate. Focusing on only infrequent ultimate goals takes much longer to attain and condition reward to sustain your motivation. Frequent success creates a pattern that affects your personality development. If your traits, like insecurity and low self-esteem change at all, it is a slow process that evolves from increasing your awareness of the personality patterns of successful performances, and repeating them. I wish there was one common personality pattern displayed by every successful performer, but there are literally thousands of patterns specific to those performance tasks.

Understanding your personality development in concert with your natural drives will help you to define your needs and motives, abilities, and values that increase or decrease your personal motivation to improve your performance. These are learned skills that increase your purposeful intent and motivation to experience success. When you know your purpose and understand what and why you are choosing to learn and perform a specific skill to demonstrate improvement, you condition your knowledge or what you actually know. Knowledge for performing tasks is a powerful intrinsic motivator. Encouraging yourself or performers to understand their personality patterns and natural drives provides purpose when they set goals to improve.

Initially your personality patterns evolve from your traits and natural drives. However, your emotions, and unconscious reactions without purpose and understanding of behavior can cause you to be conditioned improperly and perform poorly. A perfect example is how you develop a phobia for spiders, dogs, deep water, or heights or any object or event. The phobia is a conditioned response which can be conditioned differently when understood. You observed how your mother responded to a spider one time, and even though a spider had never hurt you, your response was fear enough to kill it before it could hurt you. If you took the time to understand more about spiders and how they make webs to catch bothersome insects, you would react differently. Any time you can focus your attention to increase your conscious awareness of specific cause and effect behaviors, you will create opportunities to increase your PI and motivation to improve your performance for anything. You can choose to change or modify your behaviors in a positive way.

The effect of early discipline in the home affects later performance. When parents and caregivers allow children to disagree with specific directions and focus on lower order thinking skills for the time to go to bed, take a bath, potty, brush their teeth, etc., they will establish a behavioral pattern that does not focus on higher order thinking skills later in personality development. The early performer will be more dependent on others to continually perform simple tasks they can learn to do with some thought on their own. Difficulties begin to appear in early learning awareness skills which are reasons why so many children are being diagnosed with ADD or ADHD attention deficit disorders. They have not been conditioned to focus their attention on any one task for any length of time. Somewhere we picked up this notion that a child must be entertained by someone or something every minute of the day. Consequently, the child never learns to explore, develop all their senses, and entertain themselves. Reading comprehension skills suffer, too. The brain will not be ready to recognize, receive, organize, store, and retrieve valuable information.

Lack of early discipline has huge implications for how you learn to improve your early awareness skills. Primary needs like food, clothing, shelter, and water are met early in life with regularity. Next are safety needs that your mother teaches you to feel security. If a mother does not kiss, stroke, hold, cuddle, and speak softly in caring tones to their infants, their children will be conditioned to feel insecure. The awareness cues that become conditioned and reinforced are entirely different than for a secure infant. How would you feel if every time you were picked up you sensed you would slip out of your mother's grasp and fall on your head? How would your mind be conditioned to respond today if you were left alone in a room for long periods of time as a child, and no one responded to your cries for help? You respond to early conditioned sensory patterns learned from your environment which helps to create your personality that is indirectly related to the development of your awareness skills and capacity to learn. It is how a mother bear teaches its cubs to locate and eat food. There are no meaningful verbal discussions on manners in the animal world. You get it or are punished until you are conditioned to perform that skill on your own.

As you mature, you must increase your perceptual awareness skills. As a parent, with teenagers seeking the natural drive for independence, you will be in conflict the more you micromanage their behaviors. Learn to use this and other natural drives. A better idea is to take parental accountability to teach your children how to hold themselves accountable for their behaviors and learning. But at the same time, your child must understand your purposeful intent to have them understand how to take care of themselves, and they must be able to demonstrate those skills before you stop micromanaging their behaviors to provide for their safety. This kind of balance poses conflicting views of the parent and the child. At some point a parent can no longer protect the child from all manner of harm in their environment, and the child must learn to take risks and suffer the consequences of their failures in order to learn valuable feedback.

Purposeful intent bridges this gap for parents and leaders to teach these skills that will allow the performer to learn how to learn and stay motivated and on task to seek their own rewards and reinforce positive behaviors. As the leader, you must provide your performers with positive choices that establish behavioral guidelines and realistic expectations. You want to increase the probability for their success to feel rewarded more frequently and reinforce those kinds of behaviors. Stop using the traditional 90-80-70-60 comparison performers have less control over, and start using the immediate past performance to set a goal only one point better that they can control with greater purpose. Then you can hold your children accountable for improving those performance behaviors with a little more hard work, purpose, and concentration. The skill components to increase your awareness are intuition, imagination, visualization, reflection, thinking, creating, commitment, valuing, projection, understanding, cue recognition, and vision to name a few.

Innate in all human beings is the <u>drive to improve</u>. No one purposefully seeks to be a failure and feel miserable, and things that are free, readily available, or provided by others are valued less. By educating yourself about the strategies for learning how to be self-motivated, you can make personal adjustments and use your innate motive to improve. Often, however, the personal value and reward-reinforcement system is not conditioned by our educational system or in the home. David, my 13 year old neighbor was patiently waiting in the car for his mom to take him to school. I walked over to say hello and asked him how he was doing in school. He said, "Yah, I'm doing OK, but I hate school; it's boring." His reply did not shock me. It's a typical response to public education. Perhaps this is a verbal conditioned response from the playground. More likely, students are not being taught a self-evaluation system to learn self-approval and improve their conscious sensory awareness to take in more information and make it meaningful to value it. The playground response becomes a "water-cooler response" by working adults who express their job satisfaction daily to co-workers. This practice reduces personal initiative and creativity as well as company morale and job performance. A "why bother" syndrome sets in. To get by, employees and students learn to perform the boss's way of doing tasks. This is familiar and less upsetting to the boss or evaluator's personality that may create stress or intimidate their thinking process even when you are encouraged to think outside of the box. When talented workers make positive suggestions for improvement and are not given credit, it kills morale and professional growth throughout the company. Companies struggle to improve professional growth without knowing why it is stagnant because the workers are unable to connect personal reward with reinforcement to be intrinsically motivated.

The word personal is in the word personality. You can use your personality to identify and create your needs, and better understand the needs and motivation of others. To learn how to increase your awareness involves understanding your personality and those of the people you may lead. Perhaps you know people in your work place that excessively smoke, drink, or overeat. None of these excessive behaviors is good for our bodies or our performance. Those who lack the awareness of their immediate and long term health needs, are less capable of making the appropriate choices for those needs in order to improve their quality of life. Perhaps you are trying to eliminate one of these excessive behaviors, but you lack the personality trait of will power and persistence. If so, consider that your behavior is altering your personality to fulfill the need to avoid the stress of changing your routines, habits, and personality. You can learn to consciously rationalize any behavior to justify it, but it will still have a negative intent. Successful performers, leaders, coaches, and teachers have the personality to hold themselves accountable for their performance and behavior. Great leaders and coaches make an indelible impression on performer's personalities by altering and refocusing their behavioral patterns. They can instill and exemplify the strong will power, commitment, and persistence necessary for success. Great coaches and performers can win anywhere because they personally create higher drive levels and needs for the will to win with each performance. They keep life in perspective, love helping people improve, and are passionate about the quality of their work, adjusting the personality patterns of their performers to raise their expectations and need for achievement. There is evidence that coaches recruit athletes with similar personality patterns to their own. These coaches use stimulus cues to focus their performers and produce the highest level responses to be successful in their activity. They have ethical principles and discipline their players even when this could cost the team a win because they are committed to doing what is right for each player. Leaders who embrace the "win-at-all-costs" philosophy may be successful in the short term but not in the long run.

Most successful coaches are mother-father figures to welcome their performers into their family to teach family values, build teamwork, and a common mission. This same family success formula is finding its way into school systems and corporate America, as these leaders <u>align the needs of the group or company with the personal needs of the performers</u>. This builds intrinsic motivation, and explains why effective leaders empower rather than spend time micromanaging their performers. If you have to micromanage your employees, you have identified and hired the wrong employees or your manager is a control freak caused by their lack of ability and leadership skills. It is highly cost effective to motivate your front line employees who do the work, and eliminate middle managers who apply boss management styles to improperly motivate them. This will always increase your company growth and net profit. Great coaches, like great leaders, care about their followers. Most will never ask anyone to do something they would not do. They develop strong teams of cooperative performers who understand their roles and are willing to align their personal needs with the team. These leaders create a purposeful intent in identifying specific needs for their performers to consciously desire meeting. They center the focus on group needs, and get the individuals to suppress their personal needs to win as a team.

Your most basic needs have been described by Maslow's introduction of the need hierarchy in 1943. When your basic needs for food, clothing, and shelter are readily provided by others you do not have to worry about how to acquire them, and you focus on higher order needs. The ultimate need to be satisfied after all your other lesser needs have been met is to self-actualize which is to lead and pass on to others what you have learned or materially acquired. Rich people form trusts, and philanthropic foundations to give back and satisfy their need for self-actualization. Need based psychology is the study of behaviors seeking need satisfaction. Purposeful intent is the leadership skill that teaches you to become consciously aware of your needs and develop your abilities to acquire the knowledge and skills to meet them. Every day you can project your immediate and future needs through your imagination and visualization. These skills create associations and nerve conduction pathways, with any practice, of what you know and need to know.

Personality plays an important role in motivation. Permanent behavioral changes to produce consistent success by improving your purposeful intent skills cannot occur within you without working toward a similar change in your personality patterns. Top performers in various skills appear to have similar personality patterns. Changing your personality patterns takes time, and understanding why specific patterns are necessary for top performance. This knowledge will help you to make changes in your thinking and personality while working to consistently improve. Specific personality patterns have been observed in top performers who are intrinsically motivated. Those patterns evolve as a product of your personal needs, goals, and values that increase or decrease your motivation to perform to satisfy them. For example, top performers display a strong personality pattern known as persistence. They keep trying to improve, and learn from their mistakes enhancing a self evaluation system by rubric or feedback system to continuously perfect their skills. I conducted personality research testing our 1972 Men's Olympic swimming team (Andersen, 1974). I found that their personality patterns changed as they became more familiar with a non-familiar task. The subjects moved from being less confident to more confident, more apprehensive to less apprehensive, and insecure to secure. Learning how to apply new intrinsic motivation skills to improve a personal performance is like learning a new unfamiliar task that will require the same kinds of changes to your personality.

Steps to improve your personality:

1. do unto others as you would have them do unto you
2. control your emotions; do not over or under react
3. be your own best friend
4. get familiar with more tasks to gain confidence
5. practice empathy for others by putting yourself in their shoes
6. ask yourself, "What would Jesus do?" or, "What would mom say?"
7. be happy; keep your expectations in line with reality
8. be kind to animals, small children, the elderly and helpless

9. be honest with yourself, and you will gain integrity with others
10. be on time, true to your word, and complete jobs

Goal Setting

Goal setting strategies have also been linked to personality and the perceptual anchoring point used to shift a personal goal up or down. An appropriate goal setting strategy is the cornerstone of teaching and learning about purposeful intent. It is natural human behavior to want to repeat rewarded effort, and avoid behaviors that lead to perceived failure. You can rationalize your behaviors by lying to others making excuses, but you do not lie to yourself. The intrinsic goals you set for yourself are always more powerful than extrinsic goals others set for you to meet their needs. It is equally important to know the role of personality in the kinds of goals selected. For example, performers who set very high goals or negative goals display an unrealistic personality pattern, and have less intrinsic drive motivation. This can be corrected by setting low positive goals only one point higher than your own immediate past performance or performance average. This goal strategy will provide the highest intrinsic drive motivation as you would have no excuse for not achieving your goal. You also add power to your motivation to achieve:

- first, understand your purpose for performing and trying to improve,
- second, focus on the cues to recognize and connect with correct responses to perform specific parts, and
- third, self-evaluate each performance part using a feedback model to use performance output to adjust input cues for each new attempt.

Having used the 1967 version of the 16PF personality factor questionnaire, the new 2008 version is much improved to indicate sub scales, too, that can further help define personality related to ability. How top performers score high to low on each of the 16 measured traits from top to bottom indicates their personality pattern. Poor performers and underachievers display patterns that are generally low on realism and confidence, and high on insecurity and apprehension. Individuals who select positive goals only slightly better than their own immediate past performance or past performance average display personality patterns that are more confident, higher in realism, and lower on apprehension and insecurity because they experience more frequent success to build their confidence. The drive motivation for a low positive goal that is only slightly better than your immediate past performance or average is higher than for a high positive goal way above your past performance. Yet we keep telling performers to set high goals when we know that successful personalities do just the opposite. By setting low positive goals, they enhance their probability for success. The more frequent they experience success, the more reward they feel to reinforce succeeding attempts that reinforce the personality pattern of persistence. Persistence eventually leads to success, and the term success breeds success. All performers like to feel good about their performance. However, when the goal is set unrealistically high, the probability for attainment decreases that will not reinforce the personality pattern of persistence like more frequent success can achieve to feel good and increase intrinsic motivation.

Group, Verbal, Self Personality Types

How you establish personal goal standards and use performance feedback have been linked to personality factors. While conducting personality and goal setting research (Andersen, 1976), I tested our 1972 Men's Olympic swimming team and six of the top 10 NCAA Division I teams that year. Three personality types emerged by observing their feedback preference or perceptual anchoring point (PAP) for setting new goals on a novel unfamiliar task and correlating those scores with The 16PF personality factor inventory scores. I named these personality types, *group, verbal*, and *self*. Like Type A or B personality types, it can be dangerous to categorize personalities as one type or another because of the interaction effect of a host of personality variables. When setting goals performers prefer to use specific types or combinations of performance feedback based on their personality. This preference is known as the perceptual anchoring point or PAP. The perceptual anchoring point is a hard to control dependent variable which is why this subject has not been studied very well. The PAP is a perceived standard about which performers make a decision to shift their personal goal up or down. Those three personality preferences are: Group - past performances of groups of performers, Verbal – your spoken goal to others, and Self – your immediate past performance or average.

The classic sports examples are boxing champion Muhammed Ali predicting to the public what round he would dispose of an opponent and Willie Joe Namath predicting a super bowl win for his AFC team over a powerful NFL team. From my research, I learned that the *self* oriented performers were the most successful at consistent improvement by relying on their own immediate past performance or average feedback. Least successful were the *group* oriented performers. Since we are not completely one group or the other but a combined mixture or blend, the usual higher performers are those who are mostly *self* and part *verbal* blend of personality patterns. As a leader you must not get offended by the boasting of above average performers and put conceited or arrogant labels on them. It is their goal setting personality preference to make verbal statements to increase their drive motivation and PI. It also shows how important it is to provide valuable past performance feedback to performers by asking them to keep a personal log, journal, chart, or graph to encourage the *self* personality type who display higher achievement results. This self personality type understands that they cannot control the performances of others in groups, but they can control what they consciously choose to focus on as a goal to improve. When you record your work achieved, you build value that is necessary to increase your awareness and intrinsic motivation. When you are aware that you have paid a price and worked hard to improve, you build a stronger need or intrinsic motivation to achieve results for your efforts. Top coaches condition their teams mentally and physically to win. They outwork their competition which makes them feel more deserving of the reward. Winning is rarely a fluke or chance occurrence. In schools this is known as a portfolio. This also suggests that collaborative group and team work in cooperative learning environments does not necessarily create top performers or increase intrinsic motivation unless you can define the role and achievement value for each performer. The value of having top performers on your team is that they demonstrate the intrinsic model to improve their own immediate past performance or average, and hold themselves and their teammates accountable for doing the same things to ensure performance improvement.

Each personality type appeared to display similar personality patterns with high positive correlations between their goal preferences and 16PF patterns. Personality Interaction Effect for Goal-Set Preferences shown indicates the overlapping of the perceptual anchoring points used. Leaders, like coaches, need to instill the idea in their performer's personalities that they cannot control the performances of another, and to stay focused on their own performance that they can control with purposeful intent. It is far better for leaders to teach the skills for performers to hold themselves accountable than to personally be their "watch dog" and try to extrinsically motivate and hold them accountable with threats. There is a need to know and understand how and why you are practicing and learning specific performance details to increase the

Personality Interaction Effect for Goal Set Preferences

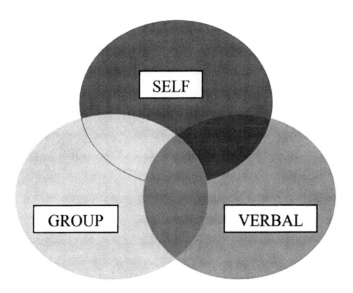

awareness level and purposeful intent of all your performers. By teaching how to look for and use natural drives, and personal performance feedback you create personal value to increase intrinsic motivation. Self evaluation skills that use your performance feedback can demonstrate consistent improvement to reinforce reward when you learn to set low positive goals only slightly better than your own immediate past performance. This naturally increases your probability for success to feel rewarded more frequently, and reinforces your positive intrinsic motivation to continuously improve. Using those defined details, then set personal performance benchmarks based on each performer's immediate past performance to stress the need to consistently improve in measurable increments to feel rewarded. This will reinforce positive intrinsic motivation to satisfy personal needs and values. When all of your performers understand how to perform this skill by retaining their immediate past performance in their short term memory, you will have highly motivated performances, see people show up for work on time, report fewer sick days, and offer more creative ideas to improve team performance. Besides keeping a log or journal to record your immediate and past performances to increase the value of your work to improve your performance, you also need to become aware of how you compare to higher performers and set benchmarks that are appropriate. It would serve no purpose to feel good about your performance scoring all A's compared to local competition, and then learn that you cannot pass a standardized test over the same information compared to others nationally. You can survey a variety of factors to help you select your new perceptual anchoring point (PAP), but your own immediate past performance will provide the greatest intrinsic motivation for you to work with a purpose to improve. Leaders wisely make this intrinsic feedback comparison process important. Great coaches know the personality traits of their performers and will manipulate positive goals in the mode (*group, verbal, self*) their athletes use to increase their personal drive motivation. For example, if a player is verbal goal oriented, you want to gather several of their peers together and start a discussion of the goal capabilities of that athlete and suggest a bit higher or sometimes slightly lower goal than the goal the athlete stated. This would manipulate or adjust the goal to increase the drive motivation and purposeful intent of the player. Leaders need to be aware that top performers in specific roles display similar personality patterns that suggest higher performance standards. This is also a form of conflict resolution. If the leader or coach puts the performer in the dog house for falling below expectations, the performer will resolve the conflict by changing their personality pattern to perform what the leader/coach expects. Great leaders/coaches are also able to see the needs and abilities in their performers and hold them accountable to reach their potential because they care about their performers. This caring application uses extrinsic motives to improve intrinsic performance.

Learn to be your own control group and compete within yourself. Your personality preference for group, verbal, or self feedback plays a key role in your future success, and to be a top performer you may need to change your personality patterns in how you think and recognize stimulus cues during performances. In all cases, you set your personal goals based on one of the three feedback personality preferences or sometimes a combination of two of them to form your perceptual anchoring point or PAP. There are top performers who are a combination verbal and self preference who rely on their own performance feedback and also state their goals to others to increase their motivation. Your PAP can be what you think you can do, hope you can do, or what you have achieved from prior experience. The latter is more common, as this kind of feedback is more realistic and appropriate to judge the worth of your next performance.

The commonly used variable by top performers is their immediate past performance or past performance average in the self personality preference pattern that becomes their PAP and benchmark. If you cannot plan to better yourself, how will you plan to compete against another better performer? Research studies have linked personality types with the kinds of goal shifts set from the PAP. Goals are personal private bits of information top performers do not often share with others. Goal setting research is difficult to conduct because you have a host of extraneous variables to control that you use to make up your goals. In the early 1970's, for my doctoral dissertation (Andersen, 1973), I reviewed every piece of goal setting research also known as level of aspiration at that time since its inception by the pioneer psychologists Lewin and Dembo, (1931) and later Festinger (1942). Replicated research studies have determined a standard of human behavior that under similar conditions top performers will set goals and behave in a consist manner. The process of setting a goal will increase your motivation. The closer you get to your goal will increase your drive stimulus. Your personality is also tied to goal setting behaviors. Weaker ego strength personalities tend to set unrealistically high goals that are unachievable and then make excuses or blame others for their failures, or they may set goals lower than their own immediate past performance to feel false pride without holding themselves accountable for the improvement needed.

Festinger (1942) was first to describe conscious goal shifts about a perceptual anchoring point (PAP). When you have past experience with similar tasks you develop that perceptual anchoring point or benchmark about which to predict the value and probability for achieving your new goal. If you set a goal lower than your perceptual anchoring point, it is a negative goal shift. If above your PAP, it is a positive goal shift. The deviation of your goal from your PAP determines the strength or weakness of your motivation to attain your new goal. Unrealistic goals that deviate far from your PAP produce less stress and motive to achieve. You have nothing to risk, and can shrug off your failure to hold yourself accountable and achieve this kind of goal. Negative goals indicate a fear of failure when you feel inadequately skilled, unprepared, or have an intense need to ensure your success. Your risk-reward ratio may also be unbalanced. Personality patterns create different perceptual anchoring points (PAP) to set new goals based on your past performance experience with a group, your verbal statements made to others, and by your personal self-experience which is what I advocate to do in PI intrinsic motivational skills training. The strength of the positive or negative goal shift also indicates personality type.

Unrealistic insecure personalities set very high positive goals that are unachievable to reduce or eliminate the stress or pressure to attain them, and make larger goal shifts. The drive stimulus is greatly diminished to a point of non-existence or ambivalence. Internal motivation is low. Top performers set low positive goals only slightly better than their own immediate past performance or average to increase their drive stimulus. Their mental toughness is conditioned to want to be in a position to win with the game on the line. Necessity is the mother of invention. Tough love is teaching your children how to provide for their own needs instead of providing for all their needs that enable the very behaviors you wish to prevent. We live in a literal society. You do not pay attention to your personal needs provided by others until they are taken away. Will your education hold up for forty years as jobs and markets change? Good parenting is not to provide for all your needs as you mature, but to show you how to provide for your own needs over time. When you can demonstrate meeting your own needs, it is because you will have purposeful intent leadership skills. The highest form of intrinsic motivation that great athletes use consistently to gradually improve their performance and confidence in attempting future performances is their own "self" performance feedback. Students as early as the 2nd and 3rd grade know enough about their chances or probabilities for success with many tasks. Kids can flip a coin and learn about probabilities.

Goal Setting Strategy Review:

1. The strength of your motive to achieve your personal goal is highest when you set your goal only slightly better than your own immediate past performance or average.
2. Merely setting a goal increases your motive to achieve success (MaS) over having no set goal.
3. Your motive to achieve your goal gets stronger the closer you get to your achievement.
4. Low positive goals only slightly better than your PAP have stronger motivation than high positive goals well above your PAP.
5. Your immediate past performance and performance average help you form your personal "self" perceptual-anchoring points.
6. Past performance feedback is essential to set realistic new goals.
7. Keeping performance logs or graphs with recorded strategies and cues, practice and trial results and efforts enhance your conscious awareness to set realistic and achievable new goals.
8. Performers who are more experienced and familiar with the task set more realistic goals.

9. Performers respond with positive goal shifts when they think they are better than a reported average score from a lesser intelligent social group, or physically skilled group.

10. Intrinsic goals you set for yourself are more powerful motivators than extrinsic goals set by others.

11. Immediate and short term goals are stronger motivators than long term and ultimate goals.

12. Realistic and high probability of achievement (PoA) goals provides a stronger motive stimulus than unrealistic or low probability of achievement goals.

13. Early successful attempts with high probability of achievement (PoA) goals build a personal reward system that reinforces work ethic behaviors to achieve future goals.

14. Writing goals down on paper or in performance logs create higher conscious awareness levels to increase their value and motive to achieve.

15. A worthy goal is worth working toward achieving.

The Low Positive Goal Strategy Works

0		58 59	74 75	100
		1　2	3　4	

The Goal Setting Strategy That Works, illustrates how top performers use goals that condition their personal reward system and motivate their performance, the third sphere in The Triad.

Key to the figure:

1) First immediate past performance.

2) New goal-set strategy, one point better to increase your drive motive

3) Probable actual performance when you read/study with a purpose

4) New goal-set strategy frequently rewards improvement - increases motivation

It is not where you start but where you finish that counts. Place more emphasis on consistent improvement with a purpose in your mind and set low positive goals that increase your probability for success. Frequent success reinforces the connection to your personal reward system. This increases your motivation to improve each new performance that you can control with greater purpose, and not have to wait for the approval of others.

You can tell a performer to set high goals, but you cannot condition this behavior because it is not the strongest motivator. Telling a performer what their goal should be is always extrinsic and less powerful that an intrinsic goal based on a personal need that the performer sets for their performance. The premise for high goals is that if you set your sights high you will achieve high. Research with Olympic swimmers suggests the opposite (Andersen, 1973). An ultimate goal is more a dream than reality, but is better than having no goal at all. To dream is healthy, but your drive motivation is strongest to achieve focused goals that are only slightly better than your own immediate past performance. You have no excuse if you practice known predictable and purposeful strategies with a positive intent to improve your skills and performance. Your focus is consciously stronger, and you increase your probability for success. The more frequently you feel success, the more likely you will be reinforced and conditioned to continue working harder and smarter to ensure your successful feelings on your next performance. This comes from your ability to self-evaluate, create value in work accomplished, and set realistic achievable goals for your abilities, skills, and experience. The ideal is to have your performance evaluation confirmed by significant and knowledgeable others who are top performers of the skills to provide congruence that validates your correct work. Congruence is a comparison process strategy used to help you establish the necessary personality trait of realism that produces self-esteem and self-confidence. When you increase your probability for success, you have no excuse. You become a stakeholder in your commitment to perform that greatly stimulates your motivation. You can create your personal need for achievement if you increase your awareness of what the immediate and long term needs are. You consciously choose to attend to your academic and physical study skills with known predictable strategies and cues to focus on with a purposeful intent.

The Application for Leaders/Managers

The perception and feeling of success or failure is a state of mind in the performer and not the observer. For leaders it is far more important to teach the feedback model and create a success strategy with purposeful intent. This focuses on self-evaluation for the performer to judge the worth of their performance against a known or personal performance standard such as their immediate past performance or average. Help your performers identify key components like personality patterns in top performers, define their job description, and self-evaluate their performance. Let them set their own sales and marketing goals based on feedback from past performance. They will be intrinsically motivated to perform and hold themselves accountable by having more control and ownership of their need to improve their performance. Managers, trainers, teachers, and coaches can extrinsically praise or reward a performer all they want, but if the performer does not feel they have earned and/or value their performance, you still have a problem. This is why self-esteem psychology using undeserved praise does not work. Individual performers, like athletes, quickly learn from their coaches that they cannot affect the performance of others. As the leader or manager you must work to reinforce the need for personal improvement through consistent hard work from every team member. Performance improvements will plateau or level out in a plane at times, but learning is still taking place. If you keep working, there can be larger gains forthcoming and your performance will jump up to another plane. This is the pattern of persistence created by a work ethic and increasing your sensory awareness to value more your own performance feedback to control what you perform. You can learn how to mobilize all of your PI skills and focus all of your energy to perform at will on demand for a given moment and not exhaust your efforts trying to put out 100% of the time to be successful. What separates top performers from average and poor performers is their ability to sense when to turn up their performance a notch when it counts the most.

Learning How to Focus

When you create value for your performance output intensity, you raise your intrinsic motivation. Your ability to focus on any given activity for any length of time to improve your performance must begin with a PI. Highly successful performers make their performances appear to be fluid in motion and easy. Top performers have a variety of performance experiences, and through specific practice are conditioned to instantly recognize the best predictive cues to focus on (stimuli) and connect the correct response for better results. Here are several strategies to use to improve your focus:

- Experienced top performers recognize when to raise their level of performance when it counts the most to create value in their brain. Pro basketball legend, Michael Jordan, was not "on fire" every minute of every game, but he had the awareness when to elevate his performance when it counted the most.

- Focus on key elements that consistently produce quality results. Practice enough to readily recognize and reinforce those specific connections in concentrated periods of time. Skilled performers increase their focus in manageable increments. The strategy is to concentrate on specific elements or parts of the overall performance in the sequence that will be performed. This has the effect of making the performance appear to be on "autopilot." They do not spread themselves too thin in order to concentrate on doing a few tasks well before moving on to the next task. Attention spans vary by individual, but they are generally increased when you have a purposeful intent and decreased without purposeful intent. If you suffer from attention deficit disorder, you would do better to focus on reading only parts or one section or paragraph on a page at a time, and immediately recalling what you read to create value that will increase your memory and reward your effort to concentrate. Then slowly try to read longer passages at a time in a concentrated effort with value.

- Use more of your senses brought up to a conscious level to bring tasks into focus by increasing your awareness for the purpose of each sensation. To make conscious meaning of sensory information requires the development of your perception (see Increasing Awareness Flow Chart in the Mind-Body Connection chapter) or the meaning you attach to the stimuli to get the response you want.

- Use your performance output to provide feedback about the success or not so successful result that can be associated to the senses that provided the most information. The output is evaluated and modified to effect a change in focus for the new input that will create a better result. This is learning. The process increases your task familiarity, and planer thinking. As you improve your PI and task familiarity, you will increase your focus to think of more specific cues in higher planes to consistently improve your performance advancing one level at a time.

- Keep working on your PI skills even though no change in performance may be demonstrated. Learning is still taking place. You will experience performance plateaus, but as you continue to practice your skills and become more familiar with the stimulus-response connections to perform, you will jump to new planes and improved performances by advanced cue recognition and higher order thinking skills (RROSR) to receive more new information, organize, and store it in easily retrievable bit maps. To organize sensory information requires perception. Projection and prediction are perceptual to know how your abilities will help you set and approximate your goals with actual performance.

- Work on your personality. A function of your personality is to take your past experience, in the form of familiar response patterns with various tasks, and compare them to an expected performance. For example, if your personality is high in realism, you are more likely to predict what you will perform on your next trial or performance. If you are low in realism, your expectations will exceed reality or what is logically possible in light of your past performance history. Top performers are higher in realism than poor performers who like to think they can get lucky.

- Top performance is based on a planned purposeful intent, and not on luck. As you become more familiar and experienced with a task, your confidence and security to take risks increase. If you manage groups of individuals who have a hard time concentrating for lengthy periods, try several of these strategies to increase their perceptual awareness: 1) help them identify their needs and abilities and create a PI for performing smaller parts of an activity well. 2) Explain each performer's role in the quality of the finished product or service. Then they will reflect and visualize more value for the work they accomplish. Old behavior is hard to shake. If their attention decreases, provide smaller incremental time periods to help them refocus on only ore or two specific cues you have taught. For example, if a reader suffers from attention deficit disorder, instead of reading an entire page before taking a break, you might suggest a paragraph or a certain number of sentences to read before getting up to stretch or get a drink. Another purpose is to transfer old familiar knowledge to new unfamiliar information, and allow time for the brain to organize the new information. This kind of achievement and reward system disciplines your mind to complete small tasks while also focusing on retention of information for future applications.

- Use a <u>keyhole strategy</u> to imagine looking through a small keyhole and picking out specific objects in the background to see more details. Such kinds of awareness training improve cue recognition skills, the first event in RROSR. Baseball players can learn to focus on seeing a black dot on a spinning baseball. Beginning readers can enhance their reading comprehension by picking out groups of related words and key elements or concepts the author is developing.

- Another useful strategy for improving focus is the <u>third eye.</u> With this strategy you visualize your performance from behind to see what your body is seeing.

- It's not possible to take back a mistake, so refocus skills are another important strategy to master. If you have difficulty in the beginning or middle or end of a performance, you must refocus rather than reinforce the negative feelings or remorse over something you can no longer control. PI skills help you to refocus on the original needs and purposeful intent of the activity to bring it into perspective and redouble your positive motivation to succeed. Successful performers learn to use these strategies at will on demand.

Steps to increase your focus:

1. attach significant value to the work you accomplish
2. take ownership and hold yourself accountable for your behaviors
3. remove prejudice and your personal bias about what you think you or a performer can learn or not learn
4. think positive thoughts; restate negative thoughts into positive terms
5. think nothing but caring and loving thoughts to help others succeed as this emotion will increase your focus
6. whatever you think in the frontal lobe of your brain will be translated into your body language for people to read
7. add realism for reinforcement value
8. set realistic goals
9. keep your expectations in line with reality and you will never be disappointed
10. understand your needs and abilities before you do anything
11. know your purpose; know what you are doing and why you choose to do it
12. lead yourself before you expect to lead others
13. learn skills you can master and teach others

14. set low positive goals you can frequently achieve to enhance your personal reward system
15. master the important cues and forget the rest

Role Models

As a behaviorist, I do not believe role models have as great an effect on modifying human behavior as most people think. Role models provide less powerful extrinsic motivation to copy. Unfortunately, some top performers are not great role models and know very little about themselves or the world around them. There are countless examples of troubled kids who had two educated and successful parents, but who provided little attention and purposeful motivation for that child's life in the home. Those kids were given gifts they had not earned and therefore had no value to them to provide a purpose. There are examples of exceptional kids who grew up in ghettos without motivated parents. Unfortunately, there are far too many successful athletes and entertainers who are not good role models.

Frequent success is what motivates any top performer which is why you have to keep your goals only slightly better than your own immediate past performance that you can control with more hard work in practice. As your leadership skills improve, you need to understand your personal motives to appreciate what is potentially going on inside yourself and the other performers you lead. Your personality is the sum total of your experience. Performers have different experiences also that make them unique personalities, and it is up to the leader to recognize and use these skills. Performers like to fulfill specific roles when they are recognized. The lessons I learned from my parents are the ones they learned from their parents: they need to be modified to suit the times. My parents were teenagers during the depression and never trusted the stock market to invest their earnings. Because they did not learn how to invest earnings, there were no discussions to invest early and often in my portfolio, even though I had the benefit of a college education to know better. Similarly, your model as a leader has no effect without defining a purposeful intent in your performer. You can be a good second baseman and show your player how to be a good second baseman, but until your second baseman understands the purpose for performing second base skills it is doubtful that your role model will make any difference.

The replication of skills without fully understanding purposeful intent to build intrinsic motivation will not achieve consistent quality performance. The older leader may blindly admonish younger performers who have different ideas from the old familiar ways because their personalities and experiences are different. An older manager does not adapt to newer efficient technology and changing markets when they have not maintained their awareness to redefine their purpose. When purposeful intent principles are taught early in the training of new performers, they will be better motivated to adapt to change, achieve, be less dependent on management, and experience long-term success to benefit the company or organization. My six children all grew up with the purposeful intent model, and knowing that they would not be able to live with me after they turned 18 and graduated from high school. This expectation was to prepare them to accept responsibility and having a purpose for becoming educated in high school to prepare for the next higher level of education. I planned to help them with part of their college tuition, and they had to earn the balance of their living expenses and be partners to value to their education. They made tough decisions that defined their daily PI: "Do I want to have money to eat or to drink beer?" It is amazing how focusing on basic needs strengthens PI. I instilled PI early in their schooling to intrinsically motivate personal accountability for their learning. I illustrated the choices they had about how to spend their time and money. If, I said, you pay for your tuition and skip class, you may as well make a paper airplane out of a $20 bill and sail it out your dorm window, or skip 20 silver dollars on a pond. Higher education is not free which makes it more valuable and harder to pay back a $10,000 student loan with a minimum wage job if you flunk out.

When students or performers are committed to a task, they have a purpose that drives a positive intent to succeed. Top performers hold themselves accountable for reaching their goals because they understand their needs to be satisfied have a purpose. Over time, my children were conditioned to increase their personal PI strength because they were held accountable for their early decisions and behaviors. The acquisition of knowledge was considered a valuable investment in the future as sure as an early investment would have been in a financial portfolio. I would emphasize to them that the turtle, not the rabbit, won the race by steadily plodding along, improving toward the end goal with each incremental step to reward and condition success. How do you eat an elephant? One-bite-at-a-time. Success is not measured in leaps and bounds but on continuous steady improvement over time that sets small goals to increase the probability of your frequent success which reinforces successful behavior. This all starts when performers can identify their personal needs and define their purpose for learning and performing.

Trying To Do Your Best

To not try is certain failure. Your immediate past performance is your perceptual anchoring point about which you judge the worth of your next performance. Your greatest drive motivation comes from setting a goal only one point better than your immediate past performance. There is no shame in defeat if you gave your personal best performance. In many work environments too much emphasis is on "standards" and defining failure outside of these standards. A more realistic goal is to focus on specific cues to continuously trigger positive improvement in small increments over time. If you try to work a little bit harder each time, there is no excuse for not succeeding. You increase your PI strength and your probability for success the more you increase your connection between reward and reinforcement. In the long run, it is not an outside standard but your own measurement of success that matters most. Need based intrinsic motivation is having a purposeful intent to know why you are working and performing to improve upon your past performance. You can increase your need to succeed by setting up a system to put yourself in position to succeed more often than fail. This has the effect of reinforcing your personal reward system that will increase your motivation to improve on any manageable task. Kids get to experience a variety of activities to find out what kinds of skills they have. Once they see their skills, then they can begin to understand the underlying needs that motivate them to improve. As you begin to understand your own skills it is essential to learn and understand your purposeful intent for each activity in order to see its value. When you learn and understand your purpose and intent, you create your need to achieve.

If you are stuck in a job with little growth potential, an exercise you can use to create your PI to be educated with personal motivation is to calculate your earning power with more education. Without an education in a global economy, you can generally expect to work for an hourly minimum wage. In a year you will work 2080 hours. In a forty year working lifetime, you will work 83,200 hours. A $1 per hour raise at the start and paid throughout your career will yield an extra $83,200. However, with an education you may have an opportunity to start making $10 more per hour. In your lifetime this would yield $832,000. When you say you hate school, think about what you are telling your brain. You need to change your focus to a positive reward system fast. What has conditioned you to believe that you cannot achieve by motivating yourself from within when the quality of your life can improve so greatly with a little daily effort on your part? Remember, the turtle plodded along and won the race. It is important to know and understand your purposeful intent in order to increase your drive motivation based on your needs. Your needs are value based when you have to work for your rewards. No one can program you to give you an education. You have to put the knowledge into your brain, set low positive goals to frequently achieve, and be aware of your performance improvements so that you can reward and reinforce your work ethic and achieve your goals. Taking pride in the quality of your work will pay off over time.

Frequently achieving your low positive goals will create learning purposeful intent and enhance your personal reward system. The disgrace is in not trying or blaming others for your failures. Begin by breaking down larger more difficult tasks into simple subroutines and eliminate your negative thoughts or traits by focusing on the smaller positive successes. Focusing on a negative reinforces it. This process will reinforce your tolerance to complete mundane tasks like homework broken into subjects or housework room by room with greater regularity. These kinds of positive mental choices create fun learning opportunities when you can see a smaller intermediate reward. It is all in how you approach the opportunity: work can be a "job" or your passion; work tasks can be boring or exciting. Choose to keep your mind motivated from within: nothing is worse than seeing yourself standing in an unemployment line, or wondering how you can earn enough money to feed yourself and your family if you lose your job. There is no disgrace in failing when you can learn and grow from your mistakes. By applying your skills to these suggestions you will see improvements as well as increased achievement quality which helps reinforce your efforts. Having trouble staying motivated? Go back and review how to increase your awareness skills. You have to be aware of your abilities and skills to create your passion and do something valuable with your life.

Work Motives: Positive Self-Talk, Visualization, Setting Goals

When faced with less than desirable household or work related paperwork and tasks like cleaning leaves out of your gutters, you can increase your awareness and work motives to get the task done by using positive self-talk: One example is, "those gutters aren't going to clean themselves" or, "that homework isn't going to get done all by itself." I will speak of the heart of a champion to an audience, and ask, "What would a champion do if the average person she competed against did 20 push ups?" Most people realize that the champion will do more than 20, and a few people will believe they do twice as many. Athletic experience teaches that you can outwork your competition to win and feel successful if you have lesser skills.

Great athletic performers practice another awareness strategy called visualization. You practice imagining yourself with the performance on the line and little time to make a difference, but you associate a positive result image while practicing drills. You specifically learn the sequence by imagining the performance repeatedly in your mind, perfecting your skill, to become familiar with as many of the sensations you can expect from your actual experience. The primary function of your prefrontal cortex is to gather data from long term memory to create a corrected short term executable program. Your focus is a positive <u>intent</u> to do better, and the efficient use of your associational neurons creates fast retrieval pathways of stored information that skilled performers apply at-will-on-demand. Positive self-talk and visualization are basic PI skills that take place in your prefrontal cortex in sequential order. You can mentally rehearse your <u>purposeful</u> performance program and then physically perform that performance more successfully than if you left it to chance. Once you learn your PI skills, you will need to continuously practice them to improve your performance over time. Success seldom happens by chance, but from purposeful intent. If your learned skills are not used, the associations you practiced to improve your responses will be reduced to the Law of Disuse. This is how great performers like Michael Jordan and Tiger Woods continue to improve in any task they choose a purposeful intent to perform.

The mere act of setting a goal creates a purpose and value system to reward and associate reinforcement behaviors. Writing down your goals provides a stronger image to store and retrieve in your brain. Journaling, work logs, and performance portfolios are valuable self-evaluation tools to remind you of your quality accomplishments to reinforce the connection between quality of effort and quality of reward that motivate increases in your work ethic behaviors. Making lists of tasks to complete provides a goal-reward-reinforcement connection to feel good about getting tasks accomplished to cross off your list. This is purposeful intent in action. Someone has to do the work, and someone gets to take the credit even when no one is looking. This may as well be you. A job worth doing is a job worth doing well! I don't know who said that, but it makes good sense. Simply having a goal will increase your purposeful motivation. The more you can become conscious of those little things you perform everyday that count, you will begin to appreciate what you do and feel more gratified. This is what purposeful intent seeks to achieve. Try to understand what motivates you to do a good job? Why do you work? Why do rich people who no longer need to work feel so unfulfilled and need to become charitable?

Energy Mobilization

As you increase your PI awareness skills, you can increase your ability to mobilize all of your skills and abilities to apply at will on demand to produce a better than average performance. This is how you achieve top performance when it matters the most because you cannot be at your best 100% of the time you perform. Your purposeful awareness skills help you learn to transfer more identical elements from one successful performance to the next. To produce consistent quality performances by mobilizing energy normally takes years to acquire these fundamental skills by trial and error. However, you can learn how faster by mastering PI skills. As your PI strength increases with practice you learn to associate the best cues with successful performance. Prior to performing, create a pre-performance routine. Then mentally rehearse the personal cues you associate with performing correctly. Pay close attention to details. Use more of your senses. Make a mental movie of your performance as you visualize it in real time. This improves your spatial (body positions) and temporal (timing) awareness of all the specific stimulus (cues) – response (sub routines) connections you have conditioned through practice in proper sequence. Physically practice what you visualize and feel in warm up routines for the mind and body. Similarly, you can use positive self-talk to place positive images of what you can perform in your brain based on your performance experience. It is rare to talk yourself into performing anything you have not come close to doing before. Obviously, more experienced performers can make better images of their performances.

Less successful performers exhibit erratic behavior and inconsistent performances because they do not understand their abilities and skills well enough from past experiences to focus and mobilize all of their energy for a given moment in time. Their personalities borrow from role models, celebrities, or what others in the group display, and this is not a good practice to learn your personal skills. Bring your personal drives, needs, and motives up to a conscious level to increase your PI strength. Top performers are consciously more dependent on their own personal performance feedback or immediate past results to value the worth of the past performance and set a worthy and realistic new goal to achieve. As most athletes learn early on in sport, it's not possible to control the performance of another person. You can control how you work and modify how you perform to a realistic level when you are consciously aware of your abilities. Your personal goals are an outcome of your needs, which help you define your purpose driven behaviors. When you have no specific goal, you have no purpose motivating your positive behaviors.

New information is initially stored in your prefrontal cortex, until your brain assigns relative meaning and value compared to stored information readily retrieved by associational neurons. The more associations you can purposefully create, the more information you can recognize, receive, organize, store, and retrieve (RROSR) to increase your intelligence. Simply yelling out negative instructions without purposeful understanding creates negative reinforcement. The only way to get positive reinforcement is to focus on the positive behaviors through repetition or positive self-talk, and not talk or think about creating any negative image that can be reinforced. When boss-managers criticize performers, they often stress and reinforce the negative behavior they want to eliminate.

My college roommate, Chet Jastremski, held several world swimming records. He chastised me for getting a little cocky keeping up with him in practice repeats. He said, "It is not what you do in practice, but what you do in the meet." This statement had awareness value and has stuck with me. I listened and learned how to focus and mobilize all of my skills, talents, and abilities for a given moment in time when it would matter the most to become an All-American. This quote became my trigger cue to value my practice work enough to want to earn my reward in the competition. Similarly, if you study and review for a test, you should be more confident of a positive reward. My personal best rewards came in my late 50's and early 60's to set world records for my age group in United States Masters swimming competition after eight years of steady improvement. This strategy reinforces the point I made earlier that all great leaders and performers are not 100% all of the time; you do not have to be to achieve great success. You do need to learn to recognize cues to mobilize your energy to peak perform *at will on demand*. This one performance skill separates great performers from average performers over time. It takes skill learned from practicing identical elements you plan to experience during competition, and applying them during your performance. Michael Jordan returned to pro basketball after a two year layoff to try baseball. It took him a year and a half to score consistently at will on demand. Even though he was in great physical condition, he had to condition his mind to perform the mobilization skills he had before. The mind and body must work together to mobilize energy at will on demand and refocus skills to score and defend for high skilled pro basketball.

Planer Thinking helps mobilize your energy and comes from your task familiarity to think in higher planes. Perfect practice makes for perfect performance means to practice the specific identical elements you expect to perform in competition. Increase your awareness of all the most important cues that predict in your mind a high level performance based on your feedback experience. Only you know how you feel prior to and while performing to make the necessary adjustments mentally and physically. Having a passion and purpose for what you choose to know why you perform makes a huge difference. You store and retrieve more valuable feedback information by increasing your associational neurons to readily transfer knowledge from practice to performance. As you gain experience your comparator operator in your lower brain stem along with your prefrontal cortex will make adjustments to fine tune your practices and transfer identical elements to actual performances on demand; provided you practice those elements or conditions you expect to experience. During the performance visualize positive performance skills by creating what you need to do from your stored past or present experience. Your selected pre-conditioned cues must be aligned with your specific ability to perform correct responses. Be sure to set low positive goals that you are more likely to know what your immediate past performance or average have been. If you like to state your goals to others, this provides little value unless you are speaking to significant others who have feelings about your performances like teammates, a boyfriend, or girlfriend. *Your actual performance value is based on exceeding your goal, and your goal was based on a positive shift above the perceptual anchoring point you were using at the time.* To instill intrinsic motivation, ask your performers to only focus on improving their immediate past performance to feel success. Build personal accountability by explaining how your expectation for success starts with exceeding your immediate past performance that can be ensured with a little more effort and focus on your goal. However, immediately prior to performing focus on the specific cues and timing you have conditioned and trust in your performance. Worrying creates a negative affect to lose your concentration for the cues you must focus on performing. This is why you need to focus on what you can control and perform and not waste your time trying to control what your opponent will do. A pro golfer does not need to look at the leader board if they are focusing on performing each shot to the best of their ability. Let the other guy worry more about you. With each successful performance, a new perceptual anchoring point will be created that must be slightly better than the immediate past performance. As you may expect, the higher your performance, the tougher it gets to exceed that performance. This will require more work and a stronger purposeful intent to make it happen, but the personal rewards will also be greater.

Going through the motions in practice will not provide a purpose to mobilize your energy as you have just learned. By learning purposeful skills in The Triad, you learn how to mobilize your efforts over time to consistently outperform others without a purpose. You don't have to be super great in every performance to be a star performer. Remember, in Aesop's Fable, the turtle beat the rabbit by staying focused on the goal line with each intermediate step and not by leaps and bounds.

Here are a few strategies I have used to mobilize my energy to set world records in masters swimming:

1. Remind yourself every day to not take what you do too seriously to put more pressure on yourself than you deserve. This can limit your performance.
2. Focus on the smaller intermediate steps that you can handle and frequently achieve to connect your reward with reinforcement to maintain your motivation.
3. I often recite to myself that, "I am just an average guy who tries to do a better than average job," or, "Jobs do not get done by looking at them."

If you can do this for the better part of your life, you ultimately will be very successful at whatever you choose to perform. Your passion is nothing more than a highly successful feeling from doing a special activity consistently well. When you hear the phrase, "The heart of a champion," you know a champion stays focused on their PI that motivates them to practice harder and longer to outwork their competition and overcome their deficiencies. Average people who are taught PI skills can achieve uncommon results because they are able to focus and transfer the identical elements from practice to competition.

Reflect back on your good performances compared to your poor performances. For all your good performances, you knew your purpose and why you were doing the activity and had a positive intent to do well before you started. For most of your poor performances, you had no conscious purpose or intent. You went through the motions and had only partial haphazard success. Performance attempts without a purpose or goals are like trying to hit a moving target blindfolded: results are inconsistent and haphazard. Luck is when preparation meets opportunity. Consistently achieving goals is not based on luck but on your personal elevation of PI strength. However, if you do not choose to understand your needs, limit your awareness of past performance to improve, fixate on inappropriate role models, participate in mindless activities, blame others for your poor performance, and do not set goals or cultivate your imagination for what you could be, then you will be bored with your job and your life and unable to mobilize any energy. You cannot expect to achieve quality rewards when you build a weak system for yourself. If you do not learn to connect quality of effort with quality of reward, you can only dream about being a star because it's not going to happen.

You will get out of life what you put into it. If you are trying, there will always be someone there to help you. If you easily give up and you do not try to change and learn to master all your PI skills, performers with PI skills will surely step over you. Others who work harder to perform for personal rewards will resent having to take care of you. The feelings you create in your mind by choice play a significant a role in your success perhaps more than cognitive visual, verbal, and kinesthetic cues coming from your body's senses that you use to enhance your awareness.

When you have practiced long enough to demonstrate consistent quality performance you may get to experience the "zone." The "zone" occurs when your talent, abilities, and skills all come together from recognition or awareness of a pre conditioned response to an initial success that triggers a sequence of pre connected reward-reinforcement reactions. You get emotionally into the game and your performance goes well. Your senses come alive, the hoop is three feet wide and the ball is the size of a grapefruit in your hand. Time slows down. You can see every move, and anticipate exactly what everyone is going to do before they do it. Successful performers sense when to raise their personal level of performance at will on demand. They do not doubt their ability to perform, and trust in their execution of practiced skills. In practice they get mentally tough by creating a make believe game or competition on the line. They visualize performing all their skills correctly to a positive outcome. They become familiar with all the stress and pre-condition a good response when the event occurs during competition. They condition accepting the pressure and responsibility for the valued outcome. They practice increasing their conscious level of awareness, and pre-condition mental toughness. They accept the responsibility for their performance. They extensively practice the physical and mental conditions to have the familiar reserves that project positive outcomes to motivate their best performances. With PI skills training, you can learn to recognize (the first R in RROSR) cues to get into the zone more frequently at will on demand.

Steps to mobilize your energy:

1. learn to set low positive goals you can frequently achieve to condition holding yourself accountable for performance improvement
2. learn to mentally image and rehearse familiar skills
3. use your PFC to create and perfect a successful subroutine in short term memory as a video you can stop, and run in slow motion backwards or forwards
4. visualize your performance as if it were correct; the cues, timing, pace, feelings, sequence, etc.
5. create positive associations to other successful past performances; how you felt during and after performing
6. know your purpose for training and performing
7. review all the highly predictable cues that improve performance for every specific task
8. increase your awareness through use of all your senses
9. focus on improving your immediate past performance every time
10. fully understand your needs and abilities
11. understand how your mind and body work together
12. have no doubt that you have paid your practice dues and refuse to lose
13. pre-condition mental toughness by visualizing yourself in position to win close competitions
14. get off to a good start to experience early reward
15. practice identical elements of skills you can transfer to your actual performance

REALIZE

Predicting potential even with the multiple regression approach explained earlier is a task for experienced trained eyes. If you are a beginner, you may want to consider having your talents evaluated and improved by a successful professional. This will save you a lot of time, and teach you the specific cues to selectively attend to that will be connected to the proper sequence to get the best performance. For reasons that we still do not fully understand, an early learner when taught properly at the beginning has greater probability to reach their full potential. Children can learn a language and sports skills easier than adults. Students who learn to play a musical instrument before they are teenagers generally show higher aptitude in math, and we do not know why. Mel Tillis is a country singer who has a stuttering problem when speaking, but sings beautifully in sequence. His brain is less confused when the response becomes the next stimulus for the next response in a sequence of musical lyrics that affords the brain less confusion having to think. Could this apply to learning sports skills using the proper cues to connect with good responses in serial learning sequences? Similarly, adult learners have been confused by learning to associate the wrong cues for the correct responses and the right cues for the wrong responses when they have teachers/coaches with no high skilled experience. Think about how this notion is applied in other fields. You do not want poorly performing and inexperienced surgeons doing your brain surgery or engineer building a bridge or tall building, but people routinely accept poor teaching and coaching because they do not want to accept the responsibility for doing those jobs. The point of learning purposeful intent is to condition The Triad skills. These interrelated skills can teach you to be intrinsically motivated to consistently improve your performance in activities you find your needs and abilities are good at performing. You easily make this job fun and exciting to learn more and make them your passion. I hate to think of how many people are doing jobs simply because it pays more money, or they have to because they have not learned their purpose to focus on the positive rewards those skills can provide.

You can develop your purpose using The Triad to develop each of the three interrelated skills: Increase Awareness, Enhance Self-Evaluation; and Connect Reward with Reinforcement. Like most kids and adults today, we want to know the meaning and purpose for life. All our motivation seems to hinge on this answer that is individually defined. One answer is to improve the natural drive - quality of life. No one has found the fountain of youth to guarantee quantity of life. So why are we here? I think it is for us to be tested to learn of our faith in humanity. We are given talents, and our job is to discover those talents. We have to trust in others before us to teach us those valuable skills and share their knowledge. Knowledge is the king of values, and when freely available is valued the least. Our gift back is to be the best we can perform, and then teach others how and what we know to pass it on. This is where motivation comes into play. If you have been conditioned to be outer directed and micromanaged, it is less probable like the early learner versus adult learner analogy that you will be able to make your own decisions. You will prefer to be motivated by extrinsic means like a paycheck. You will also avoid having to manage others because you are not as able to manage yourself. If you have been conditioned to be inner directed to learn and create meaningful and relevant information you value in your system, you will not wait for the approval of others. You can make decisions, manage performers, and provide vision. You will avoid people who try to control you.

Most people think of motivation as a locker room pep talk between halves of a game, or a speaker telling you how to be a success like them without providing you with any blueprint or roadmap other than to copy what they did. Those talks motivate you for about 72 hours. The Triad can teach you how to motivate your mind from within to consistently improve your performance over time for the rest of your life. This is as valuable a skill to learn in school as English, math, and science, but our public schools do not teach these concepts. We condition a micromanagement model where the teacher defines what is most meaningful and relevant for the learner instead of teaching the learner how to make new information meaningful and relevant in their system to value it. It is one approach to teach someone that something is valuable. It is another approach to teach someone how to value what they learn. More schools are now turning to a value based curriculum, but if you read and comprehend Purposeful Intent and The Triad you do not have to depend on your school or teachers to motivate you to improve. You can learn the skills to be intrinsically motivated, and apply them to improve your performance. These applied skills work because they adhere to laws of behavior. If you apply physics, you cannot refute the physical laws observed and written about by Sir Isaac Newton.

In the first part of The Triad – Increase Awareness, you have been introduced to a wealth of new knowledge to help you increase your awareness for how to intrinsically motivate performance improvement. Terms have been defined and new concepts introduced to get you to think, act, and do for yourself and eventually others. Several paradigm shifts have been discussed such as equating quality of effort with quality of reward. A major shift has been to set low positive goals only slightly better than your own immediate past performance or average that you can control. This increases your probability for success and frequency of reward that conditions your motivation to improve your performance on each new trial. This is the opposite of what you have been told to set high goals. It has been pointed out that schools condition micromanagement of mass behavior. Schools and teachers micromanage what you learn and think to be meaningful and relevant to value because these skills are not taught to early learners. I am not sure that the professors that teach the teachers how to teach understand intrinsic motivation. Teacher preparation curriculums spend very little time teaching human behavioral psychology to understand what motivates student behaviors so that a good teacher can refocus misdirected energy for a worthwhile purpose in the mind of the learner. This is a problem when most students cannot define their needs and abilities to learn their purpose and make it their passion to learn all that they can.

A brief explanation for how multi sensory learning creates greater numbers of associational neurons to link knowledge in the brain. This same practice was used by Albert Einstein. Associations are stimulus-response connections that with practice become conditioned. You have to increase your awareness for how your knowledge and personality has been conditioned by others and your environment. It is harder to improve on anything until you know where you have been. The feedback model developed by B.F. Skinner was introduced to help you learn how to use your performance feedback as output to adjust your input by modifying a cue to get a different and correct response. Top performers are dependent on using their own immediate past performance as their perceptual anchoring point to set the next low positive goal. This is another skill that can taught by using portfolios, graphs, workout logs, diaries, etc. to remind you of what your immediate past performance was and reflect on how you achieved it to know what to focus on to improve and keep getting better.

Complex tasks have to be broken down into smaller parts. This creates a specific sub routine you can focus on to improve, and increase your opportunities for reward. Later you can chain the parts or practiced and perfected sub routines to improve the whole skilled performance. Even huge cruise ships are built in sections then welded together. Each sub routine has its own set of specific S-R connections. Each S is a specific stimulus cue, and each R is a specific response you will hopefully make depending upon the strength of your conditioning from practicing identical elements you expect to see in the actual performance. To support this skill development you can use mental rehearsal, visual imagery, positive self-talk, and pre competitive routines to mobilize your energy at will on demand when it counts the most. You can create a subjective multiple regression equation that beta weights the most important cues to focus on learning correct responses to perform any criterion skill. In education they call these best practices, but not everyone uses them. All throughout the first part of The Triad you have been given suggested steps to increase your awareness for specific concepts like needs and abilities, values, personality, goal setting, focus, and energy mobilization.

RROSR

One of the best practices for learning purposeful intent through The Triad is to understand and use RROSR. The Triad is three interrelated skills. Each can be practiced and learned to improve. RROSR applies to all skill learning. The brain is a micro processor that does not know right from wrong. It is designed to process sensory information sometimes reflexively looping through the spinal column and lower brain stem to provide an instantaneous response to prevent severe injury like when you withdraw your hand from a hot pan on the stove or a speck of dirt hits your eye causing you to blink to protect the eye. The brain also makes meaningful and relevant information by taking sensations and turning them into organized information with a process called perception. How you learn to turn sensations into meaningful perceptions and improve your performance is better practiced by knowing your purpose to value the process, new knowledge, and performance all linked together. RROSR is a simple way to recall the process for how the brain works to learn and understand. RROSR is the anachronism for recognize, receive, organize, store, and retrieve information.

You have to be conditioned to recognize the correct cues to condition correct responses or learning suffers immediately. It is harder to unlearn a conditioned response than to have learned the correct conditioned S-R connection in the beginning. Refocus skills can recondition a correct response to the same stimulus, but it takes more time. A blatant example is when I was a swimming professional. The Red Cross advocated teaching side stroke before breaststroke because it was easier for inexperienced teachers in their system. Breaststroke is easy to teach and learn when you chain together sub routines. But once a student is conditioned to perform a scissors kick, this is what they perform on their stomachs doing the breaststroke kick. The motor panels that control the dorsi flexion of the one foot is confused. However, if I taught breaststroke first, I could teach side stroke in 5-10 minutes because the breaststroke kick is far more powerful and necessary for survival.

Once you recognize the correct cues using selective attention, you have to receive the information into the brain as sensations. This is where multi sensory learning has a distinct advantage over acquiring knowledge in only one sense modality. The dominant sense is vision, but performance is improved best by creating more associations using more senses that later improve retrieval.

While all the information is being taken in it is believed that it is temporarily kept in short-term memory. The pre frontal cortex or PFC in front of your frontal lobe

RROSR – Circles of Interconnected Brain Lobes

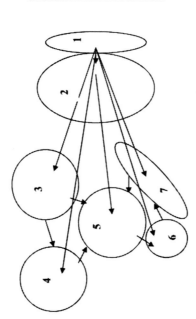

The pre frontal cortex takes in information from the senses and organizes it into tiny bit maps for easier storage and retrieval with similar data. With purposeful and valued experience the brain is organized to respond and perform efficiently.

1. Pre-Frontal Cortex- associated with planning, reasoning, and short term memory to organize information into bit maps

2. Frontal Lobe- associated with thinking, reasoning, planning, parts of speech, movement, emotions, and problem solving

3. Parietal Lobe- associated with movement, orientation, recognition, perception of stimuli

4. Occipital Lobe- associated with visual processing

5. Temporal Lobe- associated with perception and recognition of auditory stimuli, memory, and speech

6. Cerebellum, or "little brain", is associated with regulation and coordination of movement, posture, and balance.

7. Brain Stem. This is your spinal cord where all the information to and from the brain travels through bundles of nerves.

where all your thinking takes place is believed to serve this function. The PFC organizes all the new information by turning sensations into perceptions. Visual patterns that are observed are probably compressed and stored as bit maps through the optic nerve back to the occipital lobe. Each lobe has specific storage functions, and they are connected by brain cells and associational neurons. As the "organizer" the PFC also has the ability to create a sub routine to perfect a skill by retrieving already stored information to compare with new information. Visualization and mental rehearsal techniques create a mental movie of the spatial and temporal operations taken from the associated lobes of the brain.

Each lobe compresses information into a bit map and organizes it further for easier storage with other like information to improve the storage efficiency. Capacity, with the billions of brain cells, is not the problem. This is why I find it hard to accept that a child cannot learn if taught RROSR and multi sensory sequential learning to condition the number of correct stimulus-response connections to improve performance and thinking capacity.

With each lobe properly storing the information and all the associations having been created, the brain is ready *at will on demand* to retrieve all the information it needs to perform skills. As the information is passed through the brain, the PFC and other centers, make comparisons of past performance as stored knowledge with new performance knowledge to improve learning and performance.

Earlier I made reference to the hypothesis for <u>Purposeful Intent</u> that the brain stores information differently for valued information created with a conscious purpose in mind. Information that is valued is more readily retrieved at will on demand. This accounts for top performance. This also accounts for how to improve learning consistently adding to your knowledge to become more familiar with tasks by their S-R connections, and think in increasingly higher and higher planes to create new knowledge and understanding in your system.

Parts two and three of The Triad will place emphasis on self-evaluation and connecting reward with reinforcement skills. These two parts together with increasing your awareness from part one will help define your purpose and improve your intrinsic motivation for each task you choose.

It's YOUR Job

"Uphill climb not so hard as downhill with heavy burden."

Andrew Christian

Objective: How to use intrinsic motives to accept personal accountability and reduce dependency on others for your motivation and success.

Performers who are taught how to self-evaluate and self-reward their purpose setting proper goals, hold themselves accountable for improving their performance, and become independent upon extrinsic motivators provided by others. Purposeful practice reinforces good personal behaviors. By practicing PI, you increase your awareness and value for any activity to personally account for your learning that enhances performance. Performers who understand and practice PI become more engaged and accountable for their performance.

Introduction

This chapter has two components: Education and Learning, and Management. How you learn and manage is determined by how you were conditioned for performance accountability, and the skills you will need to recondition yourself and teach to others. How accountability is taught and conditioned in school and at home or on the job are very important issues. Purposeful Intent offers strategies to increase personal awareness and accountability for performance improvement without having to create rules and regulations to coerce performers.

Accountability is defined as responsible, liable, or explainable. In the traditional sense, accountable is what someone else expects of another performer. The thought process is associated with external forces outside the performer. The concept of purposeful intent is to recondition your mind from within to think of holding yourself accountable rather than expecting others to make you do something based on their expectations. To know the difference in how you learned and were conditioned to be held accountable for your behaviors, performances, and partnerships can help you change to intrinsic motivation with a purposeful intent.

Whether you are conditioned by others or have learned to hold yourself accountable in all aspects of your life, there is an association to performance evaluation. In Part Two: Enhance Self-Evaluation, pre, during, and post-evaluation will explore this subject. However, to fully appreciate and value the transition from expecting others to hold you accountable to you holding yourself accountable, some time should be spent on increasing your personal awareness.

Top performers, on average, hold themselves accountable for their performances. They do not blame others for their poor performances when they occur. They take responsibility. External forces still exist in that others who are unable to perform at that level do not understand and show their displeasure when the top performer gets mad at their performance by cursing, or displaying anger. Boos and whistling are common forms of external forces used to condition appropriate behavior. But what internal forces have you learned to apply, modify, or change to improve your performance?

This chapter creates a dichotomy between how you are conditioned by external forces or you have conditioned yourself by internal forces to hold yourself accountable for your performance. We already know that intrinsic motivation is more powerful than extrinsic motivation, therefore by increasing your awareness for how you have been conditioned is necessary to improve your purposeful intent skills. The Accountability Paradigm offers a contrast between micromanagement and empowerment leadership. Reflect back on how you felt you were educated and permitted to perform by your teachers and then on-the-job training by company management. Empowerment increases intrinsic motivation with management's expectation of performance improvement. Micromanagement uses extrinsic motives to coerce compliance with the company mission. You decide which company or organization you would like to work for.

When you think of conditioning which is a stimulus-response connection that becomes repeated with greater efficiency, you think of schools, education, and learning. Your parents should have been the first to condition specific behaviors and hold you accountable for performing them prior to school. Between your parents and teachers who are the first to evaluate your performance, together they form a powerful external conditioning force by their expectations. Some of those external

Accountability Paradigm

Micromanagement	vs.	Empowerment
No choice		Many choices
Loss of control to paranoid control freaks		Control of your ideas
Loss of creativity for ideas, methods, processes		Creative sharing of ideas, methods, processes freely
Boss managers		Professional learning community culture
- Little coaching		Lead managers
- Perform or be fired		- Strong coaching to build knowledge, skills, and teamwork
Extrinsic motives		- Recognition of personal needs of the performers
- Needs of the boss or corporation to be met		Intrinsic motives
Non-caring		- Personal needs satisfied
- Cold; impersonal; no fun atmosphere/culture		Caring
- Work, job, non-satisfying		- Warm; personal; fun helping others atmosphere/culture
Excuse		- Family values; work, job, satisfying personal needs
- Can blame others for poor performance		- Personal efforts recognized by co-workers
- Can spread false rumors and beliefs		No excuse
No personal accountability		- Blame yourself for poor performance
Lower morale		Hold yourself accountable
- "Why bother syndrome"		Higher morale
- Learned helplessness		- Can take personal credit
- Leader steals your ideas		Able to equate quality of effort to quality of reward
- Leader takes the credit for good; blames workers for poor performance		Positive continuous small incremental performance improvements are recognized and celebrated
Employees finger point and blame others for weak performance outcomes		Personal reward system is reinforced to repeat positive behaviors
No regard for what worker thinks		Take personal responsibility to achieve outcomes
Workers do not care what co-workers think		Desire to care what worker is thinking
Collection of individual performers doing their own thing		
Lost sight of company mission		

Inconsistent decisions; personal skill development; and performance Ignorance and bias = bliss Resistance to change keeps personality and stress management in check for short term Whole world passes you by Fly by the seat of your pants	Teamwork - Workers care about what co-workers are thinking and doing that reflect on overall group performance Focus on mission and outcomes Consistent, stable approach to continuously improving personal skills, decisions, that reflect best practice, and overall performance Knowledge and performance outcomes = bliss Adapt to change recognizing temporary state of stress to manage for the short term and produce long term personal growth and satisfaction You keep pace with your profession and the world by planning

expectations are biased and unrealistic because the evaluator is not the performer. You are the performer. Therefore, you need to learn how to be your own evaluator.

Purposeful intent is a skill that teaches you how to not only hold yourself accountable, but to teach others how to hold themselves accountable. For example, instead of passing judgment for a performance, ask a question that gets the performer to reflect on and judge their performance. Did you do the best that you could? Did you try to do your best? What did you have to do to get that grade, score, or evaluation? Did you improve? Are you happy with your performance? There are all kinds of questions designed to get the performer to reflect on and review their performance, but to whom and what?

Accountable also implies there is a standard to apply current performance, but what is that standard? There is also an expectation, but what is that expectation? The expectation seems to account for a performer's ability level as well as a standard they should be able to meet given the circumstances. It was already noted that top performers set private goals based on a perceptual anchoring point that is usually their own immediate past performance or past performance average. If you are going to use standards and have expectations, then use the patterns of top performers and condition those kinds of stimulus-response connections.

To condition personal accountability, whether at home or in school, provide the realistic expectation up front prior to the performance. Be able to support your case with evidence. However, if you are the parent or teacher evaluator, refrain from stating the expectation until you can determine what the performer feels is realistic for their ability. In this way, each performer becomes their baseline control. You base expectations and standards on what they are individually capable of performing based on their immediate past performance. The nice concept about kids is that they don't know they are not supposed to know. They can learn to condition their own behaviors if you teach them to self evaluate their own performance using the feedback model to compare for improvement. I can guarantee you that your child does not care whether the neighbor kid improves at anything, or that classmates are improving and making all A's. Therefore, condition what the child is naturally driven and knows how to perform; improve and feel successful.

After the performer has some experience with the task to provide them with feedback they can observe from their performance, you can condition them to keep improving slightly with each new performance. Children who are fearful of trying or make exaggerated expectations are those who have been conditioned to behave this way by external forces in the home or at school. The normal human organism does not learn in this way. The natural drive is to improve. The more often you can condition the performer to observe their performance improvement they will learn to hold themselves accountable for their performance. They will develop correct personality patterns of realism, persistence, and will-power displayed by top performers. Realism is when the goal expectation is more closely aligned with the actual performance feedback observed. This kind of behavior teaches children to learn what their abilities are and keep their expectations in line with reality to avoid serious frustrations that lead to disrupting classrooms and other bad behaviors that reduce their capacity to learn how to learn. Usually when performers make mistakes, others want to manage their behavior instead of teaching them self evaluation feedback skills to take accountability for their performance and behavior. This brings us to two more behavioral rules:

Behavioral Rule # 2: You cannot build accountability in a micromanagement system.

Behavioral Rule # 3: You will be less frustrated if you keep your expectations in line with reality.

This chapter implies that it is your responsibility to hold yourself accountable for your performance. But it also means teaching others to learn the skills to hold themselves accountable for their performances. Our society is quick to judge and hold others accountable when the evaluators or critics cannot perform those skills to meet standards or expectations any better or hold themselves accountable for their performances. Be more reluctant to cast the first stone until you get your own house in order. Hold yourself accountable; it's your job.

Leadership and Personal Accountability

Purposeful intent is everyone's job, but mainly it is your job. When you learn purposeful intent skills you accept personal responsibility for your performance, and not blame others for a poor performance. You can learn purposeful intent skills to lead yourself first, and then lead others to apply the PI Triad to their daily lives and become successful over time. Leaders are administrators, directors, managers, supervisors, commanders, professors, teachers, coaches, captains, students, parents, civic volunteers, and organizers of all kinds. Each leader has to identify specific needs to create a uniform purposeful intent in their followers, keeping in mind that their own needs cannot supersede the group's or performer's needs.

If you want your performers to be partners and accountable for positive outcomes, help them identify their short and long term needs. We are in the age of immediate gratification and a literal functioning society – "I am hungry, feed me" - with increasingly less emphasis on behavioral accountability and more emphasis on "big brother" micromanagement. The problem this creates is that most performers do not know how to perform basic process skills to motivate performance improvement. Performers like you or your employees are motivated best by guiding intrinsic motives that satisfy personal needs or goals by focusing on a specific purpose and positive intent.

Development of PI skills takes time. Historically leaders are achievers that continuously acquired their PI skills over the course of their careers in order to achieve their icon status. No one, at an early age, knows how they will turn out. What difference will you make? For certain, if you are dependent on others to meet your needs, you will not be one to make a difference in the lives of others. Top performers focused on their passion to get results, and so can you if you define your purposeful intent for your performances. Top performers try to understand their PI for each task. They prioritize their attention to details that compute the most to their success. They are driven by higher order needs to acquire skills that reinforced their behaviors and passion to increase their awareness, higher Planer Thinking, and clearer goals. Top performers see the big picture, and base their vision on their individual diverse set of experiences. They can imagine how success will change the quality of their life. All behavior is driven to improve quality of life. That is your <u>Intent</u>. Your <u>Purposes</u> are different. Fulfillment of our needs is what drives all our behaviors, and is a function of the environment we create for ourselves. When you do not learn PI skills to identify your needs and how to help yourself with awareness and self-evaluation skills to effect positive changes steadily improving your performance, you cannot reward and reinforce your performance to build your confidence. This makes it hard to get out of poverty, the ghetto, feeling sorry for yourself, or your depression caused by lack of performance achievement you value. Unfortunately, most people are not taught how to be fully aware of their needs beyond the most basic ones for food, clothing, and shelter. They do not understand their own human behavior. All over the world, many people live hand-to-mouth even in the U.S. because we are not taught PI skills to alter our thinking and environment and meet our needs. Those who lack purposeful intent seem aimless and spend their lives as victims without any awareness of their choices or of how to meet their needs to be self reliant. Perhaps you have been tempted to let others fulfill your needs or make your decisions. Giving up your choices, though, weakens your personal leadership capacity and accountability.

EDUCATION and LEARNING

It would be hard to function in the adult world with a sixth grade brain, but you have to wonder when Jay Leno does his Jay Walking segment on the Tonight Show to interview average Americans on the street. The answers to simple questions that college education majors should know is sadly incredible; the lack of awareness and knowledge. This is one example to support the need for PI instruction and conditioning in our schools. When students do not value knowledge it is not retained and readily retrievable in the brain. Intrinsic motivation skills must be taught in a way for each performer to construct meaningful and relevant value to that knowledge. This means taking sensations and consciously converting them to perceptions that think of how to improve upon past performance with similar tasks. The best way is to personally learn to create associations to what you already know also known as transfer learning. Associations are a series of S-R connections in a sequence also known as sub routines to what you already know and have task familiarity. These S-R sequences and associations create knowledge as they are conditioned to recognize specific cues and connect them with the correct associated response. As a behaviorist, this type of conditioning does not require native intelligence. Sequential learning and task familiarity require the serial S-R connections be correct. Subjectively choose the best cues that have demonstrated learning associated responses efficiently for those kinds of learners in the past. This is done using the subjective multiple regression analysis approach to pick out those top cues that best predict learning the criterion.

Educators have resisted subscribing to a conditioning approach to learning because it has been associated to Pavlov's experiments with dogs. Pavlov, if you recall, conditioned the dog with a bell and introduced meat for the reward. Very soon, any time he rang the bell, the dog would salivate. Educators question whether understanding takes place. The constructivist view is that how can you not learn when you need to acquire more information to store and retrieve familiar knowledge of tasks to transfer and acquire new knowledge. The brain, don't forget, is a micro processor. It is designed to perform RROSR very well. RROSR is recognize the cue, receive the information into the brain with your senses, organize the information in the pre frontal cortex and compress into bit maps, store the bit maps in various lobes designed for that information, and retrieve the compressed bit map data efficiently at will on demand. However, remember the hypothesis for purposeful intent is that value is what creates the meaningful and relevant associations to readily retrieve stored knowledge. Non-valued knowledge is stored differently in the brain. Your intelligence is in your ability to retrieve stored knowledge. If you think learning is a pain, boring, and no fun now, wait until you have to work two jobs at minimum wage to put bread on your table and gas in your car. You, not the teacher, must be motivated in your mind to make learning fun. Your brain doesn't know its boring until you tell it. Reverse the message and tell your brain how exciting and fun this new incoming information is to learn and pay attention; increase your awareness – Part I – in The Triad. Do you see or sense that there is a pattern or sequence to connect the new information with what you already know? Use that personal performance feedback model to compare your new performance with your immediate past performance or average to increase your awareness of improvements that you can reward. If you are improving your performance, you can be proud of the practice and attention you have given to earn the self reward.

Starting at home and early in school, conditioning the correct behaviors is imperative or the mechanism for learning will not be in place to develop higher order thinking skills later. More parents have poor parenting skills because they do not know how to say no to their whining children, or effectively discipline them when they disobey their instructions. The object of parenting is to teach your children to eventually provide for their own needs. But instead, parents keep enabling poor behaviors in their children by providing for their needs much longer than necessary and wonder why the child has not learned to be accountable for either their behavior or learning to acquire more and more knowledge. So the dumb get dumber and the smart ones figure it out to get smarter, but the educational system is conditioning underachievers because educators do not know how to teach intrinsic motivation skills. They have not learned how. The affluence of America has created a literal society that is getting fatter and dumber because we do not know the skills to motivate our behaviors to consistently improve our performance. People are not motivated to use perceptual skills to project for future need satisfaction or even stay healthy. They are motivated to value pleasurable experiences over work because work does not provide them with a conditioned satisfaction of a need they do not know they need. Therefore, eat, drink, and party especially when someone else is paying the bill. They are not conditioned to hold their learning and performance improvement accountable when they can blame others for their mistakes, and those significant others accept the blame as if it was their fault to enable that behavior. To enable that kind of behavior is their fault. Do not play the blame game. Take responsibility for your learning each day.

Change your BS to RS

You have the natural ability to sense more than you think, and so does your customer. To paraphrase Abraham Lincoln, 'You can fool some of the people some of the time, but you can't fool all of the people all of the time.' In business, you fake it until you make it. The fact is BS can mean bull—, or a Bachelor of Science college degree. It can also be the abbreviation for bright stuff or back stabber. Who are you kidding when you lie to a customer? You are the customer when you do not learn to hold yourself accountable for your performance. Why are you not improving? What's your problem? What do you need to succeed? Quit making excuses or blaming others for your inability to learn or do more work to ensure your success. Even if your IQ is 80 like Babe Ruth was supposed to be, you can condition a sequence to learn anything. Anyone can be conditioned to improve their immediate past performance by setting a low positive goal expectation only one point higher than their own immediate past performance or average. It takes a little more purposeful effort and concentration of your abilities to learn to perform that skill at will on demand, but it's your job.

RS is the right stuff. It is what astronauts are made of or any top performer in their field. If you are an employer, how do you find and determine those top performers who demonstrate and know what they are doing to guide the company with a forward vision to improve? Obviously it will not be someone who has all their needs provided by others. Look for those who have had to work to make it, and give them the chance to keep improving. Objectively you can compare past performance to plot performance improvement on a visual graph or chart to observe positive growth and changes over time to predict future growth, expansion, or leadership opportunity. Subjectively, each performer is different in unique ways and these kinds of behaviors can be observed by what motivates them: money, promotions to want more responsibility, recognition from superior or respected colleagues, job satisfaction meeting personal goals, personality patterns of stability, realism, persistence, and will power. Right stuff performers are inner directed; they need no job description. If I had my choice, I would always choose intrinsically motivated performers to work for me. Otherwise, you will always question what that performer will be doing when you are not looking. You will also have to spend more dollars hiring a staff to micromanage those employees to extrinsically motivate them more and more with greater and greater rewards.

Purposeful Objective

Your purposeful objective is to create more positive feedback of your performance based on an increased awareness of your own abilities in comparison to a standard, your previous performance, or performance average. The purpose of self-evaluation is to gauge the level of your output compared to your past performance by creating a positive pre connection between quality of effort and quality of reward. It is not what you <u>guess</u> about your performance, it is what you <u>learn to know and value</u> about your work by learning to increase your personal awareness skills. You can consciously choose a negative or positive view of any task. English play write William Shakespeare was credited with saying, "Nothing is either good or bad, but thinking makes it so." You have a choice to control your thinking and learning by knowing your purpose beforehand to create value that increases knowledge retention. Letting others do your thinking does not increase your knowledge retention. When you learned to ride a bicycle no one could ride the bicycle for you. You had to learn to ride it for yourself. You made initial mistakes and crashed a few times. The pain made you increase your awareness to learn the strategy to keep your balance by keeping the wheels rolling straight. Intrinsic motivation can only be improved by increasing your awareness and perception of the quality of your work through self-evaluation and reflection. This skill enhances your personal accountability and motivation to continuously improve your performance.

Make the learner your partner in the learning process so that they – not we – will learn to decide what is meaningful and relevant knowledge to value so they will consciously store and be better able to retrieve information when it is needed most at will on demand. *This is the acquired skill of every top performer.* We have many understood instructional practices such as do-overs or mastery learning that allows a learner to continuously learn a task until they can earn an "A." That A grade using a performance mastery rubric allows a learner to self-evaluate their performance before turning in their work for a final grade evaluation. In the adult world, we get multiple chances to correct our errors until we get it right. This manuscript went through multiple revisions by me and a skilled editor. In a kid's world, they usually get one shot at it, and then they are made to feel like dog do-do if they did not get it right the first time. In business, that sales flyer or brochure you intend to send to 1,000 customers will have multiple reviews by a variety of people BEFORE it is printed and sent out.

Children have no bias or prejudice; these are learned behaviors. They are naturally curious to experiment and try new things until adults' condition them to do the opposite or what they want. It is our educator and system bias that limits the capabilities of our students and has produced a mass of underachievers in our society for lack of understanding about how to build intrinsic motivation and accountability within students. Students are conditioned to believe that only educators can tell them what performances are good or bad, meaningful and relevant. They don't self-evaluate and few teachers provide and explain the rubrics for their lessons so that students can begin to evaluate their performance. Almost all students, including primary grades, know a quality performance when they see it but cannot describe it. Quality performance provides one standard; however, the best standard to improve is your own immediate past performance. You can reward your personal improvements more frequently to stay motivated than to surpass the performance of the top performer. It does not matter where the performer starts; only where they understand and perform at the end. We all perform based on a feeling for good, not so good, or bad.

Literal Society Model

Our personality is influenced by our experiences. Our ability to apply previous experiences to new ones is a measure of our awareness. Teaching kids to connect experiences is not necessarily a part of our school curriculum. Personality has been associated with how you choose to set goals, and identify your needs that drive your motivation to act. This is in part because teachers do not understand or possess the awareness skills necessary to help students form cues and strategies. In our literal education and culture, our basic needs are usually unidentified and met by others like parents or bosses. Allowing others to identify and meet our needs does not build personal accountability or any value for learning. The literal idea is, if you see X respond with Y, and do not bother to think or understand the relationship. Simple associations are difficult to project or to imagine an outcome. Without the ability to create these associations, it's hard to transfer knowledge or skills to a similar new skill. A literal model will not help you create more associational neurons to provide efficiency of movement or thinking capacity. The more literal we become as a society, we lose our ability to think and invite others to micromanage our performance. To improve personal performance, we need to give credit to the performers who do the work so they will have intrinsic motivation.

You are the product of your environment. The choices you make for all the wonderful opportunities you are provided in your lifetime can be positive or negative, but they depend on the development of your awareness skills.

Purposeful Educational System Change Builds Accountability

We can create in all learners the need to learn how to learn, to think, act, and do for themselves and eventually others. The current educational system does little to help each learner create a personal feedback system to learn how to hold themselves accountable for their learning and performance. Identifying their personal needs and the strategies to satisfy them with a purposeful intent would be a start. Focused driven behaviors with a purpose are known to provide greater probability to succeed on any task. You read, write, and speak with a purpose. With more success you condition the motivation to work harder to continue the pleasurable feelings of success. Charter schools attract high quality students because they require higher enrollment standards not every public student can meet. This education has a standard that comes with a price, is not free, and therefore more valued. This brings the next behavioral rule:

Behavioral Rule # 4: It is normal behavior to want more of what you cannot readily have and desire less of the commodity that is free to all.

In the United States, a free and public education is provided to all students up to the age of 16. Because public education is free and accessible to every child, it is not valued. Therefore, we need to change school systems to value based curricula where students know their purpose and needs to be intrinsically motivated to become educated. This is in keeping with the hypothesis of this book and The Triad that value is the key to how information is readily stored and retrieved in the brain.

Our educational system needs to change to a leadership system that focuses on teaching intrinsic motivation with purposeful intent strategies and skills. You already know students of the same age who learn at different rates. Within the curriculum students learn various core subjects at different rates, but school systems apply a one-size-fits-all approach by throwing all students of the same age range into the same class. Instituted learning modules to perform until mastered based upon achievement ability could create differentiated and diverse instruction to meet the learning needs and improve the motivation of every student all of the time. Students can progress at their own rate of readiness and motivation, and be taught by a variety of specialized highly qualified teachers. Performers who display more frequent success are self-rewarded and self-reinforced to learn more. They learn the tools to apply to be successful more consistently. They are less confused and more motivated to achieve consistent performances. Through PI skills training, they will connect their minds with their bodies, increase their awareness, enhance their self-evaluation, and connect reward with reinforcement.

Children born today with average heredity will predictably live to be 120 years old if they exercise, eat a well balanced diet, don't get shot, have an accident, do drugs or drink alcohol or lack a purposeful intent for their lives to focus on achieving independence. Due to changes in longevity and maturity, our school systems must change the educational delivery system. Student maturity by grade level can increase by slowly changing the age requirements to six or seven years to enter kindergarten. Pre schools can be jointly funded on the Federal, State, and local level. Schools can change their curriculums to make grades 7, 8, 9, and 10 a junior high school with core subject specialists just like senior high school. At the completion of the junior high core curriculum standards students will be 16 years old, and are no longer required to be in school in most states (Illinois just passed a bill to require this age be increased to 17). Students can be given a choice to focus on their academics or find a job to support them, and pay for their personal needs. This will help low achieving students quickly understand their needs. There can be two kinds of high schools with similar core curricula to ensure that a fundamental education will be required in either a vocational or college prep focus. The new high school would be for grades 11, 12, 13, and 14 to complete at age 20. Students would be more mature and need to maintain a purpose and intent to do well or temporarily lose their opportunity to continue their education by having to sit out a semester to experience the "real world" outside of school to meet their needs. Disruptive students would be asked to leave providing teachers more time to teach. To put this in perspective, assume the average life span was age 68 in 1950 and two generations later in 2020 may easily be 100. In 1950 giving the car keys to a 16 year old meant they had lived 23.5% of their life, but today it seems like only 16% of their life and would be like giving the car keys to a 12 year old back in 1950. The car insurance industry would believe this fact. Today maturity, a knowledge explosion, and confusion by educators deciding what is meaningful and relevant to learn create a problem understanding the best sequence for learning to

145

associate knowledge and skills to transfer to new and unfamiliar tasks. We continue to adhere to the old "receptacles" model instead of the "facilitation" of knowledge model that would create a purposeful intent to understand why to meet personal needs that change over time; A serious problem in all societies that must change to survive. Mankind must learn how to survive on earth without predatory killing each other for a cause like religious beliefs to acquire "eternal life." Instead, we need to enter into a new age of cooperation.

Our society is fearful that uncontrolled students lose hope and do not acquire workplace readiness skills. They lack learning how to equate quality of effort with quality or reward, drop out of school, become drug users, and prey on others to support their bad habits. There is no learned accountability. However, necessity is the mother of invention. If parents keep providing for all the needs the child should be learning to provide for themselves, they will only keep enabling the wrong behaviors. If you are taught PI skills to motivate your work starting in the home and pre-kindergarten to identify your needs and improve the quality of your life, you will achieve full independence to make your own decisions and be "free" from the control of others who are dependent upon you to meet their needs. You may realize that if the purpose was explained to you all those mundane school homework tasks and turning in assignments on time was important work to value your education. You can build intrinsic value in any task that you purposefully choose to store and retrieve meaningful and relevant information. Otherwise you store non-valued information in hard to retrieve sectors of your brain.

Extrinsically directed performers lose when their parent, manager, or leader leaves them. Increasingly more parents are not involved in the education of their child as the child matures. Children are also maturing later due to changes in the longevity curve. In 1950 the life span was projected at 68 years. A 16-year-old teen today with healthy eating and exercise habits, and anti-oxidant vitamin supplements can expect to live to be over 100, but now has conceivably spent only 16% of their lifespan. At age 16 in 1950 this person had achieved 23.5% of their lifespan. With much less maturity coupled with the knowledge explosion, mass media, technology and the Internet, we continue to expect far too much of our youth to learn at the same chronological age. They cannot predict their future needs that would normally motivate their behavior to want to learn, but unlike the animal world human beings allow their young to be dependent on them much longer despite the conflicts for independence. Modern medicine has saved more infant lives that have further decreased the maturational from the chronological age to require more differentiated instruction to handle the variety of learning needs in the early classrooms. There is no time for play to develop an imagination or to organize the fundamental motor and verbal sequences. PI skills emphasize intrinsic motivation and personal accountability. Adult leaders create a grossly dependent world with extrinsic motives to control youthful behaviors rather them teach them how to be in control and responsible for their own behaviors. More extrinsic control and disciplinary rules do not reinforce good behavior. Good behavior and frequent success motivate more good behavior. As the child matures and naturally gains confidence, self reliance, and independence good parents shift the needs, motives, and accountability for responsible behavior to intrinsic beliefs and values. On the other hand, overprotective parenting enables the child to be irresponsible and remain dependent on extrinsic motives such as bribes for good behavior from parents. It is hard to identify and create your needs and transition to intrinsic motives if you have been conditioned by external forces most of your life. You will not learn to make the choices necessary to hold yourself accountable for your learning performance. The inherent natural intrinsic value of learning is contaminated by the extrinsic motives of others to fulfill their personal needs, and not act in the best interests of the child. These forces come from misguided school board members, administrators, teachers, and coaches. In business you have board members, CEO's, managers, and trainers. All your natural drives are laws of behavior that lend themselves to enhance intrinsic motivation, but they are continually violated by others to control behaviors to meet their needs. All leaders would do well to know how and when to apply these natural drives to motivate intrinsic behaviors in the people who do the work.

Beacon or Reflection?

I keep a small painted plaster lighthouse on my desk as a constant reminder that we need to be the *beacon* and not the *reflection* of society. We can teach intrinsic motivation skills to improve the quality of life, the most basic of all drives, using purposeful intent. Since 1960 our public school systems have drifted away from their primary mission as academic institutions towards more highly complex social institutions where being popular is more prized than being smart. Despite nonconforming dress, there is considerable social pressure for students to perform like one another. The opportunity to stand out academically is not always desirable in a social conforming atmosphere. Sameness creates a weaker motive to produce quality. The same factors occur in unions that protect less productive workers who have no purposeful intent to produce quality performance.

Changed Model for Education

Traditions are like phobias: hard to break even when intelligent people know otherwise. When you assume that what has worked in the past will always work, you introduce a subtle bias. You resist progress because changing your familiar routines promotes stress to your personality. The Internet has dramatically changed the ability to acquire knowledge. This has forced the model for education to change from "receptacles of knowledge" to "facilitators of knowledge." When you hear, "we don't do it that way here" or, "we have never done it that way before; it won't work here" these are leader statements that negatively impose bias and beliefs on the performers they should be encouraging to become intrinsically motivated, creative, and independent and productive thinkers to be efficient. Technology and creativity facilitate knowledge. Albert Einstein and all the smartest performers also had teacher-leaders to facilitate their knowledge acquisition. As a leader when you apply your bias and beliefs to control your followers, you stifle your performer's creativity and intrinsic motive to succeed for you, for the team, and for themselves. This has the same effect as micromanagement to destroy intrinsic motivation in the performers who do the work. This creates conflicts between your leader role and those high positive performers with strong purposeful intent who consistently get results. As life long learners, average performers need to be empowered to improve the quality of their performance and hold themselves accountable for achieving specific goals and outcomes. Leaders who only teach what they know follow the *receptacles* approach to knowledge acquisition which quickly becomes outdated. The personal needs of performers are what drive their behaviors. Knowing your intrinsic needs and purpose for performing are the keys that unlock your door to success, but these needs are seldom sought after by boss-managers who impose their will, goals, and needs on employees. Because the global economy is rapidly changing what knowledge is currently meaningful and relevant to the teacher and the learner, learning to learn is a more important life-long skill to master that is continually enhanced with PI training. Your leadership role is to *facilitate* knowledge with technology by teaching critical thinking skills. What you read on the Internet is not always the truth. You must learn to consider the source and quality of the information, and how it was derived. When you are less than secure about the current knowledge you want to pass on to performers, you will feel intimidated by anyone who appears to question your authority, knowledge, or intelligence. This occurs when you accept the bias that performers cannot learn who lack native intelligence, motivation, or a home support system to reinforce what is taught.

Caring Builds Accountability and Creativity; Coercive Rules and Conformity Do Not

The ultimate theme of caring is to teach accountable independence in each performer. This includes everyone from the CEO on down. Value is the key component to intrinsic motivation. The lack of a value based curriculum is what leads to a system that conditions unmotivated performers that corporations must eventually deal with by offering their own brand of training programs. New employees who subscribe to the motives of the company survive; those that do not get fired and look for another job. This turnover is so costly that corporations have developed a science for trying to hire the best employees based on their personality, work ethic, history, and other past performance criteria. These variables are hard to spot until the leaders learn PI skills to apply to their own performance before judging others. Intrinsically motivated performers need creative leaders who have vision, understand how to identify and train talent, minimize turnover, and have performed the work they ask of their employees. This is most evident in highly successful professional sports organizations: top coaches who have played the game are better at selecting and coaching new talent. They provide their performers with the knowledge of specific successful strategies and cues to recognize information, receive, organize, store, and retrieve at will on demand for top performance when it is needed the most. This is the RROSR.

When a program does not know how to motivate its performers, they will create more coercive rules to instill conformity that may control the masses but destroys creativity in the intrinsically motivated that could become the future top performers. Unskilled teachers teach to the lower end of the performance spectrum, and the *system* produces a wealth of underachievers. Weak governments that don't trust the masses of people to make decisions for their own welfare seek to control them by providing more dependent social programs. Education is talked about but really a non issue because educated people are able to meet their own needs and are not readily dependent on their government that keeps a few in power. Poorly trained managers who feel threatened by top performers tend to find more faults than positives to reward that produce stagnation and malcontent. Graduates accept positions that have become dependent on external forces to motivate them to improve their performance. To counter this effect, states have enacted mentoring laws to assist new teachers in the application of teaching skills and classroom management. However, even skilled teachers report that they must *teach to the middle*. Similarly, corporations and their trainers are trapped in the middle and become top heavy in management spending billions to try to increase work output in unmotivated performers. Because public school systems are free and mandatory, many students behave in a manner that they do not value their education. They regard their curriculums as meaningless and irrelevant.

Thomas Sergiovanni (1994), <u>Building Community In Schools</u>, wrote that the #1 reason why students did well in the classroom was because they felt the teacher liked them. Excellent leaders also have charisma to convey a caring feeling to all performers if they expect their performers to sacrifice some of their personal needs to satisfy the needs of the organization. Sergiovanni explained that a caring community of teachers had a lot to do with the overall success of students. Similarly, a caring community of leaders and managers can have the same impact on the production value of their performers in an organization. Performing with a purpose for those who care builds self-reliance, confidence, self-esteem, and intrinsic motives to value success and avoids a co-dependency. This concept is the exact opposite of political leadership that thinks they can use other people's money to provide services to a select group to "buy" their vote. To get elected the "quid pro quo" favor builds co-dependency, extrinsic reward, and reduces the motivation of the recipient to learn how to provide for their own needs. This keeps the politician in power when the people should be the empowered. Increasing social programs may redistribute the wealth of a nation, but it does not teach a man how to fish and provide for his long term needs. This fact should make more companies embrace a family-like caring atmosphere and value the opinions of every worker. This and Total Quality Management or TQM was the model that W. Edwards Deming used to rebuild Japan after the Second World War. Each intrinsically motivated performer works to achieve a higher personal standard they create for themselves based on the knowledge of their own immediate past performance or average. Companies and organizations must continually devise and provide objective data to track the performance of everyone to gain positive feedback about their improvement. In any company, quality production can only be achieved through personal performance satisfaction and reward beyond the extrinsic paycheck. Providing a personal means to obtain positive feedback about performance improvements compared to immediate past performance or average is required. This builds the intrinsic motivational value of objective accountability.

Rewarding irresponsible behavior or modeling responsible behavior will not improve personal accountability. What is certain is the behavioral principle of Rule #1: *The more you do for people, the less they will learn to do for themselves.* When organizations and systems need to use rules and conditions to coerce and qualify performance behaviors, their micromanagement costs increase, which ultimately hurts their profitability and shareholder confidence. Another behavioral rule to apply is Rule # 6:

Do not make unenforceable rules or laws that regulate extrinsic accountability.

More rules lead to a drop in morale and change the focus as the performers feel less in control over their work environment and will hold themselves less accountable. As performers, students often focus on the negative, what not to do, instead of the positive effect of learning.

Intrinsic Model

You are intrinsically motivated if you perform quality work when the boss is not looking. The quality of your work matters most for you to attend to details. You must have observable and realistic goals to meet your personal needs to establish your PI strength. You hold yourself accountable for achieving your goals. You become more aware of what goals are being satisfied in order to reinforce your efforts. You understand the value of an education and need to share your knowledge with other performers. How can more performers be motivated to achieve continuously higher quality performance outcomes rather then increasing their social calendars? Performers only want those things that they cannot readily have: In Europe and some oriental countries, students have to meet stringent requirements in order for the government to pay for their education. They take their academics seriously because they are required to meet benchmark standards to continue their education. This points out how needs motivate purposeful intent behaviors associated with values.

When you rely on extrinsic motivation in the form of praise, grades, or some form of judgment of the performer's work you create a dependent approval system that requires more management for higher cost.

Congruent RROSR Awareness

Not only can greater awareness create numerous multi-sensory associations to enhance the way you respond; awareness skills can also help you develop an efficient valuing system using your multiple senses to increase your motivation. Motivation conversely improves your awareness skills which increases your intelligence defined as your ability to recognize, receive, organize, store, and retrieve (RROSR) knowledge at-will-on-demand. Your perceptual awareness is the most seldom learned and practiced awareness skill that assigns value and meaning relevant to previous and future performances. Your past must always be less important than your future, but your awareness will apply the memory of feelings from past experiences to anticipated future goals. Your immediate past performance provides a valuable perceptual anchoring point about which to judge the value of your next goal.

The more closely you can learn to align the perceived value meaning with actual performance results, the easier it will be to connect greater reward with reinforcement and to strengthen your motivation to repeat those behaviors. By reflecting on your past performance and associating a value to your new goal that increases the probability for attainment to slightly improve with each new attempt and feel rewarded is how you teach intrinsic motivation. This is a skill that you learn to do; not what someone says or does to you for their expectation that would be extrinsic. Motivation, awareness, and intelligence have a complex interrelationship that builds synergy. As you work to improve one area, your performance affects the other two by the interrelated associations that you create from your past experience and task familiarity which allows you to think on higher planes. If you're on a team, several quality performers can raise the awareness level for their teammates. Opposing teams raise their awareness levels to become more motivated to do their best against a better team. When athletes greatly increase their awareness during a performance, they are described as being in a "zone." After Michael Jordan joined the Chicago Bulls, he spent the first four years realizing, as his talents grew, that he could not win an NBA Championship by himself. He led team members and elevated their performances in practices and games by focusing on teaching them specific higher awareness skills relevant to the task. Success breeds success, although few successful performers can tell you how this works. Purposeful intent is the answer. The strength of your awareness comes from the affective discipline created by being able to identify and understand your personal needs, drives, motives and goals, and aligning them with actual performance outcomes.

Thinking Outside the Box

The American educational system has created the notion that if you cannot learn as efficiently as another person in the same classroom that you have a learning disability. What explanation can you give for not learning what everyone else is learning? No one suggests your lack of motivation as a potential problem. An educational system that conditions predominantly extrinsic motives to induce your motivation cannot expect you to enhance the quality of your performances outside of the training environment without increasing the external reward. When external rewards and bribes do not work in the long term, poor leaders and teachers resort to boss-management styles of leadership to control performers.

Performance below what an average person can do creates a negative motivation that gets reinforced. Students give up and often disrupt the classroom to remove the stress of their unsuccessful attempts to learn. If the task is broken into manageable parts, there are more opportunities to experience some success to reward and reinforce learning. Like coaches, emphasis should be on continuous performance improvement, and noting the purpose for learning each part at the beginning to motivate and reinforce learning.

It has never been possible to beat education into performers. The newly named personality disorder (ODD) Oppositional Defiant Disorder describes the defiant behavior of performers towards educators and parents. Extrinsic motivation doesn't work with these performers; educators must stress that learning for its own sake is a personal reward that comes from an increased awareness of your PI to satisfy a personal need or goal in smaller, realistic, and manageable improvements.

In a social context, we all want to be loved and wanted. For some misguided leaders to feel loved, they display a need to control their performers who have to learn and do as they say. Performers who have different learning styles and personalities will create conflict in the process for learning and the outcome. A secure leader will facilitate and let the person who does the work have some control over how the work gets done as long as the performer meets the mutually agreed upon outcome.

Emphasis on Positive Motives

PI emphasizes positive motives to increase the probability of success. Negative motives to avoid failure cannot happen. You must learn the proper goal-setting strategy to produce high-quality results over time that will be self-reinforcing. Inconsistent and poor performers have not learned how or why specific goals work to hold themselves accountable for performance improvements. When management uses coercive penalties or extrinsic goals, performers readily lose their focus and purpose, and learning becomes secondary. Coerced performers do not learn to see the value of their education or performance for life long learning. They are so conditioned by micromanagement that they do not easily acquire the ability to assess their personal needs and be driven to achieve a higher quality of life or standard from within. When you learn your PI and are involved in the process, you enhance your motivation to produce higher quality results, experience higher achievement and reward, and hopefully, a higher quality of life. Then when you give back some of your knowledge to help others in need, you will also achieve a higher self-actualization in Maslow's Hierarchy, first introduced in 1943. (See figure in chapter one).

[M a S] > [M a F]

The motive to achieve success must be greater than the motive to avoid failure. You learn and achieve what you focus on performing more with a positive purposeful intent in your mind. When you focus on how to avoid failure, it becomes a coercive extrinsic motive that produces inconsistent results. You can change your perception and learning strategy to provide a PI at will on demand. Homework and on the job training is practice designed to reinforce learning outside of school, and to provide feedback about the rate and progress of your learning that can be tested or other assessed. Assigning zeros for incomplete homework reinforces a negative motive to avoid failure and decreases intrinsic motivation. Relating the homework problems to what the assessment will be like and providing additional credit in the amount of correct work accomplished reinforces a positive motive to achieve success, and increases intrinsic motivation.

Positive Learning Is Self-Reinforced

Purposeful intent is a leadership skill to enhance intrinsic motivation that can be taught using The Triad. Just as a coach would break down a physical skill like shooting a basketball free throw into three or four specific skills or subroutines of the entire skilled movement to teach each separately with a conscious focus, you can also learn how to increase your purposeful intent to improve any performance. Each Triad is a separate but also interconnected subroutine with its own specific set of skills to master that when combined with the other two complete the purposeful intent to be intrinsically motivated in that activity or any other chosen activity. Learning can be its own intrinsic reward if performers are conditioned to be more aware of their feelings of success which helps them build value in their effort and conditions its relevance in their consciousness. You can condition an awareness of your personal performance by comparison to a standard or top performer. However, meeting or exceeding these two variables, the probability is very low and less likely to reinforce your motive to succeed. Whereas, by comparing your immediate past performance to each new performance when you set a low positive expectation for success, you increase your probability for success than can reward and self reinforce your continued effort to learn.

These skills can be taught by leaders who employ strategies that create your need to focus on specific connections to your past, present, and future experiences that you become more familiar with performing. Your leader can add their past success experience to increase your familiarity with each new task. Leaders become leaders when their performers determine that events unfold as they were prepared to perform. What you learned from your leader was a replay of the future experience before the performance to become aware of what to expect and be familiar with how to perform successfully. This approach meets personal and organizational needs, and increases intrinsic motivation.

Performers can be conditioned to use positive self-talk to review their performances for value to gain a level of reward they can connect to reinforce future attempts. How you feel is intrinsic. How others think you should feel is extrinsic. It is never what you think as the leader, but what your performers think that matters the most. By learning to recognize selected cues through conscious awareness with a purposeful intent, learning any skill is immediately improved with additional practice. As the correct cues provide for your early success, this success reinforces your positive feeling to work harder to ensure feeling good and getting better at that skill – whatever it may be. At the other end of the spectrum are failure or negative feelings that are as painful as accidentally touching an electric fence. A small electric shock conditions tremendous negative reinforcement avoidance feelings. It is normal behavior to expect your poor performers to avoid remote learning opportunities. Early experiences in the home or at school reinforce you to continue to avoid not as successful activities. In affluent or nurturing homes, moms positively encourage a variety of activities for their children to try without retribution for early failures. The risk is worth the reward. Highly successful performers report their moms effectively disciplined them to teach commitment and perseverance after experiencing normal early failures. This is a huge difference! When children reach school age, failure is no longer an option. Because of harsh early penalty feelings such as being called a loser by peers, being admonished to "apply themselves" by teachers, and/or disciplined for misbehaving in the classroom to avoid the painful truth that you are not learning what you are supposed to learn conditions a negative reinforcement and more avoidance behaviors. Here are some positive strategies to reinforce your motivation to improve your performance:

1. Take calculated risks. Set a goal only slightly better than your own immediate past performance to increase your probability for success and reinforce your personal reward.

2. Be more consciously aware of the reasons why you are working at improving in any activity so that you will increase the value of your learning and time spent practicing to perfect your performance. Keep workout logs, journals, diaries, etc., to reflect and record your intrinsic feelings.

3. Increase your motive to achieve success and eliminate your motive to avoid failure.

4. Evaluate your own progress for improving in smaller incremental steps instead of trying to be an overnight success. You will be less stressed and more in control of the specific cues you will need to focus on to perform well and be rewarded.

5. Make every attempt to hold yourself accountable for your learning and performance. Blaming others for your lack of performance will not help you achieve your goals.

6. Learn to be coach able. Accept criticism from those who are trying to help you succeed that have more experience to acquire knowledge and understanding that can help you learn more.

Predictive Accountability

You can create predictive equations in your mind to help you consciously focus on the most important strategies to perform smaller parts or sub routines of any skill.

This increases your opportunity for improvement and reward. Each strategy or cue is your personal choice for a variable in your equation to perform a specific criterion skill like pitching a 90 mile per hour fastball, hitting your golf pitching wedge, closing a sale, or the sequence in a presentation. Top performers, leaders, teachers, and coaches define the best three to five strategic variables to focus on learning a skill more efficiently than an inexperienced person choosing a different set of variables that do not predict as high for learning the skill. A rubric table defines a critical value system to self-evaluate variables that motivate acquiring and developing new performance skills. To acquire knowledge, or study and comprehend any criterion task of value, you will need to define with a purposeful intent by moving from subconscious sensory to conscious perceptual states. See the Increasing Awareness Flow Chart in chapter three. With purposeful intent you learn to continuously evaluate your improvement compared to a personal set of criteria using your immediate past performance as the benchmark. This simple performance improvement strategy can be taught on any level.

It is vital that you learn how to self-evaluate your performances. The best model is B.F. Skinner's "black box feedback loop" shown in chapter three, Growing Antennae. Your ability to predict your future performance skills will improve as you more often surpass your goal expectation as the criterion to feel successful. This is the process strategy you must learn to self-evaluate with a predictive goal equation that drives or motivates your behavior prior to performing. You can coach yourself and analyze your behavior to motivate your mind from within to improve. At some point your teachers and mentors will go away, and you will have to know how to learn on your own if you expect to improve. If you want to be a top performer, your long term success will be determined more by your predictable personality patterns of perseverance and determination to achieve your goals than by what others think of your work. Society and cultures create criteria, but so can you to judge the worth of your performance. Taking accountability for your learning and performance is a leadership trait, and critical to all successful performers. You are conditioned to be judged by others who apply their bias for what they think is meaningful and relevant based on their set of experiences that may not apply today or to you. First, your parents, or hopefully a parent, provides praise or scolds you about specific behaviors to judge their worth. Then schoolteachers further condition the notion that they will judge the worth of your performance. When you get home, there are chores to perform and an adult again is judging the worth of your performance. When you become employed, a boss will be judging you periodically to ensure they are getting their expectations in hiring you, and frequently evaluate your performance against a realistic standard or not. If you get married, spouses have performance expectations, too, and make frequent judgments about the worth of your behavior. Think how important your learned skills for self-evaluation are to predict your future performance without the bias imposed by others. Do you know of any top performer that ever waited for the approval of another person? This learned skill is the second part of the Triad to achieve your purposeful intent.

Leaders must embrace quality standards and positive expectations to challenge their performers to achieve those standards. Standards are goals and must be posted for your performers to see and raise their conscious expectations to achieve. This creates your purposeful intent.

RTI and NCLB and IDEA

In 2004 IDEA or Individual with Disabilities Education Act was reauthorized. States felt vulnerable to recent court cases that changed the entire outlook for how students are identified and qualified for special education services. As an outgrowth of IDEA, the No Child Left Behind Act was also reevaluated that requires states receiving Federal Title funds be held accountable for how those funds were being issued to low performing schools and those with high poverty. As a result, RTI or Response To Intervention was created. This is a three-tiered system to help identify students with early learning difficulties, and provide specific interventions in the form of Title I reading and math assistance, and after school tutoring programs. One aspect of the RTI program is to separate those students who disrupt classrooms for behavioral reasons from those who truly have a learning disability. PBIS stands for Positive Behavioral Intervention System that promotes systematic ways to handle typical classroom disruptions caused by under achieving students who are frustrated with learning and unable to see improvement. The missing link, however, is intrinsic motivation. Purposeful intent is a systematic way to instruct teachers in how to motivate all students using The Triad. Simply controlling behavior does not imply intrinsically motivating behavior that is needed in a free and public education often taken for granted and less desired by poor performers who have not been taught how to identify their needs and abilities, reward small improvements, and motivate themselves. The Triad can indoctrinate early learners to be motivated and hold themselves more accountable for their learning by placing more emphasis on rewarding improvement, and less on grades and 90-80-70-60 percentages of perfection.

A New Suggested School Grading System

Grades have become a symbol of coercion more than an indicator of a student's progress on the path to learning, comprehension, and understanding. Alfie Kohn supported this notion in 1993 in <u>Punished by Rewards</u>. Kohn describes grades, gold stars, praise, and other incentive plans as extrinsic motivators that detract from students learning how to learn to be accountable for their own behaviors. Kohn's book details over 400 research citations that offer proof that our schools are not working properly to teach students how to be self-motivated and achieve higher performance.

Schools need to create a new grading system that rewards striving for positive improvement. Scores can be weighted on improvement that still fall below the A and B range. The system would look something like the golf handicap system. Initial scores would be recorded as raw scores. The amount of improvement in raw score points would be added to the previous raw score. As an additional incentive for any improvement in the raw score on the next test: Any raw score falling below 50 would have 15 bonus points added; below 60 would have 10 bonus points added; and below 70 would have 5 bonus points added. For example, the first 100 point test is a 38 raw score or 38%. The raw score falls below 50 and would have 15 bonus points added only if the second test shows any improvement. On the second test, the student has improved the raw score from 38 to 62 or a total of 24 more points over the first test. These 24 points along with the 15 bonus points for improvement would be added to the very first test to provide a new total point score of 38 + 24 + 15 = 77. For the third 100 point test, the raw score still is improving but not as much. The raw score is improved from a second test raw score of 62 to 74 or 12 more points, plus the 5 bonus points for scoring below 70 to provide a new total point score of 62 + 12 + 5 = 79. For the fourth test, the raw score is 78 for an improvement from 74 to 78 or 4 more points that can be added to the third test raw score. However, the raw score is above 70 and does not qualify for bonus points. The third test is scored 74 + 4 = 78. After four 100 point tests, the new adjusted scores are 77, 79, 78, and 78 for a 78 average and provides hope and motivation for the individual to improve upon their knowledge as opposed to feeling there is no hope and give up having started out so poorly with little or no motivation to learn. The whole idea behind this new grading system is to provide a system that will get each student to equate quality of effort with quality of reward and increase their personal intrinsic motivation to learn and improve their knowledge. Compare to the actual raw test scores of 38, 62, 74, and 78. It should be obvious that this student can learn and has demonstrated their knowledge with scores in the 70's on the last two tests. However, when averaged in with the early mistake of 38, and even though showing great improvement on the second test was still below average was at this point averaging 38 + 62/2 for a 50 average and failing. Under this old system, this student would have to score two 90 point exams to just be passing with a C or 70% average. Under normal laws of probability this is highly unrealistic and not likely to happen, and the motivation would be a lot less. The new system is more realistic and does not penalize good students. The example presented demonstrates that students who are rewarded for improvement cannot generally score higher than those who are already scoring above 80.

Needs and Values Analysis

In the end, it is not what you think of another performer's performance that matters as much as what that performer has learned to think, evaluate, and value from their performance quality and effort to build accountability. This process varies from performer to performer based on the value system they bring to the organization or that you can teach them. If you want to create intrinsically motivated people, periodically do the needs analysis to align the needs of your organization with the personal needs of your performers. Leaders need to value and respect the opinion of every performer to improve their accountability and intrinsic motivation. You build value with trust. Empowering performers to write their job description and do their job in a creative way according to their personalities will put them on the same page and produce expected outcomes. An intrinsically motivated performer with the ability creates the need to improve. The leader needs to provide them with the training and tools to do the job. The organization creates the need in the value of the outcome or final quality product. This is what you learn from chapter 7, Post Performance Evaluation.

By taking a personal needs assessment survey in the Appendix, you can learn who provided for your past, present, and future needs as well as what those needs may be. A sample personal needs assessment survey in the appendix can give you an idea of your personal areas of strength and positive tendencies that with PI can consciously indicate your personal passion to succeed. Once you discover your passion, you will no longer need positive reinforcement and approval from others as you will find it from your PI strength and knowing your talents, abilities, and skills. Leaders can make up personal needs surveys that are conceptually similar for education, banking and finance, business management, engineering, product development, human resource management, leadership management, information technology, or any job related skill.

Alignment of Needs Improve Performance Value

After you become aware of your needs, you must align or prioritize them into preferences. You may be selecting preferred activities subconsciously because your performance makes you feel successful. Think how powerful it would be for you to be aware of why you like to perform selected activities. Then add what more you could accomplish with a purposeful intent to increase the value of what you are learning with each practice. Or, instead of learning to develop this skill on your own, you can remain dependent on others to direct you. There were two swimmers who made the 1972 men's Olympic team that did not display the typical personality pattern of all the other 18 members. I could only attribute this to the good coaching leadership they had been conditioned to perform. A good leader or teacher will create the need for you to learn a task with a variety of activities to reach the personal learning needs of all learners. They will provide meaningful and relevant value to the learner by relating the activity to prior knowledge or a familiar activity they have already learned to perform. A good teacher will relate to the age level of their learners to describe in greater detail how they will apply their new knowledge to create performance value. They will also select challenging activities that they can perform successfully to build value. Some learners prefer to learn with visual skills seeing the demonstration first. Others can verbally hear the specific selected cues to attend to spoken to them and make an image of the performance. Still others simply have to perform the skill to kinesthetically feel the movements in their muscles and even finger tips. The more visual, verbal, and kinesthetic cues you can associate with your learning will create a more powerful resistance to forgetting. This psychological process is called paired-associate conditioning. If you really want to learn, you must take notes. Writing down notes or underlining in the text with an instrument builds the kinesthetic part to the visual and verbal process of learning to value the knowledge and make it more resistant to forgetting. This creates intrinsic motivation when you make the conscious choice to work on those skills with a sense of value in your purpose.

Goal Setting

Your early trials may not have been thought of as successful because your goal-setting strategy was wrong. If you think of any goal greater than one point better than your own immediate past performance, you condition a higher probability for failure to avoid. Whereas, you increase your probability for success to focus on the positive improvement you can make over your own past performance. When you follow this goal-set-performance improvement sequence, you will eventually condition yourself to be a good performer. You listened to others who evaluated you and conditioned your failure even though you may have scored better than half of your performance correctly. To not try is to fail. Any performance attempt provides a great start to focus on getting better at any task when you learn to provide your purposeful intent to your realistic goal. That goal strategy must be only slightly better than your immediate past performance. You cannot control what others think or do. You must learn to control what **you** think and do. Learn from your mistakes, adjust your goals, and keep trying. Be more aware of your small improvements to stay motivated from within to fulfill your goals. Use your own feedback to increase your awareness and improve upon your next attempts to keep rewarding your effort. Then when you improve upon your last score, you can feel success more often. This strategy boosts your confidence. There is no such thing as learning how to be a good loser or giving up by conditioning more responses to avoid than responses to succeed. Both take the same energy to perform, so choose a strategy to succeed?

When you evaluate someone's performance, that automatically changes the value of that performance for the performer from 100% intrinsic from learned self-evaluation skills to hold themselves accountable and consistently improve their performance with feedback they identify as cues and strategies to 100% extrinsic; if I screw up, it is not my fault because I did what you told me to do and I am no longer accountable for my performance, the leader is accountable. Think of what we condition in our schools. Pre kindergarten to seniors in high school, then college, and finally in workplace training by all the teachers we instruct the masses by teaching to the middle. The recurrent teacher theme is, "I will decide what is meaningful and relevant, and be the one to tell you if your work is good or bad." Yet, even a small child knows quality when they see it, but cannot describe it. All performers can learn to self-evaluate their performance by learning feedback and awareness skills to continuously improve when they know their purposeful intent. Our schools and parents seem more bent on controlling student's behaviors than teaching them how to use personal performance feedback to hold themselves accountable for their learning and improvement.

Parents as Leaders

The greatest job a parent leader has is to teach your children the skills to be successful. When you allow your children to fight you in the home at an early age about mundane tasks like begging for candy when you take them along food shopping, staying in their seat belt, going potty, brushing their teeth, taking a bath, and going to bed, they are not focused on higher order thinking skills or a greater purposeful intent that must be learned by effecting early discipline in the home and at school. Your child is making the wrong choices to satisfy lower order personal needs or goals. Your child's underlying needs and goals have been misdirected and need to be properly taught starting at an early age. Early pre-school needs are to know a number sequence, an alphabet, shapes, and patterns by reading to them with good voice inflection to create imagery and build positive inquiry. Your strategy is to smile your approval instead of frown your disapproval when your child has lots of questions. Why this? Why that? Your child is in trouble when they do not ask questions because they are not thinking. If your child is not thinking, they are not learning. If they are not learning to master skills, their frustration with mastery of higher order thinking skills will be self-evident by the time they are a teenager. Frustrated learners seldom become the leaders or top performers. If you do not like to read is more reason to expect your child to read fluently and be successful by the end of the third grade. Kids will read more with early success and conditioned enjoyment. If you introduce extrinsic rewards, you take away the intrinsic reward and feeling of accomplishment to condition the motivation to read more and more. Excellent readers become good students. Purposeful intent leadership skills training can provide you with your foundation to be intrinsically motivated to teach the performers you will lead.

My boys had college roommates whose parent's micromanaged and met all their needs. They could not figure out how to use a coin laundry to wash their clothes. Many of their college friends did not know how to cook a meal to meet their need for food. Most had never been camping to know how to find shelter, rough it, and survive with few means. Their parents enabled their dependency by not teaching independence and personal accountability. After initial failures and no developed personal feedback system of accountability or conscious reward-reinforcement strategy for positive behaviors, they would leave school for the security provided at home.

The great honorable task of teaching your children may be more a matter of conditioning early skill sequences than knowledge acquisition. Managers and parents who instill PI skills more can micromanage less and improve personal accountability in their performers. Parents initially need to micromanage their children to provide for their safety needs. As children mature as performers they become more familiar with tasks and have a natural drive for independence. However, most are conditioned to report to and be evaluated by a boss or manager after parenting ends. The conditioning to learn and grow from one's mistakes to improve performance that comes from within to prove their worth to themselves or the organization is not taught. Micromanagement boss-type leaders that includes over protective parents routinely violate the use of this natural drive. These managers are closed minded to new ways to perform tasks more efficiently within the organization. Even a mother bear will teach her cubs how to forage for food to meet their needs, and once that process is achieved, she will swat the cub who tries to return to the den. More coercive rules such as an expanded list of phrases that begin with a negative, "don't" do, will reinforce the behaviors you want to reduce. Micromanagement behaviors are often associated with task familiarity: The less familiar you may be with a task, the more you feel the "need" to manage others. Worse, people in this situation often believe their performers cannot perform the task because *they* cannot perform the task. Micromanaging introduces a bias that limits company and employee growth. Bias is the unreasonable personal judgment or prejudice of an expected outcome prior to the performance. Introducing bias is a dangerous subtle motivational force that has negative consequences if you require your performers to complete tasks exactly as you would. This may serve to eliminate your stress however it will increase your performer's stress level as you take away their personality patterns to act. PI training focuses on the outcome and the process using realistic goal setting strategies that will produce frequent success. Success generally reduces stress and initiates the third part of The Triad to connect reward with reinforcement. Companies can use PI training to develop quality performers who hold themselves accountable for their performance, gain satisfaction by being aware of the quality achieved, and connect quality of effort with quality of reward. This reinforces work ethic as a learned behavior. What the leaders think of performance is not as powerful as getting the performers to evaluate and feel accountable for their performance. More often good to great performers are harder on themselves than their managers are aware. Be wary of your top performers developing self-imposed negative reinforcement patterns to reduce their motivation. Leaders *need* to frequently talk with or at least recognize every performer to reinforce all the good intrinsic motives they have been observing in order to provide congruence between the performer's self-evaluation and their leadership evaluation.

Value of Purposeful Improvement

My daughter struggled to do better on the girl's golf team her sophomore year. She did not practice as much as some of the other girls during the summer, and her first few rounds were not very good. Her confidence level was low and the pressure was high. She did not have a purposeful intent. She went through the motions of being on the team for social reasons. Her motivation to improve was not purposeful, and she had fallen behind in her skills development compared to other team performers who were clearly more passionate about their game. As she became more familiar with the tasks and developed a routine to set realistic performance and practice skill goals slightly better than her immediate past performance, her scores started to improve. She did not enjoy golf because she saw failure comparing her scores to the top players on the team. It was not until I taught her to compare to her immediate past performance that I could see a change in her positive performance outlook to feel some success and motivated to improve. She could see and feel performance improvement more frequently to boost her confidence and motive to continuously improve. She began to enjoy the game by seeing her performance through a different lens. She learned the strategy for continuous improvement. As a parent-leader practicing purposeful intent I can agree with her and applaud her scores to build her confidence. Most parents take this traditional approach. However your approval process changes a 100% reflective intrinsic performance to completely 100% extrinsic motivation with less personal accountability. Your judgment about your child's performance transitions a good intrinsic motive to an extrinsic motive with short term benefits. You would do better to ask your performer how they felt about their performance, and where they think they can improve. They must learn to change their perceptions for evaluation and feedback expectations by gradual improvement. It was their goal and purpose to succeed and they did the work; give them all the credit. You want your performers to recall positive images to reinforce those behaviors that created the success. This must be a reflective perception in the performer and not the evaluator to increase intrinsic motivation.

Learned Helplessness

When a child is conditioned to whine and cry to get what he/she wants, it reinforces a negative consequence. The child is not learning to solve problems or beginning to understand that every problem has a solution if his/her bad behavior is enabled. Enabling only reinforces negative *learned helplessness* and more stress. For kids, doing homework can be very enriching if they maintain a positive attitude and purposeful intent. A positive experience in smaller more manageable increments or steps automatically creates a more meaningful and relevant purpose for learning the new information. Every lesson can begin by stating, "The purpose of this lesson is...." Parents who do their child's homework are not leaders or models of correct behaviors. They enable learned helplessness by not teaching the child how to learn purposefully. Coercive punishments are designed to achieve conformity; prevent disruptions but seldom deter the behavior that is motivated by the needs of the student at the time. It is easier to send a student to the school's disciplinarian to serve a detention or be suspended than to help the student understand what motivated their behavior which is usually the result of frustration not having mastered the early skills to solve new problems. Intervention helps students assess where the breakdown in learning occurred and relearn the necessary steps to master new concepts that reinforce a positive feeling of success to value. When students turn in incomplete or underachieving work, it goes unrewarded and cannot build value or accountability. These performers are confused about the purposeful intent of their work. Failure feels shockingly painful and quickly reinforces the desire to not repeat that behavior. A student who is failing algebra may become labeled by the teacher or other students, so to avoid this pain he/she will block out learning anything that has to do with algebra. The only way to overcome this reinforced feeling is to start over rebuilding a step-by-step confidence in correct performance behavior. Having a positive purposeful intent will enable the student to recognize, receive, organize, store, and retrieve valuable information and master the subject. This way, when you are learning, your brain cannot be on sleep mode; you have to recondition the broken link S-R associations to reinforce learning the chain for each sub routine. Teachers who see this happening in their students can begin by providing them with the opportunity to get one problem correct to build their confidence and earn extra credit. You reward only the positive behaviors and extinguish the negative behaviors as inconsequential so they will not be reinforced. You only want to reflect on successful positive behaviors that can be reinforced. The smallest personal accomplishment can have great intrinsic value within the mind of the performer and trigger a whole new set of drive motives.

Extrinsic Motives as a Zero Sum Incentive

I believe the world is about to enter into a spirit of cooperation so that all peoples can win and experience sustained success with personal improvement and by helping others to succeed. There will be fewer class distinctions, and fewer reasons to kill each other when belief systems may clash. As in athletic contests, when performers sign a contract to compete only to increase their bottom line, it is a "zero sum" incentive. For every winner, you must have a loser. Teams of people often focus on the motive to avoid failure or "what's-in-it-for-me" (WIIFMs), than the motive to achieve success with a common need or vision. The "winner-take-all" philosophy will stimulate competition, but competition against others is not the only strategy to provide success. Competition within yourself to continuously improve upon your own immediate past performance is a better strategy. Within each of us is the natural drive to compete and succeed. This natural drive can be channeled to improve your personal performance. Successful performers rarely achieve success in leaps and bounds; they pay the price to pay their dues. When leaders impose and reinforce their value system they must use extrinsic motives to shape your behaviors that threaten you to accept their system. However, your personal needs are not satisfied, and your motivation is reduced. As the leader, you want to align your needs with the needs of others to reduce or eliminate the dichotomy and work as a team with a common mission. There has been too much reliance on extrinsic motives like higher salaries to get people to work. The history of successful performers is not always known by the casual observer who believes they can achieve the same results without paying the same price. Consistent among high achievers is that they have learned how to <u>control their behavior</u> – what they think, the choices they make, and how they work to achieve goals; and <u>set low positive goals</u> only slightly better than their own immediate past performance to enhance their personal reward system.

Top performers are consistent in that: 1) they do not wait for the approval from others they perceive are less than successful at performing what they do; they already know quality when they perform it, and 2) they continuously self-evaluate their personal performance against a personal standard — that usually being their own immediate past performance — so they can control how they focus, work, and reward their behavior. These two factors are what motivate top performers to hold themselves accountable for incremental performance improvements. Improvement is the personal reward that continues to motivate reinforcement of the positive behaviors they find successful. How to hold yourself accountable does not happen when you allow others to micromanage your behavior, and for not demonstrating performance improvement. The question becomes why do we need to teach others to be intrinsically motivated for top performance when so few performers, managers, or teachers seem to understand how to instill this kind of motivation in others? The answer centers about personal performance improvement as the main strategy that will serve to enhance the overall quality of life; to enjoy the fruits of our labors rather than to be victims deciding there is no hope or future. By learning purposeful intent skills, you learn how to help yourself and others. God helps those who help themselves. We must teach performers how to learn, to think, to act, and do for themselves and eventually others to hope what they have learned they will "pass it on." If you catch a fish, you feed a man for a day; if you teach a man how to fish, you feed him for a lifetime; if you teach a community how to fish, you feed them the motivation to continuously improve forever. Learning how to provide for your own needs is good parenting. A behavioral rule for government to understand is Rule # 7:

The more you tax a people, they become conditioned to demand and expect a government to provide a social service to meet their needs and recoup their loss of income.

Simply providing for others instead of teaching them how to provide for their own needs will cause the one in need to accept the offer, but not respect the giver. This has always been the behavioral mistake of our foreign policy.

Cooperative Learning

When you are engaged in cooperative learning you are less competitive in hoping to outperform your co-performers. However, high performing team members will still feel it is unfair for them to do all the work or more work than others, and they will still get the same amount of credit. The goal is to help each other learn and understand the principles and concepts that will become reinforced by the exercise of explaining your knowledge to others. Some students learn more from other students. Learning is achieved for its own reward. You are evaluating your performance only. You attach your personal frame of reference to your performances whether working alone or cooperatively in groups. You must learn the proper goal setting paradigm, and use it consistently to motivate your personal performance-reward system and connect your reward to reinforce your behaviors. This is the third Triad, and vital to your personal performance improvement. You will more often experience the feeling of success and reward to want to hold yourself accountable and repeat those behaviors. The object is for you to connect quality of effort with quality of reward, and to enhance your own personal reward system with frequent success. Then lead others to perform the same process. Break those complex group tasks down into manageable assignments for your team to accomplish in a given realistic time frame.

Whether you participate in a cooperative group, corporate or individual personal training program, you can gain the knowledge and specific skills to lead and improve your performance more with a purposeful intent. There are social and cooperative teamwork skills blended with personal discipline to persist in a work ethic to focus on specific skills that are parts of a greater task to demonstrate small improvements over your immediate past performance to build your confidence and achieve success with any task over time. However, none of these qualities will have a meaningful effect to improve individual performance and the team without a common defined purposeful intent. You can learn to identify and provide for your needs, gain personal satisfaction, and perform at a level that is acceptable to you and your team without having a manager or trainer to make you feel bad because you are not achieving their biased expectations for you. Define what your cooperative group expectations are early in the process. This will increase your PI strength and motivation to improve. You only gain confidence by self evaluation of your personal performance feedback to feel success when you consistently improve your immediate past performance or average measured against a cooperative group standard. Your creative talent is an intrinsic motive. Boss managers and other performers who lack creativity and vision will not evaluate your creative or visionary talents favorably. To be in control of your performance improvement to build your confidence and hold yourself accountable for your role in the cooperative process, you need to develop your purposeful intent. Performers who fail do not focus on their core knowledge for lack of interest or motivation. They are conditioned to be dependent on others or rely on a literal system of immediate gratification to meet their needs. When the goal is too large, unrealistic, or not readily achievable, the performer will give up without becoming aware of smaller improvements they can feel rewarded to reinforce persistent attempts. In cooperative systems, all performers need a defined job role and not rely on the "star" performer to win and create the reward for them without having to step up and do their part. This is no longer a cooperative team effort to improve the system performance. Project managers need to explain jobs and roles for each and hold their performers accountable for meeting realistic mutual expectations on a time table. You have to learn how to self-reward and condition your positive behaviors to hold yourself accountable for your personal behaviors.

When you do not feel frequent success, you have to stay motivated and keep working to improve. Change your strategy to focus on smaller incremental improvements you can reward, and delay your greater rewards by projecting the fulfillment of your long term needs with a purposeful intent. Without a purposeful intent, you can wander aimlessly dependent on others to meet your needs. To stay on task, reinforced, and be intrinsically motivated to fulfill your identified needs, you must have a specific positive purposeful intent. Public schools and training programs need to focus more on conditioning self-evaluation skills for students to learn self-reward that can increase their PI strength. This slight change could motivate more students to be quality performers. Imagine if you were created to mostly use the motivated by positive performance half of your brain. You were designed to use both halves equally well, and there would be a number of talents you may have but ignore without having a purposeful intent. To improve you need to develop your personal educational system that will relate to and reward the functional performance of both halves of your brain in order to discover all of your abilities. You may surprise yourself to find a hidden talent. Boss leaders, that can include classroom teachers, too frequently apply their personal bias in the false belief that their performers (students) are incapable of some tasks. If you are taught to recognize (the first R in RROSR) a proper sequential order you will connect and associate increasingly familiar prior learned sequences with new ones to achieve phenomenal outcomes. When your fate is decided beforehand by poor management, your personal outcome potentials are never achieved. It would be wise to move on to another job or manager to make better use of your abilities. By learning to self-evaluate your personal performance behaviors, you eliminate your need to wait for the approval or direction from others.

MANAGEMENT

Behavioral Rule #2: You cannot build accountability in a micromanagement system.

Leadership

You can learn intrinsic motivational skills through leadership training, and this skill is becoming more important in our changing society and world that has become increasingly dependent on external motives. For a long time, the attitude for effective leadership was not to care about or be involved in the personal lives of workers in order to separate emotional feelings, maintain order, and discipline in the organization. Counter to this idea has been the emergence of highly successful companies who treat their workers like family. These successful companies have grown profitable by focusing on the individual needs of their workers to feel successful and personally rewarded to value their opinions. These needs range from a family friendly atmosphere providing day care for working mothers on the premises to more relaxed dress codes, fitness centers, excellent in-house cafeterias, and accessible parking. It is essential to help performers identify and create their personal needs and purposeful intent to motivate them from within to increase their intrinsic motivation. Every performer should have an identified role to play in the growth and development of any group or organization. Performers become burned out and stale and underappreciated when their minds feel that they are not accomplishing any goal or making any progress to demonstrate personal performance improvement that is essential to maintain intrinsic motivation. Companies like Google, Smuckers, and Wal-Mart work at this kind of personal leadership to treat workers like family members, and help them routinely identify their performance improvement. Their success formula is what P.T. Barnum used on each occasion to make, lose, and remake millions of dollars. Barnum's three-point formula that all leaders would do well to improve purposeful intent and intrinsically motivate every individual was simply to:

> #1 Dream the biggest dream
> #2 Market the living "heck" out of it
> #3 Treat your workers like family.

Labor is a commodity. Management has traditionally sought to control the efforts of others for their own material gain, and used extrinsic means to boss manage through coercion and retaliation to get workers to conform. For low level task environments, you want people to be smart to follow simple directions, but not too smart to strive for more out of their work environment in a valueless job. If you observe any system, whether it is education, business, religion or politics, the object is to use external rewards to modify the mass behavior of individuals. The object is to control and not motivate individuals to think, disagree, or question the practices inherent in the system. Dissidents disagree with dictators because they want the freedom to control their personal lives within the system rather than have the system tell them what they can or cannot do. The freedom of choice creates more intrinsic motivation to achieve and help others. Dictators are like boss managers who fear they will lose their power with loss of control. There is no trust in the relationship between the boss and the performer. This suggests that individuals can be taught strategies to learn intrinsic motivational skills to willfully improve their personal performance and ultimately effect a change in the quality of their life. Extrinsic motives are only effective for the short term to result in a Quid Pro Quo – you do this for me and I will do this for you. One key question to ask in any organization is, "What will this performer do when the boss is not looking?" When the cat is away, will the mice play?

Self-motivated performers improve their personal performance to meet their needs, benefit the team, and prefer to lead by example. High achievers are often misinterpreted and mistreated by managers who are not as personally successful and are challenged by their ideas and purposeful success. Talented performers are aware of the winning cues and strategies that fit their job descriptions to ensure their success. Poor managers allow their bias, egos, and jealousy to not recognize talent in their midst. When a quality performance happens on their team, they often criticize that performance to control the performer. Criticism of a personal best performance reduces the intrinsic motivation of a high achiever. Organizations or companies need to remove managers who have a personality that can be threatened by quality performers who would like to be left alone to do their job. High achievers are often labeled whiners and complainers because they are frustrated that their company is not taking positive steps to help it succeed, and those leaders need to go. They are branded as not a team player by the micromanager system when they are highly motivated to win and feel personally rewarded for doing their part. Leaders can recognize their top performers with a pat on the back, a kind word, or sometimes a thank you note of appreciation, which means far more than winning an extrinsic company contest or trip. Top performers want to see management create a positive PI atmosphere that encourages winning. The complainer-achiever wants all the other players on the team to work as hard and have the same will-power strength to win. Vocal performers are often misinterpreted by management as threats to their leadership, and are removed to avoid embarrassment. It was good for the Chicago Bulls professional basketball organization that head coach Phil Jackson allowed Michael Jordan to be critical of his teammates to value teaching them his knowledge. Scottie Pippin became one of the top 50 NBA players of all-time. After the success, the general manager, Jerry Krause, wanted to take the credit for building the team. By micromanaging the achievers who did the work and taking the credit, morale dropped, players opted to be traded or retire, and the team dismantled. You see this happen on professional athletic teams all the time, and the player in question leaves and has an outstanding year. The Chicago Cub's executive management from 1908–2006 is a notorious example, but this same error occurs repeatedly in not so successful organizations and companies. Whether it is sport, business, or government, you have to observe the top performers and copy what they do; how they think; how they act when they perform. Then figure out a way to teach others in the organization how to perform in the same success pattern. When every performer on a team learns and understands how to apply PI skills, the results become conditioned and infectious. More performers in your organization will know and understand what it takes to succeed with a purpose, and develop stronger relationships to each other. This translates to fewer turnovers where your training dollars will pay dividends. Winning breeds success and happiness creates value that reinforces a positive work ethic. Performers and their egos learn to get along for the common good. When professional sports management takes away the credit the players are due because they want to keep a wrap on their contract negotiations to save salaries, you will find a weaker PI strength among team members. Similar examples occur in large corporations.

Leadership Personality Traits

Promote performers to leadership positions by first understanding their personality make up and whether the personality patterns inherent in the top performers are similar for the promotion to be effective. Secure leaders are familiar with performing the tasks they lead others to learn and improve. Tiger Woods changed an already great golf swing to take his play to a higher level. Would you change your personality to be a more effective leader or performer? Leaders know and accept their purpose to lead by creating and communicating positive strategies that predict success. They accept suggestions from subordinates as positive feedback to improve their leadership skills. Insecure leaders tend to be bosses who are not familiar with the performance tasks and surround themselves with buffer agents who are rewarded to protect their egos from the critical scrutiny of subordinates. Insecure leaders are intimidating and controlling personalities that will create more stress and less creativity within your organization. You must eliminate these managers from your organization as you will be less likely to alter their personality traits. Your human resource department can be invaluable to your organization to eliminate this problem in the hiring process. Hire secure leaders who understand personality psychology to build teams of intrinsically motivated performers who subscribe to a common company philosophy, needs, values, and mission as their own. This conserves your company dollars by eliminating costly middle management salaries, decreases employee turnover, and personnel costs to advertise, interview, hire, induct, train, and mentor new people. The purpose of a leader is to improve the bottom line company profit. It is important for leaders to empower their performers to be creative and come up with new ideas. Yes-men employees cannot achieve the same level of creativity. Intrinsically motivated performers go outside the box to learn and improve according to their preferred style for learning. Boss leaders who perceive defiance of their authority will use retribution or punishments such as poor grades, fault finding, demotions, or poor evaluations to diminish performer's intrinsic motivation and to maintain their control. When used, this coercive discipline consistently holds back a company's growth potential. More successful companies are led by people whose vision and purposeful intent permeate the entire organization. When you see company leadership at the top with insecure egos that cannot be challenged, growth is retarded, morale is low, they are top heavy in "yes men" managers to protect the boss, and there is higher than average worker turnover that seriously hurts company production and profit margins.

Giving and Behavioral Respect

A person who is poor or homeless because of some unfortunate event like losing their job will accept charity, but may not respect the giver because no value has been perceived. If the same person had to earn monetary help in some small way, he/she would have his/her purposeful intent restored to respect the giver. "Help comes to those who help themselves." "Teach a man to fish and feed him for a lifetime." These ideas describe purposeful intent leadership skills. When a country dependent only on oil for profits suddenly has no oil and the profits have not been used to teach people how to irrigate and grow crops to feed and provide jobs to the people, it will be a disaster. Dependency does not create intrinsic motivation. People's dependence on charity or governmental aid, reinforces their victim behaviors.

Leaders such as Thomas Jefferson, Sacagewea, Abraham Lincoln, Horace Mann, Thomas Edison, Henry Ford, John F. Kennedy, and Martin Luther King had a strong purposeful intent. They stayed focused on their passion to achieve outstanding success over time. They used their purposeful intent skills to overcome objections and hardships to achieve positive outcomes. As leaders, they did not wait for the approval of others: they had their principles, knew they were right, and went forward. Good people with strong motives to achieve a purpose perform good deeds because they understand their needs and the needs of others. Only through your own intrinsic effort can you build value to have a purposeful intent that can lead to your success over time. Modeling is external and inadequate to modify behaviors. Drug addicts come from excellent family models, and successful athletes can come from very poor family models. Modeling is not the answer. Learning and using PI strategies is the answer. You must learn to internalize your performance feedback to judge the worth of your own behaviors and compare them to your own immediate past performances to learn if you are continuously improving your performance skills to achieve success. You quickly learn that no one can do the job for you. You learn to think and be independent. Like the immigrant, your purpose is embedded in your personal needs that create your motives and drives to achieve success measured simply by how you feel about each performance. As you acquire PI skills, you become more aware to recognize and connect rewards with reinforcement to repeat like behaviors that over time prove successful. These frequent successes become your passion. This model never changes. You have to learn to associate quality of effort with quality of reward. No one can tell you. You have to feel it and know it for yourself. Once you learn to establish a purpose for all your performances, you will more often succeed than fail.

When leaders enable maladaptive behaviors by doing more or part of the work intended for the performer to demonstrate or model by example, the behavioral consequences on the learner are very grim over time and resistant to change as performers become more and more dependent on the extrinsic reward they have little or no control over. Your work ethic can only improve your performance by connecting your reward with reinforcement. The more reward you feel, the more you want to repeat and reinforce those behaviors to keep that good feeling. Performers who are ethically positive can learn to be bad if that performance is rewarded and reinforced. The road less traveled may also be the high road. Think it through before you choose the path of least resistance to understand what you need and value by your personal efforts to achieve that you can control. Know and understand your purpose and intent to increase your (MaS) motive to achieve success.

When you lead other performers, it may appear easier to use simple extrinsic motivators when dealing with small children or less intelligent people to get them started on projects or tasks to shape their behavior. If you think that you can later convert performers to prefer intrinsic motives without learning the PI skills, you will lose valuable practice and learning time to develop intrinsic motives that are based on your performer's needs and not yours or the organization. Performers become dependent on the extrinsic reward and lose sight of their purposeful intent through intrinsic means. *Performers never learn to identify their needs when someone else always meets them.* Grade school classroom management is too frequently enhanced using extrinsic or external rewards for good behavior. The typical strategy used is, "If you do this, I will give you this." When external rewards are more frequently applied, students become conditioned to expect them, and they may not behave as well in order to get the rewards. Students begin to connect good behavior with getting an external reward; learning becomes secondary to the primary rewards.

Forward Thinking

You can do nothing to change the past. You can focus on your future to make a difference in your performance. Your awareness and use of your environment through your unique personality is critical to continuously improve. By constantly improving your awareness skills, you will have a greater appreciation for teachers, coaches, friends, and family and how these people in your environment help you. You can comprehend more and become more aware by thinking about the meaning of events and how what you read will affect your life. People help people when they value the worth of every performer. No one performer is more important than another when you increase your awareness of others as messengers sent to help you.

A positive attitude provides more meaning and purpose to your life. According to the 80–20 rule, 20% of the people account for 80% of the objections in your life! You must learn to focus on the majority and the body of your work. When you think positively, you are the majority and have the power of your faith to lead yourself and others. When you learn awareness skills and practice them, you will be able to perform and achieve more positive good that will benefit you and those that you will lead.

You cannot take your learning to a higher plane without increasing your awareness and task familiarity. Visionaries, inventors, and artists have strong passions: they are willing to make huge sacrifices to follow their dreams. They are the perfect models of purposeful intent. By learning how to create meaningful associations, you increase your awareness of your environment, natural drives, and needs. Contrast your awareness behavior with that of many successful performers by making a list of similar compatible awareness skills. The average performer has lower awareness skills that reduce his/her purposeful intent strength. Tuning out through television, portable music players, and video games seldom provides the level of awareness that great performers display. The models of the great performer prototypes are never the same, so learn to acquire your personal awareness skills to make yourself a unique performer. While leaders are more aware, whole societies are decreasing their awareness skills. You are unique. God gave you talents to improve to make a difference with greater awareness. Experience is still the best teacher. Practicing a positive focus that reflects on your abilities, skills, needs, and goals you gain from past experiences will help increase your awareness. You can learn to convert negative thoughts to positive thoughts by simply restating them in your mind. Avoid borrowing make believe experiences from Hollywood personalities, musicians, or athletes, and applying their unrealistic personas to your world. A better strategy is to read about industry leaders. These experienced leaders know what works under a variety of conditions and can teach you selective attention strategies and cue recognition awareness skills to improve your task familiarity without having the prior personal experience. Great leaders communicate and share their personal performance awareness skills to provide more meaningful and relevant cues in the proper sequence. This provides a more proficient response to greatly improve your learning and cognitive processing time. Cognitive cues come from all your senses, but you rely more on the dominant visual and verbal cues. Kinesthetic or physical cues come from sensations in your muscles and tissues, but these are not dominant unless you become more aware of the specific feelings associated with good performance. The most seldom learned and practiced are the affective cues that come from feelings generated by your awareness of your needs, drives, desires, and motives. It's important to take time to get in touch with your feelings by frequently reflecting on your immediate and past performances that will help you judge the worth or motivation for your next performance. They intrinsically motivate your mind from within more than you may believe. Effective prayer creates this same kind of reflective focus on your inner feelings.

Growing Company Trends

The growing trend for highly successful companies today is to align their company mission stated as a need with the personal needs of the people doing the work. These companies develop strong employee loyalties, less turnover, and outstanding production. They realize, as educators must, that you cannot beat performance into people with a stick. You must create needs, and then be able to demonstrate to others and yourself how to fulfill those needs. This is intrinsic motivation, and is by far more powerful than extrinsic motivation and all of its worthless incentive plans. Nothing means more to a loyal employee than for the boss to recognize the worth of their small contribution with a handwritten note as opposed to the cold fact you were not the best to win a vacation trip.

Value of an Intrinsic Motivational System
(to build personal accountability)

The value of learning an intrinsic motivational system is to help you understand and manage your personal accountability. The choices you make determine how you are behaviorally conditioned by systems. The nature of your personal drives and motives are often pitted against those imposed by the organization you work for to improve. Nature versus nurture also creates intrinsic motives to satisfy subconscious needs. With certainty you must learn to identify your personal needs and understand how they will change as you mature and acquire more knowledge. This is an awareness skill that can be taught. You need to learn a personal performance feedback system that can create a personal need for achievement and provide an awareness of feelings of satisfaction that can be reinforced to enable more like behaviors to continuously improve your performance. You must first increase your awareness to increase your intelligence. This will allow you to make the best use of the information you are given to improve your skills and performance over time. Be more aware of the effect of bias and beliefs imposed by others that influence your purposeful intent. The evaluation from others is always extrinsic and never as valuable as what you learn to self-evaluate from your performances against a realistic personal intrinsic standard. If you are improving your performance, you are successful; no one can argue with that. Learning how to self-evaluate your own performance feedback is essential. The feedback model created by B.F. Skinner serves this purpose. You must learn to know yourself, your capabilities and limitations, better than others including your parents and spouse.

Extrinsic Value

Activities that are promoted by others are not as valued as those you self selected to perform. Job descriptions, quotas, and homework are intrinsic and more powerful if you define your purpose and role. Your leadership must help your performers define their purpose and roles. Your performers need to feel their reward to reinforce their positive work ethic behaviors for job satisfaction learning how to self-evaluate their daily performance feedback. When your performers are not involved as partners to achieve a common objective or know their purposeful intent for the activity beforehand, those activities will have less value. For your less motivated performers create the need to learn by starting with, "The purpose of this lesson, project, or exercise is _____ _____." This brings the personal need to learn and intrinsic value of the activity into focus to achieve a higher state of conscious awareness. As a good leader, appeal to your performer's perception of the value for any activity to increase their PI strength. Good leaders do not take credit for the work and achievements accomplished by the performers who do the work. Ask for input from your performers that work to learn what activities produce positive rewarding experiences with intrinsic value. Like sales persons who motivate performance behaviors, you create the need and communicate how your performers can fulfill their needs and the common company or team objective. If you want to improve performance, you must move away from total extrinsic and move toward intrinsic values your performer's feel from doing the work. Be less specific in your job descriptions. Allow your performers the freedom to use their personality and creativity to produce a quality process of intrinsic value. Focus on the positive outcomes, and let your performers define the process to achieve the outcome. They will feel job satisfaction from achieving daily success and look forward to coming to work. You will find this worker freedom to do the work as they define the process and achieve the same outcome one of the last freedoms to produce job satisfaction and lower employee turnover.

Modeling Versus Purposeful Intent

Behavioral Rule #15: Rewarding irresponsible behavior or modeling responsible behavior will not improve personal accountability.

Modeling is an extrinsic motive that has little effect on performance improvement without also practicing PI skills. Positive communication and trust are essential for leaders to motivate their performers. It is important to say what you mean, and mean what you say in order to condition the right behaviors. Making threats you do not plan to enforce conditions the wrong behaviors. Rather than make threats, make positive steps to recognize personal achievements with a smile, kind word, or simple note. Great leaders' strength on their PI is built using intrinsic motives to satisfy the personal needs of their performers, and by so doing meet their personal needs, too. By modeling their PI, leaders can motivate performers, even if that performer does not have a good model or support network in the home, to improve their PI skills and performance to meet their own needs, and once learned the effect of the model is much less. PI skills are intrinsic and respective to every performer's needs. Leaders cannot apply group needs and goals and expect outstanding individual performance accountability until those individual needs are aligned with the group goals.

Strategies for Discriminating Extrinsic from Intrinsic Motives

A leadership mistake would be to think that extrinsic motives can build personal performance accountability. If the need or goal comes from outside the performer, he/she has no control over reducing or increasing the goal. The value attached to an extrinsic motive cannot be as great as an intrinsic motive. Performers are less motivated to be accountable or take ownership of the performances demanded by others. The biggest trap is to believe that more micro management of poor performance will increase personal accountability.

A wise leader, teacher, or parent first asks the performer how they felt about their performances. This creates a reflection of the work accomplished to value the effort and the reward. To learn personal performance accountability:

The first strategy is to begin to evaluate your performance effort and reward for value; to create this self-evaluation a paradigm shift occurs in which performers begin to equate quality of effort with quality of reward. If you overly manage and make accountable decisions for your performers, they will not learn to develop their personal intrinsic motivational system. To lead others, it is important to learn and practice these principles on your own performances.

The second strategy is to focus on creating an immediate positive feedback system to self-evaluate and critique your own performances over time. The gaming industry is built on this notion. While the game may win big or more often bust, it does not deter the player's motive to succeed on the next trial. Similarly, performers have built-in intrinsic motives and drives that are not deterred by an occasional poor performance. When focused, a purposeful positive intent leads to success more often compared to having no conscious intent and inconsistent performance. Reflecting on your immediate past performance continuously creates a new benchmark to be a little bit better and feel successful again.

The third strategy, also known as displace-replace, is to learn to consciously restate negative thoughts or images into positive statements or images. Performers know when they make errors, and it is important to refocus negative energy into positive results! When you state or mentally visualize an image of the negative, you reinforce that performance to happen. Your brain is a microprocessor that does not know right from wrong.

The most common mistake leaders, teachers, or parents make is violating Rule # 16:

To provide too much approval or disapproval of another's performance immediately reduces the intrinsic value and increases the extrinsic value.

This is the hardest concept for leaders to grasp. Leaders must create a strong focus on the purposeful intent of the expected outcome that is closely aligned with the personal needs of the performer and the company needs to make a profit, and stay in business to employ those performers. There has to be a feeling of mutual trust between the performers and management to work together in an efficient way that fits their past experience and personality.

Can you discriminate between an extrinsic and intrinsic motive? Take the quiz found in the Appendix. The answers are at the end of the Appendix.

Promoting a Positive Leadership System of Need Satisfaction

Consistently successful performers know how to identify and regularly meet their own needs. They are not dependent on others. They learn self-reliance, and seldom blame others for not meeting their needs or for poor performances. They are accountable to themselves to raise their personal intrinsic value for all their activities. Organizations and companies that provide a positive leadership system that encourages empowerment, growth, and more efficient operations can promote their need to change for success by using these low-cost suggestions:

1. Move from boss management to lead management.
2. Align the mission, vision, and needs of the organization with the personal needs of the performers doing the work.
3. Allow performers who do the work to have some say in how they would like to accomplish the results.
4. Become more results oriented and less process oriented; managers must remove all conscious thought for "my way or the highway."
5. Value the worth of every employee and their ideas to remove formal titles and lines of communication.
6. Everyone gives credit where credit is due; no one takes credit for another performer's ideas or job performance.
7. Treat your workers like family.
8. Set performance goals only slightly higher than the immediate past performance or average performance of each performer.
9. Develop a positive feedback system, and show each performer how to use it.
10. Encourage routine self-evaluation of performance congruent with semi-annual performance evaluations from management.
11. Reward the positive by looking for the good in your performers.
12. Extinct the negative by placing emphasis on MaS>MaF.

13. Have your performers periodically assess their needs and the needs of the company to determine the impact of their job or role in the company growth.

14. Recognize and celebrate personal performance improvement without an extrinsic reward.

Alignment of mission, values, beliefs, and needs – Company and Personnel

Leaders create and identify the personal needs of the performers who do the work and try to align those needs with the needs of the organization. You must trust your performers to buy in to doing the necessary work to reach established quality performance standards, and still meet their personal needs. This will happen when you align the needs of the performers with the needs of the organization. If you want intrinsically motivated performers who improve their performance and have realistic and stable needs, then do not micromanage them. When you control a top performer's thinking you lose their creativity and intrinsic motivation to improve. Perception is in the eye of the beholder. It is not what you think about a performer's performance, but what they learn to think or value about their work motivated by their drive to satisfy personal needs. Performers are naturally motivated to improve. How they become consciously aware of their improvements has been the problem. All throughout our lives we have been conditioned to set high goals, but in reality higher goals are not frequently attained to condition the work ethic to get them. Top performers have a positive attitude because they set low positive goals only slightly better than their own immediate past performance that they feel more in control. They feel successful more often because they increased their probability to succeed. This creates a positive work environment because more people can see the immediate results of their efforts to feel accomplishment and enjoy doing the work. Their work success satisfies their personal needs. Performers are the valued workers in the system. When they care, they will have better ideas for how to be efficient or lighten up the place. Factories and offices do not have to be boring. You are a performer in a work system, and you must have some say in how you will meet your personal needs to take ownership and accountability to do the work, produce quality, and feel rewarded to reinforce more of the same quality work ethic behavior.

As the leader you must continually model a work ethic and sincere caring to enhance the personal needs of your workers if you expect them to learn new skills to improve their performance. Simply, if you want the performers to care about the organization, the leaders have to care about the performers who do the work and their role in the organization. If you do not create the need to learn and improve performance quality through awareness of self-evaluation and reward-reinforcement, you cannot expect to achieve consistent quality results from the performers doing the work. Disruptive climates occur because performers feel their needs are not being met, or that they cannot envision the quality product or service they help to achieve. Morale drops when performers do not connect reward in meeting their personal needs often enough to reinforce their motivation to repeat the work to benefit the company and themselves. Instead, they achieve the "why bother syndrome." When management has to question performances, it is because they have not identified the personal needs of the workers to provide them with a purposeful intent for doing the work. This also applies to good parenting skills. For example, one of those needs is a natural drive to belong to something bigger than ourselves. This can be both spiritual and an organizational blunder for not explaining how each performer has an important team role to play in the quality of the finished product.

The most common mistake leaders make is applying generic group needs - a mission statement, vision, values, beliefs - and then indoctrinating every member into believing these general ideals must be their personal mission, too. This is an extrinsic practice. Although common goals are essential to team development and performance, to be truly effective, leaders must be more aware of what drives human behavior and motivates every performer, and develop a mission to help meet the personal needs and goals of the people doing the work.

False Assumptions of Management

A false assumption is that group needs are stronger than the needs of the performers doing the work. As a leader, you need to align your organization or company needs with the personal needs of the people doing the work. This is not an easy task to accomplish, but the dividends are huge. The biggest mistake a leader can make is to take some or all of the credit from those who do the work. Nothing kills motivation or morale faster than making this big blunder, but it is done all the time by leaders who climb a political, social, or corporate ladder. Insecure leaders exhibit strange behaviors to protect their personal ego and how their bosses evaluate their leadership performance. When performers do well, the insecure leader-manager takes the credit, but when events go badly, they deflect the blame to the workers. By applying PI skills, these same leaders can improve performance by systematically teaching the PI strategies to their performers and building their morale and confidence. Increasing morale and confidence changes the work performance framework: there is trust in others to do their job, workers are more self-reliant, empowered, and not as dependent upon the system to be intrinsically motivated to do their job consistently, and workers take pride in their work. Accomplished work has quality value and intrinsic reward.

Micromanagement Pitfalls

When leaders mistrust their employees it results in more micromanagement, which creates more worker's dependency on an inefficient system to provide for needs that they must learn to provide for themselves. This kind of decision making leader does not have a strong educational foundation in psychology to understand need driven behavior. Performers leave jobs, or become apathetic, more for lack of some control over how their work is performed than for more money. Having some control over how you use your personality to do your assigned work is one of the last freedoms in America. Job freedom is violated the most often by people who do not know how to motivate their teams and resort to bossing to ensure compliance. These boss-managers stifle company creativity in an effort to find new, more efficient ways to perform. They also threaten performers who lack experience performing tasks in a way that they are familiar; thinking outside the box is unfamiliar and stressful to these managers. It's their way or the highway; however, some very successful people with PI skills have left unrewarding jobs to form companies that eventually took over the company they left. Therefore, do not doubt your abilities and purpose.

Unfortunately, most performers are conditioned to work and live within micromanagement systems that do not encourage personal accountability and purposeful thinking capacity. Otherwise, you would not perform routine repetitive tasks that are boring. Someone has to do those jobs so more performers are conditioned what to do rather than think how to perform those tasks better. Micromanagement systems serve no purpose other than to control your behavior with coercive extrinsic means, which are not effective motives for lifelong learning and performance improvement. By providing positive alternatives and opportunities to make purposeful choices, you can create awareness and value to enhance your personal accountability. As you mature and are allowed to make simple mistakes you learn a personal feedback system. You learn to make better choices to discriminate your responses to the proper cues. If other performers have to hold your hand and do your job, they do not need you. Your primary job is to improve your performance, and hold yourself accountable to accomplish your role. If your home life or work environment does not allow for personal accountability, then you will have difficulties managing yourself and improving the quality of your performance to feel rewarded. There is a natural drive to improve and be independent that must not be denied in the teenage years. However, to wean a dependent child, they must be able to demonstrate they can identify and meet their own needs. A failure to do so, for lack of proper education and conditioning in the home and school, will only create more micromanagement to increase dependency and conflict. This can be very frustrating. If persistent, more micromanagement leads to loss a positive intent to succeed in new tasks and of hope; you learn to give up easily.

Boss versus Lead Management

Psychologist Dr. William Glasser, (1990) <u>The Quality</u> <u>School</u>, has described a dichotomy between boss-managers and lead-managers. The boss-manager is controlling to achieve conformity; the lead manager offers choices to allow the personality to create value from their work. "Boss-managers firmly believe that people can be motivated from the outside: They fail to understand that all of our motivation comes from within us." Boss-manager types continually lament how their performers are not motivated; what they are really saying is they do not know how to motivate their performers. The boss-manager type does not believe that internal rewards can possibly motivate a performer because *they* are not internally driven; *they* are driven by the external reward of the pay increase and more power to provide temporary job security from a promotion. These managers believe it is their demeanor and coercive leadership style, along with fear of reprisals that motivates people to work harder to please them before themselves. In their mind, the performers are incapable of deciding when and how much effort to put out on the job. Inexperienced boss leaders believe they can motivate performers to conform to their thinking with the promise of a good evaluation or grade. Leaders who are not able to discriminate between extrinsic and intrinsic motives by interchanging motives will confuse performers and achieve inconsistent results because they have not established PI. Consequently, the boss-managed performer is focused more on keeping the boss happy than to be motivated in ways to improve their performance. The motivation to meet personal needs is reduced, and so is accountability. You can blame the boss management for your failures and mistakes. Boss management leads to unproductive status quo and avoidance behaviors. Your motive to avoid failure is greater than your motive to achieve success (MaF > MaS).

Conversely, lead-managers recognize the innate needs in others and align them with the needs of the company in fulfilling their roles that contribute to successful job performance. They align the mission, and needs of the corporation with the personal needs of the workers who gain personal satisfaction beyond the paycheck for their results. The corporation can turn a fair profit but not at the personal expense of the people doing the work. Success comes from a positive focus on a mutual goal to align the needs of the corporation to build a familial trusting partnership with the personal needs of the performers. The motive to achieve success will be greater than the motive to avoid failure (MaS > MaF). Highly paid performers still leave their jobs for less money in order to achieve personal job satisfaction. Underpaid top performers who are made to feel valued and are able to meet their personal needs develop company loyalties and remain on the job improving their work.

Lead-managers consistently recognize and increase their awareness skills to look for the good to point out positive feedback in every performer that communicates a feeling of value about the work quality. Performers for lead-managers report their performances are enriching and fulfill their personal needs for survival, love, power, fun, and freedom. Intrinsic motives are a matter of trust. The boss-manager does not trust the worker to be self-motivated by thinking of their needs; they focus on the company's or group's needs however, which when achieved, satisfy their personal needs. The lead-manager, however, trusts the workers to fulfill their needs and by accomplishing those needs to give back to the company or organization their quality services. Lead-managers can turn their organization or team around by embracing and practicing PI intrinsic motivational skills training.

Resistance to Empowerment

In boss management organizations, lead managers who attempt to empower their performers will meet large scale resistance. If the culture of your organization is to find fault with your performers without recognizing their positive strengths or achievements, you will have a morale problem. For example, the CEO is held accountable for the company performance so that the lay board can enjoy the power and authority without personal accountability. If performance does not improve, boards can blame it on their CEO. Organizations must begin to set minimum qualifications to be an effective board member to lead, and hold individual board members accountable for their actions.

What happens at the top trickles down to the bottom? Performers are conditioned to blame others for poor performance as a team and not take individual accountability. Performers resist empowerment because it means they will be held accountable for performance improvements that require changes in their personality patterns. If they fail to improve, it is easier to blame management for not providing the proper training or tools. When you change from a boss management to lead management culture, you can expect your performers to feel stressed and resist your efforts until they feel comfortable and secure making personal improvement decisions without manager criticism. Move slowly to establish new evaluation guidelines to encourage self-evaluation and performer evaluation for how to improve the company or system without fear of retaliation or retribution.

Encourage performers to perform their personal evaluation using the same instrument or parameters prior to receiving the manager's evaluation. Check for congruence, act like a coach looking for the positives to improve, and build a partnership with the performers doing the work. Set up a system for recognizing outstanding performers who make consistent positive contributions. If you are a teacher change your belief system. Personally, I would rather have in my third grade 20 little engines that could than to have 20 dynamos that can't do anything without my help. Empowerment and expectation are learned behaviors. If teachers have lower expectations of their students, it will consistently affect the quality of their work. For any organization, you cannot motivate quality performance by coercion, or have the belief that your performers cannot learn to improve.

Boss managers do not believe performers are intrinsically motivated and capable of working independently or understanding their needs. Boss managers extrinsically motivate their performers through micromanagement, and frequently resort to negative reinforcement – "Do this or be fired!" Needs are never given a thought, other than from an extrinsic point of view to meet the needs of the manager and not the personal needs of the worker. The choices you make for yourself and others are based upon need satisfaction. As the leader/manager you do not know the company or your needs because you have not defined your purposeful intent, you are confused about how to improve performance and display erratic behaviors trying to control things beyond your control. PI leadership skills training identifies your intrinsic personal needs, the organization's needs, and the personal needs of others that produce your drives and motives to be satisfied independent of the extrinsic motives and needs of others applied to your performance. Take the personal needs assessment in the Appendix.

Where organizations fail to perform and improve they lose their focus on the PI skills process. They are top heavy in boss leaders engaged in fault finding more than on the quality product or service outcome. This is because the boss leaders are conditioned to keep their job by finding the faults in others. It is their job to correct errors in the organization to make it more efficient. The focus should be more on positive ways to improve employee and customer relations to produce the product quality or service outcome. These are the needs and values that must be aligned. Lay boards who micromanage their professionally educated CEO's will have personality clashes just as companies laden with boss managers do not intrinsically motivate their talented and creative performers. You can begin to understand why lay boards of education have retarded the growth of American public education. You can also begin to understand how legislators, without knowledge of behavioral psychology, have enacted poor legislation that rewards performers not to work and be held accountable for meeting their own needs because the government services provided are free and have less personal value for accountability.

Use the natural drive to conserve energy and resources to increase your conscious awareness for an efficient outcome. Have your performers suggest strategies to improve performances. Work to educate lay boards to eliminate boss management style of "my way or the highway," and build trust between management and the performers. Then creativity and intrinsic motivation will be improved and everyone wins in a spirit of cooperation.

Traditional Organizations

Traditional organizations do not understand how to intrinsically motivate and empower their personnel for fear of loss of management control. Management and control provides the fuel for power and job security in a competitive autocratic environment. In a democracy, human rights are the purposeful intent of the society; trust is with the people. If you study this book and practice the exercises to perfect your skills in The Triad, over time, you will become a top performer. You will be intrinsically motivated to work independently and make creative performance improvement suggestions. You will become a threat to management because their job may be eliminated. Your manager will be threatened by your success in that to your superiors you appear to be a better replacement. That kind of organizational culture must change if you want more intrinsically motivated performers to increase production. Organizations are starting to recognize the value of intrinsically motivated employees to reduce higher management costs. Costly middle management has been an overseer but neither a worker nor creative producer. This hurts the company net profit and share value. Boss managers harass creative intrinsically motivated performers who see their ideas and suggestions for improvement as a threat to their leadership until they leave the organization. Personnel turnover hurts companies and organizations including volunteer groups who appoint well-meaning but insecure "boss manager" style leaders to direct self-directed people. All organizations must reorganize how they select and motivate their leaders and employees. The traditional boss-manager approach has been to assume that performers are not capable of self-motivation, and must be controlled and watched to ensure that they are doing the job. A boss will hire personalities to be assured of their management role in the organization. Performers are told what their goals will be (extrinsic) in the form of a too detailed job description or unrealistic quota motivated by the controlling boss manager to save their job. Don't forget the boss over the boss manager. Understand what the underlying motives are and who created the job description. School trained personnel managers hire performers for jobs they have no idea what kind of personality will fit in that role, or if the candidate is intrinsically motivated. Most human resource managers do not understand the job function because they have not performed that job or observed successful performers doing that job to identify and value the key components to predict success on the job. Few organizations that provide training understand leadership education and intrinsic motivation like the Quint Studer Group, Hardwiring Excellence, (2003)., to make good strides in organizational performance improvement. Typically, the bottom one-third of your personnel, if not successful, can cause harm and bring down several performers in the middle third group. If they do not change with training, they must be let go and replaced with intrinsically motivated performers.

Entrepreneurial Engines Change the Task

Corporations spend billions of dollars employing middle management with the premise that the worker is incapable of being self motivated. Boss managers who rely on intimidation and micromanagement reduce and destroy more powerful intrinsic motives in the people they manage. The major reason why change is difficult for companies to move away from traditional management is directly related to task familiarity as a personality phenomenon. Change implies improvement but it also upsets and stresses out your conditioned routine behaviors that are familiar to you. When you are made to change to a temporarily unfamiliar routine your personality patterns are more apprehensive, insecure, and less confident. Think about an accountant routinely working with concrete financial data every day and now suddenly having to draw up abstract plans for a new office. There are performers on your team who have very rigid personalities and others who are very adaptable to change. Start the change process with performers who are adaptable to change. Performers will self select various jobs suited to their conditioned personality patterns to reduce inner conflicts and stress. When companies manage personnel and focus on the outcomes more than the process, they enable the people doing the work to accomplish that work on an acceptable realistic timetable and within the parameters of their personalities. They are trusted to do their jobs and function as a part of the team to reach projected goals and outcomes. Few companies do this better than Google.

It's Your Job

You can make a difference to your co-workers or employees by looking for their positive attributes to reinforce, keeping a smile on your face, and recognizing even their smallest attempts to achieve quality. None of these cost any money but a little time, and reinforce intrinsic motives. When you recognize small qualities in others, you influence all your performers to make a difference. When you continually look for the faults in others, you condition the negative behaviors you want to eliminate by having called attention to them. Highly successful emerging companies like Google and Patagonia use lead management styles to empower their employees to create efficient production and feel rewarded for their personal efforts. This intrinsic motivation pays huge dividends because employees will be driven to work harder knowing they are trusted to perform quality when the boss is not looking. These employees are not dependent on extrinsic motives to achieve personal feelings of quality and pride in their work. They judge their own work against a personal standard they set for themselves. These skills can be taught.

Negative Consequences Without PI Skills

Negative social climates occur when a number of performers lack understanding of their purpose in the organization to be motivated to improve their performance. Poor performers threaten other performers so that their higher performance does not threaten their job and social status. Bullies and intimidators want to redirect their non-performance to other performers so they can get by unnoticed. If a top performer demonstrates their intelligence or motivation, they are put down. Intelligent faculties and administrations must continually define the purpose of a quality education for its value and how to envision its achievement by raising the expectations of their students. Students who are taught how to identify their short or long term needs and then held accountable for meeting those needs mature to provide for themselves and eventually others with their education.

Summary

After being introduced to the Science of Purposeful Intent there were three chapters to explain strategies for learning how to perform Part One of The Triad: Increase Awareness. Mind-Body Connection described how the *structures* work together. Growing Antennae concentrated on how to identify and develop your *abilities*. It's Your Job focused on how having a purposeful intent can develop your personal *accountability* for learning and managing performers.

Preview

Part Two: Enhance Self Evaluation will have three chapters as did Part One. Self evaluation will be a feedback model presented as pre, during, and post evaluation skills. Pre evaluation details how to plan and prepare to get ready to perform. During evaluation explains strategies to maintain or refocus your abilities to modify performance at will on demand. Post evaluation will describe how to use your immediate past performance as a benchmark to continually be motivated to improve.

PART TWO

ENHANCE SELF EVALUATION

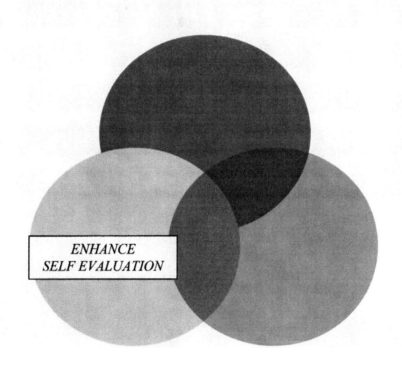

ENHANCE
SELF EVALUATION

You cannot build accountability in a micromanagement system. Do you know of any top performer that ever waited for the approval of another person? Then why do you wait for others to judge you when you already know quality performance when you see it in yourself and others? School systems, business management, and society as a whole condition you to wait for the judgment or evaluation of your performance. Top performers develop a personal set of standards based on their own immediate and past performance history. This provides immediate feedback to judge the relative value of any performance, and help set a realistic goal for a new performance slightly better to feel positive improvement and personal motivation from their effort. This is intrinsic motivation.

Part two helps you learn how to self-evaluate your performance in three ways:

Pre Performance Evaluation. How you choose to set low positive goals only slightly better than your own immediate past performance to enhance your probability for success is part of your pre planning to increase your drive motivation. Goal setting strategy is related to your personality that you can change over time to be successful.

During Performance Evaluation. You will learn how to process your own feedback during a performance, and make necessary adjustments to increase your probability for success.

Post Performance Evaluation. Taking responsibility for your performance that all top performers have is the first step to learning personal accountability. How your performance feelings agree with your evaluators provides congruence to enhance your realism and motivation to achieve quality on future performances.

Pre Performance Evaluation

"Forest full of trees provide fertile campground."

Andrew Christian

Objective: Learn to use a variety of information to predict the value of a future performance to increase your personal motivation.

A champion is willing to risk failure to test their limits and capacity to improve. They constantly measure their purposeful intent against their abilities and skills, and self-impose their immediate past performance or average as their standard criteria to improve.

Introduction

Self evaluation is a means to validate your performance against a personally selected standard. Pre performance evaluation is your review of a conscious plan to improve upon your immediate past performance or average as the basic standard used by top performers. This personal standard constantly changes as you improve your performance. Because it takes years of dedicated purposeful practice to become a top performer, forget about being an overnight success. You can also forget about being someone you're not. Adjust your personality to get real with matching your abilities, actual past performance experience, and realistic goal or expected outcome. You can change your needs and purpose once you identify their meaningful and relevant performance value. These primary factors create your intrinsic motivation.

In the first skill of The Triad, Increase Awareness, you learned how to identify your needs from your desires or wants, and your abilities that have led to your performance outcomes. Part of being smart is to learn what you are good at performing, and can feel some personal reward to motivate your need to continue to improve.

In the second skill of The Triad, Enhance Self Evaluation, you will learn how to reverse your flow of knowledge to properly affect a positive realistic plan to succeed on a given task. The B.F. Skinner feedback model shown in chapter three, and reflecting on past performance experience or task familiarity to plan to improve a new performance will be used. This strategic purposeful planning builds realism and intrinsic motivation by increasing the probability for your success. In some ways, this pre planned sequence you put yourself through prior to competition is like the pre shot routine golfers and other sports figures use to visualize their performance as a positive outcome. The process also eliminates stupid errors that could have been addressed and controlled prior to the performance.

The Pre Performance Evaluation Checklist provides you with a revue to plan your performance. After you become skilled at this revue, you should be able to rapidly run through the checklist. Almost unconsciously, you make candid adjustments and perform many of the items listed in various time periods leading up to your actual performance. The checklist order is typical but can be adjusted to meet your personal needs. As you learn these separate skills in The Triad you apply them to performance. However, in this exercise you reverse the process by identifying the task and determine how you match up those skills from the checklist.

Pre Performance Evaluation Checklist

Identify Task	Purpose – why performing	Intent – win, participate,
Difficulty	% Effort	lose Motive
Value	Need or Goal Satisfaction	
Reward	% Reward feeling	Optimal Reinforcement
		Index
Needs and Abilities	Identified	Understanding
	Assessed	Matched to Task
Mental Shift	Unconscious Automated	Routine Mode
	Conscious	Selective Attention S-R Association

Mode

Sensations   to   Perceptions   - Prediction

- Projection

Set Up Correct Standard Performance Comparison

Local Average – group PAP

State Goal/Benchmark

Stated Goal – verbal PAP

National Norm

Quartile Rank

Local, State, National, World Record

Hall of Fame

Personal All-Time Best Performance

Immediate Past Performance or Average – self PAP

Personal Personality Assessment (subjective)

Comparison personal pattern to top performer pattern

Realism   Persistence   Will Power

Feedback Awareness   Output – Input

Immediate Past Performance

Past Performance History

Personal Best

Top Performer

Set Realistic Goal   Congruence: Expectation closely

equal to Actual Performance

Use of Perceptual Anchoring Point

– PAP (group, verbal, self)

Risk-Reward Value

SMART Method

Intermediate Goals

Ultimate Goal

Immediate Past Performance + 1

Perfecting Sub Routines   Visualization and Positive Imagery
                             – Attention to Detail
                             Mental Practice – Key Hole and
                             Third Eye
                             Sequencing
                             Auto Pilot

Mobilization of Energy   Peak Performance   Zone
        High Focus Concentration
            Mental - tension control - relaxation, diaphragm breathing
                                     - butterflies in formation
                - top tunes   - music to inspire
            RROSR
            At Will On Demand
            Positive Self-Talk
            MaS>MaF
            Performance Review
            Physical - timing skills   pace
                     - taper   rest
                     - diet   nutrition

Set Up Pre Performance Routines
        Immediate   Delayed
        Mental Warm Up   Competition
        Physical Warm Up

Identify Task Difficulty

It's one thing to be challenged; it's another thing to be in over your head with no possibility for success. Be your own best friend and realistic with your activity choices. Know your purpose. Write it down. What do you want to achieve? What do you need to achieve? Know your intent; is it to succeed, just get by to participate, or lose to be accepted or liked? You know your abilities well enough to project some idea of the per cent of effort it will take to match your intent and purpose. What are the aspects about this activity that motivate you to try and improve?

Value

Value is the hypothesis for purposeful intent. Activities you value you will remember and perform better to be motivated to keep improving. Value is the amount of perceived reward divided by the amount of perceived effort or V=%R/%E. If the task is either too hard or too easy you will not feel the optimal reward to reinforce continued attempts to improve and be the top performer. If your need or goal is not satisfied frequently enough, you will either give up or get frustrated and stressed and possibly take out your negative feelings on others.

Predictive Value and PI Strength

There are two highly predictable strategies to use to build value strength:

1) Increase awareness to a conscious level, and 2) Predict how your abilities match the performance task and probability expectation to produce success. In your mind, create a predictive equation estimating which are the key variables to perform the task well, and weight each but not to exceed a total of 100%. Then subjectively evaluate your performance on each variable to compare to how the top performers in those tasks would rate. Your value and PI strength will increase the more you approximate the performances of the top performers. This is how great coaching leaders with a wealth of knowledge from their past top performers build consistently good teams.

Correlation Value and PI Strength

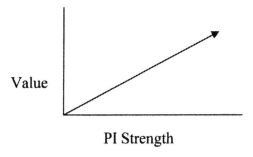

Value

PI Strength

Value for any activity must have a high positive correlation to PI strength. The stronger awareness you have of your purpose and intent for performing and trying to improve will also increase the value of the activity or performance. The predictive value of any activity will vary by performer. This prediction process occurs in two ways: First, focus the attention of your performers on what is personally at stake for a future performance to build in your purpose to succeed. Your personal stake is to improve or do the best you are capable of performing. Then let your performer's perceptions reflect on their personal value equal to their reward over past efforts. Your performers will plug in a host of personal variables such as their abilities and skills from past performances, and familiar outcomes. Top performers create perceived amounts of reward and effort for every worthy activity to increase their motivation. As the leader, if you spend more time talking about the performance event, you only increase the extrinsic motivation that can have negative stress consequences, and that is not as powerful as the personal intrinsic motivation reflected upon by each performer to focus on specifics to do their best. Second, make performances worthy with a work ethic to increase your performer's awareness and PI strength using your past experiences to familiarize inexperienced performers with images and scenarios of what to expect. The positive expectation or outcome is the criterion, and the specifics you address become the beta weighted variables in the <u>predictive multiple regression</u> equation. A representative example is in your imaginary multiple regression equation presented earlier as $V1 + V2 + V3 + V4 + V5 = C$. For example, C is your Positive Expectation or Outcome. Each variable is beta weighted by subjective priority or importance that you want to assign or focus on to perform and achieve the outcome. $V1$ can be crowd size and noise; $V2$ is officiating; $V3$ is type of conditioning – mental and physical preparation; $V4$ is your task familiarity; and $V5$ is the health of your starters. There are variables you can control and some you cannot other than to familiarize yourself with what to expect by someone who has been there to describe what the experience is like. As the leader you must figure out what and when to explain future task experience and realistic expectation. You must also spend your time wisely on the higher predictive variables with larger subjective % beta weights. This is why your leadership experience is valuable to any organization that wants or needs to improve. This is your pre planning leadership to build value in the reward from the personal efforts of all your performers. You must increase your performer's awareness level using a pre planned predictive equation. You assist your performers to narrow their focus and concentrate on the specific cues that they have been conditioned to recognize as input from their past performances and not from others. This mental planning helps your performers to have peak performances. The pre planned sequence of visualized cues to trigger a positive performance raises their level of awareness to mobilize a temporary executable program using the prefrontal cortex all of their skills and abilities at will on demand for a given moment in time. As the <u>leader</u> of others or yourself you must learn to choose to be in control of learning how to perform this process. Watching other performers during a competition is not a good practice. You risk programming the visualization of their performance into your short term memory, and confuse the program you have visualized and set up for yourself. You want to visualize with mental imagery using as many senses as possible a successful performance for each recognized cue. This is a pre performance routine, and is a learned skill to move from a routine automated subconscious practice to a conscious PI effort that has increased awareness of value. Value increases your reward feelings to desire more of the same feelings and reinforce those behaviors with gradually increased effort to ensure your success.

Perception of Value

Performing specific cues with positive self-talk raise your level of awareness to increase the value of the perception of effort and potential reward from a task. You focus on the effort you will need to produce a positive result in advance of the performance. By nature you tend to value activities that require more effort, and place higher reward value on your success. Every improvement or learning experience has reward value and is not a failure. When you have no purposeful intent and go through the motions of work with unconscious effort, the value of the activity is lost. The rewards that could reinforce your positive behaviors and create a synergetic effect to consistently improve your future performances over time do not occur. Your PI strength is diminished without reward to reinforce your positive work ethic behaviors that can ensure higher probabilities for your success in the succeeding performance(s). This worthy effect occurs within individual performers and groups. Top performers constantly review their own immediate and past performances to evaluate their pre-performances. Top performers seldom prefer to work in collaborative groups because they cannot control the performances of others. Collaborative group members use group goals and needs to form their perceptual anchoring point or PAP about which they judge the value or worth of new pre-performance goals. From personal research (Andersen, 1973) I found this to be the least effective drive stimulus to motivate performance improvement. If you must work collaboratively to learn social skills or participate in a team performance, then it would be best to break the overall assignment into specific tasks and assign those tasks to group (team) members. Each performer is held accountable to do their part, and set a specific goal to meet in a pre-performance evaluation. You would also profit from the performance feedback of other members and the group need to do well. The greatest value that top performing companies have learned is to align their company needs to earn a fair profit with meeting the personal needs for success of the people who do the work. Production and quality performance all improve as each member has a valued interest in the well being of every performer.

Value Equation

The simple equation $V = R / E$ explains how performers perceive value for any performance. Value, V, is reward R divided by effort E. Four examples are presented below the figure that indicates none are optimal for reinforcing improvement behavior. In a pre performance evaluation a strategy that will increase your motivation is to review your abilities and project how to best apply them in planning to perform a skill. You would plan to create value from your performance effort, and program a positive expectation for your success to feel rewarded. You must see yourself performing all the necessary skills to the best of your ability in the activity. Projection awareness is mentally visualizing playing a movie of your anticipated performance in your mind prior to performing. You program a positive outcome for each movie segment from start to finish building value into your performance. There are two kinds of values, expected value and actual value from the performance result. Top performers who set realistic and achievable goals obtain congruence or the same result for both values. The personality trait is realism.

Needs and Abilities

You have taken the surveys of your needs and abilities, and now is your time to apply to the selected task. If you have not identified any needs to satisfy, then you are wasting your time on this activity. Do your abilities match up with the other performers in the activity? For example, if you are built like a football tackle, you are not designed to swim like a dolphin. The more realistic you are with matching your needs and abilities to each selected task, the greater your probability for success and continued improvement.

Activity Value Index

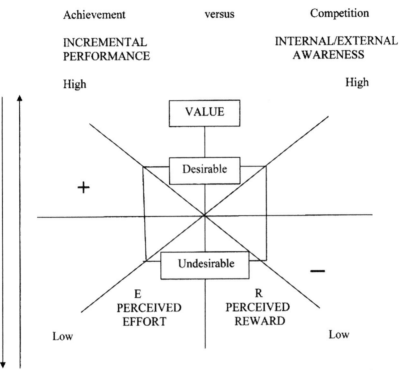

Achievement   versus   Competition

INCREMENTAL   INTERNAL/EXTERNAL
PERFORMANCE   AWARENESS

High   High

VALUE

Desirable

+

Undesirable

—

E   R
PERCEIVED   PERCEIVED
EFFORT   REWARD

Low   Low

**Optimal value comes from those performance activities that will contribute
the most to reinforce consistent incremental improvements.**

Desirable +   -   Optimal low positive realistic effort and reward in the rectangle

**These performances increase your probability for
success to enhance your personal reward system.**

Undesirable -   -   Maximum effort; Minimal reward
          -   Minimal effort; Maximum reward
          -   Maximum effort; Maximum reward
          -   Minimal effort; Minimal reward

Realism and Success Expectations

Have you ever seen an ugly looking dog? If you love the dog because it unconditionally loves you and you give the dog an identity and personality, does the dog know it is ugly? Successful performers are dogmatic and seldom question their abilities to improve with purposeful hard work any more than an ugly dog would question its beauty or purpose because they know their purposeful intent. They set achievable and realistic goals to frequently achieve. By their own evaluation to improve their immediate past performance, they can self-reward and reinforce a work ethic to maintain successful feelings. They do not wait for the approval of others that so many average performers are conditioned to wait for to feel rewarded. They perform quality performances because they create higher personal standards for improvement based on their performance history. They compete within themselves to improve their performances in small increments to maintain higher motivational levels and PI strength. They know why they compete and why they need to improve.

Identification of Needs

Our needs change as we mature, acquire valuable knowledge, and become more responsible. With change, our motives and purpose should also increase in strength to fulfill personal needs no longer met by others. Once your primary needs for food, clothing, shelter, and water are consistently met, your natural innate drive is to move on to secondary needs to feel loved, belong, and improve your performance. Secondary needs are not met as frequently by others, and vary by your experience. This can happen due to divorce, death of a spouse, graduation from school, changing your job, or losing your job. In affluent societies, primary and secondary needs are met more frequently by others to create dependencies on parents and social systems. Welfare states are created because masses of people have not been conditioned to identify and meet their own needs. The result is a lack of motivation and increased co-dependency on the system to meet those needs. The more people are not conditioned to meet their own needs, the more the system steps in to meet those needs and creates a negative cycle that does not motivate personal accountability or performance improvement. This lesson was learned as far back as the 1880's when Native Americans were confined to reservations, and the motivation to provide for their own needs was taken away when they could no longer move their villages to hunt for game. Necessity is still the mother of invention or you violate the # I behavioral rule: The more you do for people, the less they will learn to do for themselves.

Understanding Your Needs on a Conscious Level

Adult performers who are more familiar with tasks constantly need to understand their needs on a conscious level to increase their motivation. This process to increase your awareness and understand your personal needs must be purposeful or the changes that you desire in your overall performance cannot occur as readily. To continuously improve your performance, you must learn how to tune in to your environment and connect your use of the <u>awareness of mind</u> strategy to direct your body's response. When the process works in reverse its called biofeedback: you take sensations from your body and convert them to feelings you store in your mind. You can choose to condition or associate a positive or negative feeling. How to identify your needs is an on-going process of self-evaluation and very necessary if you want to understand your behaviors and what strongly motivates you to act. Needs drive your behaviors; you must know them and be able to quantify their strength and the value you gain from satisfying them. When our needs are satisfied, we begin to take them for granted and no longer value them until they are removed. A man will covet all his worldly possessions even when homeless. Our survival skills are lost in the comfort of a home, and being loved and wanted. Yet we continue to suffer through divorce seeking a more perfect partner to meet our needs. We are often motivated to do some pretty stupid things seeking to be loved and wanted by another until we find a means to love our soul and who we are to diminish that need. At times we lose our jobs and our way in life needing to become aware of how we can redeem ourselves. We can be stripped of all our worldly possessions from a fire, flood, or natural catastrophe. When disasters happen, your life is not positive, or improving, but knowing how to apply your purposeful intent skills will be valuable to motivate your personal perceptual awareness to take in more meaningful and relevant information. This will improve your temporary situation quickly as necessity is the mother of invention. Under-performers are not able to identify their needs very well because they have been conditioned to have others meet those needs and they lack purpose and intent. Their work is haphazard and aimless, and their perceptual awareness skills are very low. Conversely, top performers have very high perceptual awareness skills. Every behavior they perform is consciously evaluated for value to enhance self-improvement and feel rewarded. Top performers know why they perform in purposeful ways. They have learned how to learn and provide for their own needs and be independent from others who would provide for those needs. The longer you remain dependent on others to identify and provide for your needs, you will experience infrequent lower levels of success to feel accomplishment and pride in your work to value that can enhance your motivation. Make identifying and satisfying your personal needs a conscious activity and you will more likely change your behavior to take accountability and improve your performance. Value the work you perform to meet your personal needs, and readily retrieve the valued information stored in your brain to help you perform on a higher level. To increase the value of your work, occasionally remind yourself that you are doing work few others will perform today. More performers want success handed to them without having to earn the reward. This trend happens because they have not been conditioned to learn the skills presented in The Triad that could help them to be intrinsically motivated.

If you don't feel motivated, perhaps you are allowing others to do for you what you could do yourself. There is little value or motivation to meet needs that you do not have to work to earn. For example, if you give a baseball glove birthday present to a twelve year old, and another child mows lawns, rakes leaves, shovels snow, or baby sit to earn the $50 and buy his/her own glove, which child is most likely to absentmindedly leave the glove out in the rain? You will always value those objects and skills that you have to work to acquire. The harder you have to work to earn a reward, the greater the value; you will not give up easily.

Steps to Increase Your Awareness of Personal Needs

The first step to increasing your awareness in purposeful intent skills training is to identify your past, current and future needs; know who helped you meet them; and how you anticipate you will meet your personal needs on your own. Value for any activity comes from an intrinsic feeling of knowing you are improving and accomplishing personal goals by comparing your immediate past performance to your past performances or average. This valuing process comes from enhancing your self-evaluation skills. In the long run, it is not what others think of your performance, but what you learn to think of your performance that matters the most. To build value and accountability, you must increase your awareness to a conscious state. Place more emphasis on thinking about, knowing, and understanding how your personal needs are created, formed, and changed as you matured. Who or what satisfied those needs, and how did they make you feel interacting with your environment, people, and performances. You cannot be master to two standards: those you learn to set for yourself based on improving your own immediate past performance, and those that are forced upon you by others to meet their needs but may not have your needs in mind. This will put you in conflict to hate yourself or the one who has imposed their will upon you. You can try to please the one, but then you will not please the other.

The second step is to associate your personal needs that can discriminate between unconscious and conscious drives that lead to stronger personal motives. Then use these drives to help increase your motivation. In simple terms, learn to understand what underlying drives motivate your behavior or others associated with trying to meet their needs.

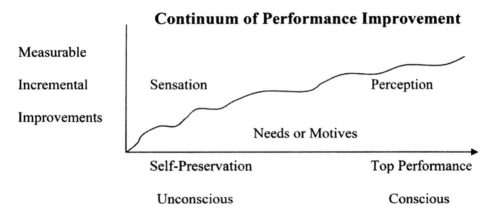

Continuum of Performance Improvement

Measurable

Incremental

Improvements

Sensation

Perception

Needs or Motives

Self-Preservation

Top Performance

Unconscious

Conscious

The Continuum of Performance Improvement helps you figure out what needs, drives and motives you can make conscious with perception or purposeful behavioral adjustments. This process increases your personal motivation to take accountability and improve your performance. You cannot control what others think or do, but you can learn to control what you think and do to affect a change in your performance: What behaviors, current and past, do you now associate to meeting your needs at that time, and are they still operating? What needs must you learn to associate to your performance improvement? For example, do you need to be independent to make your own goals and earn 100% of the rewards for doing all the work? Your unconscious drives are on the sensory self-preservation end of the continuum of performance improvement and your conscious drives are more on the perceptual top performance end. Also refer to the Increasing Awareness Flow Chart in Chapter Three, Growing Antennae.

Leadership Application

Boss leaders falsely assume that they can create stronger group motives that all performers will uniformly follow over their own personal needs and motives. Traditional leadership models separate leaders from their performers for fear of loss of control, or to effect discipline without showing favoritism. In this kind of boss-management leadership style, performers face negative extrinsic motives like loss of their job or bonus if they do not do what the boss demands. Today, successful companies demonstrate lead-management leadership styles that use positive intrinsic motives to personally reward and reinforce the good qualities that improve morale and performance output. The work environment is worker friendly, and companies are concerned enough for their "families" to provide day care, fitness gyms, extended lunch workout breaks, and other services for their employees. More men are also reversing their roles with their wives as the principal wage earner and caregiver and becoming "Mr. Mom." Needs can and do change. Corporations are becoming more worker friendly because while they need to make a profit to stay in business, the owners also realize a fair profit means they can treat all their workers like family and provide a more desirable quality of life to meet their personal needs at the same time. How they do business and treat customers relates to how they satisfy the needs of their employees who in turn care to meet the needs of the customer. When companies increase their awareness to associate their need to make a profit to stay in business and meet the needs of their customers to grow their business, they are also associating their understanding of the needs of their employees for a quality of life that will intrinsically motivate them to do a better job with higher PI strength. These companies spend the least amount of money on human resources recruiting, hiring, and training middle management to supervise and motivate their employees. They hire motivated people whom they do not have to ask the question, "What will they do when the boss is not looking?"

Mental Shifts

Purposeful intent has taught you several skills for increasing your awareness. The most important one is to take unconscious automated routines and bring them up to a conscious level of performance. You can do this with selective attention to specific stimulus-response (S-R) associations to perform RROSR found in energy mobilization. The object is to be more consciously aware of your sensations at specific times and converting them to positive perceptions. When you sense a certain key or way, you connect the pre thought out response that is designed to improve performance. That design comes from plugging in the key variables using the subjective multiple regression equation to project and predict your outcome.

Personal Prediction Skills

Your human computer constantly makes unconscious comparisons and iterations to predict potential outcomes in your daily life. Some performers call this common sense. I refer to these comparisons as Purposeful Intent. Through the process of learning purposeful intent strategy, your unconscious notions are brought to a higher conscious state to use your past performance feedback as input in pre-performance mental practice. Mental practice is closing your eyes and visualizing yourself performing successfully the way you want to program every detail. You want to build a positive self evaluation system to create a stronger personal reward system and raise your conscious levels of awareness. The knowledge or skill components you consciously select to mentally visualize in pre-performance reinforce your work ethic to ensure greater probability of success for your new performance. When you take time to reflect on all the work you have accomplished in practice, you can decide to be successful because you have earned the right to be in position to compete successfully. The statement strategy I suggested earlier might be, "Someone has to win, and it may as well be me." Successful performers create this strategy to build confidence and self-esteem that lead to consistently higher quality achievements over time. Your leadership skill is to establish your purposeful intent in the pre-performance stage.

Prediction Skills and Purposeful Intent

To preserve the human species, your brain is designed to use all of your senses to predict whether to take flight or make fight. Each sense modality is a variable you must weight because you rely on vision the most in the predictive equation and fed to your brain for processing. Your senses and your brain, based on your past experience and task familiarity in running speed, jumping, hitting, etcetera quickly make this pre performance assessment to weight the input importance for each variable. This process teaches you to create the need to increase your conscious awareness by continuously self-evaluating the match up of your abilities and skills for performing any task and predict a positive performance outcome. As you age, your needs, drives, motives, emotions, abilities, and skills will all change at varying rates. You need to select in pre performance evaluation the key practice variables to improve your predictive skills for successful outcomes. The more you can consciously perform this process you will naturally increase your purposeful intent to get results.

Key practice variables are more important than others, and require more conscious awareness skills to learn which variables should be weighted more from your personal past experience or memory bank. You must learn to assign realistic beta weights to specific key variables you feel are more important to account for the most variance and spend more time teaching, practicing, and learning. The Venn diagram shown in chapter two, Growing Antennae, indicates how variables overlap and interrelate in a predictive equation. Top performers do not waste their time with meaningless variables. Discard less relevant variables to selectively focus on only the key variables or cues to improve your learning efficiency. Your brain can accommodate and assimilate large amounts of data, but not more than five bits at a time. You can streamline the learning process to be more efficient using trigger words as a bit of information to generalize to larger amounts of stimulus - response associations. The key is having enough experience to define your needs, select a good strategy that combines your learning preferences, and the best variables for every type of equation you are consciously aware of to predict your performance quality on a criterion task.

Information Processing

Prior to 1980 your personal computer was and still is your brain, and can be compared to computer operations. Imagine a little switch at the base of your brain where the spinal column brings all that sensory information from all over your body to be processed up in your brain and turned into knowledge. When you choose to think negative thoughts your imaginary switch moves to the "off" position. Very little information will get on your "hard drive." Similarly, if you allow your senses to take in and store inappropriate and needless information like violent video games permanently in your brain they will affect your behavior. The idea that violent information from movies and games does not harm you comes from the marketers who have needs to make a profit, and their brains choose to not understand how a brain functions! This is behavioral rule # 8:

You learn what you focus on.

Your brain works like a computer to process information. It can be programmed with a purposeful intent to recognize value, and meaningful and relevant information with pre cognitive cues and strategies you have been taught and are familiar with the S-R connections from practice. Microprocessors in computers keep getting faster, and software programs function better with more ram memory. Your ram memory is your prefrontal cortex that acts like a short term bridge to your long term memory file storage. The more experience and associational neurons you can link together like Einstein chose to do with multi sensory learning, you will be more efficient at drawing upon the vast amount of your stored knowledge. Your historical hereditary DNA may also be passed on to you.

The theoretical construct for purposeful intent is that you can more readily recognize, receive, organize, store, and retrieve information you learn to cognitively choose as valuable, meaningful, and relevant from your past familiar experience and your future predicted unfamiliar experience.

Consider these logical points of view:

1) You cannot appreciably increase your intelligence until you choose to increase your awareness of what is valuable, meaningful, and relevant. Unintelligent performers, for unknown reasons, block their need to learn this valuing process.

2) Do you know of any top performer that does not display a high awareness?

3) Do you know of any top performer that ever waited for the approval of another person?

4) Top performers use their prior and past performances as the personal standard they can control to continuously self-evaluate and improve their performance.

5) Top performers know what a quality performance looks like but are not always able to describe the process strategies to be successful.

6) Average and successful performers who are conditioned to wait for the approval of others do not generally develop leadership skills.

7) To stay motivated and on task, you must experience occasional feelings of personal reward and satisfaction for your work accomplished. This is a feeling you must choose to learn and feel inside your soul. This feeling is not dependent on what others think of you. You know the feeling and choose to assign value and strength to help you persist in your work.

8) When you choose to be unaware of your work accomplished to feel rewarded, you become stale or burned out. Your work and relationships suffer when you choose to lower and extinguish your PI strength with routine subconscious behaviors.

9) Nothing valuable or good is ever accomplished without a positive PI. How you reward your smallest positive behaviors depends on how you choose to feel. By increasing your conscious awareness to reflect on the work to achieve your goals, you enhance your self-evaluation and motivation to keep improving.

Set Up Correct Standard Performance Comparison

There are all sorts of standards you can use to compare your past performance or new expected performance. I have studied top performing athletes and coaches for a long time. They all set up a model for continuous performance improvement. The premise is that you cannot control what the other performer is going to do, but you can control what you focus on and try to improve. The other fact is that it is hard for anyone, including yourself, to criticize your performance when you improve your personal best and gave it your all. This is why Michael Jordan or Tiger Woods got or get better. They kept evaluating their performance against the personal standard they created – that of improving upon their own immediate past performance or average. That is the easy part. The hard part is devoting more concentrated purposeful effort to value your work to ensure your performance improvement. Watching the 2008 Olympic Games, Michael Phelps was totally devoted to swimming. He limited the distractions because the passion for something of value in an achievement can live on forever in your heart and mind; no one can take that accomplishment away from you. You have to decide what you will give up to manage your time, and weigh that against your committed time. At least be certain that you do not rely only on a comparison to local competition or standards. I personally would hate to make all A's in high school, and then find I was just average when I went to college, or lacked common sense to direct my life.

Learning to Improve Performance

As the leader you must ask, "What will you teach your performers who are not learning how to improve?" There are skills and process strategies that have been described. They take time to learn and become familiar with each new task. You need good teachers and trainers who apply the same learning process to their performance to know how and when to expect their performers to improve. If your expectations exceed reality, there will be frustration on both sides. When you know the probability for achievement is high, you have no excuse and your drive motivation is higher. When the probability to achieve your goal is very low, you build in numerous excuses to protect your ego and your drive motivation to achieve is lower. You don't care if you improve because your high frustration impedes your learning. The process of learning is to demonstrate improvement in the application of knowledge. You must change your behavior, and this may mean working on parts of your personality. Training programs spend more time evaluating performance (extrinsic) than to teach the performer how to evaluate their own performance with rubrics and do overs (intrinsic). Research indicates that intrinsic motivation is more powerful than extrinsic to improve learning. Progressive companies ask employees to self-evaluate their performance prior to discussing the manager's evaluation. This is to determine congruence. If the congruence is high matching, your performer is more likely to be intrinsically motivated and continue to improve when you are not looking. It is that simple. Another helpful standard is W. Edwards Deming's (1982) 14 principles of Total Quality Management (TQM) listed in the appendix. Deming used these principles to help rebuild Japan after World War II, and later published them in <u>Out Of The Crisis</u>. If you study Deming's 14 principles, they still apply today to motivate management performance improvement.

Performance Criteria System

All throughout your life others have been imposing their performance criteria and goals upon you. These are extrinsic until you learn how to select and apply performance goals for yourself to be intrinsic. Select your leaders and their experiential knowledge carefully to learn from them. Some leaders may have the success credits to coach you, but more probably the criteria imposed by others can never be as powerful a motivator as those self-evaluated criteria you learn to impose upon yourself. As a leader you must be careful in the criteria you impose. Consult with your performers to devise realistic and achievable criteria that impose a mutually agreed upon quality standard to challenge every performer to improve. When you go away, you want your performers to understand how to develop this skill to continuously improve for a lifetime. <u>Top performers create their own self-evaluation system with self-imposed benchmarks, and hold themselves accountable for reaching their goals.</u> The greatest basketball player of all time, Michael Jordan, was cut from the varsity high school team as a sophomore. His North Carolina college coach, Dean Smith, rated Michael a good basketball player among the many he had coached. But no one, including Michael, could have ever predicted that he had within him the purposeful intent to keep improving his skills to perfection using a set of criteria only known to him that he kept perfecting to demand more of his ability. Michael Jordan acquired his criteria through an educational process learned in the home with a strong discipline imposed by his mother, and the standards of excellence to continuously challenge his fundamental skills development set by his coaches and teachers. Michael Jordan elevated his Planer Thinking ability to envision more and more to test his limits and be a complete player. As his performance would exceed his immediate past performance it would automatically create a new standard to improve. Using this goal setting strategy you become a top performer over time. Jordan's pre-performance self-evaluation proved a quality standard with a need to improve that set his positive attitude for each new performance. He desired and created the need to pay the price for success through learning an intense value system to try and do your best started at an early age usually by the mother. This enabled him to be in control and take accountability for performance improvement. The more Michael Jordan succeeded in small rewarding increments, the greater rewards he could feel to reinforce his work ethic.

The Quality of Individuality

Our schools strive to improve through school improvement criteria, but too often the stakeholders – teachers and students – take these efforts for granted and regard them as a waste of their time. Teachers and building administrators routinely forget the mission statement or the vision, values, beliefs, goals, or objectives of the district.

In the 1950's many Americans thought that people who played 'Rock-n'-Roll' music were sinners because those who showed free expression in the dance to these tunes looked so different to suggest a moral decadence. Two men named Gates and Job dropped out of Stanford University to work in a garage and create the personal computer because they had the vision to see a need and became billionaires! As the next leader, how do you know if you will be next? How do you know who will be the next Picasso, Jordan, Gates, Einstein, or Edison? The current example is swimmer Michael Phelps who earned eight gold medals in the 2008 Beijing Olympic Games. What is certain is that these individuals learned how to learn to think, act, and do for themselves and eventually others. They came from environments that I suggest created their purposeful intent by how they increased their awareness, self-evaluation, and reward-reinforcement, and by not copying others. When reporters tried to compare Michael Phelps to the previous great Olympic swimmer, Mark Spitz, Michael replied that he was not Mark Spitz; he was Michael Phelps. You can never be a creator as your Creator has intended for you if all you learn to do is copy other performers. There are specific PI skills to learn and then lead others to perform them as unique individuals when you have grasped them. You are created for a unique purpose. Your main goal in life is to learn what you are gifted in talent and ability, and develop those skills to eventually share and teach others to follow in your footsteps, not as copies but as uniquely talented individuals envisioning new worlds. Michael Phelps's greater vision is to change how competitive swimming is viewed in the world. This dichotomy of being a performer with needs or the need to copy others without knowing your purpose and be less innovative is a factor in self-evaluation for pre performance. Being a performer with identified needs to satisfy with a purpose will set up apart from all the rest, and will provide you with more unique success in your lifetime. The best part is you get to be yourself.

Personal Personality Assessment

Take time to reflect on your past performance behavior and learn who you are. Are you honest with yourself and others to hold yourself accountable for your performance improvement? This is your integrity. Are you in a normal range or off the wall in your behavior? Do you think things through before you act, like this exercise is suggesting you do before you perform? Are you inner or outer directed? Your ability to perform as you expected to perform suggests realism, and is an important personality trait of top performers. Obviously being persistent and committed with some will power is important. However, if you have phobias and addictions, I doubt you have self control over your performance. Assess where you are going in life, and plan for the necessary changes to succeed starting now. Write down specific measurable steps as goals with realistic time frames for their achievement. A lot can be accomplished in a year when you know your goals and purpose.

Self-Discipline

Discipline and motivation are not synonymous. They are co-dependent upon reward and reinforcement. When you apply self-discipline you understand what your needs are and why you want to perform. You know what it takes to produce a quality performance, and adhere to a strict personal set of criteria you know will more highly predict your success to produce value by the quality of your effort and reward. When others apply discipline to you it is extrinsic and less meaningful as a means to control your behavior. The effect provides negative reinforcement in avoidance behaviors, but does little to refocus on your positive behaviors for good outcomes. In an educational system, what matters most is the evaluation performers receive from others. Performers learn to limit their capacity for growth to an imposed standard. This has been the greatest single fault of American public education. Our system of education is very controlling and external discipline oriented to create order and sameness and not motivate creativity by individuality. Every top performer has had to overcome this kind of reinforcement system. Our culture looks distastefully at others who would be different by their personal success. If you talk of your success, you are arrogant and conceited. Lesser performers often add swear words for emphasis after arrogant and conceited. I do not think you have to fear success. However, winning carries the responsibility of being a role model to other performers and creates the need and sometimes personal pressure to keep improving your skills. If you are a winner and mentally tough, all you want to do is win. If you suggest your opinion to management leaders you can be labeled a trouble maker and don't get to play or get traded and sometimes fired for challenging your leaders. To understand a winner is to know what PI strength means to be consistently successful over time. Other cultures have experienced this same problem. A Japanese proverb states it best, "Tallest nail gets pounded down first." Christians learned from what happened to Jesus that people "kill the messenger." Top performers want change to create success. Average and below average performers find that change upsets their comfort zone to create unpleasant stress in their personality.

The difference lies in who directs the show. Top performers want to be more in control of their lives, and be accountable more to themselves than to others. They desire to improve their personal rather than group performance standard if they think there are a bunch of deadbeats not doing their job in the group, but who want the same credit. The extrinsic motives are much different when they are applied by others than when they are intrinsically applied from within the performer. In a group or team, each performer must know and accept their shared performance role. This is what made the 2008 United States Men's Olympic basketball team so great on and off the court. The managerial leaders, Jerry Colangelo, and coach Mike Krzyzewski, the assistant coaches, and players deserve all the credit. Personal leadership can be taught in the form of purposeful intent principles to overcome such obstacles and "stay the course," and learn to "think outside of the box." As the leader, you must trust your performers to learn PI skills to apply to their personal behaviors and increase their motivation to achieve consistent improvement.

Achieving Confidence

Your confidence is achieved by positive experiences that you feel are successful. Positive performance feedback improves the retention value for knowledge and applied skills. This brings up Behavioral Rule # 9:

It is natural behavior to remember more positive than negative experiences.

This notion has recently been supported in the research literature by K. Sakai, J Rowe and R. Passingham (2002), "Active maintenance in prefrontal area 46 creates distractor-resistant memory," in *Nature Neuroscience 5, 479-484*. You can improve your odds to frequently attain a positive experience by selecting a goal strategy one point better than your own immediate past performance or performance average. By practicing actual performance simulations, you increase your positive feedback and purposeful intent. You can transfer more task familiar knowledge to your actual performance with a higher probability of success. Confidence is having the pre-performance feeling that the actual performance will be successful. This perception is based on the immediate past performance feedback. All performers learn about the rate and progress of their learning from processing their own performance feedback. Successful sales persons value their product's features and benefits to meet the needs of their clients. Specialists in mergers and acquisitions value their market analysis before the actual performance. Understanding the valuing process is an essential component of pre-performance evaluation to achieve confidence.

Feedback Awareness Output-Input

The B.F. Skinner feedback loop shown in chapter three, Growing Antennae, helps you to understand how to use your own performance output as feedback to make changes in your input cues and strategies to create an improved performance output on the next trial. Eventually parents, teachers, mentors, and managers will go away. You are what you perform. Denial of the good or bad will not serve you. Try out new cues for input and observe the output. After some time and practice with a variety of cues, you can subjectively figure out which ones are best to teach or use that predict performance improvement. This is what the great coaches and better teachers have done for you. You can improve the skill of observing and evaluating your performance input to output when you are taught how to prioritize unconscious streams of output to a conscious value level by the purposeful effort you apply to improving that skill. Top performers continuously self-evaluate their performance and advance their personal standards to continuously improve. This is how Michael Jordan went from winning one to six NBA Championships. You can do this by learning how to process your own feedback. Processing and evaluating personal feedback can be easy by keeping a simple performance log or diary. You can keep logs to chart your performance improvements. When you see steady improvement, your motivation will be better than if you attempt to improve in leaps and bounds that are inconsistent.

Choice Psychology – Burnout, Boredom, and Staleness

If you are bored, change your focus from negative to positive. Construct your purpose for performing the activity to increase your enjoyment and reward for any accomplishment. Young performers lack a variety of experience because they choose activities that decrease their sensory awareness. They are easily bored because they have not learned to apply any of The Triad skills. The focus is on entertainment instead of knowledge acquisition. Valuable time is spent using entertainment tools such as portable music players, mindless TV, instant messaging, repetitive electronic games, socializing, and in extremes self-medicating with drugs and alcohol that do not increase their awareness. Parents and the adult society enable these kinds of behaviors to not have to deal with their children or to make a profit on their stupidity. Entertainment and social emotional learning take precedence over academic learning with an imagination to acquire more knowledge. Whether you are young or old, **boredom, burnout, and staleness comes from not having learned how to increase your personal sensory and perceptual awareness skills**. The awareness skill is essential to recognize the cues for learning new skills and smaller accomplishments you achieve and self reward to reinforce a positive feeling about your work. Hard work without awareness of smaller rewards causes burnout and staleness. You have to see the light at the end of the tunnel to stay motivated. The old adage, "you get out of life what you put into it" applies only when you connect reward to what you put in. Several strategies are shown in bold print to increase your awareness. You can **create** your personal purposeful intent by learning to consciously **value** your work and efforts that increase reward value. The simplest method is **positive self-talk**. Tell your brain how important the activity is to learn and perform, and to recognize the **sequence** to all the necessary **cues**. Prior to performing the work, remind yourself what your **purpose** must be to **focus** on the potential **outcome** goal. In this way you create the need to improve your goal and feel rewarded. This may bring physical pain to a conscious level during the work, but you can turn this negative into a positive outcome by deciding that your competition is not working as hard as you to deserve to win. This is how better than average performers become familiar with pain and block it out keeping their focus on the process rather than focus on the negative response during the later stages of top performances. In your pre performance evaluation planning, you want to mentally condition by visualizing in your personal instant replay movie a positive outcome for anticipated situations. The phrase, "heart of a champion" means that the champion has conditioned a replacement reward response to a painful stimulus to displace feeling that pain. Your will-power to block pain comes from a stronger focus on the positive reward or a specific skill strategy you pre-condition to succeed where others who are untrained in bringing physical muscle pain to a conscious level in practice will fail during the performance. Bored sensory deprived kids and adults choose to view any kind of work as a pain because they have not learned how to pre-condition a reward expectation to stay focused on a task. You always have the choice to look at your glass as half empty taking the negative view or as half full to take a positive view for all the little improvements in intermediate goal sub routines that you have made to reward parts of the larger performance.

Set Realistic Goals

You may have an ultimate goal, but your motivation is stronger focusing on each intermediate goal leading up to achieving that goal. Top performers consistently set their goals only one point or slightly better than their own immediate past performance or average. This increases their probability for success and brings up Behavioral Rule # 10:   The more frequently you feel rewarded you are more likely to be motivated to improve your performance to keep that good feeling.

Average performers compare their past performance to the performances of group members they associate with their activities. Top performers, on the other hand, prefer to use their own immediate past performance as the PAP or perceptual anchoring point about which to value a new goal. Another common goal setting strategy is a mnemonic known as the SMART method:

- **S**pecific - the goal is defined
- **M**easurable - in number term objectives
- **A**chievable – for your abilities
- **R**elevant – to fulfill a personal need
- **T**imely - close to the performance

It would be wise to use a combination of your own immediate past performance and the SMART method to motivate performance improvement.

Great Expectations

You cannot expect to lead yourself or others basing your criteria on the average performance of a group or what your critics may say. You do not want to make predictions based on your perceptions of what you think will happen more than using your own past performance history as your feedback guide. Top performers with their own criteria do not wait for the approval of another person. You may choose to increase your drive level by verbally stating your goals with positive self-talk. To avoid bruising your ego, you will be motivated to find a way to perform as you stated to others. These personality trait concepts were discussed in Chapter I, Overview of Purposeful Intent. The greatest predictor of your success in pre-performance evaluation and be realistic is to set low positive goals only slightly better than your own immediate past performance or performance average. No other variable can increase your drive level to succeed better than this one. When you increase your probability for success by strongly adhering to purposeful intent principles, you enhance your personal reward system. The more reward you feel and value, the more you condition your system to work hard to repeat those behaviors to experience more rewards. The great advantage this goal strategy has is that the personal standard to improve constantly adjusts as you improve and make it your immediate past performance. This simple low positive goal setting strategy applies to intermediate goals when you cannot expect to perform at a championship or ultimate goal level all season long. There are learning curves that look like a lazy "S" shape similar to Planer Thinking curves and plateaus as your performance will improve, plateau, and sometimes with the introduction of a new cue slightly decrease until your feedback system makes sense of the new information and performance

Typical Learning Curve

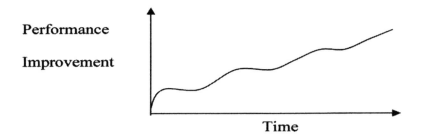

begins to improve. Coaching leaders explain this process to their performers. Teachers have not explained or conditioned this strategy for their students. In school systems that rely heavily on one-time chances to perform with no "do overs," students, especially in the elementary grades, are more reinforced to compete to turn in assignments on time rather than provide a quality effort. When extrinsic pressure to meet goals applied by others increases, the quality of performance decreases because the goal expectation has not been set by the performer to increase intrinsic motivation. To have long term success you must consciously equate quality of effort with quality of reward to reinforce your future efforts. When performers have the opportunity to improve the quality of their performance with do overs, they take more pride in their achievement to value their education. More knowledge is placed on their "hard drive" for later use. If you are taught how to set low positive goals, you will enhance your personal reward system. This increases your personal motivation and quality of effort to support the conclusion that success breeds success. You need to convince your teachers to act like coaches to strive to improve every child's performance to their fullest potential by helping them learn to see their frequent success in smaller intermediate tasks in the classroom or with homework assignments. Failure is not an option when learning is the ultimate outcome. Plan with good pre performance evaluation skills, and you will more often put yourself in position to be successful.

Perfecting Sub Routines

Top athletes make wonderful subjects to study what they do to efficiently learn and improve their skills. They succeed in short periods of time. The skills they naturally apply but are not always able to describe, we can learn from to teach other performers outside of athletics to apply to their performance skills. By questioning a top performer for any skill, you need to learn what cues and associated responses they attend to perform. These important cues probably predict higher values for learning to efficiently improve performance, and should be emphasized in practice. The problem you have is getting the top athlete to describe what they do unconsciously. Most have highly developed conditioned responses to cues they no longer have to think about to perform. For example, in 1976 I was teaching golf skills to a class of physical education majors and elective students at Furman University. Two of my students were Betsy King and Beth Daniel. Both were members of our National Championship golf team and were later elected to the Women's Professional Golf Hall of Fame. Betsy was a magician with a golf iron. She could hit cut shots to bend the ball around a bush or tree on an uphill or downhill lie, and tell you how to do it. I asked Beth to demonstrate and teach putting to the class. She had perfect form, but could not fully describe what she was doing. Today she is an outstanding golf commentator on television and Betsy heads up a foundation to help African aids victims by developing schools. Her website is www.GolfForeAfrica.org.

On a personal level, I have developed sub routines to be a five-time All-American in college swimming, and later to set Masters World Records for my age group. I strongly believe Michael Phelps could state that he had the ability to clear his mind to block out the pressure and focus on each race because he had already spent time out of the pool mentally perfecting all eight of his distinct Olympic Gold medal races as sub routines. This practice skill can be learned and applied to improve any performance task, such as taking an exam, closing a sale, prepping for a job interview, or develop a relationship with a spouse or employees.

Use your pre frontal cortex to retrieve meaningful and relevant stored feedback to create a perfect sub routine to perform exactly as you programmed it. Top performers, prior to performing, will create positive images of successful performances. Visualization is the technique of making a mental movie of your performance prior to actually performing. You can stop action, and slow motion forward or reverse for critical analysis to correct specific S-R connections. This allows you to focus on and program details you cannot normally achieve during the actual performance. The process is like writing code for a computer program to flow in the correct iteration sequence. *Mental practice* is an adjunct to physical practice that is effective when you have had prior experience with the task or activity. The more experience you have stored from practice and high level competition like Michael Phelps has had provides a distinct advantage to perfect your sub routines.

You set up your movie and practice rehearsing your physical motions in the correct sequence. This works well for specific routines where the response for the previous stimulus becomes the new stimulus for the next response in the series. Analyze your activity for a closed loop or continuous serial loop like running and swimming or an open loop with a specific starting and stopping point like bowling, archery, tennis, golf, basketball, or typing.

Closed Serial Loop

Open Serial Loop

Focus on the specific S-R connections of cues and response feelings to mentally practice the association for faster cue recognition and response. It is doubtful the actual speed of nerve transmission is much faster, but there is evidence of electrical activity in specific muscle groups during mental practice. The two strategies often used are *key hole* which is to visualize performance details looking through an imaginary key hole of a door to narrow your focus, and eliminate distractions. The other strategy is *third eye* where your performance movie is taken from the camera lens view instead of your eyes as if you had a third eye watching you from behind to observe every cue and response detail. Some performers refer to this as looking through a different lens where you can focus a close up or far away view to observe your body parts in space, and project how you might feel at each stage of your performance.

Mobilization of Energy

The expected outcome of energy mobilization is *peak performance* and getting into the *zone*. However, equally important are increasing *focused concentration* and *mental tension control*. Nervous energy, if not directed properly, can sap your energy and ability to concentrate. It will deplete your muscle glycogen or fuel needed to perform. Some techniques shown in italics are used to control nervous tension. *Diaphragmatic breathing* you inhale more by lowering your diaphragm than by raising your chest wall. *Relaxation training* initially authored by Jacobsen (1938) is also popular to control tension. You lie down and initially contract a muscle group, and then consciously feel the tension being released from the muscles. Top athletes may also prefer to listen to *energizing music* like the theme from the movie *Rocky*, or other favorite to distract their thoughts temporarily away from the competition. Energizing music becomes associated and conditioned with your response. Like *mental practice*, it is used to program a perfected sub routine ready to execute as another file in your computer. You simply add the music to your movie. *Positive self-talk* is what it implies. You focus your highest concentration on positive performance for the entire sequence of the sub routine. *Trick your brain* by telling your brain what to expect and perform. Then trust that you will execute the routine as you realistically programmed your performance. To effectively mobilize your energy for peak performance, your motive to achieve success must be greater than your motive to avoid failure *(MaS>MaF)*. You do not want to focus on and visualize past errors, what not to do or avoid, or watch other competitors immediately prior to your performance. Watching others creates a visual bit map of their performance in your short term memory. Several United States women's Olympic gymnasts made this critical mistake in the 2008 Beijing Games. Then they made unusual performance errors because their programmed sub routines were disrupted. The visual sensations are dominant to 'monkey see, monkey do.' You don't want to program their bit map, you want your bit map sub routine in short term memory. This is why you create a pre performance routine.

Increasing Your Pre-Performance Thinking

One more Behavioral Rule is # 11:
You will repeat behaviors you feel rewarded, and reduce unrewarded behaviors.

Top performers are highly aware of their performance skills and abilities to experience success more often that conditions their work ethic to feel self-reward more frequently. Performers quit or stop putting out effort to improve their skills in an activity because they have not learned to recognize and feel success from smaller parts of complex tasks. They have been conditioned to feel all or none for the whole performance. Patience and understanding are important to give yourself time to learn and master new skills. Drop outs occur when the performer cannot make these connections to feel rewarded more frequently, and know their purpose and role to be committed to improving. More than half of your life you will work alone on tasks you choose to fulfill. There will be no one but you to criticize or praise your work, evaluate, or reward. You will not be in school forever. At some point you must choose to learn to learn on your own. American school systems condition a boss-management mentality to direct masses of students instead of conditioning in each student intrinsic motivation skills to be in charge of their learning to make new knowledge meaningful and relevant. Hopefully, you can learn the PI skills to increase your awareness, enhance your self-evaluation, and connect reward with reinforcement to stay motivated, committed, and persistent to produce quality achievements you can feel proud of inside. In the long term, your body of work will speak for itself. You will know your success because your successes will far exceed your failures. Do you know any top performer that gave up because they could not connect any reward with reinforcement? Look for the positive good in everything that you do and can see in the performance of others. If you keep your mind open to believe, that higher power will also help direct you to be successful.

For any activity, you want to trigger strategies to improve your positive work ethic behaviors. You can raise your conscious level of work accomplished with every practice or parts of practice to feel rewarded by keeping performance logs to gain feedback and rate your smaller improvements to parts of the whole routine. Use mental practice to imagine successful performances with the game or contest on the line and all kinds of distractions to *mentally rehearse* a positive outcome. How will you concentrate on the skilled performance and block out distractions? This strategy works best when you have more familiarity with the task. Another strategy to use is to *be your own best friend* while being a tough self-evaluator. Many performers are conditioned by others to be overly critical of their performance. It's as if to say, 'Yes, I know I made a mistake. I am upset, and I don't need you to tell me.' The result conditions negative behaviors instead of conditioning the positive improvements to several parts to increase intrinsic motivation. When performing hands on practice or conscious mental rehearsal and positive self-talk these strategies increase your awareness and value by making your performance meaningful and relevant. Your awareness of pre-performance evaluation strategies condition your need to fulfill your performance successfully to feel rewarded to value the work content and skills learning process of that activity. Unsuccessful performers seldom pre plan how they choose to perform because they have not learned to create their own purposeful intent (awareness, self-evaluation, reward-reinforcement Triad). As the leader help your performers understand their personal needs and common purpose. Performers who do not have a strong purposeful intent automate their routine tasks that lower their values. This results in inconsistent average performances. Conversely, consistently successful performers create a purposeful intent to increase their awareness levels to a higher conscious state to value the work they perform prior to the notable performances that increases their need or drive to feel rewarded. The successful performer is better able to mobilize all of their talents, abilities, and energies *at will on demand* to perform consistently above average for a selected moment in time. This pre-planned process starts with a realistic positive pre-performance evaluation. You set up an internal clock to prepare a set time to perform like an-alarm-to-wake-up-call by having all your systems ready to execute your plan. This process is also called *peaking*, when your best performances come at the end of your season.

Choices To Make

You have many choices to make in your pre-performance evaluation. You can look at your life as half full or half empty. You will learn and achieve what you focus your efforts on to improve whether it is mental, physical, emotional, or social skills. The child's program Sesame Street often plays this catchy tune, "Be what you want to be, learn what you want to learn." Pre plan, commit to your plan, and focus on continuous small improvement of your skills over time to be successful and feel rewarded for your efforts. Why wait for someone to tell you what to do when you can do this for yourself? Much of what you practice to learn will improve your abilities and skills if you learn to value your work to feel rewarded enough to reinforce your future efforts. You need to have some idea of your rate and progress for learning to predict a future performance. I strongly suggest you keep performance logs for all your practices and performances noting specific goals, cues, triggers, and any other kind of psychological data you like to use to aid your learning and motivate your top performance. You have to learn how to use a predictive equation to select the key variable cues and strategies and focus more attention to the higher beta weighted variables to value. You need to understand how to set personal goals based on a perceptual anchoring point known to you but unlikely known by others. You have to know how you perceive value from need based behaviors assigned to your activities and knowledge gained from your personal performance feedback. You must understand how extrinsic values set by others are their goals and less powerful than goals you set. You must learn how to create significant positive thought processes in your brain with pre-performance thinking to apply at will on demand during your performance to increase your probability of a positive outcome. These are all choices you need to make.

Set Up Pre Performance Routines

Pre performance routines clear your mind of conflicting sensations, distractions, and error messages to correct at the last minute. You apply the same routine before every performance despite changes in the environment or specific task. For example, pro golfers have a pre shot routine for each club. They set up for the tee off using the driver differently than for making a putt. But the routine is always the same. You practice them as you would any other skill. But first, set them up with a purposeful plan to know ahead of time what will work best. If you have experience and task familiarity, you know what to expect. If you lack experience performing in a new environment, then ask those who have been there and done that to know what to expect so you are not surprised. Go to a quiet place, close your eyes, and run your mental movie as you want to see yourself perform your skills. In the midst of chaos, you can still block out the noise sitting in your chair, and go to your favorite quiet place in your mind that you have already programmed and mentally practiced. Create the image. It can be a favorite peaceful vacation scene like a sunset, a reflecting pool, or simply your private bedroom lying on the bed with your head on a pillow. Add your favorite music to play in your ears immediately prior to performing like Michael Phelps. This sets the program in the ready cue, and eliminates conflicting sensations for the brain to execute the performance. This is not the time to wonder if you ate the right foods, rested enough, worked hard enough, etc. This is why you perform your checklist, and make this a routine to plan pre performance evaluation. Cramming the night before a performance test is never a good idea. It takes a minimum of five days to accommodate and assimilate information or program changes to a sub routine. Similarly it takes six to eight weeks for muscle adaptation changes; you do not get in shape physically or mentally overnight. To perfect mental skills and warm up routines, prior to performing, takes time. A good example was when Michael Jordan returned to pro basketball after a two year lay off to play baseball. His body was in shape, but it took several months to get back to basketball game shape and perform on the high skill level when he left. When your programmed sub routine has been perfected with mental practice, reviewed immediately prior to performing and placed in the ready cue, set up the final trigger to start the program. In swimming and running, the horn at the starting blocks is what you concentrate on. However, in golf or target shooting, typical open serial skills, rushing your beginning does not create good performance. Getting into a comfortable stance, aiming, and exhaling slowly relaxes the muscular tension for a smooth contraction that can aid your performance. Watch the top performers and learn why they concentrate on the sequence of their routines to perfect their performance.

Summary

Whether you are planning to perform in a sport, close a business deal, or prep for a test in school, the checklist can help you to motivate your mind from within to improve your performance. True success is being consistent and successful over time. This means you know how to improve your performance, and eventually teach others to pass on what you know. Planning is the key to success in any endeavor. Success also takes hard work to create value for your achievements that continually help you to improve your performance by faster retrieval of stored information to apply. The pre performance evaluation plan helps you define your purposeful intent. When you make this a part of your performance routine, you will significantly increase the odds for a good performance to feel rewarded for all your hard work.

Strategies To Forming Your Purposeful Intent

The key strategies to forming your state of "purposeful intent" are learning to:

1) identify your personal needs to achieve a quality of life vision,

2) create a goal setting paradigm that increases your early and frequent rewards,

3) identify your need satisfaction to reinforce your behaviors,

4) know that your greatest problem as an achiever is not feeling you are satisfying your immediate needs and taking credit for them,

5) set up a personal reward-reinforcement system by bringing routine tasks to a conscious awareness level,

6) be aware that your routine behaviors become so familiar that you automate mundane tasks to inhibit your sensory awareness and conscious learning,

7) be more conscious of your smallest achievements to reward and reinforce them, then your drive motivation to repeat your routine behaviors are increased that can lead a transfer of motivational energy to higher achievements in other areas,

8) imagine how great leaders and top performers think to create their purposeful intent to overcome criticism, adversity, and succeed where others have failed.

Numerous great leaders were once miserable failures in leadership roles in several environments. Winston Churchill's early leadership years were failures until he rallied the English people and troops to overcome the adversity and persevere in victory during World War II. Struggling professional ballplayers are traded from one environment and become great the next year in a new environment. CEO's can fail to lead one company without the support of their Board of Directors, move on to a new corporation and lead them to success. <u>Change forces you to restructure your purposeful intent</u>. Do artists, leaders, or sports heroes greatly modify their personal philosophy or do their environments dictate by social approval an acceptable set of criteria they can live and grow with to enhance them and others surrounding them personally? The answer is both are more probable. **High achievers have a sound personal philosophy and high need for achievement (N-ach) that drives their purposeful intent, creates a conducive environment, and keeps them motivated over time.** High achievers become high achievers because they set their quality standard based on their personal past performance criteria which is already much higher than other performers. They are able to become more familiar with their tasks to think on higher planes. Generally, their past performance exceeds the best performance of other performers, and there is no need to compare to that group. They are the ones who set the standard for others to perform. Sports icons provide the best examples of this behavior that can be applied to teaching intrinsic motivation as a skill that can be applied to improving any kind of performance no matter what level you start at. Michael Jordan created his own personal standards to continually improve all the skills to be a complete professional basketball player. Tiger Woods completely changed his golf swing to take his game to a higher level. Michael Phelps after winning six gold medals in the Athens Olympic Games set a goal to win eight gold medals and create an unequalled paradigm shift for competitive swimming. Performers with a high need for achievement who encounter challenging environments also impose higher quality personal expectations for the two forces to merge and produce great results. This is leadership that comes from within the mind, and is intrinsic. If you practice the skills of The Triad, you will apply them for the rest of your life. Over time, you will be successful and proud of your accomplishments; hopefully enough to help others.

During Performance Evaluation

*"Wise man envisions opportunity;
intelligent man capitalizes on it."*

Andrew Christian

Objective: Learn to evaluate your feedback during performance to make
simple adjustments that immediately enhance your performance.

Introduction

Timing is everything. Top performers have the awareness to sense when to
mobilize their energy and increase their performance output a notch or two when it
counts the most. Emotion or arousal is critical to apply the energy to peak perform.
I coined the term *at will on demand* to indicate that this process is a learned and
conditioned response by all top performers who sense when and can increase their
energy level in very short preparation time.

However, performance and emotion have been linked. A classic study in 1908
became known as the Yerkes-Dodson Law, and the relationship looked like an
inverted U-shaped curve shown in the figure.
Performance improved as anxiety or emotion
increased, but only to an optimal level
after which when exceeded performance
decreased. The top performer has years of
experience with a variety of stressors, and
conditioned responses from practice and
competition to control their anxiety. They
raise or lower their anxiety to meet their
level of performance with a concept I have

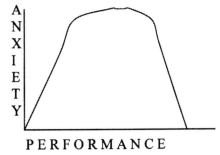

Yerkes-Dodson Law

A N X I E T Y

PERFORMANCE

introduced as *at will on demand*. Another new concept I introduced is *task familiarity*. During competition or on the job, you do not have the advantage of practice to condition a familiar response to a stressor, and your anxiety will increase more for an unfamiliar task.

Your ability to modify your performance during the performance is based on prior conditioned stimulus-response connections that you can draw upon to refocus and motivate your mind from within on the current task. Much like how a complex skill is broken down into component parts to set goals, see improvement, and reward work ethic behaviors to keep improving, the process for modifying your performance during the performance is similar. For example, whether you are performing your part in a game or making a presentation to work to close a deal, each can be broken down into sub routines or parts. Once you acquire the experience with all the parts, you can put them all together for a top overall performance. The conditioning is to connect all the stimulus-response connections you can think of prior to actually performing, and practicing them over and over to perfect those skills. This is to perform RROSR and become familiar with each task in training or on the job. There may be hundreds of small connections all linked together. After you have some experience you learn which connections you perform the best under a variety of emotional stress. These are your fundamentals that even the top performers will continually work on and not take for granted to make them mundane tasks on a subconscious level. When you automate familiar routine tasks to a subconscious awareness level, you are not as able to energize yourself at will on demand.

During your performance, you note that you have made a few errors and your performance is not going as you pre planned. What do you do? Your choices are limited already. You can continue and lose, fold up your tent and go home, let your opponent exploit your weaknesses without exploiting theirs, or you can decide to refocus on your strengths and perform as well as you can. This is where the third new concept I introduced was MaS>MaF. The odds are not good to modify any performance if you focus on your motives to avoid failure. You must focus on the specific pre planned familiar fundamental cues you perform best to rebuild your confidence. If you are the individual performer, you don't need a coach or teacher or manager to tell you to refocus and get back on track. Just do it. A classic example was in the 1961 movie *The Hustler* starring Jackie Gleason who played a pool shark named Minnesota Fats. In a match he was getting soundly beaten at his own game. He took a time out and went into the bathroom to wash his hands, look himself in the mirror, and came back to win the overall match. There are all kinds of ways to refocus, but you need to condition the responsive steps you will make into a routine when things are not going your way. Then execute that routine. There are dependent variables you need to control such as the amount of time you will have. If your performance does not have time outs, or you cannot break during an interview, you have to literally define your next move. Keep it simple so that your brain has time to process the information as input. If you are overly emotional or super aroused even mad, you need to put yourself back in charge of your brain to direct your mind and body to work together.

Rely on Feedback During Performance

You know quality when you see it even if you cannot describe it. You also know: 1) how you perform under similar circumstances, 2) have some projection for how you can perform under less pressure, 3) have a goal for how you would like to perform, and 4) have current performance input-output. Racing through your mind are many ideas that take away your ability to concentrate on performing one or two essential fundamentals. When times get tough, others who extrinsically motivate you to meet their needs could care less about your hurt feelings. They expect you to do the extra ordinary to satisfy their needs, but in reality the exact opposite is what you need to focus on performing – to meet your refocused immediate need to perform **ONLY** what you can do best now. As the leader, coach, or manager of a team of performers, you must quickly remind each performer of their role and fundamental expectations they are capable of performing. Pull your performers, take a time out, stall, but huddle up those key performers fast and trigger the response you have practiced and conditioned them to perform. Bring their anxiety level back down by changing the expectation to a specific smaller element of the whole performance that each performer can perform well as a part of the team. You are not going to get back into the game in one play. It will take more rewards than that to build their confidence. What follows are a series of strategies to evaluate your performance during performance and refocus your energy to perform what you are conditioned to do best.

The Feedback Loop

The B.F. Skinner "Black Box" feedback loop was presented in chapter three, Growing Antennae, to increase your awareness for your personal performance feedback. You cannot control what teammates or competitors are thinking, but you can control your focus to concentrate on what stimulus-response connections you can perform best under the circumstances. As a teacher-leader or coach, all you can do is present and modify the input cues and look at the performance output result. Every performer processes information differently because of their varied past experience, and you have to adjust the input cues in varied ways until you get the correct personal output. Later, during performance, those cues that work best become the most reinforced triggers to refocus that performer. In sport psychology, we call a performer who has too much anxiety, "over-amped." There is too much juice running through their nervous system. Nervous performers who are less than confident will have sweaty cold hands in a warm room. Perhaps nothing kills an interview or welcome faster than to present your self with a cold hand.

As described in chapter one, Science of Purposeful Intent, normal behavior conditions the desire to repeat rewarded and pleasurable behaviors and avoid painful responses to activities. If you touch an electric cattle fence and get a strong jolt you do not respond by saying, "Gosh, that was fun, let's do it again!" Nor does a poor job performance by a performer who cares to value their performance want to repeat unrewarded negative experiences. For the leader, teacher, or coach all you can do is evaluate the output coming from your performer's "black box" and compare it to known successful patterns of behavior. Neither you nor your performers enjoy poor performance below what was expected during a performance. Both need to lower the expectations and focus on what they do best to increase the probability for any kind of reward to motivate performance improvement. If you try the impossible, you decrease your probability for success and reward. This reinforces a further slide downward, and is often seen as a momentum swing. The ability of the performers has not changed, but their short term outlook and motivation has changed for lack of frequent reward seen as meeting what they expected to do. That expectation became the group perceptual anchoring point, and as the performer or leader you must understand the concept and make an immediate adjustment. As the leader you need to communicate the difference between what you see performed and what you expect to be performed from your past experience. If the output is not correct, you will need to keep changing the performer's perceptual input practice cues and strategies until you get the correct output.

It is extremely important to get off to a good start in any kind of performance. Focus on performing your most familiar sequences or routines. Your quality of achievement is defined by familiar cues you focus on during your performance. Your familiar task experience happens with specific practice to connect appropriate responses to the selected cues. Top performers with more experience in specific tasks are paid more to perform their skills to achieve results that other less experienced performers cannot perform as efficiently. Subtle subconscious cues for peak performance are consciously automated by skilled performers who enhance their performance feedback system to a higher level. My hypothesis is that the cues and enhanced performance feedback you use to increase your awareness with purposeful intent skills assign more value and meaning to each activity. This aids your learning and performing as these data are stored as compressed bit maps in various lobes of the brain. Then prior to and during performance, your pre frontal cortex creates sub routines by immediate retrieval at will on demand of the compressed bit maps required to execute the performance. When you unconsciously go through the motions of practice and learning, you assign less value and significance and store data in parts of your brain that take longer to retrieve. You know a quality performance when you see it. You cannot define the cues and strategies used to learn the quality performance because they are specific perceptions in the mind of the performer. The German term for this insight is called a "Gestalt" or concept of the whole. Your brain observes the performance pattern and stores hundreds of specific S-R connections in sequence as one bit of information. These video bit maps easily compare to your immediate and past performances. The strategy you need to learn is to mentally visualize an image of your performance in your brain as if you were video taping it. Actual video can be digitally superimposed over a top performer to compare subtle differences. You still need to perceive when to trigger the proper cue in the sequence that allows for information processing time.

Types of Feedback

Traditional visual and verbal feedbacks dominate your system. Biofeedback comes from your biological sensations. You can become consciously aware of your heart and respiratory rates, blood pressure, digestion, urination and bowel pressure, and adrenal gland to control before and during competition *at will on demand*. Sensory motor feedback comes from all your senses and motor or kinesthetic system in your muscles. Sensory input comes from your vision, hearing, smell, taste, and feeling. Motor or kinesthetic feedback comes from the muscle spindle that surrounds your muscle fibers and the Golgi tendon body in your tendons to measure the speed and rate of muscle contraction to apply physical force. If you focus on your fine motor skills, you can become a craftsman or highly skilled performer. If you consciously sense feedback from a specific muscle group that is not performing fast enough, you learn to condition psychological triggers to stimulate these tissues to work faster. When a muscle group is getting fatigued, you direct your brain to make the muscles work faster with stronger impulses. For example, you can say, 'faster, faster, faster.' This has the *refocus effect* of blocking the pain while specifically directing the muscle group to perform under stress. Then you want to concentrate on form. Speeding up muscles that are not applying the force correctly is a waste of your time. You learn and condition your performance speed and accuracy at the same rate. Your muscle speed or endurance is dependent upon your inherited and physically conditioned number of grey fast twitch – speed, or red slow twitch – endurance muscle fibers.

Refocus: Turn Negatives Into Positives

Take a brief moment if you can during the performance to reflect on your specific immediate past performance. When you performed a task successfully in a specific way, you had a defined purpose. When you wanted to do well, you relied on a natural drive to see improvement. This was your intent. When you put these two things together, you get purposeful intent. Mistakes happen by chance for lack of planning or having a positive purposeful intent. You can learn a lot by observing professional athletes who already have advanced physical skills. In short periods of observation you can learn the effect of specific positive or negative consequences on their sports performance. How did they refocus their attention to different cues to get better responses, and turn a mistake into a success? These are those "momentum swings." Observe what happens when a player sinks a few baskets or putts or makes a hit with a player in scoring position; their whole mood changes. You see a smile or glow that exudes confidence for the next several trials. Conversely, when an error occurs, you can focus on that mistake and make another right after it because you have not refocused your energy into a positive purposeful intent. What can you learn from these examples? In sport psychology, the strategy is to condition how to "let go" and refocus on select cues to correctly perform the next skill. You pre-condition the focus on how to recognize a specific cue to perform the correct associated response that you have simulated in practice. This specific practice helps you transfer the identical elements to the competitive situation. Rather than focus on and condition the mental image of the error, you refocus on the positive image from practice and prior experience of the correct response. If things are really going badly during your competition or in life, you must resist the temptation to try to get it all back on the next play or in one day of your life. Those would involve luck and not skills, and would not change your focus to a purposeful intent to know how and why you need to change to take the necessary steps to improve. The sports applications can be applied to your life. Look at all those different dieting plans that don't provide you with the skills to change your behavior permanently with a purposeful intent. It is harder to lead others when you cannot demonstrate your ability to lead yourself.

For all those past performances that you had a purposeful intent, whether you won the competition or aced the test, you can bet that you had better than 95-99% success that increased the value of the learning experience; you could take away something of value for your effort. Now compare these to your performances when you were just going through the motions with a negative attitude like "I hate school" or "I don't like …," and had no purposeful intent. You can bet that better than 50% of those performances were unsuccessful, had little value, and wasted your time. Your time to learn is valuable, you can earn more money but you can't earn more time. You can become more skilled at motivating the components of your mind to produce more frequent and consistent success, and over time you will reap the rewards.

Input Phase

Think about what perceptual stimulus your performer is thinking. You observe the performance output as a visual pattern you choose to compare to a standard or model. For your brain to learn and effect changes in your performance behavior, you must raise your level of conscious awareness that is Part One in The Triad of PI leadership skills training. Refocus on an already learned and practiced correct cue or strategy to change the negative to positive performance output. You can "shape" behavior by conditioning with repeated practice correct stimulus-response input cues and performance output connections in moderated sequences that are chained together for the whole pattern. A big mistake during performance is to point out the performance error. A mental comparison of the performance error with what was expected has already taken place. To talk about the error creates a mental image and conditions that behavior. The best strategy is to refocus only on the correct cue to get the correct output. In learning an unfamiliar task, your input is not yet sequentially organized to associate with similar stored information to readily retrieve and use. Consequently, your output is inconsistent as a large wavy line of a servo-mechanism in a heat seeking missile. As you learn to consciously self-evaluate your immediate performance output as feedback, your succeeding input is modified in relation to the perceptual cues given by your leader or that you find provide more success. Your inconsistent wavy output line straightens out as your performance is more consistent, direct, and efficient. Early and correct cue recognition is important. Great leaders, teachers, and coaches can envision performance outcomes to get better results with learners. Novice inexperienced leaders who cannot personally perform the skills do not have knowledge of the perceptual cues that predict highest to get more positive trials and faster performance results. You need to understand how to communicate feedback skills to your performers so they can learn to improve on their own. Rather than condition your performers to wait and respond to your evaluation, they must be taught skills in how to increase their awareness, enhance their self-evaluation, and connect reward with reinforcement. These skills will increase their desire to repeat trials to perfect their skills when you are not there to lead. This feedback strategy takes time to learn, but your performers will better know how to correct during performance errors. Biofeedback is the learned awareness of changes to your body sensations in response to activities. If there is pain, where is it located? Is it sharp or dull? What past activity did you experience that may have caused the pain? What conditioning methods are you using to block pain by overriding with greater feelings to accomplish a performance goal? Pleasure states from your success feelings condition the value of your reward and performance satisfaction from your work in the same way. If you create a higher awareness of your positive feedback input to effect learning, your performance output will continue to improve. By focusing on and practicing the correct cues and strategies, you can speed up your learning to improve your immediate performance. The way to find the correct cue is to observe the correct output. When this occurs, remember what cues you were focused on. When you make an error during performance, take a mini time out in your mind to refocus on the correct cue to trigger the correct response.

Output Phase

To learn how to learn, you must identify and process your performance feedback in the output phase. You can be taught these skills prior to performing by conditioning the verbal, visual, or kinesthetic cues for the expected output. When the performance occurs, you will recognize the cues in your performance to reinforce that behavioral connection. Experience is the best teacher provided you learn how to learn with your own performance feedback. Your brain is an information processor to tell your body messages to perform that does not know right from wrong unless you condition correct responses to stimulus cues. This is your output. Your observed output can be measured subjectively or objectively by the evaluation from others like sports officials, teachers, or managers. You have the ability to learn how to use your own immediate past performance feedback and unobservable biofeedback from your tissues to stimulate your pre conditioned motives or how you feel about your performance. Your feedback helps you reflect on and judge the worth of your next performance. The conditioning process to connect a stimulus cue with a correct response is essential to learning how to learn. Your skill to apply subjective values to your feedback to see your performance improve and predict your future success is how learning occurs. What you think of your performance must matter more than what your leader thinks of your performance. You must learn to be consciously aware of your performance feedback to self evaluate the worth and value of your own performances to condition reward with reinforcement. This is the functional sequential process for learning The Triad for purposeful intent leadership skills training.

To evaluate your immediate performance feedback consciously condition specific cues to associate with correct performance responses. If you performance is not correct or as you expect, then refocus on the pre conditioned cues with a purpose to demonstrate positive performance. Use your performance feedback to set realistic goals and judge the worth of your next performance to determine your improvement even during the performance or competitions. Top performers play a significant role to visually and verbally present new performance standards to achieve by the cues they recognize and correctly respond to perform. You can reflect on the worth of your performance in comparison to approach that standard. Initially leaders provide the standards from their experience performing and studying top performers. Through repeated trials great performers and learners develop their own performance standards to challenge as their need to improve all skill components. They develop their Planer Thinking skills as they become more familiar with each level of skills performance. Top performers practice and develop their sensory motor nervous pathways to significantly improve their response time to the selected cues that predict positive performance outcomes. You are familiar with your own feedback to set realistic and achievable goal expectations for performance segments that can be adjusted during your performance evaluation. If you have the flu you tend to lower your performance goal expectations. If you have trained hard all season and now rest to taper, you can raise your performance expectations.

Types of Performance Applications

The length of performance time allows you to make gross or discrete adjustments to your conscious thinking and application. Performance time is defined by the type of physical or academic stimulus-response (S-R) skill, continuous or discrete, closed or open loop. The closed loop figure represents a repetitious continuous skill that is a series of S-R connections. The open loop figure represents a repetitious discrete skill that form an open straight line starting and stopping point in a series of S-R connections. Each response becomes the stimulus cue for the next response. By increasing your knowledge for how to successfully perform, you also increase your probability for success to reward and improve intrinsic motivation.

Open Serial Loop

$$S_1 \implies R_{S2} \implies R_{S3} \implies R_{S4} \implies R_{S5}$$

Closed Serial Loop

$$S_5 \quad R_{S1}$$
$$R$$
$$S_4 \quad R_{S2}$$
$$R$$
$$S_3 R$$

A freestyle swimmer has a repetitive closed loop response. To correct a performance error requires you to project at least two S-R connections ahead of the error connection to locate the stimulus cue to change or insert a new one. This will allow enough information processing time to recognize the new cue and connect with the proper response. Then you can condition the specific perceptual cues to trigger specific motor or muscle responses to improve their skill in practice before and during competition. The discrete open loop series in the figure are specific S-R connections to perform one time like a golf swing, basketball shot, bowling, or archery. There is a specific starting and stopping point. Once you start the application and release, you do not have time to make even minor adjustments during the movement unless you pre program them with mental rehearsal prior to performing. To strengthen the specific S-R sequence will usually produce initial practice errors or breaks in the chain links. This means the last link gets practiced the least as you start the sequence from the beginning. This is called forward chaining. To practice and reinforce the last and sometimes most critical connections, you can practice segments in reverse called backward chaining. In this way, the critical release of the bowling ball from the glide step gets more attention so that if you make an early in your sequence you may still have time to recover and complete the chain.

Top performers increase their awareness to condition fine motor finger tip control pressure of the release of a basketball in a jump shot. A golfer may have a terrible swing path but makes the final correction to square out the club head at impact. You learn to pre condition your performance using mental rehearsal to create an image in your brain like watching yourself perform on a video tape correctly as you program BEFORE you compete. You learn to control your heart and respiration, adrenalin response, and anxiety to get your butterflies to fly in formation. Every top performer learns how to mobilize all of their energy, abilities, skills, techniques, strategies, and cues or triggers for a given moment in time *at will on demand*. For any during performance evaluation you must take a "time out" moment to reflect on and retreat to performing your conditioned and most practiced fundamentals. More than any other learned skill, this is what separates the top performers during performance to know when to ratchet up or down their performance of fundamentals when it counts the most. Get ready to compete focusing on the triggers to use during your performance evaluations to get your correct pre planned responses. Focusing on the outcome creates more stress you cannot control to cause fatigue and will not aid performance. Great marathon runners are known to condition a subversive response to pain when they "hit the wall" and go beyond normal limits to near death. With pre conditioned triggers you can have faster responses to perform correctly than if you leave your performance to chance. You must learn strategies and cues to recognize and speed up your during performance evaluation to make positive adjustments. The purpose of practice is to condition your mental and physical performance stimulus response skills. With purposeful intent you create value based on your needs to increase your awareness for cue recognition to respond correctly faster as you conditioned in practice to readily recognize, receive, organize, store, and retrieve information.

You can apply the same skills top athletes use to your specific performance. Sales training pre conditions your responses to customer objections, and connects customer benefits to every feature you mention about your product or service to meet your customer's needs. Students study for types of tests differently to practice pretests to prepare for their actual test performance with similar or identical elements to increase their task familiarity. Great teachers lead their students by explaining how to study for their course and learn from their lectures and test. You learn math differently from science or English or social studies. However, noting the specific cues and creating meaningful and relevant relationships are still common to all learners and performers who want to improve. You pose anticipated questions to be familiar with what to expect as you read the text and review your class notes. This reduces your anxiety and increases your confidence. Top performers use strategies that will calm themselves down to perform more skillfully. Your study skills become familiar and repetitious to think on higher planes to raise your level of achievement. You have more time to think to apply your skills that during performance evaluation strategies and skills will improve your overall performance with faster adjustments you pre planned.

This form of mental practice will pre program or automate their execution. Your pre performance evaluation system is more helpful. You want to visualize "check points" for every specific skill. By having a plan in place, you can move to correct during performance errors very quickly to stop the bleeding. For continuous closed series loop skills you can only attend to one or two perceptual check points during the performance. One strategy is to slow down your performance application speed to give your brain more time to process the feedback to make discrete changes in your motor output in practice, but this will not help you in a race. You can slow down your backswing in golf. Another strategy is "smoothing" and as it sounds attempts to make your movement responses more fluid. The downswing and follow through of your golf swing for a short chip shot to the green and rolling the ball to the pin off your putter are examples. With practice you can increase your awareness of feeling cues in your fingertips to apply small pressure adjustments that modify the ball flight prior to release. Your wrist snap contact in the golf swing must square out the club head at impact. Your aim in archery or shooting is a breath holding smooth release or pull of the trigger. You can pre set your focus on specific stimulus-response cues to recognize as you perform and automate a correct response provided you have extensively practiced them before your competition. Then you can gain a moment to regain your composure to lower your anxiety, reflect and evaluate, and refocus on the necessary pre programmed fundamental cues to perform. Your feedback is simple. You hit or missed your target because you were able or not able to perform the correct S-R pattern.

Academically, in a timed test you have to increase your conscious awareness of the specific body of knowledge you must demonstrate for that given moment. You are only tested on a portion of the whole. Practice and condition the specifics to pre program your test taking strategies. Then execute your plan. If you encounter or need to modify your plan, stop for a moment during the test to reset your awareness mode keeping track of your purposeful intent and concept of the whole. Make your adjustments and continue your positive plan. In a sales presentation, gain feedback from your audience. If they have puzzled looks, you need to ask for questions or explain the benefits to your customer for the features in your product in a different way.

Two Digit Error

My two digit error hypothesis is that on average two bits of information must be processed before you can physically respond to the perception of the error. This is significant because when you modify a perceptual cue on the input side of the "black box" you must look at two S-R connections in the sequence or two cues before the actual performance error is displayed. Interruptions in processing feedback while speaking causes stuttering. However, when there is continuous flow in singing the feedback is not interrupted. Mel Tillis, stutters when speaking, but can sing as an entertainer. What is more mind-boggling is why elementary students who learn to play music are able to develop better math skills. As a performer creating personal mental movies, you can perfect your sub routines by correcting specific stimulus-response connections prior to and during the actual performance. As the leader or coach of a physical skill you must subjectively project back in the sequence two bits of processed information prior to the error to re condition a change in perception for that specific S-R connection to repair that link in the chain. Your art of coaching will try one cue after another until you unlock the stored code to repair the link and improve the output performance. As a leader, teacher, or coach, all you can do is keep modifying the cues in the input phase until you get the correct output from each performer. You can focus on these kinds of corrections to think about on a conscious level, and then practice to program them to happen during the performance evaluation of your personal feedback.

You can program automated responses using visualization to mentally rehearse your performance. Golfers will visualize striking their ball immediately before hitting each shot to program a positive result. Swimmers during the meet between events will quietly visualize a complete rehearsal of each coming event, sometimes stroke by stroke from kind of start to finish, and then trust they will perform the same result programmed into their short term memory. This is a strategy also known as *auto suggestion*. Michael Phelps did not touch out Cavic by .01 seconds on the finish of the 2008 Olympic 100 meter butterfly race based on luck. His impulse to take a short half stroke propelled his finish while Cavic lifted his head and put on the brakes in his glide. That possible and the action taken was pre programmed well before the actual performance to make the change during the performance possible. It was already conditioned by Michael for any close race. The trigger was the awareness for being slightly behind coming home and realizing his finish was going to be on a half pull stroke. For my first U.S. Masters Swimming national title in the 50 yard breaststroke for my age group, I had to take three much quicker strokes without breathing normally every stroke to out touch a competitor by .2 seconds who was easily one and a half yards ahead with four yards to go. Top performers are able to visualize changes and adjustments to their performance during competition to trigger positive performances. You can learn and apply these techniques as mental skills to improve your performance with The Triad and a purposeful intent and apply them to any mental or physical performance.

Positive Performance Value

When you attach a purposeful intent value to your actual practice work and performance your brain stores valued information for faster retrieval to your pre-frontal cortex to set up a perfected sub routine and execute a short term program. This is like pulling up a word document file stored in a folder, and cutting and pasting the words from other word documents you attach into a readable sequence. When you have no defined value or purposeful intent while performing your work, your achievements will be inconsistent. Denver Broncos NFL quarterback, John Elway, was noted for his last minute fourth quarter heroics to win games. He practiced with a positive purposeful intent in mind. He used PI skills and mental rehearsal strategies to raise his level of consciousness to visualize a variety of game situations with positive outcomes. He pre programmed his behavior to respond to specific purposeful awareness triggers during performances. Elway connected the practice work with his earned reward by commenting that 'it is harder to surrender when you know you have paid the price for victory." This enabled him to draw upon that body of work at will on demand. All great performers are not able to perform consistently at this high level all of the time. Top performers have the learned ability to perform higher skills at will on demand. They benefit from the past experiences of top coaches who were great players for the top coaches of their era to learn the predictable cues and strategies to achieve success. This is why skilled performers with potential choose these coaches to learn how to be top performers. In the United States we practice self-selection to make these determinations. In China, performers are screened for potential very early in sports and academics and offered the opportunity to learn from their top coaches and teachers. Leaders bring a variety of experience to adapt and change your performance during performance evaluation periods like time outs and halftime. In sales you have reflective down time between sales calls during your performance day. While driving or commuting to and from the office or your job, you can review your positive accomplishments and set goals for the new day. When you know a variety of strategies to use and adapt from your performance feedback you will be consistently successful over time.

Skill Comprehension Purposeful Intent and Congruence

When you comprehend and understand your needs through purposeful intent teaching and construct the correct goal setting paradigm to increase your motive to attain your goals, and then perform your goals you achieve congruence. This builds your intrinsic motivation and confidence faster than any other evaluation method. True learning occurs when you can consistently demonstrate congruence between your expected goal and actual performance. You are intrinsically motivated by your purposeful intent skills. The achievement or skill is observed in how the correct nervous pathways you constructed to see and respond to the correct feedback cues with greater efficiency. This cannot be possible without purposeful intent skills to store the information differently with an attached value based system in place. To retrieve, irrelevant volumes of unvalued information would only serve to bog down your processing speed and resultant output. This hinders small adjustments during performance to enhance your positive outcome.

Error Correction

Picture a basketball free throw shooter during a game. They miss the first free throw and what have they practiced to do? They refocus to mobilize all their skills and abilities to perform the top cues that predict positive performance. They make the adjustments using the immediate past performance feedback to make the next free throw. You take your last output feedback, and a host of comparative cues to adjust the new input to get a better output on your next attempt. Performers who acquire a purposeful intent skill for this learned process continually improve their performances over time. PI skills condition you to create more associational neurons to increase the neuronal transmission pathways to make your performance output appear seamless. Performers without PI skills go through the motions, and do not learn to process their own feedback with a purpose to build value and appropriate associations to improve neuronal speed, and have a more difficult time becoming high achievers. The central idea of learning to process your feedback in the loop is to learn to attend to and condition responses to the appropriate cues for faster and better responses in succeeding performances. If you experience an error during performance, you evaluate that specific S-R connection and mentally visualize a positive response to repair the link with the correct association. This strategy is a refocus skill that is dependent upon having a purposeful intent to decide what you need to identify as your S-R connection error and correct with a visualized response you can associate. Shamefully, many public school students cannot tell you what their score was on their last math or science test to use as a personal benchmark to motivate their improvement simply because they have not been taught this skill by their teachers. So learn this skill with a purpose on your own, and teach it to your children. If you are clueless about your intrinsic needs, you will be confused about what you are learning and display inconsistent responses. This will frustrate you and your coaches and teachers who lead you with the proper cues.

Getting in the "Zone"

Great performers are not able to perform at a high standard or peak performance every practice, game or day. What you learn to do is mobilize all of your talents, abilities, and energy to apply and focus on a performance at will on demand for brief moments in time. This is getting in the "zone." To get in the zone you must have extensive experience to be familiar with the task. Athletes in the zone display exceptional performance skills for brief periods. Highly successful life long performers also display exceptional performance skills for brief periods. They mobilize their energies and skills similarly with practiced skills and *Planer Thinking* to envision pre planned sub routines and achieve greater performance results when the opportunity is present. They also use their immediate performance feedback while performing to compare to preset standards they created to apply *at will on demand.* This is intrinsic motivation, and the leadership skill that can be taught.

In the 2005 NCAA basketball playoffs, the University of Illinois was down 15 points to a talented University of Arizona team with only 3:28 remaining in regulation. Coach Bruce Weber in a post-game interview admitted he had quietly given up hope of making the final four, but stated that his boys took over the game and he simply watched. All throughout the year, I watched and listened to his interviews. He did not make the crucial leadership mistake of taking credit for what his players had accomplished. He added a subtle trigger statement that few sportswriters and fans may have heard. All year long during their 29-0 unbeaten string, the boys should listen and be energized by the crowd. This subtle trigger and talented team play was programmed into all the players to perform during performance evaluations. During performances, close ones and blowouts, the players increased their awareness (the first Triad) to grow antennae to take in more specific and relevant information to compare and make necessary adjustments. With past practice to recognize cues to pass the ball and score or defend and steal the ball or be in rebound position to enhance self-evaluation with immediate feedback (the second Triad) the nervous pathways were connected. What happened next was Williams drove to the top of the key and sank a 3-point shot to reduce the deficit to 12, and the Illini crowd vainly applauded with hope. The Illinois players heard the crowd. They were programmed to be energized by the noise. The players grew their antennae. The ball began to appear like a beach ball in slow motion to pick off passes. The hoop suddenly became much larger, and the next 3-point shot quickly made it 9. The crowd grew louder, and the boys' antennae grew longer. Time slows down to make 3 seconds seem like 20 seconds before impact in a car crash. The boys are in the "zone." Extraneous insignificant stimuli are totally blocked out. It is a brief outburst of mobilized energy. The positive feedback is coming in and compares well with past input already in the highly practiced retrieval system to reward and reinforce the next attempt (the third Triad). Confidence builds with each new successful attempt. The output is positive and congruent with previous results that produced a good outcome. They keep it going to win the game with a huge comeback. You can teach performers how to get in their zone using triggers consistent with their level of talent, ability, and experience. These consist of a variety of cues and responses that also include pre-set goal routines to value minor positive achievements as you learn to evaluate during your performance and trigger your mentally rehearsed response.

Personal Standards

To develop your purposeful intent during practice you must learn to self-evaluate your performance feedback against some quality standard. Your standard can copy a top performer, but to be realistic and congruent in the standard that predicts the highest you want to use your own immediate past performance or average. You cannot control what another person can or will perform, but you can control how you will perform based on your past experience and task familiarity. You must become skilled in The Triad. You want to create a paradigm shift in creating a positive view of your performance to increase your awareness, enhance self-evaluation, and connect personal reward with reinforcement to want to repeat those positive work ethic behaviors. The end objective to condition is to equate your quality of effort with quality of reward. Success does breed success, and builds your confidence. Simply patting your performers on the back to build their self-esteem does not work. Your performers need to have PI skills to believe in the work that conditions their performance success. Start with mastery learning skills that can be positively reinforced first on the level where the skills break down. Build those pathways and confidence first. This starts your Planer Thinking. As you become familiar with each tougher task or sub routine, you perform your advanced skills on successively higher planes. Then build your intrinsic value by creating the need to practice specific skills with cues and strategies that can be transferred to your actual performance. If you do not know what you are skilled at, take the personal needs assessment survey in the appendix to find out what you like to do and have some talent to perform. Your passion will emerge to increase your intrinsic motive as you experience success.

Thinking It Through

In the heat of competition, there is little time to think through the necessary stimulus cues and your physical responses to be successful unless they have been pre-programmed. Scouting an opponent and watching their game films gives you the chance to specifically prepare to meet your opponent's strengths. You develop strategies to combat the other team's positive tendencies. You put your best basketball guard on their best shooting guard to improve your defense. Task familiarity and task specificity play key roles. You do not image bowling to perfect your basketball skills. Getting your mind focused on the specific task ahead centers your thinking. You cannot be thinking about a past error and expect to have a positive focus for the next play. You have to learn to let go, and refocus. You cannot let your emotions get the best of you or the Yerkes-Dodson Law will take effect. You must stay in conscious control, or your performance will suffer. Queen Elizabeth said, "Anger may make dull men witty, but it also keeps them poor." By thinking it through you get to pre plan how you will approach a task and use your skills for a purpose on the next play, point, swing, or deal. During a performance you use specific cues to trigger specific responses you have pre planned to perform. You can trigger a cue during your performance in the time it takes you to take a breath. You learn how to make adjustments with specific S-R connections. This is a hallmark of all great coaches at half-time. Beating on lockers and yelling at players to excite their emotions has been replaced by an intelligent stimulus response approach to create a winning strategy with a focus on a common goal. A strategy helps identify your weaknesses and provides a positive means to improve your performance. This is accomplished by creating a higher order need. In a team environment, you must align the needs of your team with the personal needs of your performers. Finger pointing fault sessions lower your morale and performance focus. Focus on specific skills you can perform correctly to build your confidence. Program a practical positive visualization of your performance as you plan for it to happen. Keep your expectations in line with reality. You cannot expect to achieve what you are incapable of physically performing. But neither do you want to introduce negative thinking that you cannot perform higher with proper conditioning. Set low positive goal expectations like stepping stones during the performance to create a more highly probably reward-reinforcement effect that all your performers will notice and put forth more effort. If you get off to a bad start, your team will not be crushed and give up. Teams that exceed early expectations are more motivated for the rewards they are conditioned to value and feel. Your performers need to be taught how to self-evaluate their effectiveness during performances and give themselves a short pep talk (positive self-talk) to refocus on the correct S-R connections to be successful. Focus on your positive performance as you think it through to a positive result. You condition in all your performers the response that has been practiced to be task familiar. You will know what to do, and then must go do it. The value of a great leader is that they have been there before. An experienced leader can more fully describe the task to familiarize their performers about what to expect to decrease their apprehension and increase their confidence to improve overall performance. Remind your performers that they only need to focus on doing their job playing the one position well. Your opponent puts their pants on one leg at a time just like you do so outsmart them with your pre planned play. Learning to visualize an expected outcome is to create a purposeful intent prior to performing. This learned process helps mobilize your energies to peak perform at will on demand. Consistently successful performers and leaders are able to perform best when it counts. The great leader is better able to paint a more vivid impression of how an expected outcome can occur to focus all the performers on a common realistic and achievable goal effort. The key is to align the goals of the mission with the personal needs of the performers to feel successful. Leaders clearly outline the positive steps they will take to accomplish their mission. The task as described becomes more familiar to all the performers, and is more likely to turn out the way the leader explained it would happen. When you lead yourself to accomplish a realistic goal, you perform the same steps to motivate your mind from within that you can do it. Then you go do it. Plan your success and execute your plan. When your success happens as you planned, your confidence is greatly improved because you know it was not by chance and you can do it again.

Increased Expectancy of Reward

Congruence is important during performance when events are turning out as you predicted. Your expectations are in line with reality. Based on early during performance evaluation sampling and doing as expected, your confidence fuels your intrinsic motivation to keep putting forth the effort to ensure your success. Your performance equals or slightly surpasses your realistic and achievable goal. Your self-evaluation must be closely aligned with the evaluation provided to you by others. If you are a top performer and your manager or leader is not, then you must move on or suffer the conflict. An organization is only as effective as the leaders who recognize and encourage talent to perform above average and provide a means for self-satisfaction on the job. Confidence is anticipating an event will occur as you predict. You have the right to adjust your goals during the performance. By setting and frequently achieving low positive goals only slightly better than your own immediate past performance, it is easier to predict your future performance and condition a positive reward than to set unrealistic goals, condition failure, and be miserable. When you rely on a group or total team performance, there are too many variables to control. Lesson #1 you learn in a team sport or competition is that you cannot control what another competitor will do, but you can learn to control what you will perform through practice and hard work. During competition you cannot control the other team or teammates, but you can control your reaction and feelings to respond and perform in a positive way. Setting goals follows this same premise. How can you predict what another person is thinking when you have trouble getting in touch with your own thoughts? You know that if you practice hard, your learning and conditioning curve will get better to allow you to improve upon your immediate past performance. When you exceed your personal goal – no matter how slight – you take away a personal feeling of satisfaction or reward. You have learned to equate quality of effort with quality of reward. You no longer have to wait for the approval of others to feel rewarded. You are self-rewarded and reinforced to repeat the work or practice trials to get even better. You can refocus on your positive purposeful intent. You can will what you want to happen if it is within reason. You approach each practice and competition with a purposeful intent to improve. You begin to see how your needs form and the benefit of both short and long term goals, and how to take positive steps to achieve them consistently without fear of failure. The closer you get to your goal your intensity and motivation naturally increase in proportion to your expectancy of reward. Once you learn self evaluation skills, no one can take away from your performance if you know you tried to do your best. You will be able to apply this skill to all things measurable and immeasurable for the rest of your life.

Conscious Execution

To increase your awareness during a performance you must work on your conscious execution of smaller movements. This means processing your output as feedback to make immediate input adjustments during your performance. This will assist your recall of cues and responses to events while practicing and during performances. Always keep in mind that your mind and body are set up to automate responses, and you must learn to override this natural occurrence at will on demand. Focus on a specific cue and response connection that you know you can always perform well, and apply that first during your performance. Continue to set realistic intermediate goals based on how you last performed. Any subjective skill can be made into an objective raw score to record in your performance log and compare with your past performances and expected new goal. Break complex skills down into sub skill components to provide each part a subjective-objective rating. Select no more than five sub skills to describe the whole skill performance. Create a rubric table that describes a 1-2-3-4 or 5 score for each sub skill of the total skill. An example is provided in the appendix. When you become more familiar with your standard, you will enhance your personal self evaluation system that is the second part of The Triad.

Auto Suggestion

You can increase your awareness in activities by practicing visualization also known as mental practice during the performance. You mentally rehearse your association for specific cues and responses to speed up your performance reaction in sequence. The more you associate specific cues with repeated practice responses, you improve your efficiency. Prior to competition, when you know your pace or type of performance you expect and it is probable and realistic based on the wealth of your past experience, you can use the strategy of *auto suggestion* to motivate your mind from within how you will perform. Auto suggestion works as if you had put yourself into a hypnotic trance, snapped your fingers to come out, and then respond to the trigger cue that was pre programmed. Did you ever get excited about getting ready to leave on a trip, set your alarm to wake up an hour earlier than normal, and find that you wake up ready to go 30 seconds before the alarm goes off? This strategy lets you step back and trust your system to respond and perform as you had pre-programmed your responses during the time out or between plays. If all is not going well during your performance, you need to find a way to remove yourself from the competition or fray for a moment or two, and reset your stimulus-response approach. During the performance, focus on your pre-shot routine. In golf you *visualize* your stroke and ball flight to take dead aim at your target (goal). Then you relax with a deep breath to trust in your performance. You will make a fast evaluation of the cues and responses you have been making that forced errors in your performance. Then *mentally rehearse* a correct response for the same kind of cue. This is called *stimulus generalization*. It is non-specific, and provides faster nerve transmission rates that improve reaction time and performance. Through this auto suggestion strategy, you can come back into the competition and expect to perform as you programmed yourself to perform. If you have the talent the skills are already in place to perform. Self-induced hypnosis works on the same principle. Go to a quiet place in your mind during the heat of competition, put yourself in a trance and mentally rehearse what you want to perform, set up the cue recognition trigger, and go for it. The entire process requires a positive purposeful intent to be effective, create the need, and value for the activity to have a positive effect.

Endorphin Release of Pleasurable Feelings

Pleasurable physical activities that are perceived successful tend to release endorphins. Endorphins block pain and provide a euphoric pleasurable feeling of well-being that conditions your motivation from within your mind for a repeat performance. You can exert more physical effort to win that third set when you are winning, than if you were falling behind. If you associate your small successes with a feeling of satisfaction you experience enough pleasure that can condition or reinforce that pleasurable feeling enough to want to repeat the experience. When you permit yourself to set unrealistic goals– even as a high achiever – you play a marginally successful game that is more miss than hit. You have effectively lowered your probability of attainment, and therefore the reward and pleasure that you can feel. With infrequent reward, you do not readily condition or reinforce your desire or motive to want to work harder to potentially experience the same reward or pleasurable feeling. When you analyze your performances or your performers, you must take into account your talents in relation to the competition. Past experience and task familiarity are essential to perform at a high level. If you are not performing up to your expectation, you need to drop your expectation back down a level or two to ensure your mastery with any task to rebuild your confidence and reinforce your skills with more specific practice. You must increase your awareness to associate quality of effort with quality of reward, or you will see no marked improvement. You must also create a need to perform quality by focusing on a purposeful intent taken from the performance nature of the activity. If you have no need to perform quality, you can expect mediocre performances, and your personal satisfaction is rewarded less to produce less value that can be associated with success to want to repeat like behaviors. Your subsequent performances will always be inconsistent.

The application for leaders is to provide reasonable expectations for those inexperienced newcomers who are not accustomed to the standards for unfamiliar tasks. The easiest standard to present is to use your performer's own immediate past performance. Every new goal must be slightly better than their immediate past performance. Over time, everyone can learn to work harder and smarter to continually improve and achieve quality performance. This is how you enable intrinsic motivation, and build accountability. You need to plan periods to set aside new performers with unfamiliar tasks so they can process feedback during the performance from the sidelines observing others performing well. Inexperienced performers need time to recognize and associate proper cues with appropriate responses and through repetition increase the efficiency of those nervous pathways. These proper cues will have been practiced and their associated purpose understood prior to actual competition to "trigger" their execution during the performance.

Summary

During performance, the Purposeful Intent Triad is put to the test. You can use the principles found in B.F. Skinner's feedback model to increase your awareness of performance output during the feedback loop that can be compared to your past performance, others, or a standard. Top performers create personal performance standards and need to keep improving their immediate past performance to keep the success feeling. With each succeeding attempt proper cues and responses become conditioned and reinforced as realistic low positive performance goals are met with greater probability and frequency. More frequent success builds your personal reward system that improves your confidence, and self-esteem. Your inconsistent or poor responses must be eliminated by refocusing on your pre conditioned cue response connections with positive visualization during reflective time outs. Find time to practice mental rehearsal to visualize the correct association between the cue and appropriate response. Then trigger the response with a brief visualization prior to performing or during the time out. Your goals must be adjusted to increase your probability for success to create reward that can reinforce your positive work ethic behaviors and consistently improve your performances over time.

Post Performance Evaluation

"Imaginary signs not always coincidence."

Andrew Christian

Objective: Increase your awareness to evaluate the details to improve, value success, and reinforce your attempts to keep improving.

Introduction

During your performance you learned that there are specific strategies you can use to adjust your performance. These strategies involve the immediate use of your performance output as feedback to adjust the quality of your input. Your input comes from your awareness skills to recognize cues you have become familiar with in practice or other competitions from experience and have been held in memory. In post performance, you are still working on the development of your prediction and projection skills by analyzing what you did right from what you did wrong that is in your control and you can improve for future performance. You compare your performance output and the adjustments you made to your input to effect a positive change in actual performance. Your reflection of the intensity of your response is equally important to learn how to control your emotions. You must learn how to think clearly and stay focused while performing, and not expend too much nervous energy that will deplete your blood sugars and muscle glycogen prior to performing. In sport psychology, Dr. Bob Rotella, of the University of Virginia and advisory board of Golf Digest magazine, coined the phrase, "getting your butterflies to fly in formation." Rather than pass off your performance, take the opportunity to review and plan how you can purposefully improve your next performance. What follows are some strategies you can use to increase your intrinsic motivation:

Congruence -This means that your personal evaluations of the actual performance are closely aligned to what you predicted would happen with realistic and achievable goals. This requires an understanding of your needs, values, abilities, and skills as they improve over time to maintain a consistent intrinsic motivation. In simpler terms, do your performances indicate that you are improving? If you are not improving, why are you not improving? It could be that you are not being fair with yourself, and are setting goals that exceed reality to cause your frustration. Frustrated performers seldom learn to self-reward and reinforce work ethic behaviors. There is an optimal performance reinforcement value when your performance more closely approximates or slightly exceeds your goal. This demonstrates the personality trait of realism and when you also increase your frequency of improvement has tremendous reinforcement value.

Personal accountability – Top performers learn to hold themselves accountable through this process of self-evaluation. They do not wait for the approval of others, and tend to be tougher on themselves than their coaches and teachers. They set personal standards that promote and reward consistent improvement in small increments to maintain their high motivation. Those personal standards are based on their own immediate past performance that they can control by improving their awareness skills to recognize the more important cues to process from their performance output.

Value perception - Value is created by the amount of perceived reward divided by the amount of perceived effort. Value leads to increased purposeful intent over time. Therefore, any activity must be assigned a relative value using the equation that becomes purely intrinsic; increasing your frequency of success.

Common goals and mission – These variables are improved when each participant pays an equal price for success that can be shared by all. This factor is why companies try to ferret out the lowest one-third of all their employees who can damage this perception and reduce the group motivation to succeed. When all pay the same price, they can value the same benefits and enjoy working together for a common purposeful intent. When this happens the common purpose is aligned with the personal needs and values of all the team members who learn to work collaboratively like a family in a common bond.

Personality components – Do you have what it takes? Are you willing to change your personality to be successful? Top performers exhibit common personality traits to believe in their work, performance effort, and success. They do not look to take shortcuts. They find ways to work and remember their practices more efficiently. Many keep workout journals and logs to track their progress.

Reflective thinking - Comparing traditional post performance evaluations by others with your learned post performance evaluations. The value of teaching each performer self-evaluation skills; key elements; building confidence; traditional organizations;

Dichotomy comparisons...

Extrinsic versus intrinsic evaluations – personal evaluation; organizational evaluation; peer evaluation; resistance to empowerment. When done correctly, your personal intrinsic evaluation is more powerful than an extrinsic evaluation provided by your boss or organization.

Post performance actual versus goal expected – To gain realism, a personality trait found in top performers, your actual performance should closely approximate your goal expectation to provide you with the greatest intrinsic motivation. See the figure, Optimal Performance Reinforcement Value Index under the section on congruence later in this chapter.

Individual and team satisfaction of needs – winning is just another measure of your performance improvement. Whether the team wins or loses, how well did you perform each sub routine that is taken from your whole performance? What areas did you perform well to perform your team role that contributed the most to the success or failure of the team?

Overview - There is a distinct difference in how others see your performance and what you see in your performance. It should matter most what you think of your performance more than what your critics think. In good teaching and coaching, leaders teach their performers how to self-evaluate their personal performance in relation to a number of factors they introduce to gain the personal motivation of every performer. Teaching and coaching leaders cannot be with every learner every moment, and must depend on a positive system that will continuously improve every performer's performance over time if practiced. One strategy has been to reflect on immediate and past performances in relation to expectancy of future performance that develops the personality trait of realism inherent in top performers. When the expectancy goal and actual performance approximate each other this is known as congruence. This reflected comparison helps you identify and learn what specific parts of sub routines to correct and reward to improve the whole performance. Personality traits play an important role in how realistic and achievable goals are selected. By selecting low positive goals only slightly better than your own immediate past performance or average, you increase your probability for success. Frequent goal achievement increases the personal frequency of reward to increase intrinsic motivation through the post performance reflection process. This is what top performers play through their minds to hold themselves accountable for performance improvement to value. As you improve, your immediate past performance also improves to challenge you to set another slightly higher but low positive goal. Over time, this reward-reinforcement strategy increases your intrinsic motivation to keep improving and work harder on conditioning the physical effort and the mental skills of purpose, commitment, dedication, sacrifice, focus, and concentration on the specific cue-response connections. This also leads to Planer Thinking as tasks become increasingly familiar to perform at higher and higher levels.

Purposeful Rules

The key concept to learning the PI motivational skills training evaluation system is to understand that: **Judging another person's performance automatically converts the valuable intrinsic motive into a less valuable extrinsic motive.**

Your performer is not able to accept all or a major portion of the credit. Imagine a small scale.

The more you take credit, you reduce that amount of credit the performer can accept and feel positive reward to reinforce succeeding attempts. When others accept portions of the reward you worked directly to earn, they diminish the value of your personal intrinsic connection between quality of effort and quality of reward. This reduces your desire  to increase your work output on succeeding attempts to ensure your success and feel good. By reducing your 'feel good' awareness to build value, the repeat valuation and reinforcement of the work activity is lost. Performers may not know how to define their personal needs, but they still know how their performances make them feel.

Rule #1: *Routinely self-evaluate your performance to be consciously aware of positive feelings you can take away.*

In excellent organizations, performers are able to ask the opinion of their peers without fear of ridicule or retribution to reinforce additional assurance. This provides congruence or a match between how you see your performance, and what others see you perform. When performers experience repeated failure, they are not easily motivated to do more work to achieve the same feeling. You must be able to see some signs of success to want to attempt working harder. If failing, you must first change your perception of success by adjusting your personal goals to be more achievable and realistic.

Rule #2: *Your drive motivation will increase when you set a goal only slightly better than your own immediate past performance or average.*

Wanting to do better is a natural drive.

Rule #3: *Plan for initial success.*

Serious morale problems result when:

a) a poor start in early trials is held over the head of the performers in the name of accountability,

b) leaders accept the credit for the suggestions or work of others, and

c) blame their performers for poor results.

These set up a negative cycle and mistrust. Performers learn to hate their job because they are not reinforced how to be aware of their roles and that success comes in small positive incremental steps to feel rewarded by consistently improving upon your own immediate past performance.

Rule #4: *When your expectations exceed reality it leads to frustration.*

Performers enjoy working when they can feel a personal reward for a job well done. Contrary to the issue of money, workers leave jobs because there is little or no job satisfaction they can feel to take the credit. This is why intrinsic motivation leadership skills are so valuable to help performers define their role in the organization, and keep people on task. Successful performers are generally happy on the job to reduce job turnover, and transfers to all the other employees they have contact with.

Rule #5: *It is not what others think, but what you learn to think of your performance that matters to produce consistent effort to achieve success.*

You learn best by increasing your level of awareness from processing your own feedback, projecting feedback from the mistakes of others, or predicting what may happen in a new trial from past positive experiences you have learned to readily store and retrieve with your awareness skills.

External evaluations performed by teachers and bosses are extrinsic and less powerful motivators. Internal evaluations performed by you are intrinsic and more powerful motivators. It takes more than talent to be a top performer over time. You must also know your purposeful intent to increase your motivation to continuously improve. Once you lose your purposeful intent, you are easily beaten because the intrinsic value of doing the work it takes to succeed is lost. Being talented on the athletic field, in school, or on the job is no guarantee of success over time. Learning skills to be in tune with your purposeful intent will take time but make you a more consistent winner. The successes of great coaches over their careers are usually the athletes who had more heart with a purposeful intent than physical talent, and achieved great success. The Notre Dame "Rudy's" put success in life into perspective.

Creativity and Planer Thinking

Planer thinking is your creative ability to process increasingly more complex information as you learn to perform a skill efficiently in varying levels or planes when you become more familiar with a task. When performers are labeled as right- or left-brain dominate, it creates a negative focus and conditions a limiting bias. Our school systems often socially penalize artistic talent and creativity; however these kinds of performers more closely identify with purposeful intent skills for the kind of awareness and creativity others can benefit from. Right-brain learners have artistic talent and left-brain learners learn core subject skills as long as teachers/coaches model purposeful effort and focused intent on a positive outcome. We are created to use both halves of our brain. Modeling PI skills can help performers begin to create value for what is most meaningful and relevant, which produces unlimited learning freedom without bias.

You will create a personal higher level of aspiration based on your need to achieve the next higher personal standard you set. By studying the great leaders, artists, and creative geniuses who have invented what we take for granted, you get a snapshot of how they became motivated with a positive intent to achieve a purpose that was their passion. The philosophical question is whether leaders or creative geniuses created works and made decisions to please others or themselves first? The real critics in a free market economy are the people who buy your work, deeds, or thoughts that stand the test of time. Your intrinsic motives keep you on track to persevere and commit to your personal standard of quality and achieve what no other man has achieved. Leaders enhance their vision, endure criticism, and achieve greatness over the test of time. Great performers are less concerned about the performances of others and more concerned about their own performances that they have control over. When you set goals, concern yourself with the most familiar input you can gather from your own immediate past performance or past performance average. Use this input to advance your planer thinking in higher task familiar levels to boldly envision what you can be achieve. This sets the benchmarks for your purposeful intent to increase your personal intrinsic motivation. This is a learned leadership skill that all successful performers perform. As an outcome, your leadership vision will be misunderstood by lay performers and critics who are unable to think on your plane of thought.

Thomas Edison was repeatedly told he was a failure for trying to build a battery. He continued and was not persuaded by critics to quit the project to preserve his reputation and avoid embarrassment. Edison knew a key principle. Every problem has a solution. Critics by themselves never create anything of value. Critics are self-proclaimed authorities without personal experiences to create any kind of planer thinking. Top performers learn to rely on their own self evaluation feedback to judge the quality of their work.

Successful performers who are passionate about their work reach much higher *Planes* in their thinking based on their greater knowledge of a specific task, and are able to envision more than the average performer. All performers improve to a point and then level off for a while until they become more familiar with new tasks by performing RROSR. This same process occurs for all IQ levels and why brains cells can be organized to process sequential information and continue to improve to higher functional levels with proper motivation. Learning is still taking place but not displayed consistently in some kinds of assessments. Due to Gardner's work with multiple intelligences, we now know that intelligence is specific probably because of task familiar patterns learned in sequences. Planer Thinking supports this notion. If you can keep improving your PI strength to increase your awareness, your performances will eventually improve again to the next level or *Plane* as you become highly familiar with each performance level. This suggests that you must continue to work on your purpose to meet a specific need and understand how your positive purposeful intent will motivate and sustain your work ethic even when it is not always justified by a continuous performance improvement. The repetitious jumping from one plane to a higher performance plane is the result of practice that develops task familiarity and is closely tied to a performer's personality: top performers are not quitters and seldom say, "I can't." They are also tough judges of their personal performances; committed to their goals; have natural drives to want to be loved and wanted and belong to something greater, and strive to be independent of others. Top leaders understand that when group needs are aligned with individual needs, average performers can begin to perform above average skills. This is called synergism, and one way great leaders have accomplished incredible events in history. On a smaller scale, good marriage partnerships seek to provide for the needs of each partner. Behind every good man is a good woman, and vice versa. Good loving and caring partners learn to focus on the higher order needs and tasks of the other, increase their awareness of the specific cues to attend to, and consistently provide more appropriate responses. Your frequent success provides a stronger self-evaluation, and enables you to perform better by connecting or associating your feelings of being loved as reward with reinforcement to repeat the kindness. Increased success increases your need to do more to improve your performance and that of the others associated with your group. You moderately increase your work ethic to ensure continued good feelings from the affective domain. Thus, the successful activity becomes self-reinforcing and needs no extrinsic reward.

Purposeful Intent and Social Systems

There are numerous post performance applications to social systems like education, business, and sports that PI can address because these performers have been conditioned to perform in a specific way without having to think. These violations of human nature create diminishing returns, but can control the universal behavior of the workers. As presented in chapter four, It's Your Job, Dr. William Glasser (1990), described how "lead management" has replaced "boss management" styles of leadership. Lead management is more practical at intrinsically motivating performers to work independently and stay motivated to continuously improve their performances. There are principles that create successful leadership. One of the specific functions of PI intrinsic motivational skills training is to develop personal leadership. All performers can learn to be a little bit better tomorrow than they were today. You learn something new everyday when you are focused in your awareness to pay closer attention to using specific cues and strategies observed in top performers of that skill. This idea is like the notion for playing tougher rather than weaker competitors in a sport to improve your skills. When you open the receptors of your brain you choose to create an awareness of value to gain knowledge. This helps you to make the new information:

- more meaningful and relevant to readily store and retrieve in your pre-frontal cortex.
- readily available *at will on demand* to improve your performance.

In a dichotomy the opposite would be to condition a negative attitude to hate school and learning, and turn off the imaginary switch at the base of your brain. Try to create a word document on your computer with the monitor off. Not much is going to go onto your hard drive for later use. What little information does reach your brain gets parked in a less ready mode.

The age of accountability is driven by economic and social reasons. This creates demand for equality and fairness, but will not account for every worker every minute or how talent and skill play important roles in pay scales and other mostly extrinsic rewards that are determined and applied. Few corporations still believe that a trip to the Caribbean is the motive that sparks sales performers to excel. What matters most is that top performers know they are doing their job well by how they are improving or producing performance numbers of higher value compared to other performers in the corporation or on the competitive field within the team guidelines. Top performers have respect and confidence in the quality of their work that is also valued by their leaders with an occasional simple kind word, pat on the back, or sincere note. Quality performers do not need others to gush all over them. It is not what they need most. They do, however, need a true and fair evaluation system that recognizes and rewards their efforts to give them credit for their work, and that they can self-evaluate. Most leaders do not have a background in psychology to know how to apply this simple practice. It is why corporations pay big bucks to have others teach them how to do it. The economic benefit to even a small corporation translates into millions of dollars if 95% of the workers improve their performance a mere 5%! Technology can only take a corporation so far. While technology has helped to make your quality of life more efficient, it has also reduced your dependence on your senses to increase your awareness skills. Our very literal society – I have a problem and I want an immediate answer – is built on immediate gratification. A problem is always caused by someone else, and not your fault. You are overly conditioned toward micromanagement and perhaps have willfully given up some personal freedoms to avoid personal accountability. Purposeful intent seeks to counter this conditioned response to rebuild a whole new set of internally conditioned responses to help you become a top performer in your lifetime!

Evaluation Leadership

For your post performance evaluation to be beneficial, you must pre design several key strategies or rubrics to focus your desired thinking or thought process. See the Table: Post Performance Evaluation Rubric on the next page. The goal of your post performance evaluation is to learn how to process your own performance feedback, make positive adjustments, and efficiently improve your performance consistency. You will selectively attend to specific strategies you feel predict your performance improvement. Top performers who have achieved consistent success look for more. At the top of Maslow's Hierarchy is self-actualization. This is the need to give back that top performers feel the need to achieve. They become driven by a higher power to give back to others what they know and have achieved. It disturbs me to see leaders, coaches or teachers spending all their time on the best performers or well-behaved. If you manage or coach a team, whether in sales or athletics, this practice to only work with the best leads to serious morale problems. A few top performers may be happy for one or two events in the short term, but overall growth from the everyday contribution of the entire team will not improve very much. As the leader you must find a simple and personal way to recognize the contributions, struggles, problems, and improvements of every performer in your organization. If not by you, then delegate your staff to permeate personal recognition in the organization. The greatest coaches have remarked that they viewed their success more by the development and improvement of their average performers who were able to achieve greatness through diligent hard work to continuously improve until they became a top performer. In college, I was fortunate to be one of those performers for Doc Counsilman. If you are in the business of helping performers improve, then you must help all your performers find a way to improve. This includes the troubled, mentally weak and misguided, and unfortunate performers also. School systems do not ordinarily use rubrics to teach you how to self evaluate your performances and hold yourself accountable. Schools condition you to believe that your teachers, parents, and coaches know what is best to evaluate in your performance. Then, after you get your evaluation or grade, little is done to suggest how you can immediately improve your next performance. Rubrics help you learn how to self evaluate your performance to upgrade the value before the final external evaluation by your teacher. As valuable as rubrics are, they are seldom used by teachers and less by coaches to teach physical skills. Leaders must use strategies to teach their performers how to continuously evaluate and improve their performance as individuals or within a team environment. You want to learn how to process your

POST PERFORMANCE EVALUATION RUBRIC

External Evaluator _____   Self Evaluator _____

Rubric	Score 0	Score 1	Score 2	Score 3	Score 4
Improvement	0 part of whole	1 part of whole	2 parts of whole	3 parts of whole	4 parts of whole
Purpose & Value	had none	knew for this part	knew for these parts	knew for these parts	knew for these parts
Congruence	not even close	+/- 6-10%	+/- 3-5%	+/- 1-2%	right on target
PAP	had none	used performances of others in group	based on stated goal to others	combination verbal & past performance	immediate past performance/average
Sub routines	looked at whole performance	broke task down into two parts	broke task down into three parts	broke task down into four parts	connected cues and responses each part
Accountability	blames others & finds excuses	has idea to do better next time	identified needs & abilities to develop	created steps to improve	gives credit for success to others
TOTAL SCORE					

0 - 3 You are wasting your time.
4 - 10 You are starting to get a clue how PI skills can improve your performance
11 - 17 You have the idea and it is a matter of time until you are a top performer
18 - 24 You have what it takes to be a top performer

own performance feedback, and assign a relative value to reinforce the input-output and goal-performance relationship. The more you increase your awareness of the goal objective and actual performance outcome as you predicted, you will improve your conditioned responses through post performance evaluation that build your confidence and realism to lead. You speak with more believable conviction to lead. Your performers will believe what you suggest to raise their positive expectations and follow your leadership when more often, performances turn out as you stated they would. *Your leadership is to familiarize your performers with what to expect performing unfamiliar tasks to build confidence.* Your consistent positive winning behavior will benefit yourself and the organization. You motivate your mind from within to continue working hard to enjoy successful feelings.

To sustain or improve your intrinsic motivation, you must increase the probability for your success with a low positive goal, and learn how to self-reward your performances. If you focus on your mistakes, you condition that stimulus-response connection the same as if it were a positive performance. If you discipline your performers by focusing on all their mistakes, they will be conditioned to make more performance errors. You want to condition positive performances and extinct negative performances by not calling attention to them. When you focus on all the faults of your performers, they will stop being creative and contributing, and fly under the radar of management. You do not want to reinforce negative performances by talking about them when your leadership focus must be on reinforcing the positive steps that are taking place within your organization. Performance improvement requires leaders to understand the psychology of human behavior. No one likes to have someone find fault with every little part of a more successful overall performance in order to strive for perfection. That strategy does not reinforce positive performance improvement. Your performers are driven to improve to feel reward not criticism for trying and taking some risk to increase the reward. Hindsight is 20/20 vision after the performance. How you choose to lead is your choice. If you continually find fault with an intrinsically motivated performer, they will reduce their intrinsic motivation to improve their performance for the good of the company or team.

A better strategy would be to *increase awareness by focusing on specific steps for improving each task within your organization.* Another strategy is to continually *focus on the positives and not talk about the negatives* of performance improvement. Boss leaders have an intrinsic need to seek power and set extrinsic goals for their performers to meet their needs first, and then wonder why their performers are not motivated to extend their work effort. Lead managers believe the opposite that their performers can be intrinsically motivated and trusted to do their job well when they are not looking. The performers doing the work are empowered with a conscious purposeful intent to improve their performance and achieve quality that is self rewarding. If you want long-term training gains performers must evaluate and reflect on the quality of their own work in relation to other performers or to a standard you set with the performer as a realistic expectation to self-reward and reinforce increased work ethic behavior. In the classroom, grades consistently create a competitive climate, but once that grade is achieved, the value of what was learned is greatly diminished. New knowledge gained is short term and temporarily stored in the prefrontal cortex of the brain until value is assigned to make it meaningful and relevant compared to prior knowledge in storage. The prefrontal valuing process improves with PI skills training so that the new knowledge can be stored in short and long term memory through the structure of associational neurons that make the new information readily accessible. When prior knowledge is stored in long-term memory but readily accessible because of the value that has been assigned, you can recognize and receive more new knowledge to compare for value to accommodate and assimilate in short-term memory.

When self-esteem psychology was popular, evaluators praised performers when they had accomplished little work to deem their success. The false thinking was that performers would feel success even though they had not earned it, and want to improve their performance behaviors to earn more praise. This strategy backfired because performers at any age know if they are doing the job and resent false praise. False praise creates loss of respect and oppositional defiance. The reverse effect is conditioned.

Finally, be careful who gets or takes the credit. Evaluation leaders from boards, managers, parents, teachers, coaches, and significant others who take personal credit away from you and your accomplishments, automatically reduce a potential 100% intrinsic reward response to improve your personal reward-reinforcement relationship. Think of that balance or scales again.

As you take any credit for an achievement, you tip the scales down from providing your performers with 100% intrinsic reward for doing the work. Valuable reinforcement of work ethic behaviors and morale is lost in this scenario. Over time your

performers will not be motivated from within to put forth any extra personal effort. Performance and personal accountability will steadily decline as your performers will be conditioned to accept the "why bother syndrome" – nobody cares what you do. As the experienced leader who has walked in your performer's shoes, you do not need to take any credit. Your reward is to see your performers improve, feel job satisfaction, and have an increased desire to want to come to work and do a better performance every day. Your job is to lead!

Motivating Progress

Evaluating the progress of your performers like coaches do for skill based learning on athletic fields is hard work with more record keeping. Every performer has specific needs, talents, and skills both physical and mental that they bring into the classroom and on the job. All performers require some form of differentiated instruction to learn. Learning is no longer a one-size-fits-all. Performers who are challenged to produce quality become more motivated. The quality you produce and learn to self evaluate against a standard will be reinforced when an unbiased teacher or leader provides a *(similar) congruent evaluation*. Leaders are able to recognize and encourage developing talent and guide your effort. Enhancing your self-evaluation system will help you learn to be intrinsically motivated to produce quality that you can be proud of seeing your improvements. You can reflect on your personal efforts to improve upon your last performance and not have to compare your performance to others in a competitive environment. In a purposeful intent leadership system, failure is not an option. All performers learn to succeed to gain self confidence and self esteem through self reward. You learn to value your personal efforts that you can control, and you don't have to wait for someone to tell you.

Congruence

Whether or not you succeed in achieving a standard, goal, or outcome, you must learn to evaluate the effectiveness of your performance in relation to the work accomplished to assign relative value. When activities are going right, there appears to be no need to evaluate your performance. This would be a mistake. There is always something to learn from every performance using post performance evaluation strategies. You need post performance evaluation skills to keep your conscious awareness higher, and prevent automating your responses. Automated responses have less value in your feedback system. Hypothetically, low awareness information is not recognized, received, organized, stored, and retrieved as readily in your brain. In the post performance phase you learn to evaluate all kinds of performances – big and little. Never take anything for granted, including relationships, if you want them to improve with a purposeful intent. Using the congruence strategy implies that you have a pre set goal from a pre performance evaluation that you will compare to how you actually performed. Ask yourself, "What can I do differently to affect a better result?" Do other evaluators rate your performance close to what you expected? Ideally, a self-made rubric can help you evaluate your pre performance goal and actual performance relationship. An example is presented in the Table: Post Performance Evaluation Rubric, presented earlier in this chapter.

Your immediate past performance is the main standard for you to judge your effective value of each goal performance relationship. There are optimal values to perceive and achieve that enhance your reinforcement probabilities. The figure Optimal Performance Reinforcement Value Index was presented in chapter five, Pre Performance Evaluation, and is shown again in the next section of this chapter, Congruence of Predicted Value and Performance Result. Non-valued non-reinforced behaviors seldom improve over time. Nothing stops you from setting up your own standards and determining how close you come to meeting your personal standards to feel rewarded. Create a strong purposeful intent to motivate your mind from within by aligning your basic needs and drives with your talents and abilities. Successful performers do not wait on critics to judge the worth or value of their performance. Leaders, teachers, parents, and coaches unfortunately condition performers to be more attentive to their evaluation to meet their needs than to teach their performers self-evaluation skills. Consequently, you are conditioned to wait for the approval of others before making a new attempt or trial. Performers are conditioned to be "coached" instead of learning how to coach themselves. Imagine the great painter Picasso, being hesitant and timid to paint his new "modern art" form because he felt the critics might not approve his work. What if Edison and his staff responded to the critical evaluations that a battery could not be invented to avoid being called a fool or worse, an idiot by the nay-sayers? Highly successful people learn early on to set their own standards of performance that are highly realistic and achievable for their talents and abilities. You develop Planer Thinking by enhancing your self-evaluation skills as a top performer to continuously improve and challenge your skills and abilities on higher planes as you become more familiar with each task. Top performers set low positive goals to increase their frequency of success to enhance their personal reward system. This establishes a reward-reinforcement schedule that increases your intrinsic motivation to continually improve. In all post evaluations, the more congruent your goal and actual performance relationship are you will be more realistic, confident and secure in your personality to lead. These are the essential qualities of every successful performer and leader.

To improve personality patterns for realism, it is important to have the performer learn how to judge the quality or worth of their performance. Rubrics, portfolios, and written performance self-evaluations, allow performers to rate the quality of their performance against the quality of their effort to determine relative personal value. As the leader provide your evaluation after the performer has learned how to self-evaluate their performance skills and provided their own evaluation. The purpose is to determine congruence or agreement in yours and their evaluation to improve realism. The concept of congruence is a conscious awareness activity. When the performer is not given the opportunity to self-evaluate prior to the performance evaluation by their manager, their PI strength and intrinsic motivation is decreased. The motives and needs to be satisfied become the extrinsic needs of the company and not the personal needs that benefit the performer. This will not build personal accountability or intrinsic motivation, and can weaken morale and loyalty that increase company turnover. Companies that do not get this concept provide layers of middle management to oversee that the work gets completed, and spend additional dollars in human resource management recruiting and training to make up for the turnover. This proves very costly, and hurts the net profit that could be used to share with the workers to help their families and improve their personal quality of life. These workers develop the "why bother syndrome."

Congruence of Predicted Value and Performance Result

When you consciously work harder and record your efforts in a performance log, you increase your perceived effort and your PI strength. You feel more like you deserve the reward for all your hard work, and you are more likely to persist in your efforts if you know and understand your purposeful intent or why you are working to improve to meet a specific personal need and goal. Top performers have many hours of practice and performance experience to form realistic goals and values. Any top performer will come very close to what they predict they can perform. When the predicted performance value closely resembles the actual performance result, you have congruence and realism. This is a highly desirable personality trait of leaders and top performers. They know what they have to do to be successful, and are less likely to mislead other team members for their personal gain. Using the Activity Value Index from chapter five with some modification, you get a scaling effect for % of perceived effort and reward and performance value to create an Optimal Performance Reinforcement Value Index.

The Optimal Performance Reinforcement Value Index is formed with an upper and lower-half mirror image. The index is applied to actual performance results after you have performed in the usual way by dividing the perceived reward R by the perceived effort E. After the performance, you will self evaluate your actual performance results. There is a positive and negative scale to 100% with the base line in the middle and intersected by the % reward and effort lines. If your performance has improved over your immediate past performance you will use the positive scale upper half. If your performance has declined from your immediate past performance you will use the negative scale lower half. You will still subjectively estimate your perceived effort and reward scale to compute your index.

Value can also be represented as an empirical index. V is a value index from 0 to 10 found by dividing R, the perceived % reward strength by E, the perceived % effort strength. The optimal reinforcement is a perceived value index of a positive 1.0 to 1.5 when you can expend 30-50% effort more often to increase the frequency of valued reward. If your perceived reward is approximated at moderately high 70% and easy to attain 30%, you have a Value index of 70/30 = 2.3. If your perceived effort is easy (20%) and your perceived reward will be slight (20%), your Value index 20/20 = 1.0, but not optimal because you have not expended more than 30% effort for the value to condition a reinforcement effect. If your perceived reward value is a high 80% and your perceived effort is 80%, then your value index would also be 80/80 = 1.0. However, the difference is above the 50% base line, and because you had to expend a great effort to get a great reward you are not likely to want to repeat this activity very often. Therefore, this activity would also have less motivational value to reinforce your future efforts. An index below the base line still has relative value to improve your motivation, but probably is half the strength of a positive index of the same value. When you work harder and increase your training effort, the perceived effort comes easier with more physical practice conditioning and knowledge 50%, and your perceived reward may stay the same or slightly increases to 80% to give you a value

Optimal Performance Reinforcement Value Index

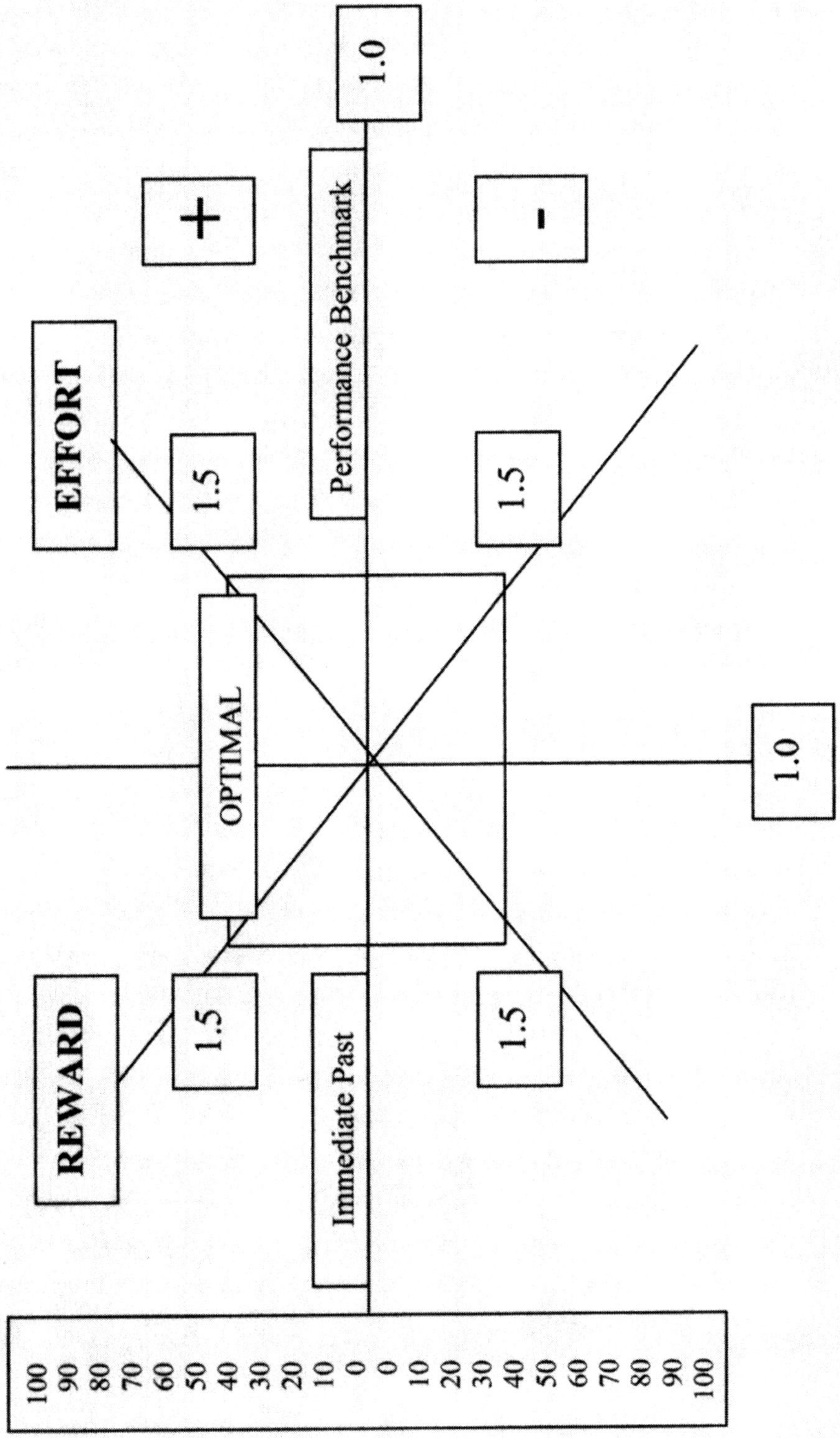

EFFORT

REWARD

OPTIMAL

Performance Benchmark

Immediate Past

+

-

1.0

1.5

1.5

1.5

1.5

1.0

100
90
80
70
60
50
40
30
20
10
0
0
10
20
30
40
50
60
70
80
90
100

index of 80/50 = 1.6 slightly above the optimal reinforcement range. With improved performances your perceived rewards will begin to exceed your perceived effort. You will gradually become more aware of a higher index value that will increase your PI and connect reward with reinforcement. Conversely, if the reward is perceived to be very high 90%, and the effort is 100%, the value index would be 90/100 = .9 or less than 1.0. This lower value index reflects a slightly lower probability for positive reinforcement over time. Consistently lower values do not generally increase your motivation or drive stimulus to achieve without also having a greater number of high value indices to reinforce taking more attempts or practicing the specifics to reinforce intermediate rewards. Thus, the strategy to increase your intrinsic motivation will be to increase your conscious awareness of your purpose, and projection of perceived value, and can adjust your thinking to positive optimal levels in the value index. This will gain realism and congruence between your expected performance and actual performance that is a trait found in consistent top performers. The table of Purposeful Intent Value System provides examples of how value perceptions affect performance.

Understanding the process strategies to use like *visualization* and *projection* from your pre performance evaluation will help you to plan your performance improvement rather than leave this to chance. Top performers are professionals that plan for their success. To hold your performers accountable for their early mistakes made with lack of training or your direction will not motivate your performers to take risks. You must help your performers balance risk with reward by how you choose to hold their early learning attempts accountable. Early trials will have higher perceived effort percent scores and lower perceived reward percent scores. As performers become more familiar with the tasks and their physical and mental conditioning improves, their perceived reward-effort percent scores will reverse. They will perceive the work to be less effort and the reward greater. They will associate the quality of effort with the quality of reward. This is a huge paradigm shift in your performer's thinking as they become more intrinsically self-motivated. The outcome must always be viewed as more important than the process, but this process is complex and must be learned or you will take your chances to produce haphazard success. The process to develop your purposeful intent is a learned skill that increases your motivation through pre-performance evaluation using feedback from your past performances kept in your portfolio or performance log.

Purposeful Intent Value System

TASK DIFFICULTY	+	AMOUNT OF EFFORT	+	DEGREE OF OBSERVED CHANGE	=	VALUE OF ACHIEVEMENT
PAP perceptual anchoring point		ability & talent required		new performance compared to past performance or average		expectation of success
past experience		task perceived as easy or hard; familiar or unfamiliar		computed probability of success		feelings of self-worth
knowledge of abilities, skills, needs, strategies		level of commitment		increasing the odds to succeed		positive reward
knowledge of competition & standards		knowledge of performance conditions		need to decrease odds to protect ego		positive reinforcement
		emotional make up; will-power, persistence				

<u>Examples</u>

SIMPLE TASK	+	LOW EFFORT	+	LOW DEGREE OF CHANGE	=	LOW VALUE OF ACHIEVEMENT
DIFFICULT TASK	+	HIGH EFFORT	+	HIGH DEGREE OF CHANGE	=	HIGH VALUE OF ACHIEVEMENT

Table ___. Achievement Value and Goal Orientation Related to PI Strength

VALUE OF ACHIEVEMENT	+	GOAL ORIENTATION	=	PI STRENGTH

<u>Examples</u>

LOW VALUE OF ACHIEVEMENT	+	WEAK GOAL OR NO GOAL	=	VERY LOW PI STRENGTH
HIGH VALUE OF ACHIEVEMENT	+	HIGH POSITIVE ULTIMATE GOAL	=	VERY HIGH PI STRENGTH

Increasing Your Frequency of Success

In your post performance evaluation, if you do not feel significant feelings of success your goal or outcome was not realistic and achievable, or you have been conditioned to automating lower levels of accomplishments. You must overcome this natural tendency with stronger awareness of all your personal feedback in the post evaluation phase. Give yourself more credit to reinforce your positive behaviors. Make adjustments in how you approach and select all your goals – not just significant goals. Goal setting is a function of your personality. Start reviewing your personality traits and patterns in relation to the kinds of personal needs you identify for yourself. A typical list of personality traits and patterns is in the appendix. You may be surprised to see that others describe your personality differently than you see yourself. If your pattern is to be outspoken and boastful about how good you are to others in a verbal way, you may want to rethink this position. Highly skilled performers seldom look outside their own performance feedback to compare the rate and value of their success. A common mistake of high achievers is to not consciously recognize and self reward the little things they do to be successful. Setting unrealistic goals do not increase your probability for success to reward your personal work efforts frequently enough to condition your responses. As the leader you can make the mistake of pushing your performers too fast. They will not enjoy frequent rewards enough to condition a positive work ethic and confidence. By increasing the frequency of your success and selecting smaller incremental and measurable goals, you also increase your reward-reinforcement schedule. This is the final or third Triad in purposeful intent. Nothing creates stronger intrinsic feelings of success and reward to want to repeat those work ethic behaviors that will ensure your continued success than becoming more consciously aware of your significant role and all the little things you do that count. In an excellent leadership system, your team members learn to recognize and praise the efforts of fellow team members. Writing a simple thank you note showing your appreciation gets the recipient to reflect on their behavior to be intrinsic. If you rate their performance value, your note becomes an ordinary extrinsic motive. A happy heart is a learned perception of self reward that is reinforced by peer recognition. Your biological system is set up to automate tasks. The only way to self-reward in the post evaluation phase is to increase your conscious awareness of all the gradually improving incremental steps you took to reach your achievements. Your ultimate goal plays a role but is not the strongest motivating influence. Achieving your conscious daily goals increase your reward frequency to gain more job satisfaction. Performers who never learn to observe small changes in their personal achievements report low job satisfaction. Society and schools condition you to wait for the approval of parents, then teachers and professors, and finally bosses to evaluate your work to feel satisfied. Purposeful intent leadership skills train you to self evaluate your work using your performance feedback and other strategies. You evaluate the quality of your own efforts to provide self-reward, increase your intrinsic motivation, and perform consistently at a higher level or plane than others who have not learned these skills. Remember: <u>No top performer ever waited for the approval of another person</u>.

Building Confidence

Nothing will build your confidence faster than your immediate and consistent success. Success is a perception in your "black box." How you evaluate or value your success is a result of your personality that is largely formed by the environment you are driven to control. Most performers are unaware of their needs to know when to feel success when it happens. If you are conditioned to meet the less powerful needs of others who often condition the awareness of your faults, these will be extrinsic motives. If your leaders take credit for your work or ideas, you can:

a) put them in writing to prove where they come from,

b) get mad and purposefully slow down your performance output and convince co-workers to do the same,

c) pout, yell, and call in sick the day before an important group presentation or deadline to send the message – the team needs you,

d) refocus on your PI and do your job to eventually get noticed, or

e) confront your leader who took your credit to learn where you fit in the organization.

What choice will build your confidence faster?

Key Elements

The key elements to learn are how to identify and create your own needs to fulfill your *purpose*, and a positive goal setting paradigm that builds your confidence by increasing your frequency of success and reward feelings. This conditions your intrinsic reward and creates a positive *intent* to approach all new tasks with a commitment to succeed. Successful performers do these skills without knowing how or why they perform them. You build your confidence by creating a personal paradigm shift that equates quality of effort with quality of personal reward. With increased awareness all your activities in life have more value. You lead a fuller, more satisfying and happier life that is infectious to your circle of influence. When you are aware that you have put forth more effort in your training by recording your work in a performance log, you do not want to surrender or give up. Failure is not an option. You make success happen. When you learn how to increase your conscious awareness of what that value means to you, you condition a reward-reinforcement for all your self-evaluated performances. Learn how to be your own best friend and not beat yourself up for failure to achieve unrealistic goals is another elemental strategy to follow. If you find that you are really hard on your post performance evaluation, consider that this was conditioned in you by others who had a need to manage your behavior. Their way of managing was to point out all your faults, to keep you in check, and under their control to avoid embarrassment to them for your behavior or poor performance. Let your failures become your future successes by making your goals more realistic and frequently achievable. Steady progress and self improvement is the best strategy to motivate your mind from within. Be happy with this strategy; the tortoise won the race with it.

Evaluation Strategies

There are many strategies to help you increase your awareness of your performance evaluations and connect the reward-reinforcement value of your activities:

1) Allow a skilled outside evaluator to rate your performance. If you rate your performance the same as the evaluator, you will have congruence to reinforce your behaviors. This confirmation by a skilled performer develops your realistic behaviors and confidence in those tasks.

2) Hold yourself accountable for your performances by not making excuses for your mistakes. Turn your mistakes in positive opportunities to learn.

3) Set goals your personal abilities and skills can perform to regularly achieve success and reinforce your personal reward system.

4) Create a job description that defines your role and expectations to perform.

5) Center your focus on applying the skills you possess that are required to do a job well and create your purposeful intent.

6) Create a personal portfolio to compare past performances with goals for future performances.

7) Build a resume to reflect on your accomplishments.

8) Collect reflections or snapshots of your work with references and letters of recommendation from others to help increase your performance awareness value.

9) Use a rubric and/or the B.F. Skinner feedback model to help other performers create the need to self-evaluate their personal performances.

10) Align your personal needs with the needs of the organization.

11) Reflect on ways to provide an objective means to connect reward with reinforcement in the evaluation process.

12) Compare your own written personal performance evaluation with your boss' evaluation.

13) Take a personal needs and abilities assessment survey (see Appendix) to rate yourself. Then ask significant others who know you to rate your performance on a separate survey, and then compare your scores. This kind of exercise can provide you with more insight into your expectations and needs that affect your personality patterns and motivate your behaviors.

14) Keep a personal journal or diary of your day-to-day accomplishments to reflect on your past performances.

15) Improve your performances in small increments each day to enhance your personal reward system.

16) Practice continuous assessment of your needs and your performance skills to satisfy and reward them.

17) Track positive performance results in a work log to reinforce your positive work ethic behaviors. Great process for athletes.

All these strategies contribute to developing your higher PI strength that over time will produce successful performances of greater value.

Summary

The purpose of learning to perform a post performance evaluation is to learn how to process your own feedback without having to wait for the approval of others to help you judge the worth or value of your efforts. Your comparison must focus more on your own immediate past performance or past performance average. As you learn to increase your feedback awareness of your past performances to form a "self" perceptual anchoring point, you will judge the worth of each succeeding performance better. You cannot control the performances of others. You can control how you approach your goals using the needs you identify and create in your mind, your work ethic, and setting realistic and achievable goals based on your awareness of your talents and abilities, purposeful training, and immediate past performances. To condition your reward-reinforcement system, you must "connect" your quality of effort with your quality of reward consistently improving and learning that good performances are not haphazard luck. You are blessed with God given skills, and your mission is to gain a variety of experience to learn them. In return, your gift back is to learn and perform your skills to the best of your ability gained from hard work, and then pass on what you have learned to lead other performers.

No one who has experienced an electric shock thinks that was fun and wants to repeat the accidental behavior. Neither would you want to perceive not being able to better your own immediate past performance with a little more purposeful intent and work ethic. This is your best strategy for motivating your mind from within. Your intrinsic motivation and personal drive motive is highest when you set a low positive goal. With a little more work and concentration, you will improve and feel success. You have no excuse. When others accept any portion of the credit for your work accomplished, they automatically exchange that amount into an extrinsic reward system that will never build accountability. Research consistently indicates that extrinsic rewards offer little when compared to intrinsic motivation within the performer for long term success. Every success has its price to build value and confidence. You cannot build confidence by heaping praise on performers who know they have not earned it to boost their self-esteem. Conversely, every performer must know what qualities they perform in their role and who does the work to get the credit. Extrinsic means in the form of outside rewards or setting a goal or outcome for your performers to meet your management purpose or needs are not effective motivators for the long term. It is not what the evaluator thinks as much as the performer knows to self-evaluate their work that matters the most. If you select the goals and set up the desired outcomes as the manager or leader, your performers will have less purpose and value to perform the work because the performers doing the work are not intrinsically involved in the plan. Confidence must be earned from feelings of success in the mind of the performer not the evaluator. This leads to positive reinforcement where you want your performers to improve upon and repeat the work accomplished to "feel" the same reward. By selecting low positive goals only slightly better than your own immediate past performance or average, you greatly increase your probability for success. The more frequent you can experience success, the more likely you want to repeat and improve upon those work ethic behaviors. Learn to increase your probability and frequency for success by selecting low positive goals. This strategy raises your level of confidence and expectation for success to hold yourself accountable for achieving *your* goal.

Boss leaders who assume their performers are incapable of self motivation lose their ability to lead. No self motivated performer will desire to improve their performance when they are micromanaged and controlled. Remember Behavioral Rule # 2: You cannot improve accountability in a micromanagement system. This is a form of slavery that causes a reduction in intrinsic motivation and creativity because the goals of the organization are not aligned with the personal goals and values of the performers. The surest way to kill off any form of intrinsic motivation in a person is to:

1) boss manage and control how they perform their personal skills,
2) take credit for their work, and
3) not provide working conditions to meet their personal needs.

When you demonstrate that you care about your performers, their opinions, and how they feel about the work they accomplish, you'll find an improvement in work performance. Your management must find time to effectively listen and communicate with every performer. Ultimately, it is not what you think or evaluate in another person's performance but what they learn to self-evaluate that matters most. It is always what the performer perceives to be success or failure. Any performance improvement is success that can be conditioned to be repeated. Society has falsely created the notion that only those who are passing, make good grades, or perform outstanding achievements are successful. With purposeful intent skills, you condition your own success as you improve upon your immediate past performance or average. The longer and more continuous you make this quest you become a high achiever over time. You learn how to reinforce your own efforts to continue and persevere where others will quit and move on to another task.

In any organization or system, micromanagement will not instill personal leadership and performance improvement accountability. Lead management will raise the level of your performer awareness with positive feedback so that each performer can learn from their continuous performance a developed self-imposed pre, during, and post performance evaluation system, the second part of The Triad. True evaluation and performance improvement grows from a value system inherent in the performer that comes from elevating the quality of their work performed to a higher conscious state of awareness learned from self evaluation. By increasing the conscious awareness of the value of the work performed with a purposeful intent, you can more readily store and retrieve information to process faster. This helps you make better decisions to think it through for potential outcomes, and set more realistic goals that, when achieved more frequently, help you to establish a stronger personal reward system. By consciously increasing the value of the work performed and perceiving yourself as successful by getting better compared to your own immediate past performance, you will learn to evaluate-reward-reinforce positive behaviors that over time will define your achievements with results.

PART THREE

CONNECT REWARD WITH

REINFORCEMENT

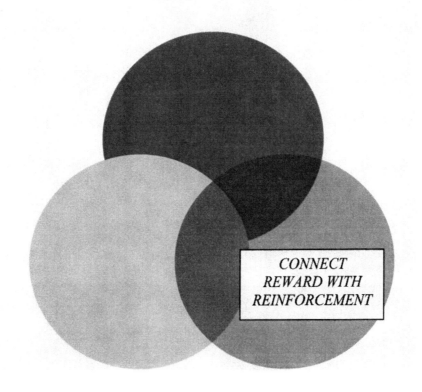

CONNECT
REWARD WITH
REINFORCEMENT

The biggest mistake a leader can make is to take credit for the work or idea of another person. Nothing will kill the morale of your performers faster. Empowerment systems imply that all performers can connect reward with reinforcement to provide lead management. Boss management systems imply that they are not capable of motivating the performers. However, when performers have some say in how they can perform the work to feel rewarded, they are more motivated to produce quality products and services.

Part three helps you to understand the behavioral relationship between reward and reinforcement of behavior by examining two points of view:

Principles of Reward-Reinforcement. Something so simple can be greatly misunderstood. You can learn to reward your own purposeful behaviors, and reinforce your performance skills to continuously improve until you become a consistent top performer in a specific task. This is how to motivate your mind from within.

Leading Purposeful Intent For Success. Every great leader communicates a positive vision that creates "buy-in" from the performers doing the work. Leaders hold themselves accountable. Building a sense of purpose with a positive intent to succeed is how leaders connect with the people doing the work. Every performer must build a connection between quality of effort and quality of reward to want to repeat those behaviors over time to produce success.

Principles of
Reward-Reinforcement

*"The quality of your excellence is
measured by your heart's desire."*

Andrew Christian

Objective: Learn how to create personal rewards to reinforce your
motives and work ethic to achieve positive results in succeeding attempts.

**The object of purposeful intent is to increase your intrinsic motivation
to learn how to learn, to think, act, and do for yourself and eventually
others.**

Introduction

Webster's Dictionary defines the prefix "re" as to go back again or anew. Reward
and reinforcement provide recognition for an improved performance. Re-cognition
is to think again or reflect on your achievement. Re-inforcement is to strengthen by
adding new material; the facilitated connection between a stimulus cue and a response.
Re-ward is to give something for something achieved. An extrinsic reward would be a
tangible prize like money or a gift from an outside source to recognize an achievement.
An intrinsic reward would be the feeling for improving a performance or exceeding
a personal goal enough to desire wanting to repeat the performance. It is harder
to reinforce unrewarded behavior. Therefore, use your mind to create the value of
reward for any small performance improvement that will reinforce the connection.
The greater the number of small reward-reinforcement connections the greater the
increase in intrinsic motivation to desire a renewal of the performance or activity. The
first principle of reward-reinforcement is Behavior Rule # 11:

You will repeat behaviors you feel rewarded, and reduce unrewarded behaviors.

Reflect back on your successful performances. Were the performances pleasurable and somewhat gratifying or painful and a waste of your time? What needs were you trying to fulfill? Were you aware of your purpose? What was your level of awareness to generate a purposeful intent to succeed? Did your success happen by chance, or by purposeful intent? Did you want to repeat successful performances and avoid activities you perceived you were not as successful performing or as satisfying? When you become dependent on extrinsic rewards to shape your behavior, you do not learn how to self evaluate your performance to define or create your personal needs that operate from within your framework of experience. This forces you to change how you create or adapt to your environment. One strategy is to control your environment rather than let your environment control you. If you choose not to become educated, you lose your opportunities for rewarding jobs. What environmental choices do you think will help you succeed? You can choose where you live and work, the kind of friends you keep, the marriage partner you select, the courses you need to take, the church to attend, and even the amount of time you devote to exercise and nutrition to be healthy for a higher quality of life. If you are insecure, you do not risk choosing new unfamiliar experiences to learn and draw upon to fulfill your future perceived needs because this process will create change and stress. This will not effect a change in your environment to learn and grow more to achieve satisfaction.

Society is not kind to outstanding performers when the expectation is to be humble and respectful, and not talk about their achievements. If you should mention your pride in your accomplishment to others, this is a means for you to personally increase your awareness of your achievement so that you can enhance your evaluation and sense of reward to reinforce your behavior. But society, instead of being happy and sharing your pride to motivate the personal interest of others to improve their performance, make up nasty labels. People will often remark that the top performer is a conceited b _ _ _ _ _ _, or an arrogant son-of-a-_ _ _ _ _. Learning how to self-reward and reinforce your outstanding performance behaviors is a difficult task. This Part III of The Triad, Connect Reward With Reinforcement, is perhaps the weakest skill of any top performer. However, in order to increase your motivation to work harder to keep improving your performance, you must learn this skill. If you don't learn to have confidence in your abilities, no one else will either. The extreme in sports has always been Muhammad Ali's comment, "I am the greatest!" If you make public comments like that, you better be able to back up your words. To open your mouth prior to a competition and guarantee victory only motivates the opponent, and even though it provides a verbal perceptual anchoring point to live up to your prediction, it is not a good idea. This is where *positive self-talk* comes in. You can verbally state your accomplishment privately to your brain to increase your conscious awareness for the meaningful and relevant value of what you just performed. Your body language will display a quiet confidence that your performers will sense in you and help build their confidence. This is OK, and should be practiced more often. It is great to give yourself a pat on the back for a job well done. You don't need to wait for the approval of others, including your critics; you know quality when you see it to compare your performance.

You are probably unaware of how conditioning is taking place to make your daily life dull and routine, or exciting and challenging. Repetition and routine creates boredom and staleness, and automates responses placed in unconscious sensory reaction mode. Instead of planning and acting to improve your performance to get ahead, your life is centered on following and reacting to maintain the status quo. The latter certainly entertains less stress as change is non-existent, but so is your knowledge acquisition and income to provide for your future needs. You must take control of your life and hold yourself accountable for learning and performing new skills. If you wait for others to approve your work or have to motivate you to learn and improve upon your God given abilities, you may have to wait for a long time. It does not matter that your parents were not motivated to model the correct go-getter behaviors. What matters is what you think of your purpose in life. What are you here for? Do you really want others to provide for your needs for your entire life? It is truly sad to see so many people in the world and especially in affluent countries with loads of opportunities who cannot learn to provide for their own needs. It is as if they have given up on themselves, and so has everyone else but this is a real concern in public education why this is happening in such great numbers. The answer is in the details of reward and reinforcement and the first principle. If you really want to help people, you have to teach them how to govern themselves to build value in their minds for the minor successes they can feel rewarded and condition another try to improve upon the immediate past performance. If a student does not score above 60 or 70 per cent on the first try, the public school system labels them a failure – a loser who is not trying. This is what gets conditioned and reinforced. If school systems would change their grading systems to reward improvement, then improving your immediate past performance – no matter where you start – would be the goal to increase the probability for success and feel reward enough to want to repeat the effort only harder to improve again and again. This is why Aesop told us about the turtle winning the race. This is why we must teach men how to fish so they can feed themselves for a lifetime.

Change your thinking right now. Practice self reward by viewing your success as any kind of slight improvement over your own immediate past performance or average. Forget about that 90-80-70-60 or A-B-C-D idea. You cannot control what other performers do, but you can control what you plan, decide, commit, and work to achieve. Rejoice in even your smallest of achievements to improve. Keep in mind that as you improve, your last performance becomes your immediate past performance, and your new goal must be one point higher to feel success. If you did it with any kind of purposeful effort last time, you are already reinforced to do more of the same things to make it happen again on a higher level. Your mind knows you can learn, and your body feels it is in condition to get stronger. You already have the mind-body connection in place; use it or lose it.

Key Principles to Follow

1. <u>Listen with your heart.</u> Your "ear" for listening is in your h(ear)t. Your purpose and value are connected to satisfaction of your need or goal and continuously measure the quality of your excellence.

2. <u>Know the quality of your work.</u> Leaders do not wait for the approval of others to motivate their behaviors. When you learn to self-evaluate and reflect on your work using a set of predictable personal standards that work and principles to assign meaning and relevant value, you will have a vision and realistic goals to understand how the quality of your performance will affect outcomes. You must hold yourself accountable to your personal quality standard and be committed to achieving your goals. This is how you connect reward with reinforcement.

3. <u>Be consistent in your work ethic and motives.</u> You learn skills in planes. Your performance may not be markedly improved during performance plateaus, but learning is still being conditioned by valuing the small rewards of success. See the Typical Learning Curve figure that resembles a lazy "S" tipped on its side. Stay focused on consistently achieving your intermediate goals that lead to a final outcome. Know why you want to achieve your goal to meet a specific need. This is your intrinsic motive defined by your purpose.

4. <u>Understand how to increase your awareness to meet your personal needs,</u> When you know your purpose, you can achieve more. You will more readily recognize, receive, organize, store, and retrieve (RROSR) information you have created the need to be meaningful in your pre-frontal cortex. This process executes and reinforces your performance with a purpose focused on a higher level or plane. When you have no conscious purpose and go through the motions with your performance, the information is less meaningful and stored in the less retrievable parts of your brain. This information is not readily available at will on demand when your performance counts. If you are conditioned to expect or depend on others to meet your personal needs, you will never achieve consistent performance improvement to reinforce your work ethic and energize your internal system. You will be conditioned to work to meet the needs of the person directing you as opposed to learning to be inner directed.

5. <u>Get in touch with your feelings to build value.</u> Your desire to create and meet your personal needs comes from your heart, i.e., "The heart of a champion." To become highly aware of your personal feedback use the Skinner feedback loop to continuously self evaluate the worth of your performances and improvements. You determine the rate and progress of your performance improvements over your immediate past performance that condition your feelings of success or failure. You evaluate the value of every performance experience in getting slightly better. Great performers seldom reach the pinnacle of their success overnight. They all pay a price, and suffer set backs but learn to overcome errors and obstacles with frequent smaller successes that reinforce their work ethic behaviors and positive success feelings. Top performers stay positive in how they choose to feel about their overall performance. You simply do not give up, and remain persistent. Remind yourself why the turtle won the race with smaller more manageable continuous improvements with each step focused on the finish line goal.

6. <u>Keep it positive.</u> No good feeling was ever achieved by negative thinking. Stay focused on visualizing positive outcomes for all your activities to increase your awareness that will enhance your motives and provide you with your purpose.

7. <u>You learn what you focus on,</u> Our educational system and society is focused on producing immediate gratification. This creates a literal behavioral

sequence dependent on short rather than long term need gratification. As a conditioned response you do not learn how to project, understand, or plan for your future needs and how to fulfill them when your focus is on immediate gratification. When you become increasingly dependent on others to meet more of your personal needs, you tend to blame them for your shortcomings and have a difficult time achieving your goals and a quality of life. This behavior creates victims, and conditions "learned helplessness." All throughout your life you must condition a positive response attitude to focus on your motives to achieve success, and make them greater than your motive to avoid failure.

You will always have your critics. Never lose sight of your hopes and dreams or the P.T. Barnum circus model for success. He said dream the biggest dream you can, market the living 'hell' out of it, and treat your workers like family. Successful companies are beginning to follow this leadership model.

Approval System

No highly successful performer ever waited for the approval of another performer. Successful performers learn to connect reward to reinforce their own performance evaluations. They keep a positive focus on the purposeful intent of the activity. Reflect for a moment on your past activities over a two to three year period. For any activity that you understood why you were working hard to improve with a purposeful intent, you were probably successful for a good portion of your activity better than 95% of the time. There was always something positive you could take away from your purposeful performance. Conversely for activities that you went through the motions with no purposeful intent, your success was haphazard and inconsistent. If by chance you had a good feeling for a successful performance, you made a positive connection between your effort and reward. This increased your motive to want to repeat those like behaviors to enjoy more of that feeling. With more repetition and success your passion grows. You begin to self select more time for activities you feel successful at performing because you condition your relationship between reward and reinforcement. You subconsciously assign high to low values for each activity. I doubt the great modern art painter Picasso ever contemplated what the critics might think of his creative work. Critics are more often average people who cannot create and do what you have achieved. This is why you need to learn how to evaluate your own work for quality, and reinforce the personal value you attach to your effort and results. As you become more reinforced to produce quality and your repeated success becomes routinely familiar as if automated, you will also have to increase your conscious awareness of this fact to continue to self reward your work or you will lose interest. Most successful performers fail to recognize this fact. Much of what you successfully perform each day you take for granted because your performances become routinely familiar and common. This does not create a desirable reward-reinforcement schedule, and why the strategy to increase your conscious awareness of routine tasks is necessary to create value to motivate performance improvement.

Behavior Premise

The simplest behavioral concept to understand is that you tend to want to repeat behaviors you feel are rewarded or successful, and avoid those that create pain, or stress associated with unfamiliar changes in your routine. Negative results or feelings are associated with changing a familiar sequence of behavior or performance whether good or bad to an unfamiliar trial or effort. There are two key premises to all behavior:

First premise: Change is difficult because unfamiliar new tasks place unwanted stress on your familiar personality patterns to create discomfort and anxiety until you become familiar with the new task. You have no proof from your experience whether those changes will create a better quality of life or efficient performance.

Second premise: You know quality when you see it, but you are conditioned to wait for the approval from a parent, teacher, or boss. You have not been taught how to condition and self reinforce positive behaviors using your own performance feedback. This process is learned from your work ethic to build value for all your performance activities. If success comes too easily, you will not place a high enough value on that kind of activity to want to repeat those work behaviors that lead to increasingly more success and feeling good inside about your work unless you change and raise your personal standards to improve.

If you have any concern for either premise, try these two strategies:

First, increase your awareness for your brain to demonstrate that you can learn.

Second, understand the relationship between quality of effort and quality of reward to self-reinforce your work ethic that will enhance your personal reward system.

These strategies can be achieved by regularly setting low positive intermediate goals only slightly better than your own immediate past performance or performance average as you visualize each smaller goal to increase the probability for your success and reward. Continued success will keep you on task. The turtle won the race to ultimately succeed by focusing on trying to be a little bit better with each new trial (step) or performance opportunity. This is Behavioral Rule # 3:

If you keep your expectations in line with reality, you will be less frustrated with your performance.

When you attempt to achieve higher unrealistic goals that you are more likely conditioned to perform by others to meet their needs that you will **become frustrated and discouraged**. This leads to disruptive and bad behaviors. Intrinsic motivational processes are least understood to be taught as a leadership skill, but provide higher drive levels than extrinsic motives in the form of goals and objectives created or demanded by others. You know your goal achievement probability is created by your desire and will to win inside your heart. If you take your goals seriously and stay focused and positive in your motives to meet your personal needs, you will increase your PI strength and probability for success. By having no goals to meet your identified needs, you do not feel rewarded to condition your motive to repeat work behaviors to improve your learning and physical skills. You feel less worthy, lose interest, and accomplish very little for your efforts to waste your time, and decrease your PI strength and probability for success.

Micromanagement and leader evaluation reduce the personal empowerment and self-evaluation that can increase workers' intrinsic motivation. What you learn to think of your performance is far more powerful than what your evaluator thinks. Leaders must help performers make the connection between quality of effort and quality of reward. The connection of personal reward to reinforce the intrinsic motive and continuing effort is reduced by the performer's perceived amount that the leader has taken credit. As the leader, and this includes teachers and parents, when you go overboard externally praising a performer for a good effort on a task, it automatically creates an extrinsic motive and sets the bar height for the performer's next expectation. The goal is for the performer to establish a purposeful intent for all their performances and to continuously improve their immediate past performance so that they can challenge themselves with no set limits. You want your performers to want to do well when you are not looking. When there are specific rewards achieving a group goal, the extrinsic motivation diminishes the personal intrinsic effort of every team member. Therefore, a strategy to control for this behavior would be to *define and assign specific team roles and hold each member accountable for performing their part.* To reinforce good performance behaviors, you want your performers to exceed their personal goals. This will not happen as frequently when you have established extrinsic group goals with pre-set limits. Asking a performer to journal how they feel about what they accomplished will help them reflect on the purpose and value they attach to their effort. Creating personal value is a far more powerful motivation than the extrinsic praise because it puts the performer in charge of his/her work ethic behavior, fulfillment of his/her needs, feelings of success, and intrinsic reward, all of which are necessary components to building personal accountability, and connecting reward with reinforcement.

When leaders motivate performers using specific rewards (candy, money, gold stars, check marks, vacations, or excessive praise of any kind) these become extrinsic motivators. The more powerful motivator, though, that can alter behavior, is the performer's internal feelings about the value or satisfaction of their positive intent to achieve the personal effort. Because some tasks are easily accomplished, performers don't value them, and often these tasks are not reinforced. Leaders must challenge performers to focus on the specific parts of the process using RROSR and the outcome will have a higher probability of achievement. The focus on the parts reinforces everyone to mobilize their creative personality, skills, and abilities to achieve the result for each part to complete all the steps. There are no short cuts to consistent success. Trainers who noticed the failing results of "approval" systems instituted methods that would provide for reflective thinking to allow performers to judge the value of their performance in relation to the group objective.

Excessive social approval and verbal praise diminish your reflective thinking to self-evaluate and compare your immediate performance with past performance for improvement and form a perceptual anchoring point and new goal. The comparison can be to what another group has performed, or your public statement of the desired goal, and the most powerful would be tracking your immediate past performance which can help set a low positive goal one point higher to increase your drive stimulus and probability for success. Now with a stronger purpose to put forth more focused effort, you have more motivation to achieve your goal, and connect reward with reinforcement. This strategy is a necessary skill component to increase your awareness, confidence and self-esteem that intrinsically create the value of your personal reward. The quality or value of the reward you perceive reinforces and increases your motive to want to repeat the activity on succeeding attempts with more effort to ensure your continued successful feelings. This process of setting new goals enhances your personal reward system and intrinsic drive motive.

Need Based Behavior

Most performers do not think about their short or long-term needs that drive their behavior. Knowing your needs, even as they change, is essential in the pre-performance evaluation stage. Knowledge of how you meet your personal needs is also vital to how you reinforce your own behaviors. You cannot expect to significantly improve your performance when you go through the motions of the activity. In affluent countries like the United States, you take for granted your basic needs for food, clothing, and shelter. Things that are free or you do not have to sacrifice and work hard to get are not valued. This is normal human behavior. Most of your education is free, but there are too many students who do not value their education enough to want to work harder to obtain more quality education. However, if you were having brain surgery, I doubt that you would want to know that your surgeon only cared to have a 70% average in school. The more others provide for your needs, you lose your drive motivation to provide for those needs. You are not reinforced through intrinsic reward to be self sufficient. Performers with learning difficulties have their need to achieve reduced by others who feel a stronger personal need to provide for their needs. You can mean well, but you must learn to teach your performers how to be aware of their needs and plan to meet them. If you teach your performers how to fish, you feed them for a lifetime. All the things that you do for others will take away from their intrinsic motivation and creates dependence on you and your system. Our congressional leaders have conditioned the behavioral principle of dependence. Unearned welfare does not create an intrinsic motive to achieve anything, and steals self-esteem and pride. We learned this principle in the 1880's with the Native American Indian Reservation system. You must not condition learned helplessness. A cry for help does not mean that you perform the work. Teach your performers how to help themselves. *Learned helplessness* is a behavior that conditions others to do the work for you, and is not a desirable leadership principle. When you do the work for others who are capable, you only reward more of the same unmotivated behavior. Once again this violates the # I Behavioral Rule:

The more you do for others, the less they will learn to do for themselves.

For this reason, governments that create more social programs enable unmotivated behaviors to work and provide for personal needs. Entitlements condition the demand for service in return for paying higher taxes to get one's fair share. Leaders must communicate a strong "can do" message of confidence that their performers learn to hold themselves accountable for their performance. Over protective parents have stronger personal needs to fulfill than they can see to help their children learn to provide for their own needs. Perhaps a mother has a strong need to be loved and wanted, and conditions "learned helplessness" in the child to need mom to meet their needs longer than they should. This pattern becomes reinforced where the child behaves to not learn to meet their own needs to gain more love and attention. This is not good parenting. Good parents teach their children to focus on higher order needs to eventually take care of themselves. Good parenting is teaching your children to learn how to provide for their own needs and accepting the consequences of their behaviors. When you take the fall for your child's mistakes, you will not teach them accountability to learn from their mistakes. Your personal needs drive your behaviors.

Increasing Intrinsic Feelings

All behavior is motivated by the personal needs of your performers at the time. You must know and understand what those needs are that are operating during the performance. Erratic behaviors are caused by not knowing your immediate and long term needs. You must create a system to identify your needs to set goals. Your post performance evaluation provides the necessary feedback to indicate the strength of your intrinsic motive to fulfill your needs. If your motive is a need or performance goal set by your manager, it automatically becomes extrinsic. Extrinsic motives are less likely to reinforce lasting results from personal feelings of success. Leaders must learn how to shift the focus from a group interaction to small individual incremental achievements that increase your performer's frequency of success to reinforce personal reward feelings. This will increase their intrinsic motive while still operating within a team environment. Each team member must fully understand the role they play in a team effort, and be held accountable for performing their part. Credit is given to the performers that do the work. Effective leaders must not accept any credit for creative suggestions and work accomplished by team members. Nothing will kill your team or performer's morale or reinforcement faster than for you to take credit for a positive performance from those who did the work. The second worst morale buster is not having a system to recognize outstanding performances. You do not have to use extrinsic rewards to recognize good performance. Any outstanding performance recognized by peers or that you credit those who performed the work has intrinsic value. A sincere and simple thank you or pat on the back from the leader will do wonders. Why destroy or lessen the 100% intrinsic performance value by a percentage that will diminish that pure form if you take any of the credit? Leaders with secure egos do not need the credit, and it is far more important to reinforce the efforts of the performers doing the work.

Creating Purposeful Needs

Strong leaders display several common characteristics that develop relationships that motivate their performers. Several of these characteristics are: vision, trust, integrity, forthrightness, patient, will-power, character assessment, strong communication, focus, accountability, and realism. Good coaches are able to break down complex tasks into smaller, manageable parts to teach and learn. For each part they identify key skill components to recognize cues and create correct responses they can objectify performance data to track improvement in each sub skill. Top coaches continually condition the relationship between the sub skills and the whole skill to create the need to focus on in practice and improve performance in competition. All this leads to quality performance improvement that can be rewarded. These kinds of coaches are noted for getting their performers to delay rewards until championship play or the big contest when the stakes are more valued.

If you want to be a good leader, study the great coaches who instill strong positive relationships with their players. Players have reported an intense loyalty to being coached by Johnny Wooden, Bobby Knight, and Doc Counsilman. A key characteristic of great leaders and coaches is their vision from years of quality experience and patience. They see the potential and reinforce the good qualities of their performers. They help their performers increase their awareness of smaller positive incremental improvements to frequently reward and motivate them to consistently bring out their best performance. As leaders, they do not look for the faults, but rather the good qualities they can reward and reinforce to continually strive to improve. You cannot continuously criticize an employee or performer or child and also expect them to be highly motivated. The more you yell at your child to do their homework or chores, it is no longer their goal or reward to complete that task. They are less motivated because no personal need has been created that they can feel rewarded and held accountable for the achievement. All learners will make mistakes or they would not be trying to improve. To reinforce those errors is a fatal management error. Great leaders and managers know that your personality patterns will change over a period of two to six weeks as you become more familiar with any new task or job. Focus on only a few key points to improve performance that you can provide positive feedback to reinforce and condition any performance improvement. Sometimes, your role in management to lead is not to boss, but to listen to the questions and concerns of a new employee with understanding and patience to build their confidence in you. For teachers, the classic "do overs" are the rule until the performance evaluations by the performer and leader are similar and congruent. Where school systems adopt the policy, "Failure is not an option," students are given opportunities to get the assignment correct until they can earn a "B" or an "A." Very quickly students grasp the idea that it is better to produce quality on the first attempt. Create the need with an objective scoring rubric to enhance self-evaluation and build personal accountability. An example of a writing rubric is in the appendix.

This patient approach to learning is what builds confidence in your pupils to acquire knowledge of their subject or a workplace task. By helping your performers become aware of the key focus points or cues, you reinforce the stimulus-response relationships until the correct behaviors are demonstrated. You must provide realistic expectations to overcome obstacles. In psychological terms, you are creating conflict in the performer's personality patterns between the old and new way to perform, and the need to get conflict resolution. To resolve the conflict and stop the leader's wrath, the performer will make the necessary adjustments to their personality patterns to accommodate and assimilate the new way of performing or behaving. Performers may adjust personality patterns by increasing their persistence and will power to achieve a personal goal that reinforces the correct behavior when achieved. The performer will remain in the doghouse until they modify their work behaviors to meet the expectations of the leader. As more frequent accomplishments occur in the parts, the performer is rewarded and the correct response behavior is reinforced.

When you establish a purpose by telling your performers why they need to learn relevant information in a forthright expectation, you create the need for positive work ethic behaviors. You ensure repetitive success to condition the connection between reward and reinforcement in repeat practice trials. As you lead, project the need to improve performance over time based on the prior personal experiences of your performers combined with your experience with other top performers. Great coaches learned from top coaches they studied and/or performed under in a variety of conditions. Leaders use praise and reproof wisely to gain the respect of their performers. If you give unearned praise, you will lose respect. Morale will also drop if you do not recognize big or small contributions by all your performers who are trying to improve. Good leaders know when to give earned praise to build a performer's self-esteem. Trust is built upon forthright honesty communicated in an objective and fair way. Everyone has an ego to protect that can be hurt more by words than action. The best way to create a higher expectation of a need to personally improve performance besides breaking complex tasks into more manageable components to experience success is: a) place accountability for improving on the performer, and b) teach them how to evaluate their own performance against their personal past performance standard. Remember the behavioral rule about performance evaluations. Your evaluation automatically shifts their perception of the intrinsic value of that evaluation to extrinsic. This makes your evaluation less valuable than their personal evaluation. When performers learn to self-evaluate by comparing their new performance to their immediate past performance, they intrinsically build positive value for any kind of improvement. Knowing your purpose for performing is what creates the value for the need to improve that enhances the learning experience and makes it more meaningful and relevant. After your performers have evaluated their performance, the leader – teacher, coach, or manager – can provide their objective evaluation. If the two evaluations agree, you will have a more powerful motivational reinforcement in a <u>congruent evaluation</u> that is essential to create the need to improve and build a purposeful intent. The performer and the leader, teacher, or coach must be on the same page in how they define "performance quality." You want to look for, reward and condition positive behaviors that overlook or extinguish negative behaviors by not calling attention to reinforce them. This is the major fault for parents who have discipline problems in the home. The more they point out their child's faults they keep reinforcing those bad behaviors. The same applies to schools that create more rules to violate to improve their discipline.

Great leaders account for the psychological make up of their performers. You create needs to achieve, and personality chemistry to define performer roles in the team organization. You cannot recruit performers with character flaws and expect them to lead your team, or be self-disciplined to improve their performance when they believe other performers are the problem. The demonstration of psychological skills has become as important as the physical prowess skills. The mental aspects of sport are legendary. Great leaders are passionate and patient to teach anyone and everyone who will try to improve their personal performance, and will consciously choose to work with less physically talented performers because they know they can create a stronger purposeful need to achieve team success. The highly talented physical performer is more satisfied and less driven to improve and gain more rewards with teammates until the coach convinces them that they cannot win a championship by themselves. Your performers need to have leadership capacity to self direct their behavior and the performance behavior of others when you are not looking. You do not need to be top-heavy in middle management to make this happen. Talented performers who are not motivated to improve rely on the rewards from their past success rather than risk losing what they already have achieved. They need to be challenged with a purposeful intent to continuously self-evaluate their progress to keep improving their immediate past performance or performance average. This is the process that creates the need to increase personal expectations and intrinsic motivation.

Whether you desire success in a classroom, boardroom, or at any physical or mental skills event, a skilled performance can be broken down into several key parts also known as subroutines to work on them individually. This enables you to have a stronger focus to set a low positive goal, and evaluate the results for each part more frequently. When your performance feedback shows improvement, you can connect reward with reinforcement easier than you could by thinking of the entire performance. A great symphony orchestrates parts for each musical instrument to blend into the entire performance, and is written accordingly in parts to achieve this result. Generally your brain cannot attend to more than five selected cues at a time, and three would be optimal. There are specific cues to learn to anticipate and stimulate your conscious awareness. With each new trial, a certain amount of feedback is learned to associate and reinforce reward with the next performance. Great coaches and teachers provide you with the specific visual, verbal, or kinesthetic feedback cues to attend to that will improve each trial until a greater consistency of performance occurs. Innate in all human behavior is the drive to improve. Ideally you want every performer to see and value even small improvements frequently to build their confidence and reward to reinforce their intrinsic motivation to work harder to maintain feeling good about the work they are putting in to improve. Knowing and observing continuous improvement from your own performance feedback creates a powerful reinforcement schedule that is highly resistant to forgetting, and conditions your personal accountability for your performance.

Organizational Recognition

The central idea of your organization is to see every performer consistently improve incrementally. The most important variable to create is an atmosphere of continuous and consistent self-improvement. If every performer made timely incremental progressions that were slightly better than their own immediate past performance or average, the company or team would see monumental gains in less than one year. Performers who compare their performance in relation to others never perform as well as performers who self evaluate their immediate feedback against their immediate past performance. Large organizations, top heavy in middle management, want to build immediate results using extrinsic goals that place adverse pressure and stress on all performers. The work is no longer enjoyed because no personal satisfaction of reward can be observed. A commonly accepted behavioral pattern is that people and animals tend to want to repeat satisfied behaviors and avoid painful unsatisfactory behaviors. No one touches an electric cattle fence and says, "Boy, that was fun, let's do it again." If you can learn to use your own feedback to compare your immediate performance with your immediate past performance and see improvement, then you must feel some satisfaction. When you can equate quality of effort with quality of personal reward, you will be intrinsically motivated to work harder and smarter to continually improve upon your performance.

There are all sorts of organizational recognition schemes to reward performers. Unfortunately the predominant rewards are extrinsic with no thought of how your performers feel about their performance. There are announcements in the company newsletter, performer of the week or month, closer parking space, a raise or salary increase, increased responsibility for a team role, or some other kind of extrinsic reward. However, nothing can replace how your performer feels about the quality of their efforts supported by caring leaders who show empathy and personal appreciation. Leadership can provide all the positive accolades and feedback you want, but your performers must learn how to self evaluate and value the quality of their performance. You do this by periodically asking your performers to evaluate their work post performance in relation to their personal goals. Are they on pace or target? What must they change to improve? Is training adequate, and do all the performers have the tools for success? Top performers take pride in their work, and love to communicate this pride to leadership. But too often leadership seems too busy to want to take the time to listen. As the leader you must build time into your daily routine to regularly communicate with every performer on an informal first name basis.

Leadership can provide extrinsic benchmarks, goals, expected outcomes, standards, and a company mission that is the ultimate goal. Or, your performers can select their own performance standards to increase their intrinsic motivation by improving their immediate past performance. Intrinsically motivated performers will more often exceed their personally set standards than those set by management. The strategy is to get your performers to set realistic standards they can frequently achieve rather than try to impress their manager with an unrealistic high goal that cannot be readily achieved to reinforce a positive work ethic. In your post performance evaluation, you learned how to connect reward with reinforcement, the third part of The Triad. You do not need a manager to tell you this fact. If you must have managers, ask why and overlook the fact that your performers are burdened with extrinsic goals based on the needs of the manager and not the performer. The effect of extrinsic management on personal performance improvement is not happening.

Set Up Your Personal Standards
For Success

Feelings of success are in the performer's mind from within. Success is not what you tell your performer to feel value with your evaluation, but what your performer learns to value and feel rewarded from their post performance self evaluation. Anyone can tell you with emphasis that some specific new information is valuable. However, until you create the need in your mind with a purposeful intent to make the information meaningful and relevant in value to associate with previously stored knowledge, it is doubtful you will make the connection to retain as much of the new information. <u>Your success feeling is associated with how closely you approximated your goal with your actual performance compared to your immediate past performance.</u> This is your personal standard that you have some control over to consistently improve with any purposeful intent skills training. Because your brain is a microprocessor that does not know right from wrong, you must direct the brain to make new information valuable for better retention by simply creating the need in your mind that says this new information is cool, meaningful, and relevant. If it is something entirely new you have trouble associating to already known information, then tell your brain to wake up, get out of sleep mode, and remember this bit of information. You can create your own personal associations using more of your senses like Einstein did. There is a reason why he became the most intelligent man. I am sure that when he was born he did not have the same high IQ that he had when he died. Once you learn your PI skills, you will never forget and be able to apply the principles for the rest of your life. With these skills you increase your opportunity to become a top performer moving to higher performance planes as you become more familiar with each new challenge. Your strategy to win is to increase your probability and frequency for success, and awareness for highly predictive cues and self-evaluation that conditions your reward with reinforcement to work harder to maintain your success feelings. As the leader, you must avoid the traditional extrinsic evaluation systems to provide a personal intrinsic feedback system and PI skills for your performers to learn how to correctly evaluate and improve their own performances. This is how you build personal accountability for performance improvement. Break down job performance skills into smaller more manageable components your performers can improve and feel some success while they get the "big idea" and adjust to their role. This builds a self-reward system for each performer to create a higher awareness for all their performance improvements. To feel success requires a mental comparison to some kind of standard. The traditional standard has been some kind of group performance average, or arbitrary results for grading purposes like 90-80-70-60 for an A,B,C, or D and below that would be failing even though you could still be scoring better than half correctly. However, the numbers of students who seem to lose their way in public schools is increasing. We need to create a new personal standard each learner can have some control over to see improvements that provide personal reward feelings. Otherwise, life is pretty boring when you can show very little for your time and effort. Eliminate the word failure from your vocabulary and use varying degrees of success. The immediate past performance personal standard goal strategy changes the entire perception of intrinsic motives in your performers. To not try is failure, but any score provides a perceptual anchoring point (PAP) to improve. All performers have to start somewhere. It is not where you start, but where you end up that count the most. Your immediate past performance will change as you consistently improve, and is your baseline PAP about which you self evaluate the worth of your next goal. This creates your motivation and purpose to achieve. Your goal strategy must always be to set a low positive goal slightly better than your own immediate past performance. This is what you measure the most often in your post performance evaluation to condition the improvement motivation. As you achieve and reward yourself for small noticeable improvements, so will your immediate past performance change to create a new low positive goal and stronger purpose to value your work efforts to improve.

Research with Olympic swimmers suggests this strategy creates your highest drive motivation (Andersen, 1973). You have no excuse for not improving your immediate past performance if you practice harder and consciously increase your awareness and evaluation skills with a purposeful intent. This is the success strategy of top performers. Inconsistent performers set too high unrealistic and highly improbably achievement goals that do not condition their personal reward system. You want to increase the odds for your success so that your brain will be more aware to function in a higher capacity with a purposeful intent to readily perform RROSR: recognize, receive, organize, store, and retrieve information. You have a lot at stake. It is your goal, not your manager's. It is your needs that will be satisfied. It is your reward for the taking. If you cannot better what you did the last time out with a little more focused effort, you cannot expect to go from a low to high degree of success with the same effort and focus. You cannot fool yourself. A child knows better. If your performance has less value because you have not created a purposeful need to perform, you will seriously reduce your opportunity to achieve personal satisfaction of that need from any improvement. When significant others like leaders, teachers, and bosses try to create this need for you instead of showing you how to create a personal need for yourself, you will treat the need or goal or outcome like any other extrinsic motive, and lose any benefit of long term feelings of reward to reinforce your motivation to keep improving. You also lose your ability to connect reward with reinforcement, the third element of the Triad that through your post performance evaluation will reinforce your improvement success.

Stay Focused

When you lose interest in your performance, it is because you do not see measurable improvements to keep you focused and on task. You must remind yourself that the turtle won the race because of a plodding relentless nature one step at a time. The longest journey begins with the first step. If your focus is the mountain top, it will look ominous to reduce your will to achieve. When you break down tough tasks into smaller manageable and measurable increments, you increase your reward-reinforcement probability that enhance your motivation to improve and ensure your succeeding success. Set a realistic achievable goal to climb to the first level, and reward yourself with a rest to reflect on where you have come from to start your improvement. Leaders who have higher expectations mistakenly allow their performers to set unrealistically low or excessively high goals. Unrealistic goals have lesser motivation than goals only slightly better than your immediate past performance. Your leadership goal is to get your performers to demonstrate to their brain that they can learn with a purpose driven intent. When you demonstrate that you can learn to improve, you will achieve to prove your worth and more importantly, value your effort. If you are a leader, failure is not an option; but there will always be varying degrees of success. You can choose to feel success when you focus on your performance improvement more than your performance average based upon an absolute per cent scale like 90-80-70-60 or A-B-C. If you average a 58 and a 74, you are still failing by some standards. Or, you can choose to focus on your 16 point improvement over your immediate past performance to keep your motivation positive. In all probability, with a new goal of 75 you may have another positive increase when you increase your PI strength to retain more knowledge when you study. All performers can learn when properly motivated from within their own personal need satisfaction system you help them to create and understand. Thomas Edison stayed focused on his intent to learn 1119 ways how not to build a battery before succeeding. Initial partial success you perceive provides a base line to demonstrate your improvement and produce a positive reward to condition your effort. To think negative is to learn to perform negatively. To think positive is to perform better than your own immediate past performance, and continually self reward your own behaviors that you have some control over. You can achieve any realistic standard you set for yourself that you perceive as valuable. As the leader or significant other your goal is to teach your performers how to set goals to moderately improve each day to achieve significant results over time that are valued. Focus and do all those little details that count each day. Your goal driven behaviors do not come from infrequent large incremental gains that offer less opportunity for reward-reinforcement. Although on occasion, your one lucky haphazard shot in a round of golf will reward you enough to want to play another round. If your golf game is not improving, it is because your need is not stronger than other priorities in your life. You must be committed with a purposeful intent to achieve any need or goal. Your intensity to achieve a personal goal or need is matched by your frequent successes to keep you on task and focused on each intermediate goal achievement. You do not become rich or shed forty pounds of fat overnight. You invest small change that becomes dollars or balance your calorie intake with your expenditure through exercise to gain fitness over time. To succeed you sometimes have to change your thinking and priorities.

Keep It Positive

Everything has its price. As the coach you remind your team or a performer who has not achieved their potential that they are doing work few kids are willing to do. This sets your performers apart, and builds intrinsic value for the work each must sacrifice to accomplish every day. It refocuses the group purposeful intent on the mission to keep working on the need to perform a little better every day! You have to want it, and continuously compare your immediate performance to a desired future performance that is realistic to increase your drive level and purpose of the practice. *You have to be conscious of your purpose.* Your purpose becomes your mission and a very powerful intrinsic motivator. You learn to climb the ladder one rung at a time. You can look at the top rung but your hand has to grasp the next immediate rung or you will fall to the bottom and have to start all over. If you become aware that you are making many negative statements, stop yourself and think of how to restate the negative into a positive statement. The more you increase your awareness for what you say; you will correct negatives and turn them into positives for better performance results. Therefore, it is better to do it the right way the first time with a purpose.

Conditioned Approval

Performers who are conditioned to wait for the approval of others seldom become top performers. Top performers learn to develop personal feedback systems to self reward and reinforce a work ethic that leads to continuously improving their performance. To become a successful performer and develop your personal reward system use a low positive goal setting strategy to set goals only slightly better than your own immediate past performance or average. You can only seek to control how you can perform by how you choose to learn and practice your skills. Frequently achieving your low positive goals conditions your personal reward system. This conditioned reward system gradually raises your personal standard in planes as you acquire increasingly more familiar knowledge and skills in planes to apply to your future behaviors. This strategy helps you acquire purposeful intent skills to continuously improve the quality of your life. You will recognize your quality performances and no longer feel the need to wait for the approval of others to continue to improve your performance.

The approval of others is an accepted conditioned response in many performers. Waiting for the approval of others becomes a reinforced expectation and powerful short term motivator. Do what the boss manager says or risk losing your job. Companies and organizations spend billions of dollars to hire middle management to ensure that the workers do their job and stay motivated. Management conditions how they would accomplish the tasks to improve the company bottom line with little or no thought to the personal motives of those doing the work. To put this concept in a simpler context, when you fall in love your emotions drive you to gain the approval of a significant other. How you feel about your performance courting your partner to satisfy your personal motives is what must really matter if you plan to dazzle the other party. You know if your performance is improving to achieve a happy partnership. Learning how to be self-directed and not co-dependent upon a system of learning that conditions you to wait for a conditioned response from your manager or leader is the ideal but has not been the rule. As a leader you cannot expect to externally motivate every performer every day in your classroom, at home, or on the job unless some personal satisfaction can be achieved. If you fall into this trap, Kohn (1993) points out that when you get older you seldom do anything that is not connected to an external reward. If the external rewards are not great enough in value, you are not motivated to act. Your behavior is meaningless to have less value to retain information or feel any sense of accountability. This same notion can be seen in very rich performers who are unhappy because the extrinsic reward is never great enough. The happiest performers are those who feel personal reward satisfying their needs that are aligned to the needs of the corporation, organization, or team as a valued member.

Behavioral Accountability

Purposeful intent is a leadership training method to achieve personal behavioral accountability and performance improvement. It is a leadership style interwoven in all training, teaching, coaching, and evaluation. Purposeful intent is a learned skill that can be incorporated into all forms of teaching and training. This method is not a simple learned lesson or unit. <u>Purposeful Intent is the foundation for all motivation.</u> It represents a major paradigm shift in how you evaluate your performance behaviors. It is a commitment to teach you how to reflect and evaluate your own performance, and structure a positive deliberate plan to efficiently improve upon your performance.

Loyalty

Professional sports teams that scramble at the trading deadline to improve their teams more often hurt the morale of their players who felt they were needed and counted on throughout the season. Management conditions the opposite of team play. Players are motivated to focus on their personal statistics to increase their value or fear they will be traded. Sports championships and loyal management are dependent upon unselfish team play. The manager gives all the performance credit to the performers doing the work. Teams like businesses and school systems seldom become championship caliber when their management system is faulty. The Chicago Cubs provide the best example of conflicted management over the past 75 years. On the other hand, in 2005, the Chicago White Sox traded no one and won the World Series with the players who had become a team loyal to management that was loyal to them to increase their motive to win. Loyalty is a measure of trust. As a company or team, you must align your mission with the personal needs of the people doing the work. Quint Studer (2003) quickly points out that if you classify workers into three groups based on their personal needs and job satisfaction, those workers in the bottom third who have their coats on one minute after the workday ends and complain that their personal needs are not being met are least likely to become good to high quality performers. This bottom group will detract company performance by recruiting other workers to join in their philosophy and yield poor performance outcomes. Performers who are not intrinsically motivated need to be identified and ferreted out of your system or you must change your system thinking to accept lesser performance. The middle third can identify with and become more like the upper one-third of company performers if they are regarded by management to have personal intrinsic motivation to improve their performance and help reinforce the quality efforts of others. The last question to be satisfied, after all the interviews have been conducted to conclude who will be offered a position must be, "What will this person do when we are not looking?" If you hire intrinsically motivated performers and recognize their efforts to improve the company by giving them the credit, you can improve their loyalty and productivity with less management cost. Be sure your managers understand these PI principles and apply them to their performance behaviors as well.

Increase Your Awareness of Incremental Performance Improvement

Formal evaluation systems attempt to define achievement, but have similar pitfalls as extrinsic motives. These external systems are based on what someone else believes are the most important predictors of quality performance improvement. As a result external evaluation systems provide a less reliable feedback system to reinforce positive behaviors in the performers doing the work. What organizations have begun to do is have performers use the evaluation instrument to rate their own performance and compare with the supervisor's evaluation to determine congruence. When both agree, the evaluation becomes a powerful feedback tool to reinforce learning and performance improvement. When a supervisor provides an exceedingly harsh evaluation, higher management must be assured that the evaluation is valid and not due to a personality conflict where the supervisor feels threatened by an astutely creative and intrinsically motivated employee. In this case, the evaluation and evaluator must be realistic, and the coaching or request for performance improvement must be achievable to enhance the intrinsic motives of the performer.

In traditional training programs and schools objective scores below 60% of a total possible point total are usually assigned an "F" or failing achievement grade. This kind of evaluation rarely lends itself to reinforcing new attempts or trials to experience more failure. If you take the opinion that this is not failure but a better start than absolute zero, then it must only matter whether you can demonstrate performance improvement to your brain. Any noticeable performance improvement is cause to self reinforce some kind of probability for being successful on the next trial or attempt. If you learn to keep your improvement probability high by setting a low positive goal only slightly higher by one point than your immediate past performance, you will succeed in learning how to process or evaluate your own performance with smaller incremental and manageable steps. This creates a positive value system of self reward to reinforce your own performance behaviors. It does not matter where you start, it only matters where you end up that counts. Failure is when you do nothing to help yourself learn, and blame others for your poor performance. No one expects a beginner to know all the answers and perform like a professional. Your ability to learn comes from processing your personal feedback as opposed to having others constantly having to tell you what is wrong with your performance. Continually berating a performer will never teach them how to improve and build their self confidence.

Success Strategy

One team success strategy is to maximize your strengths and minimize your weaknesses, and get off to a good start. This is the objective game plan in winning athletics. You have weaknesses and strengths. You capitalize on the weaknesses of your opponent with your strengths while minimizing your weaknesses. Not understanding your short and long term needs to project a plan of intermediate goals to reach an ultimate goal is a weakness that can be corrected. Unfortunately in our society of immediate gratification, fewer performers have learned a successful strategy for planning to meet their long term needs. We have become a literal oriented society for short term need satisfaction. Purposeful intent teaches you how to acquire leadership skills using the Triad that provide for your understanding how to personally stay motivated to meet your projected long term needs.

Another success strategy is to be aware that in life you get multiple chances to perform "do-overs". Perhaps less than 5% of your life is spent in a one-time got-to-get-it-right or lose situation. If you pull your car out into traffic your one-time decision that there are no vehicles coming to merge into the traffic flow must be correct. You may not get a second chance if you are wrong. You must learn to be certain of your decision. You cannot learn how to drive a car by going through the motions on "auto-pilot." There can be serious consequences including death if you make a wrong choice, but for 95% of your life you get another chance to improve. You can afford to continuously plan for your success, take risks, be satisfied with personal rewards, and alter your plan until you achieve your desired level of success for your ability.

Team Roles

If you are conditioned to operate within the limits of a team, you must learn to focus on the elements you can control in your team role. Teamwork is an absolute concept with numerous meanings and perceptions to performers. You may devote your heart and soul to a team effort to win only to learn that your teammates are not as serious pulling their share of the load. Leaders and coaches need to define roles for every player to focus on achieving. Leaders of high performers create the need for consistent improvement and models for teammates to follow. You want to align the team mission and goals with the personal mission and goals of the performers. Mission statements are designed to bring the company purpose and goals into focus. You should align the company goals and needs with the personal goals and needs of the people who will do the work. The strategy for acquiring your personal goals becomes secondary where others on the team can fulfill their defined roles. Your focus must be on the outcome steps that you find are successful. Once you understand the purpose of your goal or need, you are automatically intrinsically motivated to care about the outcome to find an efficient way to get the job done. You will be committed to do whatever it takes to succeed even if it takes more initial mistakes and more frustrating hours than anticipated. Top performers find a way to succeed with a defined role and purposeful intent. A trust factor is built up between the management of the work and those performing the work. You must identify your personal needs by understanding your personality patterns that allow you to perform without great stress. Top performers create avoidance behaviors toward boss-management leaders. As the leader you must never over control the process a performer defines within their personality patterns for doing the work tasks unless you care to do the work for them. If the outcome is within the parameters, why care about the process? The boss's way or the highway can stifle intrinsic motivated caring performers who may be more creative and efficient. The intrinsic motivated performer finds more efficient processes to meet their personal needs and is aware they are accomplishing them with some degree of quality to take pride in their work. Your feeling of connecting reward and reinforcement is larger than you can put into your paycheck.

Learn to Win

Failure or winning can become a conditioned cycle and habit. Both take similar energy, so choose skills and strategies for winning. Your purposeful intent, your needs, your goals, your mission, and your passion to want to succeed are all concepts you can control. Individuals or teams that consistently fail or perform below their expectations have lost their purposeful intent. They are not focused on a realistic identification of needs to fulfill. They may be a collection of quality performers with different belief systems and expectations who lack a common mission or expectation to unify their collective efforts. You have to walk before you can run. Success must be reinforced with small incremental steps by setting low positive goals you can frequently achieve. To break a losing cycle you must take two steps back to learn where your stimulus-response (S-R) breakdown occurred before you can take three steps forward. Go back to doing what made you successful to re build your confidence. Few performers are willing to undertake this process to redefine their needs, and be more realistic. Failure achieves nothing; success achieves everything.

You do not make attempts to punish or embarrass yourself to feel bad. You make attempts to fulfill a need and create a positive feeling about your performance. Frequent failure conditions avoidance behaviors. Your brain shuts down when you turn your monitor off. This makes new attempts harder to perform without a purposeful intent and positive focus. No performer wants to feel worse about a projected negative probability to perform. The strategy to work to avoid failure will never help you to succeed. You must create the need to keep your motive to achieve success greater than your motive to avoid failure. Avoidance behaviors create a negative focus that more often reinforces your failures. This is what typically happens when school systems create excessive disciplinary policies. To perform better, feel good, and want to repeat that behavior, you must learn how to create low positive needs (or goals used interchangeably) that are realistic and more achievable.

In most all educational systems, learning how to win is not what is taught. Highly successful students and performers have learned the Triad system of purposeful intent on their own by trial and error based on the driving forces that were imposed upon them from someone other than the school at an early age. All schools and training programs are notorious for imposing grades as a means for easily objectifying behaviors to qualify performers for a future performance as acceptance to college, trade school, other higher institution of learning, or employment. The means to evaluate others takes precedence over teaching your performers how to reflect and self-evaluate their performance. You must be consciously aware of your immediate past performance or past performance average to predict and set new goals that are realistic to challenge fulfilling your personal need to do well. You can graph your scores or keep a performance log or journal. How frequently you continuously improve your performance determines your perception of success or failure. When you feel personally rewarded you will want to repeat that behavior over and over again. It is how you begin to learn how to win.

All grading and evaluation systems are extrinsic motivators. Your performers will not hold themselves accountable until they learn how to evaluate their performance. Your performers are more highly driven to feel rewarded and repeat winning behaviors when they are made to feel part of the process. Learning must be its own reward, and a reflective process within the performer to continuously learn to improve and win by achieving personal goals and objectives.

Teaching Purposeful Intent Strategies

School systems need to start teaching purposeful intent leadership skills in kindergarten. Teachers and trainers need to transition performers from excessive use of extrinsic motivators to intrinsic motivators to increase performer accountability for learning and demonstrating performance improvement. Leaders or parents who micro manage their performers do not permit them to take risks and occasionally fail on initial attempts to learn how to process individual performance feedback. This practice deprives your performers of learning how to use vital feedback lessons. Independence in thought and action are critical to becoming a responsible adult. You must understand how the positive choices you make affect your performance over time. These skills are not a one time event to feel lucky. Skill based learning is sequential and dependent on reinforcing your feeling of performance improvement. If you are not improving, you try a new cue in your input phase to change the outcome of your output phase. Teens make bad choices when they have no purposeful intent. They do not understand their needs to prioritize them or have goals to achieve. When performers make poor choices you have to think what motivated their behavior at the time.

Differentiated Coaching

Coaches have used differential learning to teach their athletes for generations. Each athlete has a specific program to follow in a skill acquisition sequence to master and perform at a high level. Similar stimuli are associated in pairs known as *paired associate conditioning* to get the same response. Coaches describe "*feeling*" cues to anticipate in the muscles while making a visual demonstration of the sequential movements.

Kinesthetic, verbal, and visual cues are simultaneously used to get the same positive response from performers who process information differently.

Self-Evaluation Mastery

In the elementary grades children are getting their educational foundation. They are not typically given enough opportunities to learn how to self-evaluate through rubrics that could enhance their quality of performance. Mastery learning allows you to do over assignments to learn and continually improve. You realize that you may as well put forth more effort to achieve higher quality on the first try. The long-term effect creates the need to value what you are learning with a purpose. Having a purpose helps you achieve quality. In the adult world you get multiple tries to get "it" right. You can self-evaluate and reward your behavior for the thinking process and achievement. Learning how to self-evaluate helps you understand how to be accountable for your learning. You gain control over what and how you prefer to learn with purposeful intent leadership skills. Intrinsic motivation creates a paradigm shift for you to <u>equate quality of effort with quality of reward.</u> When the three elements of the Triad come together, you will have powerful learning skills to apply for a lifetime.

The Early Learner

First and second graders are capable of understanding or learning intrinsic motivation with purposeful intent skills. I spoke to a class of 44 first graders. They all knew when they had put forth an effort to achieve a good result, and also knew when they had not put forth a good effort and received a lesser result. They understood the story about how the turtle won the race over the rabbit. I expanded this concept to teach them to set low positive realistic goals only slightly better than their immediate past performance. This goal setting strategy increases your frequent feelings of success to reward your behavior. You keep improving in small bits and pieces like the turtle who won the race. The turtle was a plodder who achieved success over time staying focused on each new step. Create your personal portfolio system to plot your scores on a graph to see your improvement and know the effort you used by keeping a journal.

The Adult Later Learner

Most adult teachers and trainers and performers do not understand how to teach intrinsic motivation. As the leader, parent, or trainer be careful not to apply your bias about what you think your performers cannot do. Do not underestimate your performers. If you teach the basic skills in a sequence, your performers will learn to apply their skills until they become more familiar. This process will improve their personality patterns of confidence, self-esteem, security, and self-assurance. Learning intrinsic motivation skills to motivate your mind from within can be learned as easily as learning the skill to shoot a basketball free throw. Top performers learn by trial and error and the benefit of good coaches who speed up the skills learning process by teaching specific strategies that predict faster and more accurate learning. The strategies to learn your purposeful intent to motivate your mind from within are found in The Triad. The Triad is based on the fundamentals of behaviorism. You have innate drives such as to improve the quality of your life. A robin will build a better nest each year given the proper materials. The Triad provides you with the proper tools to apply and learn to improve for the rest of your life so that you will achieve quality performance over time. Once you understand your needs and how all behavior has motives to satisfy needs, then you can predict how performers will learn and act to fulfill their needs.

Legislated Behavior

Our legislators need to understand how the legislation they write creates adverse behaviors that motivate people not to perform and produce quality. Legislation has cost our government systems millions, rather billions, of dollars to fund and in the long term motivate people to "beat" the system to qualify. What are supposed to be programs to help the needy in fact create the needy problem. The costly bureaucracy cannot enforce the laws that are already in place. Business management works in the same way because most leaders do not understand the foundation for all motivation and continually hire traditional performers who are not intrinsically motivated, and have to surround new employees with costly middle management.

Athletic Model

Athletes can learn objective skills to self-evaluate when given individualized cues to enhance their abilities to their fullest potential. This evaluation has as its foundation the purposeful intent of the coach with the learner to build a congruent concept of acceptable quality performance that will lead to success. When coaches use proper cues and they prove successful, their performers are conditioned to listen to their advice to continually improve.

Micromanaged Relationships

I never knew what a refrigerator magnet was until I married my first wife. Her whole life was managing mine. You cannot lead and approach performers with the idea that you can prevent every mistake in the road. You can demand effort leading to quality to build value into the learning process. You can understand the meaning of personal success setting proper goals and establishing your purposeful intent based on satisfaction of your personal needs. These foundations for your motives satisfy your underlying needs, and all that successful performers do.

Positive Self-Talk

Positive self-talk is another PI strategy. You must learn to be your own best friend. Successful performers make mistakes because they frequently try new and creative solutions to problems they encounter. They accept small failures as opportunities to learn. They learn to take calculated risks, and learn from their errors. *Positive self-talk* is a strong strategy for building reward-reinforcement. It helps you to reflect and evaluate your performance as only you have experienced it. You can talk to yourself as you grow and learn to improve in small increments. You increase your awareness of your small successes, to stay focused on the positives. You learn to process personal performance feedback to improve your thinking in higher and higher planes that continuously reinforce your personal need to demonstrate improvement and feel satisfied by your efforts.

Positive Performance Visualization or Mental Practice

Positive performance visualization is a strategy that works like a video taped movie to see you successfully performing a skilled activity prior to the actual performance. You can attend to all the positive cues you have been coached in practice and conditioned to perform with no errors. You can mobilize your positive energy to apply at will on demand in the correct sequence. Another sport psychology term for this process is "*auto regulation*." Top athletes use this strategy to "*psych up*" prior to performing to "*program*" the skilled performance automatically without having to think about anything during the performance. These kinds of skills are transferable to a variety of mental and physical skills.

Learn From Your Mistakes

Learning to learn comes from becoming aware of your performance feedback. If you work on increasing your awareness, you will pick out and discriminate positive from negative in each performance. All performance is a sequence of stimulus-response connections. To correct an error in your performance response become aware of the proper cue to become the new stimulus-response connection you can slot in the series to replace the faulty connection. If the performance feedback loop is not what you want or expect, change your stimulus input. See the figure, B.F. Skinner's "Black Box" feedback loop in chapter five, Pre Performance Evaluation. This is how *Planer Thinking* gets started. Eventually, there will be many more positive outcomes than negative ones. You will begin to think in a familiar higher plane to take in more information to apply to your future performances. You will have increased your associational neurons to a greater degree to more readily retrieve more information than if you simply go through the motions without a sense of value or passion for your work effort when you have a purposeful intent.

Mobilization of Effort

With each new attempt, you create a personal need to perform to the best of your ability. Your purpose is to learn how to mobilize all of your energy and skills *at will on demand*. You cannot control how another person, competitor, or teammate will perform or complete tasks on the job. You can control what you purposefully decide to perform. You can elect to work harder to identify and overcome your personal weaknesses by creating the need to perform a little better each week. This implies that you know how to recognize, receive, organize, and store meaningful and relevant information you value in your learning process. You will have increased your awareness of your immediate and past performance feedback to compare to a familiar standard. The only difference between a high performer and an average performer is their ability to recognize when to raise their level of performance up a notch for a given moment in time relative to the overall performance time already spent or anticipated. The top salesman knows when to make the close. The top athlete knows how to be single-minded and focus all of their energy in a given pre programmed moment in time. The NBA pro rarely misses the second free throw with more concentration and use of the immediate feedback. Success is a learned and highly familiar sequence of psychological events. It cannot be achieved over night. A great example was when Michael Jordan left the NBA after winning three championships to learn to play baseball starting in the minor leagues. After returning to the NBA it took him one and a half years to reacquire the high skilled mental focus to apply his physical skills at will on demand when the game was on the line.

Mobilization of effort is a finite skill that must be learned over time from preparing for higher and higher levels of competition as your skills improve. Highly skilled athletes need several performances to "*tune up*" their skills prior to a "*peak*" performance. In comparison, the only difference between an average and top performer is in their ability to intrinsically motivate themselves to mentally perform at will on demand when it matters the most. The top salesman knows when it is time to shut up and quit selling. After making the close, the first one to speak loses. Similarly great athletes know when but not how to get into the "*zone*" at will. To apply these kinds of skills at will on demand are based on The Triad, the fundamental basis for all motivation. If you increase your awareness, like an atom shown in chapter two, Mind-Body Connection, you will bump the molecules in the overlapping spheres and enhance self-evaluation and reward reinforcement. This stirs these spheres into action to provide a synergetic effect to continuously learn and improve your skills.

You cannot appreciably increase your intelligence without first increasing your awareness skills. You will need to recognize, receive organize, store, and retrieve more and more information into and from your pre-frontal cortex where it is readily accessible to hold your pre planned executable files in short term memory. If your life depended on an object file or bit map you created, you would not want to store that important file in a folder in a folder in a folder. By the time you retrieved the important information you could be dead or will have lost the contest when it matters the most. By increasing your awareness skills, you learn to process more data faster with repetition. Hypothetically, this is the function your prefrontal cortex is designed to perform. You increase your microprocessor speed by building associational neurons and nerve transmission pathways as you repetitiously practice your physical and mental skills. Your brain will begin to function as if you had added a faster microprocessor chip. When you visualize a positive performance prior to the actual performance, you theoretically send smaller waves of electro chemical responses through your muscle tissues as if you were actually performing the skill. This process helps you to increase your nerve conduction pathways to process data more efficiently. You also develop your pre cognition skills to recognize and process cues more selectively.

Like a computer file in your zip drive you compress a host of data into a much smaller bit map. A video response that can be complex is compressed and stored into a smaller more readily retrievable bit-map. Trigger words act in the same way to elicit a host of information to draw upon and apply to your immediate performance. Your practiced patterned responses are critical to the development of your awareness skills. Leaders would do much better to accurately demonstrate physical skills and the specific sequence for learning and applying those skills to create efficient pathways. Practice alone does not create correct outcomes. Practice with correct cues and a feedback system that can make continual adjustments to your input with a purposeful intent will cause you to improve. That is the nature of striving to reach your potential based on your ability. You will apply your purposeful intent skills for the rest of your life and never achieve all that you can. But you will have far more successes than failures to define your life and improve the quality of your life. Never give up!

Leading Purposeful Intent
For Success

Stormy sea requires strong faith and sturdy boat."

Andrew Christian

Objective: To understand how imposed standards and evaluations by others reduce the intrinsic value of an activity to the performer.

Introduction

The Purposeful Intent Flow Chart gives you a visual summary of the schematic diagram for teaching intrinsic motivation as a leadership skill.

The clockwise circular flow figure: 7 Steps to Purposeful Intent Performance Improvement gives you a cliff notes visual summary for how to affect performance improvement for yourself and those whom you will lead. Both are found on the next pages.

Purposeful Intent Flow Chart

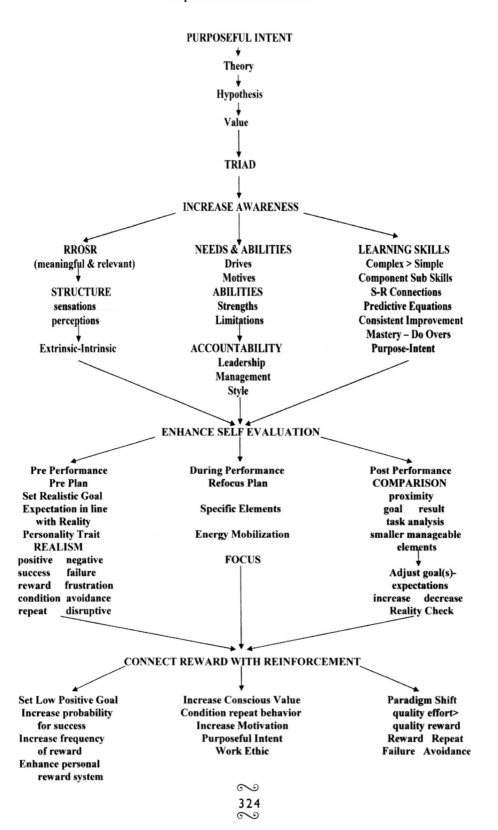

PURPOSEFUL INTENT
↓
Theory
↓
Hypothesis
↓
Value
↓
TRIAD
↓
INCREASE AWARENESS

RROSR	NEEDS & ABILITIES	LEARNING SKILLS
(meaningful & relevant)	Drives	Complex > Simple
	Motives	Component Sub Skills
STRUCTURE	ABILITIES	S-R Connections
sensations	Strengths	Predictive Equations
perceptions	Limitations	Consistent Improvement
		Mastery – Do Overs
Extrinsic-Intrinsic	ACCOUNTABILITY	Purpose-Intent
	Leadership	
	Management	
	Style	

ENHANCE SELF EVALUATION

Pre Performance	During Performance	Post Performance
Pre Plan	Refocus Plan	COMPARISON
Set Realistic Goal		proximity
Expectation in line	Specific Elements	goal result
with Reality		task analysis
Personality Trait	Energy Mobilization	smaller manageable
REALISM		elements
positive negative	FOCUS	
success failure		Adjust goal(s)-
reward frustration		expectations
condition avoidance		increase decrease
repeat disruptive		Reality Check

CONNECT REWARD WITH REINFORCEMENT

Set Low Positive Goal	Increase Conscious Value	Paradigm Shift
Increase probability	Condition repeat behavior	quality effort>
for success	Increase Motivation	quality reward
Increase frequency	Purposeful Intent	Reward Repeat
of reward	Work Ethic	Failure Avoidance
Enhance personal		
reward system		

7 Steps to Purposeful Intent Performance Improvement

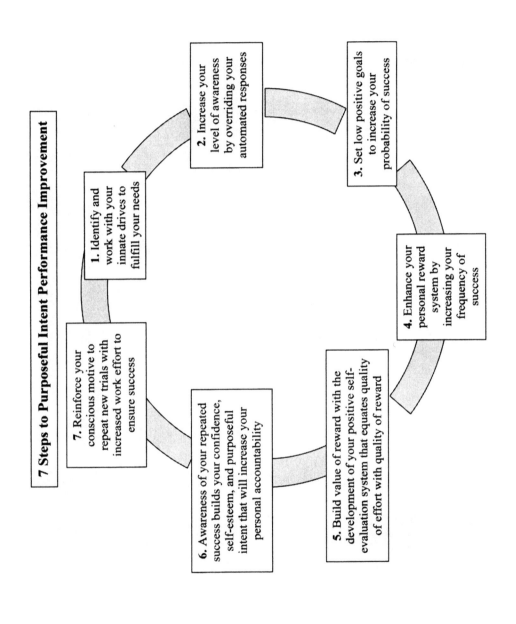

1. Identify and work with your innate drives to fulfill your needs

2. Increase your level of awareness by overriding your automated responses

3. Set low positive goals to increase your probability of success

4. Enhance your personal reward system by increasing your frequency of success

5. Build value of reward with the development of your positive self-evaluation system that equates quality of effort with quality of reward

6. Awareness of your repeated success builds your confidence, self-esteem, and purposeful intent that will increase your personal accountability

7. Reinforce your conscious motive to repeat new trials with increased work effort to ensure success

Key to the development of intrinsic motivation and personal accountability using The Triad is the development of a personal feedback system. Each performer learns to tell their brain what they feel is meaningful and relevant information to assign some kind of value. RROSR was introduced to show how the brain processes information and to suggest that Purposeful Intent is the system to introduce value with a purpose in mind. How you progress to learn the Purposeful Intent system to intrinsically motivate your performance is shown in the figure, PI Feedback Loop. This figure provides you with an easy review template to check your progress in learning the Purposeful Intent system.

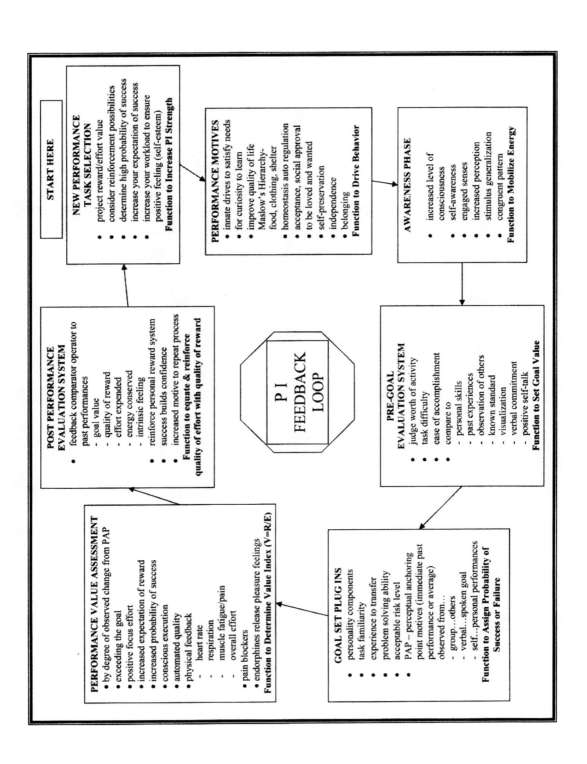

START HERE

NEW PERFORMANCE TASK SELECTION
- project reward/effort value
- consider reinforcement possibilities
- determine high probability of success
- increase your expectation of success
- increase your workload to ensure positive feeling (self-esteem)

Function to Increase PI Strength

PERFORMANCE MOTIVES
- innate drives to satisfy needs
- for curiosity to learn
- improve quality of life
   Maslow's Hierarchy-
   food, clothing, shelter
- homeostasis auto regulation
- acceptance, social approval
- to be loved and wanted
- self-preservation
- independence
- belonging

Function to Drive Behavior

AWARENESS PHASE
- increased level of consciousness
- self-awareness
- engaged senses
- increased perception
- stimulus generalization
- congruent pattern

Function to Mobilize Energy

POST PERFORMANCE EVALUATION SYSTEM
- feedback comparator operator to past performances
   - goal value
   - quality of reward
   - effort expended
   - energy conserved
   - intrinsic feeling
- reinforce personal reward system
- success builds confidence
- increased motive to repeat process

Function to equate & reinforce quality of effort with quality of reward

PI FEEDBACK LOOP

PRE-GOAL EVALUATION SYSTEM
- judge worth of activity
- task difficulty
- ease of accomplishment
- compare to
   - personal skills
   - past experiences
   - observation of others
   - known standard
   - visualization
   - verbal commitment
   - positive self-talk

Function to Set Goal Value

PERFORMANCE VALUE ASSESSMENT
- by degree of observed change from PAP
- exceeding the goal
- positive focus effort
- increased expectation of reward
- increased probability of success
- conscious execution
- automated quality
- physical feedback
   - heart rate
   - respiration
   - muscle fatigue/pain
   - overall effort
- pain blockers
- endorphines release pleasure feelings

Function to Determine Value Index (V=R/E)

GOAL SET PLUG INS
- personality components
- task familiarity
- experience to transfer
- problem solving ability
- acceptable risk level
- PAP – perceptual anchoring point motives (immediate past performance or average) observed from...
   - group...others
   - verbal...spoken goal
   - self...personal performances

Function to Assign Probability of Success or Failure

Meta-Cognitive Flow Chart: Intrinsic Motivation

Meta-cognition is your ability to construct your own knowledge as you learn on the job or in school. Nothing can replace first-hand experience to be more familiar with new tasks you must learn. However, this is when your teacher creates the need to learn by providing you with age-appropriate methods and strategies that are meaningful and relevant for your prior knowledge. Good teachers make learning fun and exciting as discovery tasks to build value in their courses. Their passion and caring comes through, and every learner feels compelled to learn because that teacher cares about them and their performance every day.

The flow chart below helps you to understand how to increase awareness for learning. It is based on the three chapters in Part One that focus on the structure of the body to use nerves to transmit and store information, the mind-body connection to transform sensations and lower levels of primate thinking into higher level perceptions, and accountability through learning using natural drives.

Meta-cognitive Flow Chart: Intrinsic Motivation

Structure → Central Nervous System
Awareness → Sensations, Perceptions
Learning → Learning Models, Natural Drives

Central Nervous System		Sensations	Perceptions	Learning Models	Natural Drives
Brain:	Body:	Unconscious	Conscious	Mastery Do Overs	Improve
Brain Cells	Nerve Cells	Automated-Routine	Irregular-Routine	Multi Sensory	Value
Frontal Lobe	Synapse	Stimulus (S-R)	Response	Input-Output	Meaningful, Relevant
Pre-Frontal	Associational	Conditioned (S-CR)	Response	Transfer	Motives: Motivation
Cortex (PFC)	Neurons	Paired-Associate	Conditioning	Feedback	Memory-Long Term
Memory-Short Term	Reflexive	Information Processing	RROSR	Identify Needs	Identify Abilities
Microprocessor	Flight-Fight	Sensory Satiation	Task Familiarity	Planer Thinking	Practice-Repetition
Fine Motor	Gross Motor	Selective Attention	Cue Recognition	Sequence	Pattern
Kinesthetic	Receptors	Stimulus Generalization	Response Generalization	Serial Loops	Chaining
Personality					
Traits	Patterns	Feeling	Reward	Open-Closed	Backward-Forward
Types	Perceptual Anchoring Pts	Intent	Purpose	Complex Tasks	Subroutines
Group	Group Perf	Immediate Past Performance	Perf. Average	Visualization	Mental Rehearsal
Verbal	Verbal Statements	+/- Goal Shift	Low + Goal	Paradigm Shift	Quality Effort-Reward
Self	Past Performance	Extrinsic	Intrinsic	Leadership	Top Performance
Realism	Top Performers	Effort	Reward	Desire to Repeat	Work Ethic
		Incr. Prob.Success	Incr. Prob. Reward	Reward	Reinforcement

Success Breed Success

Successful people know that success breeds success. When you feel successful fulfilling a need or surpassing your goal, you naturally want to repeat those behaviors and good feelings. Success is in your mind's eye. You do not have to be the best in the world. What matters is that you feel you are improving against a standard you have set for yourself. The standard most often used by top performers and the one suggested throughout this book is your immediate past performance or average. By setting a low positive goal only slightly better you increase your probability for success and frequency of reward. This conditions a positive feeling and expectation to build confidence and increase your intrinsic or self motivation. You feel success because you apply a positive feeling to having improved your performance over your perceptual anchoring point. Success is to know your purposeful intent in all your activities all of the time on a conscious level, and then performing what you choose to perform.

Outstanding Performers

Top performing athletes use their immediate or past performance as a perceptual anchoring point (PAP) to evaluate the worth or value of a new goal. They become their own control group, and do not compare their performances with other performers they cannot control. You cannot affect what another person thinks or performs. You can control what you do to improve your performance. By setting low positive goals only slightly better than your own immediate past performance you create the strongest motivation to improve. Satisfying more frequent goals also improves your personal reward system and confidence. This is why you need to break up complex difficult tasks into smaller component sub routines to provide more opportunities to experience success with small improvements. Your frequent success conditions and reinforces your need to continue feeling good about your next performance, and drives your positive motivation to ensure your success with a little more effort and purposeful intent at will on demand. You fulfill the value hypothesis of more readily storing and retrieving necessary information to perform your skills by consciously creating a purposeful intent for every work activity.

Your increased awareness enhances your nervous pathways by creating more associational neurons to assist in the speed of sensory data transmission. Good coaching and teaching provides you with the proper strategies and cues to attend to and recognize early in the skilled performance. This improves your efficient and successful performance over time with repeated trials. By mastering the B.F. Skinner (1953) "black box" feedback loop, high performers have learned to learn from self evaluation skills fostered by increased awareness strategies. They know their needs, and why they perform practice trials or homework to simulate competition and assessment. They perform highly skilled activities *at will on demand*. When it counts the most, top performers know how to mobilize all of their talents, abilities, and energy for a single moment in time. The average performer has not mastered this skill because they do not know how to apply the strategies of purposeful intent.

Get More Out of Your Life With a Purpose

You get out of life what you put into it. You were not created to use half your brain. Learn to use your entire brain. You have an artistic and analytical side, and must learn to merge the two to work in concert. This is no more difficult than teaching your non dominant hand how to perform a physical skill like your dominant hand. Performers say they are not good at math because they have not created a positive motive to succeed. Your focus is to avoid embarrassment and failure seen by others. When you learn PI skills to self-evaluate, it will matter more what you think of your performance and hold you accountable. A brain cell is a micro processor that does not know right from wrong. Your brain is programmed like a computer with built in system files to process data from your sense organs. If you practice skills in a sequence, you develop an efficient nervous pathway to readily recognize, receive, organize, store, and retrieve (RROSR) relevant data for later use. You improve your learning with a purposeful intent to focus your behavior *at will on demand*. Anyone can master PI skills to enhance their performance and quality of life over time.

Negative to Positive Conversion

Your thinking capacity for purposeful intent can greatly improve your skilled performances over time with correct practice. Try this exercise strategy. Note the sample form in the appendix. On a sheet of paper draw a line down the middle and across the top for a header. In the left header write negative thinking behaviors, and in the right header write positive thinking behaviors. Next, reflect on several of your latter performances and record your negative and positive thoughts under each header with an event description in the middle across the line. A delta ▲ symbol indicates change. For each positive thought that resulted in an improved performance, place a +▲ symbol to mark it. For each negative thought that resulted in a lesser performance, place a -▲ symbol to mark it. This awareness exercise should quickly demonstrate how your positive or negative thoughts impact your performance. My mother used to say, "Turn lemons into lemonade." You must do the same to change your thinking skill. This strategy is also choice psychology. Begin to rewrite every negative thought you stated in the left column into a positive statement in the right hand column in the form of "I can" or "I will" statements. This will complete the written exercise.

A second strategy is a *mental exercise*. You must learn to trigger a positive response to stop and convert every negative thought pattern. First, create an image of a traffic stop sign. You can imagine a red flashing stop light, octagonal stop sign, or a flat hand palm out extended at arms length. Second, condition a paired response to your visual image held in your brain and say to yourself, "Stop!" Third, if you are emotionally charged up, you can also add and condition a silent number count down to yourself. Start with the number 10 and descend your count and pace down to 1 or 0 if needed. This temporarily diverts and neutralizes your focus to easily convert to a positive thought in the heat of competition. Mentally rehearse the positive physical outcomes of your present and future expected performance. By turning your negative behaviors into positive behaviors in your thinking capacity you increase your odds to beat your own last performance. When you better your last performance by any margin, you must feel successful. Give yourself permission to feel rewarded. You will have to exhibit more and more effort as you improve little by little, but you will also experience and feel greater reward from having earned your goals. <u>Great achievements are seldom earned on the first trial</u>. You get back in the game with gradual successes to fuel your confidence. Successful people pay their dues with many smaller achievements they value that keep them motivated and on track to earn their path to success. Performers who give up easily are conditioned to set too high goals that cannot increase their frequency of reward enough to condition repeat positive responses. It is strongly suggested that you need to change your goal setting strategy so that you may begin to perceive success more frequently than failure.

Mastery Learning

If you adopt, "Failure is NOT an Option," then you let learners do over their work and use self evaluation rubrics until they can earn a "B" or "A." In the adult world, a marketing brochure gets a dozen reviews before being printed. The ultimate outcome is LEARNING! Necessity is the mother of invention. It is human nature to not act or do anything until there is a need to do so. It is not natural to learn how to identify and create your higher order personal needs that can improve the quality of your life. Most all basic needs for food, clothing, and shelter are provided for by someone else until you turn 18. The United States government has legislated so many social programs that they have conditioned its citizens to believe that "Big Brother" will take care of them. Young people are confused and behave indifferently because they have not learned how to identify and strive to meet their long term needs. Fast food, video games, toys, T.V. and electronics can retard the development of your performance feedback from all your sense organs. One thing video games prove is the natural drive to improve. Each new trial is an attempt to better the immediate past performance or average. Even after repeated failure, the motivation or drive persists. Short term needs, and living only in the moment or paycheck to paycheck are all that matter to more and more performers as we have become a literal society. You are conditioned to think only in the moment you experience. This is all driven by more and more extrinsic motives for the profit incentive of a third party who prey upon the weak mental abilities of performers who choose not to master fundamental learning skills. The predictive equation is simple. Without a purposeful intent, it is hard for you to create your personal needs to motivate and drive your positive behaviors to accomplish long term results. How you learn to approach a difficult task is important. You must learn to break down hard complex tasks into smaller incremental tasks that can be accomplished individually in a sequence. Your responses will also provide you with more opportunities to perceive and value your reward in relation to a manageable effort to reinforce your work ethic. You cannot learn all about art or science in a day, week, month, or even a year. Mastery of any skill takes time, and it helps to break down the skill into no more than five components at a time to focus your energy to get positive results.

Mastery learning means that you must master a skill level before proceeding on to the next level. Performers become confused about the conventions for a subject like algebra, because they did not master the lower level concepts. More confusion and feelings of failure do not build your confidence. The perceived pain of frequent failure leads to procrastination, stalling, denial, rationalization, and other avoidance behaviors to keep from doing the assigned work. You are not intrinsically motivated because you cannot feel any success from your lack of effort. You can spend more time thinking of excuses than it would take to get the job done by backing up the component skill to learn where there is a break down in knowledge and learn a to master those underlying skill levels first. Our educational system is set up to move performers along by grade levels and chronological age whether or not they master the concepts and benchmarks. We are fearful that students will be hurt socially if they do not remain with their peers. We assume that failing performers cannot socially adapt. Then we expect our students to adapt to learning new concepts every day. Good caring teachers are able to recognize students who have breakdowns in their learning sequence to coach them until they master that level and can move on with understanding to the next process. These teachers use differentiated learning strategies to increase mastery learning. Poor teachers blame failing students for not trying harder to apply themselves with enough practice. They do not understand the importance of early learning success to intrinsically motivate student behaviors to learn. While this may also be true, there are negative feelings generated by earlier perceived failures that are hard to overcome and tend to condition negative consequences. The more you discipline performers, the more trouble they find themselves doing negative behaviors. You learn what you focus on – good or bad.

Mastery learning provides for early and often success to build your confidence. There is evidence of performers who are required to complete modules to correct their deficiencies in a subject, and then surpass the brighter students in that subject once they get "caught up" or master the learning sequence with understanding. Subject mastery cannot readily be achieved without a purposeful intent to change your focus. <u>You identify and create the appropriate need and align your positive goal strategy that reinforces your learning with continuous success.</u> The traditional grading system used by schools forces a comparison to others and a group standard in place of your immediate past performance that can demonstrate a personal feeling of success. When you perform poorly that pain can only further your negative reinforcement to create more avoidance behaviors. Not so successful students can shift the focus from their poor achievement to their classroom disruption, or in worse cases self medication with drugs. It is all about where you shift your focus with a purpose. If you look at self improvement, you can feel good about any kind of improvement over your last performance that can demonstrate you are learning. This reward will motivate you from within to keep trying to improve. Negative reinforcement conditions you to avoid learning how to improve. Your choice, but our traditional schools and adult training programs need to look more closely at how they motivate their performers to improve. For a complete review of the research literature consult Alfie Kohn (1993), <u>Punished by Rewards</u>.

Overcome Your Fears

No one likes to continually feel pain and suffer embarrassment. When your pain, suffering, and punishment are too great, you withdraw and lower your expectations. You are conditioned to dream less about a higher quality of life. Your perception of success or failure is associated to your reinforcement and learning. If you do not experience early and continuous success in a subject like algebra, you quickly learn to hate it. Similarly performers claim to have no artistic talent because they feel they cannot draw. When you ask performers what art skills they have learned to perform, they have no reply. They have turned their brain off. You cannot acquire a skill if you do not try to improve with a purpose. You seldom learn what all of your capabilities are because you think you cannot do something. You fear failure and let your negative thinking get in the way of your opportunities to learn and practice what you learn. If you master the sequence for any complex task in more manageable sections by attending to the correct cues, you can learn to master many skills if you have the physical and mental capacity.

Create Dichotomies to Aid Your Learning

Positive reinforcement plays a great role in learning to learn. Mastery learning increases your probabilities for success to feel rewarded and reinforced to repeat similar learned activities. A dichotomy forces you to recognize both ends of a larger spectrum so that you can readily choose the correct path. Right or wrong, positive or negative, yes or no, and pleasure or pain are all dichotomies. Using a dichotomy, you can convert negative to positive images or feelings. Dichotomies increase your awareness to make the obvious correct choice. If you have a choice between a negative and positive outcome, you would choose the positive outcome. No one purposefully seeks failure. Performers can become conditioned by failure and reactive as victims instead of learning how to be proactive and positive. No one purposefully wants to repeat an accidental electric shock from a wire, or cattle fence. That negative unpleasant sensory feeling is avoided. You quickly convert sensation to perception. No rationale is necessary. Performers who repeatedly fail feel the same pain need to be taught strategies for how to master a complex skill in a positive performance sequence of smaller incremental steps that can demonstrate improvement and provide success. Otherwise, the outcome is that you easily give up and try something else. This is not a good thing for you or the people you work for.

The Triad in Action

You repeat what you feel rewarded inside about your performance improvement. You avoid activities that produce negative feelings of failure. Similarly you avoid others who negatively criticize and berate you against their personal standard. Any time you see and feel your performance improvement, a kind word, look, or pat on the back from others can condition this enhanced feeling. You can also increase your awareness to condition these feelings in yourself. *Be your own best friend.* Top performers do not wait for the approval of others when they know they have done a good job. You know quality when you see it performed by others, and you can learn to see it in your own performances. Increase your awareness (first Triad) that it is you who set the goal, did the work, and deserves all of the full reward. Cooperative learning does not always condition this feeling. Reflective thinking reinforces your positive beliefs about what you self-evaluate (second Triad) as quality. Take time to reflect and associate your quality of effort with your quality of reward (third Triad) to build value in what you are learning to learn. Creating a dichotomy will place more awareness of your not so successful feelings in early trials with your later successful trials with a purpose. How did you feel when you were not so successful versus how you feel when you know you are successful? Dichotomy comparisons enhance your personal reward system by helping you to understand the value of your correct choice to feel rewarded. The intrinsic motivation of your mind from within creates more little engines that can. You can understand the motive and process to condition the value and mastery for any skill.

Accountability Measures

You cannot build accountability in a micromanagement system. If your purposeful intent is to manage and control the behaviors of your performers, then you must assume they will not be accountable for their behaviors. As the leader, understand that most performers are conditioned to follow directions and take orders. They will resist being empowered and held accountable for their decisions and performances. You can create all the necessary rules and consequences. Your performers will still misbehave because your management controls are extrinsic. To build accountability your performers must have perceived intrinsic value to their performance outcomes to hold themselves accountable. Extrinsically managed performers do not take ownership for their behaviors or performance outcomes. They blame management for their poor performance. Management must balance the alignment of extrinsic management motives with the personal intrinsic motives of the performers. Your natural human behavior is to challenge and defy the odds to achieve what others say you cannot perform. If your self-evaluation skills are realistic, you can feel confident of your ability to perform and be willing to hold yourself accountable for your performance. When more rules are created than can be enforced or reinforced to correct your bad behaviors, they are a waste of your time and energy. Excessive rules are counter productive to improve intrinsic performance. "You can lead a horse to water, but you cannot make him drink." Public schools mandate students remain in school until they are 16, or they will be prosecuted as truant and the parents can be fined. This is a joke. In most states a parent can elect to "home school" their child with no accredited curriculum to by-pass the law. Do these regulatory laws change your behaviors? Without a purposeful intent to learn, you do not readily become aware of meaningful and relevant information to store and retrieve to aid your learning and accumulation of knowledge. Performers without a purpose can be very disruptive to learning for other performers. When you identify your needs and create your purposeful intent to learn early, you learn to store more information for your future knowledge acquisition. Bribing your performers to improve their performance with extrinsic motives like bonuses, contest prizes, grades, new job titles, pats on the back, smiles, and nods of approval are all short term. Teach your performers how to increase their awareness of their personal performance feedback to self-evaluate their performance improvement, and you will create long term intrinsic motives they can self reward. Portfolio systems, self-evaluations, performance logs, sales charts, and company balance sheets provide you with common feedback relative to your past performance standard. You would be intrinsically motivated in this kind of feedback comparison system. You would not have to beat education into your performers.

Employee/Performer Self Evaluation

When you give your performers the opportunity to evaluate their work using rubrics, portfolios, pre set objective evaluation tools, and portfolios prior to turning in new work for a final evaluation, you are developing their intrinsic feedback skills. Your performers will learn how to learn on their own and succeed in small increments with each new trial when you are unable to lead each effort. Your job as the trainer or leader is to ensure that all your performers are aware of how to positively respond to the essential cues. You can point out the essential cues before you start your educational session. Robert Gagné (1962) created *The Nine Events of Instruction* to improve rapid learning for training military personnel that still apply today.

Gain Attention	A quotation; opening sentence; or thought provoking question.
Learner Objective	A statement about what you should be able to know and do.
Recall Prior Knowledge	A brief sentence or two about the previous chapter(s).
Present Material	The written body of work about the chapter topic.
Provide Guided Learning	Thought provoking questions on how and what to think to learn from your own performance feedback.
Elicit Performance	Take a survey or quiz, practice a specific strategy until you condition correct responses, or reflect on past performances.
Provide Feedback	Evaluate your current performance to past performance.

Assess Performance	Measurable steps to improve your immediate past performance.
Enhance Retention and Transfer	You will repeat what works and apply those strategies to other performances.

The awareness of the stimulus-response connection will improve their succeeding trials leading to higher achievement and quality of performance on demand. Your performers will learn when to recognize cues to turn up their performance to a higher personal standard to seek greater feelings of reward. As the leader you raise performance expectations by simply refusing to accept poorly created quality until it meets an acceptable standard.

Choice Psychology

Dr. William Glasser (1990) popularized choice psychology in his book, The Quality School. Children have a normal drive for independence. You must use this drive to teach your performers how to be accountable for their behaviors by not making all their decisions for them. Give them choices that sometimes border dichotomies to point out the extremes to become more aware of their behaviors and the consequences for an improper choice. Human behavior is predictable. Performers are not stupid to choose pain and feel predictable failure. Give your performers choices with predictable consequences, and they will make the correct choices. You want your performers to make intelligent decisions to benefit themselves and the company or team and become independent working without a manager. This trust builds confidence and loyalty in the people doing the work. Create positive choices that lead to acceptable performance outcomes they can self-evaluate. The old phrase, "Do not add insult to injury" applies. Your performers know when they have made a mistake without you having to emphasize and reinforce the error. If your performers care about your organization, they will be stakeholders to make correct personal decisions on behalf of the company. As the leader you must decide on how to display the amount of latitude you will accept as your performers learn, and grow with the company to earn more independence in the field. Obviously you do not let two-year olds play in traffic, but neither do you treat adult performers like children. You will make decisions for children until you teach them how to self-evaluate their performances to hold themselves accountable for the outcomes. You will teach them with a purpose for their performance that is their choice to accept and value.

The Affect of Early Discipline

Your performers must choose to accept the consequences of their behaviors if you expect them to learn how to hold themselves accountable for their performance improvement. When I began to study sport psychology, a notion was presented in class that has stuck in my brain ever since. The single greatest predictor of later athletic or academic success was early discipline in the home. This was thought provoking. My professor asked, "If early discipline is a factor, which parent has the greatest impact?" Our class was split in half between the father and mother. The answer was the mother who has the most early contact time to spend with the child, and reinforce their positive behaviors. I cannot imagine Michael Jordan's or Tiger Wood's mother allowing him to get away with very bad behavior in her home. Conversely, observe children's school performance from permissive undisciplined homes. Early discipline in the home is a choice. When my triplet boys were born three months into my doctoral studies, the doctor advised that 'the kids come to live with you; not the other way around.'

I thought about raising my children especially the triplets when they were little. I was a young father and busy working to put bread on the table like most dads. I would get home and have to discipline my boys if they misbehaved and wondered why my wife did not discipline them immediately to be more effective. Children have a marvelous way of growing up despite what parents do right or wrong. As I completed doctoral studies in personality and behavioral psychology for an educational psychology minor, I thought about how we condition our children to behave or enable their misbehavior. Children who misbehave are not provided choices to make that follow through with conditioned consequences to develop their self-evaluation performance feedback system and hold themselves accountable (second Triad). For any house rule keep it simple and few, "If you do this, I will do this" and then follow through to condition your rule to effect discipline.

Natural Rules of Human Behavior

There are several natural rules of human behavior.

Behavioral Rule #1: The more you do for people, the less they will learn and be reinforced to do for themselves.

You do not increase motivation by providing your performers with answers. You want to create the need to know and be curious to discover the answers to your own questions. You provide your performers with the tools to learn how to learn, to think, act, and do for themselves. You cannot hold your child's hand all of their lives. There will be some disappointment that can be understood when you help your performers increase their probability for success. Then lack of improvement is short lived. You know welfare systems do not work because free handouts are taken for granted and not valued, and do not motivate internal drive systems within the recipient. Free handouts are unearned extrinsic motives. This process is nothing like teaching a man to fish to feed him for a lifetime. The process is quid pro quo – 'You do this for me and I will do this for you.'

Behavioral Rule #2: Natural human behavior is to accept unearned free things like money, and basic needs like food, clothing, and shelter, but the recipient will not respect the giver.

This has been the fault of our American foreign policy and why the United States is not respected in many world countries. Our policy should have been to provide tractors and plows and irrigation equipment and technology to help countries feed their people by putting them to work to keep their self respect and dignity. A man earns his self respect by working for his rewards from his own efforts. After the Great Depression our government created the WPA or Works Project Administration, and the CCC or Civilian Conservation Corps. These programs put able bodied men to work to earn a wage and do good work for the country. There are many lodges at state and national parks that were built by the CCC. Unlike welfare today, if you qualify, you do not have to work to earn your pride and dignity.

Turtle and Rabbit

Occasionally school leaders challenge the idea that you can teach very young children goals and purposeful intent leadership skills. I start by speaking to children kindergarten through grade three, and sometime all the way up to adults about the Aesop fable of the Tortoise and the Hare. I refer to the characters as that turtle guy and rabbit guy. I ask, "Who won the race?" Children can provide you with a variety of positive answers that are all correct. Then I focus their thinking about how the turtle guy won because he tried. He tried to be a little bit better tomorrow than he was today with each step he took. Those are the real reasons why he won. The turtle guy achieved success over time. He was not a "flash in the pan."

Success in learning develops over time to be a life long quest. You never learn everything there is to know. Skills are produced slowly over time. You cannot perfect the three interrelated skills in The Triad, but you will be able to apply them for the rest of your life. The skills that define your purposeful intent are based on motivational principles in behavioral psychology. As a skill you do not make one free throw and believe you will be the next Michael Jordan. Your purposeful intent leadership skills will develop as you learn to apply the principles to improve your performance for the rest of your life. Great performers are remembered for achieving their success over time. They display above average PI strength in their personality patterns. They have the will to win that has been conditioned by their frequent success.

Parents as leaders can share in the excitement and the performance consistency of their children without passing judgment to create an extrinsic reward connection. Performers have to realize from within that they can perform any task better tomorrow than they performed today if they continue to practice and work on their desire to want to be better. This process is your purposeful intent. If you go through the motions of learning, you will not value taking accountability for the process and outcome.

Intrinsic-Extrinsic Applied

There is a distinct dichotomy between intrinsic and extrinsic motivation applied to company leadership. For example, in a team sport, Phil Jackson has applied intrinsic motivation skills to win numerous NBA Championships with two different teams, the Chicago Bulls and Los Angeles Lakers. Each team had its top performer, Michael Jordan with the Bulls and Kobe Bryant with the Lakers. What makes Phil Jackson unique and successful is that he unknowingly applies purposeful intent leadership skills coaching his players to hold themselves accountable for their personal performances working as a team. Coach Jackson's philosophy and coaching style appear to be aligned with purposeful intent skills training:

1. He personalizes every player's approach to the game by providing them with purposeful intent leadership skills. These skills are to focus on improving their personal performance in all the fundamental skills of the game all of the time. This includes practice as well as games and their personal lives off the court.

2. He uses the player's own immediate past performance or average to be the personal standard for improvement rather than comparing their generalized skills performance to high performers in the game.

3. He teaches a personal feedback system for each player to self-evaluate the worth of their performance. This personal self-evaluation feedback converts the motivation from extrinsic to intrinsic where the player not the coach holds them accountable for performance improvement. Research has consistently proven that intrinsic motivation is much more powerful than extrinsic motives imposed by others including coaches.

4. When errors are made to be corrected, he refocuses on the motives to achieve success greater than the motives to avoid failure by trying to please him that would be external. Consequently, he will not refer to the error to reinforce that error and cause it to happen again. The focus is positive that infects the team with a much stronger work ethic toward a common goal or purpose to improve.

5. The players are conditioned to be more aware of their personal skills and abilities to work together as a team to improve through self-evaluation. Players know their team role and learn to hold themselves accountable for performance improvement that will help the team win games over padding their personal statistics. Players spend time focusing on their personal intrinsic strategies that they can control, and less time being critical of the performances of their teammates that they cannot control. This reinforces the proper purposeful intent strategy.

Here are a few of the named purposeful intent strategies:

1. Identify, rate, and prioritize your needs and abilities using the needs and abilities assessment survey in the appendix.

2. Identify and prioritize your top three tasks either on the job, at home, in a relationship, or learning to improve a physical skill.

3. Define your purpose, in a sentence or two, for performing each skill named that includes a personal need and ultimate goal you desire to achieve.

4. Identify what you value most about the activities you perform using the skills named.

5. Identify three to five strategies you will use to improve your skills performing each of the prioritized tasks named above. (Create a simple outline format.)

6. Write each strategy as an objective beginning with the words, "I will be able to (place the adverb to describe the specific strategy here) ... followed by a short description of the skilled performance." For example, I will be able to (type) 60 words per minute with no errors after two weeks of practice.

7. After you take an assessment performing each named skill to establish a baseline performance, also known as your immediate past performance, write a realistic goal for each that is the lowest positive goal you can make.

8. List five personality characteristics that could be used to identify several top performers in each of the tasks you have named above. (You can use the list of personality characteristics in the appendix.)

9. List five personality characteristics you would use to describe yourself. (You can use the list of personality characteristics in the appendix or you may add other characteristics not found on the list.)

10. Compare and contrast your personality characteristics to the personality characteristics you used to describe several top performers in each identified task.

11. Describe how you will try to change your personality to be more like the successful performers. Limit your response to two to three sentences, and record in your task performance journal.

12. Describe how you plan to create objective data to demonstrate learning and performance improvement using feedback taken from your immediate and past personal performances. (Keep a task performance journal)

13. Using the tasks you have previously stated, list five strategies you will use to increase your awareness to improve your performance skills.

14. Using the tasks previously stated, list five strategies you will use to enhance your self-evaluation for performing those skilled tasks.

15. Using the previously stated tasks, list the primary reward you will be consciously aware of to reinforce your motivation to continually improve that skill.

16. Describe the objective and goal you have met, and your conscious awareness of the steps you used to accomplish them in your performances.

17. State a new goal for each task when you accomplished your previous goal using the goal setting strategy suggested by purposeful intent.

18. Rate the value for achieving each goal by assigning a percentage of perceived reward divided by perceived effort to derive a positive index between 1.0-1.5.

19. Self-evaluate the performance value index for each goal accomplished to determine it's reinforcement value or suggest a need to change how you will set up a new goal and stay focused to increase your work effort to insure your success.

20. Keep a workout log to journal your daily activities and specific cues to focus on recognizing with selective attention to enhance your response.

21. Using the strategy RROSR:

- identify a specific task and list the top two or three cues you want to immediately recognize;
- list two primary ways you prefer to receive performance information (visual, verbal, or kinesthetic performance feedback);
- describe how you plan to organize the new information –
  - comparison to immediate past performance or average
  - visual bit maps of the whole performance using visualization technique having observed yourself on tape or a top performer from in front or behind as having a "third eye"
  - verbal breakdown of the complex skill into specific S-R sequence using perceptual cues to selectively focus on immediately prior to performing, during performance, and in a post-performance evaluation
  - kinesthetically to increase awareness for fine motor skills during the warm up activity to suggest a positive feeling anticipating success and performing with confidence
  - creating a complete positive continuously improved subroutine to execute on autopilot during the performance after frequent mental rehearsal trials using visualization techniques prior to performing
- describe the value of each learned subroutine to select whether you want to store for immediate short term use or archive for long-term

use later by associating and scaffolding new performance knowledge to prior knowledge and understanding also described in task familiarity and planer thinking

- Using the value index to store information for immediate short term or long term use, list several key multi-sensory associations that you will use to readily retrieve stored information at will on demand –

  - create a new visualization that includes as many other senses as you expect to make the experience as realistic as possible

  - recall from your successful performances how you felt in your warm up, or pre performance routine, kinesthetic feelings from your muscles, sounds like crowd noise, energizing music like the theme from 'Rocky', even what you ate for pre performance meals, review of your pre performance routine via visualization and mental practice

  - recall the primary trigger or cue to start the performance sequence

  - recall via reflection all the previously created and stored performance predictions and projections that came true to determine congruence between the goal and actual performance that increases realism essential for consistent top performance and building confidence

  - realism increases positive reinforcement value and raises personal expectation for success by performing all the usual routines and adding some new ones to be more task familiar

For example, if you are a salesperson visualizing an important sale in your mind to rehearse your sales pitch features and benefits, incentives and close prior to getting in front of your customer you can increase your motivation from within and be more confident because you are already familiar with the stress that will be placed upon you. You can practice with a recording of the crowd noise in the background, and imagine the game to be on the line with the clock running down. You cannot possibly practice these kinds of actual game experiences which is why you learn to use visualization techniques to make the practice experience as real as the actual experience. You can control for the emotional stress, and learn new cues to respond to more efficiently with earlier recognition awareness skills to enhance your future performance (planer thinking capacity) as you become increasingly more familiar with a task. The more familiar you are with a task, you are able to increase your awareness of new cues, focus on positive goals, objectives, and outcomes to create MaS>MaF.

APPENDIX

List of Behavioral Rules

#1.   The more you do for people, the less they learn to do for themselves.

#2.   You cannot build accountability in a micromanagement system.

#3.   You will be less frustrated if you keep your expectations in line with reality.

#4.   It is normal behavior to want more of what you cannot readily have, and desire less of the commodity that is free to all.

#5.   The principle of the path of least resistance is to want the most and do the least.

#6.   Do not make unenforceable rules or laws that regulate extrinsic accountability.

#7.   The more you tax a people, they become conditioned to demand and expect a government to provide a social service to meet their needs and recoup their loss of income.

#8.   You learn what you focus on.

#9.   It is natural behavior to remember more positive than negative experiences.

#10.   The more frequently you feel rewarded you are more likely to be motivated to improve your performance to keep that good feeling.

#11.   You will repeat behaviors you feel rewarded, and reduce unrewarded behaviors.

#12.   You cannot legislate morality.

#13.   More regulations lead to more faulty behaviors as performers are micromanaged by the regulators more and hold their performance accountability less.

14. Natural human behavior is to accept unearned free things like money and basic needs for food, clothing and shelter, but the recipient will not respect the giver.

15. Rewarding irresponsible behavior or modeling responsible behavior will not improve personal accountability.

16. To provide too much approval or disapproval of another's performance immediately reduces the intrinsic value and increases the extrinsic value.

Personal Awareness Survey: An Enhancement Exercise

This exercise is designed to help you understand your strengths, weaknesses, preferences, and ultimately your passion to excel or exhibit quality performances. In the end you will determine your past, current, and future needs to develop your personal PI strength. To increase your level of awareness may require moderate changes to your personality over time. If you are conscious of your strengths and weaknesses, you can focus your energy to improve your weaknesses to strengthen your personality and awareness to perform with a purposeful intent at will on demand.

Sections

Part I: Talents, Abilities, and Skills

Part II: Attitudes, Values, and Beliefs

Part III: Activities, Preferences, and Goals

Part IV: Performances, Achievements, and Planning

Part V: Personality

Part VI: Needs, Drives, and Motives

Measurable Objectives

- You want to raise your level of awareness.
- You want to move from an unconscious to conscious awareness.
- You want to record general and specific responses.

- You will assign a Likert Scale rating of 1-5 with 1 indicating low and 5 high strength for your personal selections.
- You will make an honest appraisal of your talents, abilities, and skills from past performances.
- You will understand that your awareness level is associated with your personality.

General Directions

- Go to a quiet place to eliminate distractions or possible interruptions.
- Your initial responses need to be more spontaneous and what you first feel to be more accurate.
- Do not dwell on any one question or spend a lot of time thinking about your responses or they are less likely to be a realistic indicator.
- Control your sensory input at the time you are thinking to access the thought that pops up in your mind.
- Close your eyes to create a mental image of a past performance or to block visual stimulation in the room.
- Restrict portable music in your ears to attend to, and refrain from trying to watch TV or people.
- This will be a time consuming exercise.
- Your first pass through will be incomplete, and you should not stop to answer any one question too long or have to complete the question.
- The object is to obtain spontaneous answers..
- You will have the opportunity to fill in your responses with additional passes.
- You can enlist help from significant others like parents, grandparents, siblings, aunts and uncles, cousins, or a close friend only after you have made it through all the questions once.
- You can ask people who know you like teachers, coaches, ministers, peers, neighbors, employers, bosses or people you report to.

You may be surprised to learn how they see things in you that you do not see in yourself. This alone is worth the price of doing this exercise.

Specific Directions

- After you have filled in the blanks, you can replace suggested responses made by others to best fit your personal description, but you must not replace any of your initial selections.
- If you want, you can add another selection and keep it beyond the number asked for.
- Make a copy of your survey BEFORE you begin your personal rating.
- Rate, 1-5, every response you have made on your personal copy.
- There are no right or wrong answers so be honest with your initial first impression.
- Reserve the second copy to ask others how they would rate you to compare to your personal ratings later.
- Hopefully others will rate you as you rate yourself to provide congruence.
- Using a blank sheet of paper, draw a line down the middle to create a dichotomy.
- On the left hand side of the paper you will include selections you or others rated as a 1 or 2.
- On the right side place all the items rated as a 4 or 5 corresponding to each question that you can shorten into a header.

For example:

1. Academic talent

1 or 2	4 or 5

Shakespeare wrote, "To thine own self be true." This exercise is designed to provide you with a better feeling for your tendencies that when brought to a more conscious level of awareness can yield more positive performance results. If honest, you will form a fairly accurate personal awareness that will enlighten you to affect future choices you make and strengthen your PI skill. Later, in Part II, self-evaluation, and Part III, reward-reinforcement you will understand how awareness is interrelated to these areas.

Carry this survey with you. Answers will come to you at the strangest times that you will want to record. Jot down your thought on a note pad or scrap paper to record later. Keep a pen and paper handy with a small flashlight next to your bed. Thoughts may come to you in the middle of the night.

Part I: Talents, Abilities, and Skills

1.   Name five academic talents you have.

2.   Name five athletic talents you have.

3.   Name five talents that are neither academic nor physical.

4.   Name five mental abilities you have.

5.   Name five physical abilities you have.

6.   Name five abilities you have that are neither mental nor physical.

7.   Name five specialized mental skills that you have demonstrated.

8. Name five specialized physical skills that you have demonstrated.

9. Name five specialized skills that are neither mental nor physical that you have demonstrated.

Part II: Attitudes, Values, and Beliefs

10. Name three attitudes you have had toward people, places, or things in the last five years.

11. State five values you have thought about in the last five years.

12. State five beliefs you hold without question or doubt of any kind.

Part III: Activities, Preferences, and Goals

13. Name five activities you have consistently strong preferences for performing.

14. When you make up a personal goal, do you take into account more the performances of...

a. groups of other people

b. what you tell people you plan to do

c. what you have performed in your immediate past performance

15. If you were given a crystal ball that you could look into and see your future, what three things would you most like to see?

16. If you were given the technology, would you want someone to program you so you would not have to be concerned with all the work required to learn?

17. In terms of how you prefer to think, circle the activities you have preference for and have been able to demonstrate some ability to perform.

Concrete	Abstract
Numbers	Concepts
Deductive	Inductive
Mathematics	Psychology
Accounting	Sociology
English grammar	Creative Writing
History	Social Studies
Reading	Speaking
Government	Political Science
Auto Shop	Art
Industrial Arts	Music

18. You consider yourself to be the most proficient in what two sporting activities (they can be non-competitive like fishing or water skiing)?

19. What two things interest you the most when you read a book?

20. What two things do you do to organize your daily activities?

21. When you see a movie for a second time, what three details do you seem to notice that you missed the first time?

22. When you write a paper and let it sit for a few days, what areas do you look for in your writing to correct and make the paper better?

23. When you are speaking face to face with one other person, what body language do you attend to the most?

Part IV: Perfomances, Achievements, and Planning

24. In the last five years, name your three most quality achievements.

25. At what age did you realize you needed to be independent enough to argue with your parent(s)?

26. How much time do you spend planning your activities?

27. How do you prefer to prepare for a significant performance...

   a. Paper and pencil test on a core academic subject?

b. National test like ACT or license of some kind?

c. Athletic contest?

d. Job interview?

e. A first date?

f. An extracurricular activity (name the activity _____)?

28. Rate your ability to...

a. Communicate

b. Understand

c. Think

d. Create

e. Learn to learn

f. Focus

g. Use tools

h.   Make decisions

i.   Solve problems

j.   Increase awareness

29. Name three performances that you demonstrated attention to details.

30. I prefer to plan my activities.

Part V: Personality

31. The following is a list of common personality traits taken from IPAT 16PF test profile (2008). Review them, but wait to rate each of them until instructed to do so.

a.	Reserved	Outgoing
b.	Concrete thinking	Abstract thinking
c.	Affected by feelings	Emotionally stable
d.	Conforming	Assertive
e.	Serious	Impulsive
f.	Expedient	Persevering
g.	Shy	Bold
h.	Self-reliant	Dependent

i.	Trusting	Suspicious
j.	Practical	Imaginative
k.	Forthright	Calculating
l.	Confident	Apprehensive
m.	Traditional	Free-thinking
n.	Group-dependent	Self-sufficient
o.	Undisciplined	Controlled
p.	Relaxed	Tense

32. Name the two best performances of your life and the activity you were doing.

33. If you had the opportunity to do these performances again, what would you do differently?

34. If you had a choice, would you choose another kind of activity instead, and if yes what would that activity be now?

Part VI: Needs, Drives, and Motives

35. I want you to think of your life on a continuum from birth to now and project into your future all of your needs you can list. Beside each need indicate who, if not yourself, has provided or will provide for that need in the future.

Infancy 0-1

Early childhood 1-5

Pre-school – elementary school 5-10

Junior High School   10-13

High School   13-18

Post High School   18-23

Post College/Trade School   23-30

Settling Down   30-49

Maturing   49-62

Early retirement 60-70 (if applicable)

36. Describe what typically drives your behavior everyday.

37. Name two prominent drives that have motivated your behavior most all your life.

38. If you could dream the biggest dream possible for yourself to achieve in the next five years, describe what that would be and how it would affect your life.

39. Do you prefer to entertain yourself with physical or mental activities?

40. Do you like to use all of your senses?

41. On average, how many minutes a day do you spend...

a. Listening to music with a portable player and earphones?

b. Watching mindless non-specific learning TV programs?

c. Reading?

d. Eating?

e. Sleeping?

f. Communicating?

g. Learning something meaningful?

42. In relation to your peers, would you rate yourself as having more or less experience to perform difficult thinking tasks to solve problems?

43. In terms of travel to gain experience in the world, you have been...

a. Out of the country

b. Out of the state

c. Visited 10 or more states

d. Flown in an airplane

e. Seen one of the Great Lakes

f. Seen an ocean

g. Been to a major city in the last two years

h. Been on vacation with a parent regularly

i. Taken a passenger train ride

j. Camping

k. Seen a sunrise and sunset in the same day

l. Gone fishing

44. What was the last project you created by yourself?

45. What is the best quality performance you have ever seen, and why did you enjoy it?

For every response you have indicated on your paper, you are to rate from 1 weakest to 5 strongest. Be patient, this will take some time. You may add another item to your incomplete lists, but you cannot replace one of your initial responses.

Know Your Purpose

Pick any activity you wish to improve your performance and complete this questionnaire.

1. Fully describe the nature and value of the activity.

2. What purpose do you expect to get out of your efforts in this activity?

3. Will your success or performance improvement be dependent on others?

4. What need or goal do you expect to meet by your performance?

5. Record your immediate past performance or average.

6. State the three most important elements you will focus on to improve?

7. What is your plan to practice and learn the cues to recognize and perform?

8. Write down your goal for improving each of the three sub skills based on immediate past performance, and describe the process used to set each goal.

Short Term Memory and/or Biofeedback Awareness Exercises

1. What did I eat for breakfast, lunch, and dinner yesterday?
2. What pant leg or shirt arm do I put on first?
3. What did I wear to work yesterday?
4. What clothes did I put on after I got home?
5. What physical activity did you perform two days ago?
6. What quantity of fluids did I take in yesterday compared to the fluid output today?
7. When did I have an activity with a heart rate above 100?
8. What one of two good things did I accomplish today?
9. What was the result of the good things I did a week ago?
10. What was my score on that test I took yesterday?
11. What were my scores on the tests I took in the last two weeks?
12. When was the last time you hugged a significant other like your spouse or kids?
13. Who was the last person you said "I love you" to?
14. Who was the last person you wrote a thank you note to?

How Good Is Your Sensory Awareness?

Try this exercise to determine your visual dominance by removing this sense and use all of the other senses.

1. Collect the following objects to use in separate trials:
   Obtain a water balloon for feel, jar of limburger cheese for smell, ticking clock for hearing, and a banana for taste. Also, obtain a blindfold.
2. Pick a familiar room in the house where you will place the sense object being tested, and be sure to remove sharp objects and breakables.
3. Allow the participant to familiarize themselves with the room by counting paces or steps to various large objects, and get an overall visual map of the room.
4. Show the object you intend to place in the room and allow the participant to manipulate.
5. Blindfold the participant.
6. Place the object in a reasonable place that would easily be seen if not blindfolded.
7. Ask the participant to make two complete revolutions standing in place, and then start your watch to determine how long it will take to locate the object.
8. Repeat the procedure with all the other objects to determine which senses provided the most information to rely on to locate them.

List of Personality Traits

From the list of traits below, circle all those traits that you feel you have. Use a separate clean list to give to a significant other who will also circle whether you have those traits. Then compare to see how others may see you or confirm your selections.

There is an excellent website that provides you with details to increase your personality awareness and fitness for specific skills:

http://www.csun.edu/~sp20558/dis/discover.html

Abstract	Creativity	High Energy	Negativism	Responsibility
Acceptance	Cruelty	Honesty	Nervousness	Rigidity
Adaptability	Curiosity	Impatient	Neuroticism	Risk Taking
Aesthetic	Cynicism	Impersonal	Nonconformity	Self Control
Aggressiveness	Decisiveness	Impulsivity	Nurturance	SelfDisciplined
Agreeableness	Dedication	Independence	Obedience	Self Reliance
Aloof	Defensiveness	Industriousness	Objectivity	Sensitivity
Altruism	Dependency	Influence	Omnipotence	Sensuality
Androgyny	Dishonesty	Inhibited	Openmindedness	Sentimental
Anxious	Dogmatism	Initiative	Optimism	Seriousness
Assertiveness	Dominance	Integrity	Organized	Shy
Authoritarianism	Drive	Introversion	Outgoing	Sincerity
Boldness	Egalitarianism	Irritability	Paranoia	Sociability
Calmness	Egotism	Liberalism	Passiveness	Solitary
Carefulness	EmotionImmaturity	Likeability	Patience	Spontaneous
Choatic	Emotion Inferiority	Liveliness	Perceptiveness	Stability
Close Minded	Emotional Stability	Loyalty	Perfectionism	Suggestibility
Cold	Empathy	Machiavelianism	Perseverence	Suspicious
Compassion	Enthusiasm	Masculinity	Persistence	Tension
Compatibility	Expedient	Mature	Pessimism	Timidity

Competitiveness	Extraversion	Melancolic	Positivism	Tolerant
Concrete	Feminity	Misanthropy	Reactive	ToughMinded
Conformity	Forceful	Moodiness	Reasoning	Traditional
Conservatism	Friendliness	Motivated	Receptive	Trusting
Courage	Gregariousness	Narcissism	Relaxed	Vigilance
Courtesy	Hardiness	Neediness	Reserved	Warmth

50 Suggested Ways to Increase Your Awareness

1. **Valued as an individual.** God has provided every living creature with great gifts. It is only fitting that every human being search out and experience what those gifts are, develop them to the best of their ability and pass them on.

2. **Make new information meaningful and relevant.** This increases value for new information, and adds to your body of knowledge through associations to what you already know from past experience. Therefore, when introducing new information be sure to relate as much as you can to what you already know in your mind. This is like adding pieces of a puzzle together until you can eventually see the big picture. As the learner receiving the information, you make choices and decide in your perception how and when to make these compassion processes to fit the piece(s) in the correct position in your brain.

3. **Foundations of sensations or multi-sensory learning.** These enable you to experience all of your senses to equalize their value. As a species we have evolved to be visually dominant. We observe behavior and form bit maps of complex patterns to compress large amounts of streaming data for easier retrieval. We read and process written words from left to right on a page. Speed readers visualize groups of words holding one group in short term memory for processing as the next group is being scanned. This is a skill that can be learned. The eyes can see far more than words can speak.

    However, there will be a time in your life when you will be dependent on every one of your senses. The foundations you learn early in life will make it easier to apply later.

    Learn to do what Albert Einstein did to create more associational neurons. He would imagine what an object would be like in another sense modality. For example, if you see an apple: What color is it? Is the outer skin waxy, smooth, tough, soft, or hard? Before you bite into it will it injure your teeth as if it were a rock? You feel the texture with your hand, your nose the aroma, and ears hear the first crunching bite. Your jaw muscles sense how much pressure to apply. I think you get the picture how you can expand your conscious awareness of other sense modalities you seldom rely on solely without vision support, but are necessary to make accurate perceptions to acquire new knowledge.

4. **Controlling for bias.** Experimental research analogy how prejudice works to cloud your thinking and reasoning to block the truth. By deciding for someone what is meaningful and relevant to be valued you introduce your bias without explaining why to draw your own conclusions. It would be better to teach others how to evaluate and make new information meaningful and relevant to value in their personal system of learning.

5. **Understanding prediction and probabilities (sampling).** Select on a subjective basis the three to five key variables to learn a specific skill. Then assign a beta weight to their relative importance but not to exceed a total of 100.

6. **Formulating a common sense.** Logic is the learned skill of understanding inductive and deductive reasoning coupled with probabilities and predictions. If you leave objects on the stairs, you increase the probability that someone will eventually trip and fall down the stairs to be injured. Inductive is intuitive. If elderly with brittle bones you can project more bones will be broken (specific > general). Deductive is probabilistic. It is only a matter of time until a serious injury occurs to project the amount and kind of traffic flow using the stairs; greater traffic increases probability for injury (general > specific).

7. **Create value and weight assign % of importance.** V = % of perceived reward / % of perceived effort. The greatest reinforcement value occurs when the value index is 1.0 to 1.5 meaning that the task is challenging and rewarding but not too difficult that you cannot achieve or improve your performance frequently to stay motivated. What does it take to make you feel successful performing?

8. **Increase your PI or purposeful intent.** Know why you are working toward an objective to meet a personal need or goal.

9. **Know your immediate past performance or average.** Keep records, workout logs, diaries, and performance graphs.

10. **Continuously improve.** Set low positive goals only one point better than your own immediate past performance or average to increase your probability for success and reward. This is the greatest motive or drive stimulus because you have no excuse for not achieving your goal with any kind of purposeful effort.

11. **Spend quiet moments observing your environment.** Take a few minutes to watch a sunset or sunrise. Take a walk in the woods and listen to the various sounds. Sit by the shore and listen to the waves and sea gulls.

12. **Identify and create your short and long term needs.**

13. **Take the needs and ability survey.** Identify your experiences with your environment, and learn how others see your performance, needs, and abilities.

14. **Focus and refocus on any given task.** Attend to the specific variables and skills that will improve your performance.

15. **Be responsible and take personal accountability.** Hold yourself accountable for completing tasks and not making excuses. Did you have a goal or need in mind? How close did your performance approximate your goal? What value did you obtain from the experience? Did your behavior help or hurt your performance?

16. **MaS>MaF.** Your motive to achieve success must be greater than your motive to avoid failure. Focusing on what cues to avoid or not perform only creates the image for the brain to process and make happen. Better to keep your brain occupied with all the correct cues to perform.

17. **Be self-reliant.** Earn your own money to pay for your rewards. Do not accept unearned gifts if they will spoil your need to learn and grow on the job. If you allow yourself to be micromanaged by others, you will soon be conditioned to slavery and meeting the needs of your boss. None of those will lead to motivating your performance improvement.

18. **Weigh the odds.** Also weigh your options to achieve any identified need or goal.

19. **Positive self-talk.** You may not be able to tell others of your success, but you can have a personal discussion about the positives you value from each successful performance improvement. Do the work prior to the performance and you will be able to use positive self talk to increase your confidence and motivation to succeed.

20. **Those gutters aren't going to clean themselves.** This refers to getting started. You can waste more time thinking about how to avoid an unpleasant task than if you were to just do it and get it over with. By getting started, the sequence falls into place, and you can evaluate your performance as you perform.

21. **Visualize success.** See your putt going in the cup. If you have any kind of negative thought, wipe it out by focusing on the positive cues you most need to attend to for success. You may have to reset your pre shot routine.

22. **Mental rehearsal.** After you have some physical practice skill with an activity, you can also practice making mental movies and images of correct performance associated with early recognition of cues. This reinforces learning between actual practice sessions.

23. **Rocky's theme song.** What's your passion? You can energize your performance using a theme song to get you motivated.

24. **Play let's make a deal.** When you encounter a tough task, break it up into simpler components and make a deal which component you will be successful in first.

25. **Do one good thing a day.** Then remember what you did the next day to reinforce more good performance events to happen with greater frequency.

26. **Break bad habits.** You can recondition your mind to focus and think about positive benefits to the performance changes you are making. First, remove all the negative triggers and replace them with positive associations. For example, when you get the urge to have a cigarette, put on your coat and take a walk around the block focusing on inhaling good, clean, fresh air into your lungs to benefit your health. This practice is also known as displace-replace where you condition a positive response for a negative trigger you want to displace. To lose weight decide your health purpose and make a realistic plan you can achieve. Measure your body parts and record them, then measure and record them each week. Plan a healthy diet and cut back the intake in half while increasing your activity levels. Park the car a block away, use the stairs, take a walk after dinner, and eat smaller portions more often to burn calories as they are consumed.

27. **Form a plan.** Create step by step benchmarks with realistic objective time frames to hold yourself accountable for achieving. Do not take short cuts, and work to perform quality you can value.

28. **Take a stand.** What do you believe? Write down your beliefs in a record book and refer to them from time to time to see if you are changing how and what you believe. This affects your purpose and intrinsic motivation. What are you accountable for? Being a dad, then be a dad. Set a good example. Give good honest advice. It is not about you and your performance, but how your child views their performance that must matter the most. Share time with your kids. Explain what your job and vocation are and how you perform, your focus, and performance improvement. Discuss your thinking process to be successful.

29. **Make your start.** First step, walk before you can run. Keep your expectations in line with reality so that you can increase your probability for success and frequency of reward to maintain a higher level of motivation.

30. **Chinese proverb** – "Longest journey begins with the first step." What will be your first step to making something happen in your life? One good step follows another until soon the time has passed and the goal is achieved.

31. **Make a realistic goal.** You can't achieve a goal you don't make. Frequently satisfying your goals keeps your rewards flowing and increases your motivation to keep improving.

32. **You don't have to be great.** All you have to do is find a way to consistently keep improving your performance and one day you will be a top performer. All top performers are not operating at 110% every minute of the day, but they do know when to increase their performance effort by mobilizing their energy at critical times to ensure their success.

33. **Mow the lawn.** When you mow a lawn you do it one swipe at a time. You can see where you have been to project where you need to go next.

34. **Cut your hair.** Change your look by getting a haircut. Sometimes a new you resets your personal image to make new unconditional attempts that have opportunity for personal reward.

35. **Smile a lot.** If you take time to notice, when you smile a lot the world smiles back at you. Body language is universal, and a smile says you are happy and confident and willing to help others. This reflects back on your soul to keep you motivated to improve your personal performance by helping others.

36. **Just do it.** Nike made this a household phrase. Why waste any more time thinking about what you plan or would like to do. Select your purpose and get started. Just do it.

37. **Where do you want to be in 5 years?** 10 years? 15 years? This will help you get a vision for your life and your purpose to guide your efforts to improve.

38. **Make up your personal bucket list and get started.** It is never too late to mobilize your energy to achieve a purpose. You only regret the things you do not try to do. Forget about success or failure and enjoy the moment when you are participating in life. It is getting later than you think, so do them now.

39. **What would your life be like if you watched no TV for 100 days?** Record what you do in each of the 100 days you did not watch TV, and consider the value of the activities and experiences you have made.

40. **Keep a log of your "free" time to see how much of it is wasted.** When you value your time, it will mean more to you than money. You will also see performance improvement by increasing your awareness of a life without wasting time.

41. **Contact an old friend to keep your relationships you hold dear.** Go see them in person or use the telephone. Relationships are what provide meaning and purpose to life but so often ignored to focus on less important matters.

42. **Highlight reel.** Recall all your favorite moments by writing them down. For the past year at first to job your memory, then for the past five and ten years. You have much to be thankful for. This helps you to learn how to dwell on the positive and forget the negatives in your life that make you unhappy.

43. **Are you getting out of life what you put into it?** Make a ledger. On the left side record things you have done that you valued enough to record. On the right side record things you feel you achieved to feel successful and good about yourself. Now rate their quality from 1-10: Effort on the left; Reward on the right.

44. **Plan to develop healthy habits each day.** Did you skip brushing your teeth last night? Did you put on clean clothes today? Did you get yourself up and dressed before 8:00 a.m.? Could you say no to a fried food? Do you still smoke? Do you still drink alcohol? Do you exercise at least three times per week for 20 minutes or longer? Do you eat too much as your age increases and your metabolism decreases? Have you learned to control your stress?

45. **Don't over react, but remember what was said in those conversations.** People will generally let you know how they really feel about you when you listen to their comments over a period of time.

46. **When introduced to new information.** Ask yourself what you already know, and what you need to know. This will create meaningful and relevant value to the new information to improve your memory.

47. **Put your brain on high alert.** Code Red for danger and safety awareness. Code Blue for depressing event or negative stuff. Code Orange for physical

skills needed. Code Green for improving relationship skills. Code Purple for improving knowledge skills. It is important to know what you know. Otherwise, tell your brain to pay attention and learn the new information by valuing it to retain it. If you can't readily recall recent information, it was not valuable to you.

48. **How do you eat an elephant?** One bite at a time. The most difficult and daunting tasks are made much simpler in smaller steps you can reward and stay motivated. Every problem has its solution, but you must be willing to search for the answer. If you are patient, you will get your answer. Hoist up your antennae or strap on your radio dish.

49. **Busy beaver.** Get busy. Find something worthwhile to do with your life. Read a book, keep a daily diary, find a sport to participate in, create a new recipe, make quilts, go camping to tune in nature, hybrid a new flower, plant and tend to a garden, read to a child, volunteer at the school or hospital. You are worthy, and people need your help. You will feel good about yourself and your accomplishments.

50. **Get out of bed with a positive attitude each day.** Life is precious and should not be wasted. You can make more money, but you cannot make more time. Take care of yourself and those around you.

40 More Suggestions to Increase Your Awareness

1. Keep an open mind to the truth
2. Understand bias and how it is applied
3. Look for the key points to trigger the rest of the story
4. Bit maps store more information
5. Understand how needs drive basic behaviors
6. For every action there is an equal and opposite reaction
7. Know what root causes create specific behaviors or human action
8. As chemicals combine to form reactions so do the interactions of human behavior

   (it is best to keep some people apart from others)
9. Constantly assess the feedback from your own performance
10. Be mindful to get your own house in order before you criticize the performances of another
11. You don't have to be a brilliant light to improve your performance over time
12. Be more aware of your purpose and intent to perform any given task
13. Cultivate and listen to that little voice within your brain
14. Never lose your faith, God has a purpose for you that requires your patience
15. Always believe that every problem has a solution
16. The Lord works in mysterious ways
17. Nothing great was ever achieved without paying a price through self-sacrifice
18. If rewarded achievement was easy, no one would do them again
19. Challenge yourself and hold yourself accountable to achieve the results you want
20. Be persistent - the greatest achievements came after numerous failures
21. Cultivate friendships and facilitate and collaborate to form an opinion
22. Scaffold your ideas to envision new planes of thinking
23. Use the Einstein Factor to develop your multi sensory associations to learn new tasks
24. Plan every day to have a restful quiet time to keep an open mind and you will hear the answers you need (Edison took cat naps; Einstein would sit and contemplate for hours even if others had to wait)

25. Listen to the common man for they too have a message
26. Know that we are all messengers that God uses to speak to us – be aware and tune in
27. Learn to keep a notepad and pen handy to write down those thoughts and images that come into your head; they have meaning but are only bits and pieces of a greater puzzle you must solve
28. God wants you to be successful to do more and help His people
29. You are unique; God has blessed you with specific talents and skills for you to learn and be able to pass on to others to return the gift – this is your stewardship
30. Be neither arrogant or boastful; be a teacher and fisher of men
31. No matter what the task, perform to the best of your ability
32. Only ask others to perform tasks you could perform
33. Provide the vision for the realistic expected outcome and timeframe, and let the person performing the work do as they wish using their specific creative skills that are aligned to their personality to get positive results
34. The last freedom any good worker has is control over how they can perform the job after the objectives are made clear
35. Micromanagers are the death knell for idea companies
36. Better to have tried and failed than to ponder and wait to do nothing
37. Make use of every moment in life, they can never be retrieved again
    (Do not waste your time; time is more precious than money because you cannot give more of it once it is gone)
38. Be kind to animals and all living things- they too have a purpose
39. God gave us Noah to show us that we must go through life as partners; share your life
40. Learn to enjoy the little things that cost the least
    (sunsets, hugs, a spoken kind word, a thank you note, a quiet place)

Dr. W. Edwards Deming

14 Points

These 14 points first appeared in Deming's 1986 book, <u>Out of the Crisis</u>. They have been paraphrased to shorten, but still provide the intent of the work. These points are being included to indicate the importance Deming placed on management to intrinsically motivate workers. The theme in the very first point is more than ironic in that it sums up Purposeful Intent; to have a constant purpose for continuous improvement.

1. Constancy of purpose.

This is the continual improvement of products and services by allocating resources for long range needs rather than short term profitability. The plan is to become competitive, stay in business, and provide jobs.

2. The new philosophy.

In a new economic age you cannot live in the past, accept delays, mistakes, defective materials and workmanship. Adopt the new philosophy for transformation to Western management style and halt the continued decline of business and industry.

3. Cease dependence on mass inspection.

If you build quality into the product, you eliminate the need for mass inspection to achieve quality after the fact of production. Require statistical evidence of quality materials and manufacturing practices.

4. End lowest tender contracts.

Stop awarding contracts solely on lowest price, and require meaningful measures as proof of quality along with the price. Qualify and reduce the number of suppliers for any one item to minimize initial and total cost and variation from your standard of quality. Move toward loyal single suppliers you can trust.

5. Improve every process.

Continuously review and improve every process for planning, production, and service. Identify problems to efficient quality production to reduce costs. Work to innovate and improve every product, service, or product. Insist that management focus on improving the system for the design, purchasing, maintenance, improvement of machines, supervision, job training and retraining.

6. Institute on the job training.

Be certain that every employee is trained to perform their specific job well and offer suggestions for improvement as changes occur.

7. Institute leadership.

Provide leadership aimed at helping each worker improve by changing the thinking from mass production to quality production. Quality automatically improves productivity as workers take pride in their work. Management must immediately respond to reports of defects, poor maintenance, inconsistent operations, and all detrimental conditions to quality.

8. Drive out fear.

Encourage every employee to communicate concerns for quality production without fear of retaliation or retribution to work effectively and productively.

9. Break down barriers.

Eliminate titles to improve communication between departments and staff in order to work in teams with a common objective to improve.

10. Eliminate exhortations.

Remove posters and slogans demanding zero defects and new levels of production without first providing training and materials to produce them. Eliminate the blame game and other adversarial relationships between management and the production work force as low quality and productivity belong to a system that needs to change.

11. Eliminate arbitrary numerical targets.

Eliminate prescribed quotas and standards for the work force, and number goals for management. Instead, focus on helpful aids and leadership to continually improve the quality of the product or service.

12. Permit pride of workmanship.

Remove the annual merit rating of performance and management by objectives in order to provide every employee to reflect and have pride and value in the final outcome of the product or service that they played a role.

13. Encourage education.

Encourage self improvement for every employee with a vigorous educational training program. Educated employees feel a greater sense of trust and loyalty knowing their knowledge is valued and transferred to other employees.

14. Top management commitment and action.

Clearly define top management's commitment to improving quality and production through an obligation to implement all the principles. Each must know their specific role in the systematic process to improve and commit to being held accountable for their work and actions to implement the necessary changes.

Name _____   Class/Activity _____

Goal Planning Record

Goal Triggers: **Reinforce, Compare, Intrinsic Value, Needs, Observable and Measurable, Personal, Visualize, Believe, Record, and Conscious**

You may want to have three to five goals for each subject or performance group.

This will be Goal # _____ . In the subject of _____ or performing _____ .

These are the following steps I must take to achieve my goal:

1. _____

2. _____

3. _____

4. _____

Journal comments: _____

Dated: _____   Signed: _____

Name _____ Class/Activity _____

Goal Reflection

My main goal for this term was:

These were the strengths I focused on to achieve my goal:

These were the distractions that did not help me focus to achieve this goal:

These are the talents, abilities, skills, needs, and motives I realized:

These are the qualities and values I learned from this achievement:

This is what I learned about my personal goal setting preference:

These are potential goals I would like to achieve next term:

Goal Reminder bookmarks and paperclip work tabs.

GOAL	GOAL
WORK STEPS TO ENSURE MAKING MY GOAL	WORK STEPS TO ENSURE MAKING MY GOAL
1.	1.
2.	2.
3.	3.
4.	4.
PERFORMANCE DATE: ___/___/___ Circle Result: Great Good Okay Poor	PERFORMANCE DATE: ___/___/___ Circle Result: Great Good Okay Poor

Goal *Setting Guidelines*

Contrary to what you may have been told, consider these points when setting goals:

1. Set goals only slightly better than your immediate past performance to increase your frequency of success to enhance your personal reward system. This will <u>reinforce</u> your work, and keep you motivated. You will have little excuse for not achieving your goal if you put forth a little more effort than you did for your last performance.

2. Before setting your goal, take into account your personal talents, abilities, skills, and past performances in <u>comparison</u> to known standards or quality performers you have seen.

3. Take into account the <u>intrinsic value</u> of your goal in relation to the perceived reward obtained divided by the perceived effort it will take to achieve.

4. Understand your personal <u>needs</u> that will be met to achieve the goal.

5. Set <u>observable and measurable</u> objective goals. Saying you want to be good at something is not going to motivate you as strongly.

6. The goal is <u>personal</u> and controlled by you, and may not come from anyone else. You are accountable for taking the positive steps to reach the goal.

7. It helps if you can <u>visualize</u> yourself performing the goal successfully. If the goal is not strongly visualized, then it is probably less realistic. If you <u>believe</u> it, you can imagine it.

8. <u>Record</u> your goal(s) by writing them down.

9. Keep track of your successes in a log or journal to raise your future goal expectations to a more <u>conscious</u> level with purposeful intent.

These underlined words trigger what a goal must do for you: Reinforce, Compare, Intrinsic Value, Needs, Observable and Measurable, Personal, Visualize, Believe, Record, and Conscious.

Name _____   Class/Activity _____

Intermediate Goals Plan

The strongest motivation comes from goals that have a higher personal need and value, and probability of ensured success do to taking intermediate work steps. The ultimate goal may be general, but the intermediate goals that lead to the achievement of the ultimate goal must be in smaller increments and only slightly better than your own immediate past performance. They must also be observable, measurable, and realistic taking into account your personal talents, abilities, skills, needs, and past performances. The group needs or performances of others are not strong motives because you have no control over the work ethic, dedication, and perseverance of another person let alone their talents and abilities, but you can use these descriptions to motivate your personal performance. While your goals are personal, you may find yourself stating your goals to others as if to boast of your prowess. This can motivate you to prove you are going to do what you say you will do, but not as strong as quietly looking to better your own immediate past performance by working harder to ensure a positive result. Therefore, set an ultimate goal, and under it select several intermediate goals you expect to meet in incremental steps as you strive to achieve it.

MY ULTIMATE GOAL IS: _____

_____

_____

I expect to achieve this goal on or before:

_____

_____

These are my intermediate observable & measurable goals and dates I expect to achieve them:

Intermediate Goal   Date Achieved Y/N

_____

_____

_____

_____

Comments:

Name _____ Class/Activity _____

Homework Survey

Directions: Fill in the blanks and circle all answers that apply. You will not be graded.

1. Homework, in general, is a:
    A. waste of my time
    B. pain because I already know the stuff
    C. pain because I don't know how to do it
    D. pain because teachers do not make the assignments clear enough
    E. hardship because the deadline due dates are too short
    F. hardship because I do not have enough time
    G. hardship because I get no help at home
    H. pain because I hate to read
    I. stupid exercise because it has nothing to do with what we are learning
    J. great way to earn extra credit points for my class
    K. dumb exercise when we don't get our results back right away
    L. pain keeping track of whether the teacher records it in the grade book to get credit
    M. ridiculous to penalize me for not doing when I get A's on my tests
    N. needs to be a student's choice to help them learn
    O. crazy when we don't discuss it the next day in class to learn from it
    P. fun experience learning new stuff
    Q. great when we have to search the Internet for answers
    R. the best when we get to work on it in groups
    S. good experience to show my folks what I am learning
    T. easier to do when we know the purpose for doing it
    U. is more fun when the teacher makes the assignment meaningful and relevant
    V. more valuable when it meets my personal needs and interests
    W. is made clearer by the teacher's learning strategy tips
    X. easier when we have a rubric to guide us
    Y. less stressful when I know I can make a do-over to get it right for more credit
    Z. neat to look back at my work and knowledge acquired keeping them in my portfolio

2. On average, I spend these many hours doing my daily homework:

    A. 3 hours B. 2.5 hours C. 2 hours D. 1.5 hours E. 1 hour F. ½ hour

3. To the left of each response record the number of minutes you spend daily doing...
    A. _____ reading (English – Language Arts)
    B. _____ social studies
    C. _____ math
    D. _____ science
    E. _____ writing (all subjects)

4. I prefer to do my homework...
    A. No set time B. Right away C. Never D. In school E. After dinner
    F. When I can

5. In addition to homework, these are the other obligations I must do each day...

Key concepts

1. You cannot build accountability in a micromanagement system.

2. When individuals are given proper choices and fair consequences for improper choices, they can be trusted to make good decisions.

3. You can question an individual's purpose; their intent is much more difficult.

4. The more you do for others, the less they learn to do for themselves.

5. Extrinsic motives work well for the short term while intrinsic motives work best for the long term to comply with the mission of lifelong learning.

6. Individuals learn to focus on rewarded behaviors and diminish unrewarded behaviors.

7. Intrinsic motivation works in concert with innate drives and needs of the human organism.

8. Intrinsic motivation comes from personal needs and goals to be met that are directly related to personality patterns and traits.

9. Intrinsic motives are dependent on schedules of reward and reinforcement.

10. The intrinsic motive increases as the individual relates the quality of effort to the quality of reward.

11. The intrinsic value of a performance is in proportion to the performer's perception of the amount of reward they internalize credit for the result.

12. The most powerful intrinsic motives are what the individual learns to value from their performance.

13. Performance value is the amount of perceived reward divided by the perceived effort.

14. The brain is a microprocessor that cannot distinguish between right and wrong.

15. To achieve personal accountability it must matter what you think of your performance more than what any other person may think.

Quality Newsletter Rubric
Name _____

Paragraphs have topic sentences	All have an informational & captivating topic sentence 4	Some have an informational topic sentence 3	All have a topic sentence 2	Few or no topic sentences 0
Writing is clear and understandable	All writing is clear with transitions and complete explanations 4	Most paragraphs are clearly written 3	Missing details make paragraphs hard to understand 1	Writing is unclear 0
The topics are supported with specific details	Many specific and meaningful details 3	Most have specific and meaningful details 2	Some details 1	Very few details 0
Illustrations are included which support the topic and add interest		Illustrations are about the topic, add interest, and are neatly done 2	Illustrations are included 1	None present 0
A variety of sentences are used		A variety of sentence type and length are used 2		Sentences are same length and type 0
Newsletter is carefully and neatly written in cursive handwriting	Handwriting is very neat and attractive 3	Cursive handwriting is neat 2	Has "write-overs" eraser marks, poorly formed letters 1	Difficult to read 0
Correct grammar, capitalization and punctuation are used	No errors 3	A few errors 2	Several errors 1	Numerous errors 0
Correct spelling is used	No errors 3	A few errors 2	Several errors 1	Many errors 0
Handed in on time	Organizer Point 1		Yes 1	No 0
Goal	Met my goal bonus 3	Appropriate goal 2	Included 1	None 0
Read and signed by a parent		Read and signed 2		Not signed 0
Is your goal specific, realistic, and measurable? Yes No	Did you reach your goal? Yes No		**Total Points** **28-30** **24-27** **18-23** **15-17**	**Grade** **A** **B** **C** **D**

Name _____

— *Quarterly Student Survey*

1. I understood the State Standard(s) because they were discussed in these classes _____ as goals and expected outcomes from our learning.

2. The activity I liked and learned the most from this quarter was _____
    _____
    because _____
    _____

3. I do my best at _____
    _____
    because _____
    _____

4. I must work more on _____
    _____
    because _____
    _____

5. When I struggled I knew how to get help from _____
    _____
    _____

6. Overall, I feel successful in school at _____
    _____
    because _____
    _____

7. The one thing I disliked the most was _____
    _____
    because _____
    _____

8. My classroom rules are posted and fair in these classes _____
    _____
    but they are not used in these cases _____
    _____

9. My school has an overall positive culture for learning _____

    _____

    because _____

    _____

10. If I could change one thing about school, it would be _____

    _____

    because _____

    _____

Added comments:

Name _____ Class/Activity _____

—Quarterly Weekly Summary

MY GOAL FOR THIS QUARTER IS:

_____
_____
_____

THE DATA WILL COME FROM MY PORTFOLIO:

_____
_____
_____

Week 1

Week 2

Week 3

Week 4

Week 5

Week 6

Week 7

Week 8

Week 9

I have met the State Performance Assessment Standard(s) by demonstrating knowledge in these classroom assessments:

I am pleased with the quality of my work:

I understand my needs and how I must meet them with purposeful intent:

Twenty hints for teachers/trainers to improve self-evaluation feedback

1. Provide a detailed course syllabus to indicate how students will be evaluated with a tentative outline of the dates for readings, assignments, and tests to be covered so they can develop planning or organization skills. Include learning objectives, expected outcomes, and exercises to apply the concepts.

2. Include multiple and varied assessments of learning and demonstrations of knowledge to lend opportunity to all learners and styles of learning.

3. Provide, post, and handout to each student copies of rubrics for numerous learning outcomes, and allow students ample time to consult with you on their work prior to the final evaluation.

4. Permit students to do a portion of their work as do-overs to provide mastery learning and improve their scores. Accept that failure is not an option.

5. Make portfolios mandatory to provide every student with feedback about their immediate past performance to be able to set a realistic goal for their next performance.

6. Encourage reflective thinking by requiring a weekly short essay detailing what they have learned the past week. This encourages positive learning and value for an education.

7. Assign at least one group project to encourage cooperative learning, and get students to verbalize with their peers what they have learned or are learning.

8. Change the perception about homework to being practice exercises that provide valuable feedback indicating progress and rate of learning course content and concepts. Permit do-overs for all homework. Do not require deadlines or penalize learners, but instead provide extra credit for successful comple'tion on time to reward and reinforce more learning. When you penalize students who already have the knowledge and can demonstrate it on tests and other work, you send a negative message about school and learning to learn.

9. Create learning progress graphs to include in the student's portfolio, and show every student how to be accountable for their learning by keeping them up-to-date.

10. Encourage students to keep a journal of what they are learning from the class each day.

11. Encourage students to rewrite their class notes to reinforce concepts to set learning, and organize for more efficient study to prepare for tests.

12. Provide in writing course strategies for reading, reading comprehension, writing, organization and study skills, and motivation and goal setting.

13. Encourage all students to keep a work log of their study habits and learning strategies. This will help them narrow their focus to apply their knowledge at will on demand.

14. Prominently post the state standards on large posters in your classroom written to the age level of your students, and discuss their meaning and relevance.

15. Collaborate with your students to select 3-5 classroom rules to post that can enable all students the equal opportunity to learn in your class, and provide consequences that you can enforce as the CEO of your classroom.

16. Devise a standard work exercise for a disruptive student to perform on average in 4 ½ minutes at the back of your classroom that will encourage them to reflect on what triggered their behavior, disruption of the classroom learning for other students who have a right to learn, and to provide time-out to settle down emotionally without effecting a harsh penalty. If the student continues to disrupt, provide for a backup plan to serve their "time-out" with a partner teacher next door. If repetitive, assign a detention to be served before or after school with you to have counsel with this student, and contact the parent. If negative behavior continues after that, then consult with school administration for harsher penalties. You must not allow any student or students to disrupt learning in your classroom any more than as the CEO of your home allow your child to violate house rules.

17. Have students write their job description for your class, and what they expect to learn.

18. Have students periodically write a short one-page self-evaluation progress report to include in their portfolio. This reflective thinking helps students to be accountable for their learning.

19. Consider demonstrated improvement in learning throughout the term in your final grade. Perhaps you drop the lowest grade and all of those points to tally a new percentage, or you apply a multiplier formula like 1.5 to that lowest score. If a student screwed up a test for a $42 \times 1.5 = 63$, this new score at least helps out the average a little without skewing the true outcome. Students who try but make one error because they had three tests in one

day, did not organize their studies, their dog died, etc. can have a chance for redemption to reinforce learning. The opposite would be to continually coerce students with harsh penalties that are like touching an electric fence and avoided because of the pain they feel.

20. Give credit where credit is due, but do not take credit for a student's learning or overly praise what they are expected to do for themselves to be accountable.

Name _____   Class/Activity _____

Self-Evaluation
Performance Action Plan

Written or stated goal:

_____

Personal need(s) identified:

_____

Performance skills used:

_____

Standard to be met:

_____

Past experiences to transfer to the task:

_____

Purposeful Indent;

_____

Immediate Past Performance	New Goal Performance
Actions Taken	Change Action
1_____	1_____
2_____	2_____
3_____	3_____
Measurable objective outcome	Measurable objective outcome expected
Scored _____ points better than goal. Circle Rating: Great Good Okay Poor	Scored _____ points better than goal. Circle Rating: Great Good Okay Poor

Resources and peope who can help me:

_____

_____

Subject "   " Performance Log   Teacher _____   Name _____

State Standards: _____
Performance
Assessment
Standards: _____

Tests (black ink)	1	2	3	4		5		6		7		8		9
Quizzes (blue ink)	1	2	3	4	5	6	7	8						
Date														
% Goal/ Score														
100														
90														
80														
70														
60														
50														
40														
30														
20														
10														
0														
Accum. Raw Score														
Accum. %														

Record a dot or color in for the % value on the vertical line to the right of the test/quiz number.   Connect the dots for test scores with black ink pen; quizzes with blue ink.

Take the Quiz

Can you discriminate between an extrinsic and intrinsic motive?

Directions: To the left of each numbered statement write "E" for extrinsic or "I" for intrinsic motivator being used. Answer key at end of Appendix.

1. That was a super great effort you did on your paper.
2. My goal is to better my last math quiz score by 5%.
3. My regional manager informed me of my quota for next quarter.
4. I need to find something to eat.
5. Mom put my "A" spelling test paper on our refrigerator.
6. I want to be an Eagle Scout.
7. Mom will buy me a new shirt if I watch my brother for two hours.
8. Dad gives me a $ 1.00 for every hit I make on our baseball team.
9. I would be happy to be in the top 10% of all company sales reps by the end of this year.
10. If I sell two more magazines, I will win a new bike.
11. My teacher writes my name on the board when I am bad.
12. If I am late to work one more time, I will lose my job.
13. I am going to catch a bigger fish than my Dad on this vacation.
14. I just found a new way to manufacture our widgets that can save the company.
15. Dad just told me I wrote the best English paper he has ever read.
16. Way to go John. I knew you could get that B! Great job.
17. The first sales rep to sell $1,000,000 in real estate this year will get a free trip to Florida for their family.
18. I want to read at the fifth grade level in the third grade.
19. I want to go to college.
20. I must mow two more lawns to earn enough money to buy my new baseball glove.
21. If I block five more shots, I will set a new school single season record.
22. I have improved my grade point average .67 points this semester.
23. I need to score five more points than my last math test.
24. Dad told me I could watch TV when my homework got done.

ANSWERS

Take the Quiz

1. E	7. E	13. I	19. I
2. I	8. E	14. I	20. I
3. E	9. I	15. E	21. I
4. I	10. E	16. E	22. I
5. E	11. E	17. E	23. I
6. I	12. E	18. I	24. E

Example Work Out Log (Swimming)

Mon 9/8	W-up 400 free-breast 1:32,	Flys 3x20 @50 lbs.
	1:50 pace HR 140 Wts.	
	Kick 400 avg. 1:02's per 50 8:15	Lats 3x20 @16 lbs.
1500	Pull 400 fr/br avg. 1:10's; 48's per 50	Curls 3x20 @20 lbs.
	Swim 100 br 1:45 counting 8 or less	
	Swim 100 fr 1:28	
	Swim down 50	
T ue 9/9	W-up 800 fr/br 1:35; 1:50 HR 150	plus Wts ditto
	Kick 400 avg. 1:02 8:17 HR 150	
1850	Pull 400 avg. 1:08 9:12 HR 150	
	Swim 200 BR br 3:33 avg. 52	
	Swim down 50	
Wed 9/10	W-up 400 fr/br	plus Wts ditto
	Kick 400	
1800		Pull 400
	Swim 2 x 200 3:40	
	Swim 2 x 100 1:49+	
Thu 9/11	W-up 400 fr/br 1:34, 1:50	plus Wts ditto
	Kick 400 avg. 1:01	
1800	Pull 400 avg. 1:05 HR 140	
	Swim 400 BR by 100's 20 rest avg. 1:48 HR 160	
	Swim 4 x 50 easy/ hard br long rest 41+, 42 HR	
	160	
Fri 9/12	W-up 400 fr/br 1:32, 1:48	plus Wts ditto
	Swim 8 x 50 easyfr/hard br on 3 42+, 41+, 43,	
	42+ HR 160	
2000	Kick 200	
	Kick 8 x 50 on 1:30 avg. 48+ HR 140	
	Pull 200	
	Pull 8 x 50 on 1:45 avg. 55+ HR 140	

Mon 9/15	W-up 800 fr/br 1:28-1:37, 1:46-1:50	plus Wts. Ditto
	Kick 400	flys upped to 60 lb
2000	Kick 2 x 100 1:44, 1:47	lats upped to 9
	Pull 400	curls still at 20 lb.
	Pull 2 x 100 1:55, 2:00	

Tue 9/16	W-up 400 fr/br 1:26-1:35; 1:47-1:50	plus Wts ditto
	Swim 4 x 100 br NS 1:37, 1:39, 1:42, 1:44 on 3	
	Kick 200	
2000	Kick 4 x 100 1:44, 1:48, 1:49, 1:48	
	Pull 200	
	Pull 4 x 100 1:47, 1:50, 1:59, 2:05	

Glossary of Terms

Accountability – This is defined as responsible, liable, or explainable. In the traditional sense, accountable is what someone else expects of another performer. Personal accountability is holding yourself to meet specific identified needs or goals.

ADD - Attention Deficit Disorder – A learning disability caused by the inability to concentrate and focus on a task for time enough to enhance learning.

ADHD - Attention Deficit Hyperactivity Disorder – Like ADD above only the disability also involves the body to make movements and not sit still for any length of time.

Associational Neuron – This is a nerve cell that connects to similarly stored information to form a network of associations to more readily retrieve knowledge. The network acts like the electrical wiring in a house. You are able to associate similarly stored information to learn new information.

Auto Suggestion – The more you mentally rehearse your performance to perfect the subroutines of the entire performance and begin to demonstrate them in physical practice, you can create an associated trigger to execute the entire programmed response.

Automate – This is to take routine behaviors like getting dressed and moving them to a subconscious awareness level to avoid stress from too many conscious sensations.

AYP - Acceptable Yearly Progress – This is a new term under the No Child Left Behind Act to ensure that schools are making progress in reaching the goal for all third graders to be able to read at the end of the third grade by 2014.

Behavior – How individuals perform is in part based on their personality learned from their environment and external factors that together comprise behavior. All behavior is motivated to fulfill a personal need or goal.

Behavioral Pattern – The typical or habitual behavioral response made to specific cues constitutes a pattern that is often predictable.

Benchmark – Either a national, state, or personal standard for measuring what you should know at a given moment in your educational process.

Bias – This is the pre judged view of an outcome without evidence that could prove otherwise.

Bio Feedback – This is the sensory feedback you receive from your biological organism that deal with your heart rate, respiration, hormone secretion, elimination of wastes, and movements of the muscles.

Bit Map – This is the compression of a computer file or series of stimulus-response connections into a more readily organized, stored, and retrieved bit of information.

Black Box – This is the term used by behaviorist B.F. Skinner to describe perceptual processing of information in a performer's brain that he could neither see nor hear and therefore did not concern himself with.

Boss Management – This is an external control system that operates under the belief that individual performers are incapable of self motivation, and an attempt to gain conformity in the work force to follow through on company generated policies and procedures.

Caring – The ultimate theme of caring is to teach personal accountable independence to each performer.

Closed Serial Loop – A series of continuous stimulus-response connections that make up a repetitious physical movement such as swimming or running.

Cognition – This is the learned process for creating knowledge through the perception of various sensations and assigning meaningful and relevant value.

Conditioned Response – This occurs whenever a stimulus cue is automatically associated to a specific and predictable response. The classic example was Pavlov's dog conditioned to salivate at the ringing of a bell the dog associated with getting a morsel of meat.

Conditioning – This is the repetition that connects a specific stimulus cue to a specific physical response. Nervous pathways with associational neurons to speed up the transmission of sensory impulses from the recognition of a cue and selection of the specific conditioned response.

Congruence – This is your realism ability to predict and perform when you set a goal and then closely approximate in your performance. This also applies to self evaluation prior to your manager's extrinsic evaluation and be closely similar in content and performance.

Constructivist Learning – A learning system where the individual learner constructs their learning by defining what is meaningful and relevant new information they can attach or scaffold and build their knowledge.

Cooperative Learning – A learning system that involves several learners to perform specific roles and share what they have learned in their own words with the team.

Cue – A cue is any stimulus agent or action generally associated through a practice set to increase the recognition to a desired response.

Dichotomy – A dichotomy is the comparison of two opposites to point out the great differences between the recognition and associated actions of the two to aid learning discriminate cues. Examples are hot and cold, positive and negative, and intrinsic and extrinsic.

Differentiated Instruction – This is a system of instruction used to teach a variety of students with different learning preferences and styles to progress at personally optimal rates and be self initiated to construct their learning to make it more meaningful and relevant.

Discrimination Learning – This is your ability to clearly see the differences between two closely associated stimuli to make a proper response.

Drive - A drive is the persistent dominant subconscious behavior until the desired need is sufficiently satisfied to temporarily reduce the drive, or the conscious awareness of the need and behavior are identified to convert the drive to a motive.

Empower – This is an attitude or belief to allow performer's to create significant improvement to their performance when allowed to perform work as they deem efficient.

Energy Mobilization – This is the top performer's ability to activate all their systems to perform a skill at full capacity for a given moment in time when it matters the most to be successful.

Extrinsic Motivation – This is another person's need or goal imposed on an individual or group of performers.

Feedback – This is positive or negative information about performance in relation to expected outcomes to measure the progress in attaining a need or goal. Your ability to self-evaluate performance feedback and make adjustments to input cues to improve personal performance is critical.

Frequency of Reward – This is an important measure for how you maintain your motivation to achieve a need or goal. More frequent reward increases your motivation; less frequent reward decreases your motivation.

Frontal Lobe – The lobe where thinking takes place in the brain located behind your forehead.

Gestalt – A German term used in psychology to describe the concept of the whole.

Goal - A goal is the objective measure of a pre-set personal standard to achieve in the short or long term.

Group Personality Type – Individuals use the average group performance to provide a perceptual anchoring point about which to set a new goal.

Homeostatic Equilibrium – A term created by William D. Cannon in 1929 to describe the natural drive to automate responses to routine sensations such as the regulation of hormones, and heart and respiratory rates without having to think about them.

IDEA - Individuals with Disabilities Education Act – An Act of Congress to protect and provide for the education of any person with a disability.

Identical Elements - Specific stimulus-response connections in the form of cues associated with specific kinds of responses are transferred to learn new unfamiliar tasks. For example, acquiring ball skills you can apply to a variety of sports.

IEP - Individual Educational Placement – A practice commonly used in schools to assist students with professionally diagnosed learning disabilities.

Innate Drive – Also known as a natural drive that is built into the human organism to preserve our species and motivate development and growth. Examples are self preservation, quality of life, independence, belong, love and be loved, and improve.

Intent – Your intent is almost always positive to succeed; people do not purposefully have intent to fail or are driven to make mistakes and not improve.

Intrinsic Motivation – This is a performer's internal desire to satisfy a personal need or goal.

IPP - Immediate Past Performance – This is the objective measure or subjective feeling taken from the last performance.

Key Hole – This is a sport psychology term used to increase focus ability by imagining you were looking at all the objects in a room through a key hole. This awareness of details improves performance.

Lead Management – This is a system that operates under the belief that the performer needs to be empowered to create newer strategies and methods for more efficient performance.

LOP - Level of Performance – This is a benchmark that objectively measures the individual performance in relation to other similarly talented performers, or one's immediate past performance or average.

MaS>MaF – Your motive to achieve success must be greater than your motive to avoid failure. Performance improvement is enhanced by focusing on the positives and not the negatives. Thinking about a negative creates a visual image in the brain that conditions the event to potentially occur with more frequency than you desire.

Mastery Learning – This is learning how to perform one segment or subroutine of a whole skilled performance well before attempting to learn the next segment.

Mental Practice – This is an adjunct to physical practice if you have enough physical practice experience to imagine and visualize going through the motions of an actual practice. You make a mental movie of the observations you make of your performance. You can put the movie mode into slow motion, stop action, forward, or reverse to make minor stimulus-response connections to perfect your practice.

Meta Cognitive – This is conscious learning to reinforce the connection between successful and pleasurable feelings associated with the desire to learn new information.

Micromanagement – This is a systematic and often coercive method to externally control the behavior of performers that does not encourage or empower personal accountability for performance improvement.

Modeling – This is to demonstrate the example for specific behaviors as an expectation, but has not been shown to improve personal performance.

Motivation - Motivation is the specific strategy used to satisfy a motive. This strategy is usually in the form of a need or goal to focus on the accurate recognition of conditioned pre-set cues to elicit a proper response represented by a series of S-R stimulus-response connections.

Motive - A motive is the conscious awareness of a drive to purposefully satisfy a personal need or goal.

Multi Sensory Learning – A practice used by Albert Einstein to imagine what a stimulus cue would be like in another sense modality that created numerous associations to aid his perception and learning.

Multiple Regression Equation – To predict a criterion such as having the knowledge and skill to be intrinsically motivated, a select number of variables are chosen that will account for the most variance or predictive strength to focus on learning before all the others.

N-ach - Need for Achievement – A psychological term used to describe a presumed identified need in a performer that increases their motivation to achieve.

Natural Drive – Also referred to as an innate drive that is built into the human organism to preserve our species and motivate development and growth. Examples are self preservation, quality of life, independence, belong, love and be loved, and improve.

NCLB - No Child Left Behind Act – An Act of the United States Congress in 2003 to ensure that every school child would be entitled to an equal opportunity to learn to meet specific outlined standards by 2014 with the help of federally funded Title programs.

Need - A need is a personal call to action stimulus to satisfy the acquisition of an object or to demonstrate a skill with a reasonable degree of proficiency.

Neuroscience – This is the relatively new science of neurological functions of the brain and central nervous system. More knowledge about how the brain works has created a whole new system of brain based learning.

Neuron – This is a nerve cell body and all its processes to connect nervous pathways that transmit sensory information to the brain to be processed into a response.

ODD - Oppositional Defiant Disorder – A personality that chooses to defy authority or direct commands.

Open Serial Loop - A series of continuous stimulus-response connections that make up a non-repetitious physical movement with a specific starting and stopping point such as bowling, throwing a ball, or a golf swing.

Paired Associate Conditioning – Two different stimuli are paired up or associated with the same response. This creates a powerful conditioned response resistant to forgetting. The usual visual, verbal, and kinesthetic cues are paired. Taking and writing notes is kinesthetic.

PAP - Perceptual Anchoring Point – This is a subjective measure about which a performer chooses to set a new goal.

Paradigm Shift – The ability to recognize a significant change in a cluster of perceptual thought processes. For example, learning to connect quality of effort with quality of reward to improve performance.

PBIS - Positive Behavioral Intervention System – An educational system for training teachers on how to help improve student learning and behavior with positive intervention that reinforce learning.

Perception – How you think to perform using past performance feedback, and based on the processing of predictable sensory information.

Personality Patterns – Patterns are the spokes that come off the wheel hub in a variety of ways to guide your habits and performance tendencies.

Personality Traits – Traits are mostly formed by the age of two and are like the hub of a wheel; once formed they resist change, but can be altered over time.

Planer Thinking – As you become more familiar with a task you are able to think on increasingly higher planes to solve problems and provide solutions with a greater vision.

Positive SelfTalk – The act of having a personal but silent conversation with your brain to reflect on a positive performance expectation based on past performance experience.

PFC - Pre Frontal Cortex – This area of the brain is in front of the frontal lobe behind your forehead and is involved in planning, reasoning, organizing, and decision making directly.

Probability of Success – This will occur when you set goals only slightly better than your own immediate past performance or average, and also increase your frequency of reward.

Purpose - The act of having an understanding of what and why you are learning to perform an activity to the best of your ability with positive results.

Purposeful Intent – This is the conscious cognitive motive to satisfy a personal need or goal.

Quid Pro Quo – You do this for me and I will do this for you.

Response – The action made to a stimulus.

Routine – Subconscious steady states require little or no thinking to perform familiar tasks with average results such as brushing your teeth or putting on your pants.

RROSR – This is the anachronism for recognize, receive, organize, store, and retrieve valuable information compressed into bit maps.

RtI – Response to Intervention - This is a three tiered system to help identify students with early learning difficulties and provide them with mandatory interventions in the form of special classes, after school tutoring programs, and focus on improvement.

Rubric – This is an important tool to enhance self evaluation by providing some kind of table this indicates several component parts or variables to indicate knowledge of a subject. Each variable is described in the adjacent 3-4 columns with each description accounting for a better performance of that variable and indicated by a higher score. If a student scored well on the fourth column for any one variable, it would provide 4 points and indicate they had performed the best possible. Total points are awarded to evaluate completeness and follow through ability to learn and improve performance.

SEL - Social Emotional Learning - This is an educational practice of placing performers into diverse classrooms to learn a variety of acceptable behaviors for students of the same grade level.

Selective Attention – A specific cue among many is singled out to focus on and trigger a response.

Self Esteem Psychology – This is the practice of praising performers to induce them into repeating the performance with increasingly higher levels of confidence, but has often been detrimental as undeserved praise and loss of respect for the provider.

Self Personality Type – Individuals use their own immediate past performance as a perceptual anchoring point about which to set a new goal.

Sensation – Any kind of stimulation from one of the five senses.

Sensory Deprivation – The brain must receive some kind of sensations at all times to process. When all sensations are removed, the brain shuts down in a state of confusion and subjects have reported hallucinations.

Sensory Satiation – A constant stimulus does not remit, and the sensation becomes suppressed at the synapse. An example is working in a cheese factory. After several minutes the smell goes away.

Sequential Learning – Subroutines are parts of more complex tasks to facilitate learning the whole skill in a sequence that is chained together as the parts are learned and improved.

Serial Learning – Specific stimulus-response connections are learned in a series to perfect performance. This means that a specific cue represents the stimulus to practice and reinforce the connection to an appropriate series of responses.

Skill – This is the demonstration of your talents and abilities in a specific activity that you have learned and practiced to improve your performance.

Smoothing – This is the practice of making a fluid action of a physical response.

Stimulus – A stimulus is any agent or action that causes an activity in an organism. The stimulus creates the sensation that reaches the brain or central nervous system for processing. Any one of the five senses can create a stimulus.

Strategy – This is a systematic and predictable set of cues to improve performance.

Sub Conscious – The sensory response of the body without having to think about the action.

Sub Skill – Also known as a subroutine or part of a larger complex skill.

Subroutine – A subroutine is the connections of specific sets of predictable cues (S) with correct responses (R) that are known for learning a skill faster. Also known as sub skill to break apart complex activities to practice and improve performance in specific parts, and then reconnect all into one performance.

Synapse – This is the chemical connection of dendrites at the ends of nerve cells that transmit sensory information along a series.

Talent – Your physical and mental attributes enable you to perform on a higher skill level than average performers of the same skill.

Task Familiarity – Your personality patterns change as you become more familiar with a task from insecure to secure, apprehensive to less apprehensive, and less confident to confident.

The Triad - These are the interrelated skills of increasing awareness, enhancing self evaluation, and connecting reward with reinforcement.

Third Eye – This is the strategy for projecting an image of yourself performing as if you were observing with a third eye placed behind you like a movie camera.

Transfer Learning – Early recognition of specific cues to perform specific responses can be transferred from one activity to learn another similar activity. For example, ball skills are used in baseball and basketball.

Trigger – This is the key stimulus used to start a subroutine, recognition of a cue, or by selective attention discriminate a specific cue from several others.

Two Digit Error – In information processing, these are the number of stimulus-response connections that pass by undetected while the brain receives and processes the perception of the stimulus error. In typing, usually two key strokes will pass before stopping to correct the mistake.

Value – This is the personal significance one assigns to an activity they deem meaningful and relevant. The equation $V = R/E$ where value is the amount of reward divided by effort.

Variable Interaction Effect - This is the overlapping effect of two or more variables resulting in a bias or un pure result.

Variance – This is the amount that each variable accounts for its portion of the total 100% prediction in a multiple regression equation to predict a criterion.

Verbal Personality Type – Individuals use what they state to others about a future performance as a perceptual anchoring point about which to set a new goal.

Visualization – This is the process of making a mental picture of a physical action you wish to replicate during the actual performance.

WIIFM – This is the anachronism for What's In It For Me.

Zero Sum – For every winner you have to have a loser that results in a zero sum.

Index of Names

NAME

Ali, Muhammad, 103, 290

Andersen, Dr. Pete, 66, 101, 103, 107, 110, 200, 000

Aesop, 123, 291, 342

Aristotle, 77

Barnum, P.T., 171, 294

Billingsley, Hobie, Dedication

Brodman, Korbinian, 50

Bryant, Kobe, 342

Burton, Dobbie, Acknowledgement, Dedication

Cannon, William D., 17, 32, 62, 405

Cavic, Milorad "Mike", 246

Christian, Andrew, 1, 49, 132, 197, 233, 258, 289, 323

Churchill, Winston, 232

Colangelo, Jerry, 219

Counsilman, Dr. James "Doc", Acknowledgement, Dedication, 76, 267, 300

Counsilman, Marge, Acknowledgement, Dedication

Covey, Stephen, 42

Daniel, Beth, 224

Dembo, Tamara, 107

Deming, W. Edwards, 9, 150, 215, 375

Drowatzky, Dr. John, Acknowledgement, Dedication

Dyer, Dr. Wayne, 30

Edison, Thomas, viii, 26, 32, 74, 90, 128, 175, 217, 264, 272, 308, 373

Einstein, Dr. Albert, viii, 50, 58, 74, 79, 82, 148, 217, 305, 373, 406

Elliott, Robert, Dedication

Elway, John, 247

Festinger, Leon, 107

Ford, Henry, 26, 175

Freshley, Mike, Acknowledgement, 89

Freudenrich, Dr. Craig, 5

Gagné, Robert, vii, 76, 338

Gardner, Howard, 79, 264

Gates, Bill, 217

Getty, J. Paul, 1

Glasser, Dr. William, 186, 265, 339

Gleason, Jackie, 234

Goethe, 42

Hull, Clark, 10

Jackson, Phil, 173, 342, 343

Jacobsen, E., 226

James, LaBron, 29

Jastremski, Chet, 121

Jefferson, Thomas, 175

Jobs, Steven, 217

Jordan, Michael, 26, 32, 112, 119, 121, 152, 173, 214, 216, 217, 220, 230, 232, 321, 342

Kennedy, John F., 175

King, Betsy, 224

King, Dr. Martin Luther, 26, 175

Knight, Bob, 300

Kohn, Alfie, 159, 310, 335

Krause, Jerry, 173

Kroc, Ray, 26

Krzyzewski, Mike, 219

Landry, Tom, 20

Leno, Jay, 139

Lewin, Kurt, 107

Lincoln, Abraham, 26, 141, 175

Mann, Horace, 175

Maslow, Abraham H., 18, 19, 41, 57, 77, 90, 93, 100, 154, 267

Murray, Edward, 10

Namath, Willie Joe, 103

Newton, Sir Isaac, 127

Passingham, R., 219

Pavlov, Ivan, 139, 403

Phelps, Michael, 50, 51, 214, 217, 225, 230, 232, 246

Picasso, Pablo, 89, 217, 294

Pippen, Scottie, 173

Queen Elizabeth, 251

Roosevelt, Eleanor, 26

Rotella, Dr. Bob, 258

Rowe, J., 219

Rudy, 263

Ruth, Babe, 26

Sacagewea, 175

Sakai, K., 219

Sergiovanni, Thomas, 150

Shakespeare, William, 30, 142, 350

Skinner, B.F., vii, 81, 91, 128, 157, 179, 198, 220, 235, 256, 281, 320, 331, 403

Smith, Dean, 216

Sorenstam, Annika, 7

Spears, Brittany, 74

Spitz, Mark, 217

Studer, Quint, 190, 311

Sunleaf, David, 99

Terhune, John, Acknowledgement

Tillis, Mel, 126, 245

van Baalen, Vinus, Acknowledgement, art designs: 44, 194, 286

Victor, Dr. Tony, Acknowledgement

Warren, Rick, 89

Weber, Bruce, 249

Williams, Deron, 249

Wooden, Johnny, 300

Woods, Tiger, 53, 70, 119, 174, 214, 232

Yerkes-Dodson, 233, 251

Key Phrases

Science of Purposeful Intent

If you expect to lead, you must empower others to succeed more often than fail.

To be highly motivated to achieve and value a new goal, you must be aware of your past performance.

The motive to achieve success must be greater than the motive to avoid failure.

It is not your failures, but your awareness and ability to act with a purpose that will define your life's work.

Trying to improve your personal best is all that I can ask of anyone and all that you can ask of yourself.

You learn what you focus on to achieve.

When you have a clear purpose for performing an activity coupled with a positive intent to improve or be successful, chances are good that 95-99% of the time you'll have a positive outcome that you can value.

Mind Body Connection

All behavior is motivated by the desire to satisfy a personal need or goal.

No one is perfect, but trying to improve is perfect.

It is never too late to start training your mind to control what your body does.

Your PI skills are always improving but never mastered.

Increased intelligence is directly proportional to increased awareness.

You cannot appreciably increase your intelligence to be a top performer until you learn how to increase your awareness.

When are we going to teach men how to fish so they can feed themselves?

What makes purposeful intent significant is the hypothesis that for learning to take place you must attach value to the information.

Growing Antennae

By defining your purpose you achieve intrinsic motivation, and consistent performance.

Align the company needs and values with the personal needs and values of the performers.

It is not where you start out in life, but where you end up which matters most.

Focus only on what you can control, and you will become more self aware of how to improve your own performance.

Align your behaviors with natural drives.

The value of any activity is the amount of the perceived reward divided by the perceived effort.

People do not value what they do not have to earn by their own doing.

It's Your Job

You cannot build accountability in a micromanagement system.

The object of parenting is to teach your children to eventually provide for their own needs.

It is not what you guess about your performance, it is what you learn to know and value about your work by learning to increase your personal awareness skills.

The model for education has changed from receptacles of knowledge to facilitators of knowledge.

You can build intrinsic value in any task that you purposefully choose to store meaningful and relevant information.

Since 1960 American public schools systems have change from potentially being the "Beacon of Society" to be the "Reflection of Society."

The ultimate theme of caring is to teach accountable independence in each performer.

Increasing social programs do not teach a man how to fish and provide for their long term needs.

When you rely on extrinsic motivation in the form of praise, grades, or some form of judgment of the performer's work you create a dependent approval system that requires more management for higher cost.

The greatest mistake a leader can make is to take credit for the efforts of another performer.

The motive to achieve success must be greater than the motive to avoid failure (MaS>MaF).

Do you know of any top performer that ever waited for the approval of another person?

Performers never learn to identify their needs when someone else meets them.

Rewarding irresponsible behavior or modeling responsible behavior will not improve personal accountability.

Work ethic is a learned and reinforced value system based on your personal efforts and task difficulty.

Pre Performance Evaluation

The more realistic you are with matching your needs and abilities to each selected task, the greater your probability for success and continued improvement.

The theoretical construct for purposeful intent is that you can more readily recognize, receive, organize, store, and retrieve information you learn to cognitively choose as valuable, meaningful, and relevant from your past familiar experience and your future predicted unfamiliar experience.

Top performers create their own self-evaluation system with self-imposed benchmarks, and hold themselves accountable for reaching their goals.

It only matters that you try to be a little bit better tomorrow than you were today.

The most powerful motivator is to set low positive goals only slightly better than your own immediate past performance or performance average.

Set low positive goals to increase your probability and frequency of success to enhance your personal reward system.

You can never be a creator as your Creator has intended for you if all you learn to do is copy other performers.

Whether you are young or old, boredom, burnout, and staleness comes from not having learned how to increase your personal sensory awareness.

Drop outs occur when the performer cannot make these connections to feel rewarded more frequently, and know their purpose and role to be committed to improving.

American school systems condition a boss-management mentality to direct masses of students instead of conditioning in each student intrinsic motivation skills to be in charge of their learning to make new knowledge meaningful and relevant.

Thinking it through is your ability to project your personal needs that will drive your behaviors.

Change forces you to restructure your purposeful intent.

During Performance Evaluation

What you think of your performance must matter more than what your leader thinks of your performance.

Post Performance Evaluation

Your leadership is to familiarize your performers with what to expect performing unfamiliar tasks to build confidence.

To sustain or improve your intrinsic motivation, you must increase the probability for your success with a low positive goal, and learn to self reward your performances.

Any performance improvement is success that can be conditioned to be repeated.

Principles of Reward Reinforcement

The object of purposeful intent is to increase your intrinsic motivation to learn how to learn, to think, act, and do for yourself and eventually others.

We tend to want to repeat pleasurable activities, and avoid painful experiences.

If you dwell on negative thoughts, you will experience negative results.

Micromanagement and leader evaluation reduce the personal empowerment and self evaluation that can increase worker's intrinsic motivation.

Leaders must help performers make the connection between quality of effort and quality of reward.

Excessive social approval and verbal praise diminish your reflective thinking to self evaluate and compare your immediate performance with past performance for improvement and form a new perceptual anchoring point and new goal.

Your success feeling is associated with how closely you approximated your goal with your actual performance compared to your immediate past performance.

Purposeful intent is the foundation for all motivation.

Failure achieves nothing; success achieves everything.

Leading Purposeful Intent For Success

Great achievements are seldom earned on the first trial.

You identify and create the appropriate need and align your positive goal strategy that reinforces your learning with continuous success.

You cannot acquire a skill if you do not try to improve with a purpose.

No one purposefully seeks failure.

Be your own best friend.

Take time to reflect and associate your quality of effort with your quality of reward (third Triad) to build value in what you are learning to learn.

When more rules are created than can be enforced or reinforced to correct your bad behaviors, they are a waste of your time and energy.

List of Illustrations

Book Cover -   *BookSurge Design Team*

Title Page - *The Triad*   *BookSurge Design Team*

Chapter 1, Science of Purposeful Intent

    The Triad with name labeled spheres

    Inside an Atom

    Multiple Regression Equation

    Maslow's Need Hierarchy

    Activity Value Index

Purposeful Intent Skills Development Model

Part One Title Page - *The Triad* with Increase Awareness label

van Baalen original artwork *"Awareness"*

Chapter 2, Mind-Body Connection

    Synapse Human Nerve Conduction

    Increasing Awareness Flow Chart

    Multiple Regression Equation

    Overlapping Variables

    Planer Thinking Curve

    Serial Stimulus-Response Loop

Chapter 3, Growing Antennae

B.F. Skinner's Black Box

    Personality Interaction Effect for Goal Set Preferences

    The Low Positive Goal Strategy Works

    RROSR – Circles of Interconnected Brain Lobes

Chapter 4, It's Your Job

    Accountability Paradigm

Part Two Title Page -   *The Triad* with Enhance Self Evaluation label

van Baalen original artwork **"Self Evaluation"**

Chapter 5, Pre Performance Evaluation

    Pre Performance Evaluation Checklist

    Correlation Value and PI Strength

Activity Value Index

Continuum of Performance Improvement

Typical Learning Curve

Open Serial Loop

Closed Serial Loop

Chapter 6, During Performance Evaluation

Yerkes-Dodson Law

Open Serial Loop

Closed Serial Loop

Chapter 7, Post Performance Evaluation

Scale

Post Performance Evaluation Rubric

Optimal Performance Reinforcement Value Index

Purposeful Intent Value System

Part Three Title Page - *The Triad* with Connect Reward with Reinforcement label

van Baalen original artwork **"Reward Reinforcement"**

Chapter 8, Principles of Reward Reinforcement

No Illustrtations

Chapter 9, Leading Purposeful Intent for Success

Purposeful Intent Flow Chart

7 Steps to Purposeful Intent Performance Improvement

PI Feedback Loop

Meta-cognitive Flow Chart: Intrinsic Motivation

Gagné's Nine Events of Instruction

References

16PF. 5th Edition, IPAT. Champaign, IL: Institute for Personality and Ability Testing, 2008.

Andersen, Peter A. *The Relation of Personality Factors of Olympic, National Finalist, and Non-National Finalist Swimmers to Unfamiliar and Familiar Aspiration Tasks.* Unpublished Doctoral Dissertation, The University of Toledo, Toledo, OH, 1973.

Andersen, Peter A. "Personality Differences in United States Men's Olympic, National and Non-National Finalist Swimmers and Seven Stroke Classes." *Motor Learning, Sport, Psychology, Pedagogy and Didactics of Physical Activity.* Vol. 7, 327-336, Quebec City, Canada: The International Congress of Physical Activity Sciences, 1976.

Blanchard, Ken. *The Heart of a Leader.* Tulsa: Honor Books, 1999.
Cannon, Walter B. "Organization for Physiological Homeostasis." *Physiol Rev.* 9, 399-431, 1929.

Cannon, Walter B. "Homeostatic Motives." in Chapter 3, *Motivation and Emotion.* Murray, Edward J., Englewood Cliffs, NJ: Prentice-Hall, Inc., 1964.

Covey, Stephen R. *The 7 Habits of Highly Effective People.* New York: Simon and Schuster, 1989.

Dembo, Tamara. "Der arger als dynamisches problem, (Untersuchungen zur handlungs- und affektpsychologie." X. ed. by Kurt Lewin.) *Psychologie Forschung,* 15, 1-144, 1931.

Deming, W. Edwards. *Out of the Crisis.* Cambridge, MA: MIT Press, 1986.

Dyer, Wayne W. *The Power of Intention.* Carlsbad, CA: Hay House, Inc., 2004.

Faculty, Washington.edu. http://faculty.washington.edu/chudler/synapse.html. *Neuroscience For Kids*. (2007, June 3).

Festinger, Leon. "Wish, expectation, and group standards as factors influencing level of aspiration." *Journal of Abnormal and Social Psychology*, 37, 184-200, 1942.

Fitts, Paul M., and Posner, Michael I. *Human Performance*. Belmont, CA: Brooks/Cole Publishing Company, 1967.

Freudenrich, Craig C. Ph.D. http://science.howstuffworks.com/atom.htm. 2003.

Gagné, Robert. "Military training and principles of learning." *American Psychologist*, 17, 263-276, 1962.

Gagné, Robert. *The Conditions of Learning (4th ed.)*. New York: Holt, Rinehart & Winston, 1985.

Gardner, Howard. *Intelligence Reframed*. New York: Basic Books, 1999.

Glasser, Dr. William. *The Quality School*. New York: Harper & Row Publishers, Inc., 1990.

Greenwald, A.G. "Ego task analysis: A synthesis of research on ego-involvement and self-awareness." In A.H. Hastorf and A.M. Isen (Eds.), *Cognitive Social Psychology*, *(pp.109-147)*, New York: Elsevier/North-Holland, 1982.

Hackman, J.R., and Oldham, G.R. "Motivation through the design of work: Test of a theory." in *Organizational Behavior and Human Performance*, 16, 250, 1976.

Hill, Winfred F. *Learning: A Survey of Psychological Interpretations*. Scranton, PA: Chandler Publishing Company, 1963.

Hull, C.L. *Principles of Behavior*. New York: Appleton-Century Crofts, 1943.

Jacobson, E. *Progressive Relaxation*. Chicago: University of Chicago Press, 1938.

Kohn, Alfie. *Punished by Rewards*. New York: Houghton-Mifflin Company, 1993.

Kouzes, James M., and Posner, Barry Z. *Encouraging The Heart*. San Francisco: Jossey-Bass, 1999.

Lazarus, Richard S. *Personality and Adjustment*. Englewood Cliffs, NJ: Prentice-Hall, Inc., 1963.

Maslow, Abraham H. *A Theory of Human Motivation*. Psychological Review, 50, 370–96, 1943.

Maslow, Abraham H. *Motivation and Personality*. 2nd. ed., New York: Harper & Row. 1970.

Maslow's hierarchy of needs. in *Wikipedia, The Free Encyclopedia*. Retrieved from http://en.wikipedia.org. March 4, 2007.

Murray, Edward J. *Motivation and Emotion*. Englewood Cliffs, NJ: Prentice-Hall, Inc., 1964.

Sakai, K., Rowe, J. and Passingham, R. "Active maintenance in prefrontal area 46 creates distractor-resistant memory." *Nature Neuroscience*, 5, 479-484, 2002.

Sergiovanni, Thomas J. *Building Community In Schools*. San Francisco: Jossey-Bass, 1994.

Skinner, B.F. *Science and Human Behavior*. New York: The Free Press a MacMillan Company, 1953.

Studer, Quint. *Hardwiring Excellence: Purpose, Worthwhile Work, Making a Difference*. Gulf Breeze, FL: Fire Starter Publishing, 2003.

Sullo, Bob. *Activating the Desire to Learn*. Alexandria, VA: Association for Supervision and Curriculum Development, 2007.

References

Svinicki, Marilla. *ALD 320: Cognition, Human Learning and Motivation.* outline and notes, Retrieved from http://www.utexas.edu/courses/svinicki/ald320/, March 10, 2007.

Yerkes, Robert M. and Dodson, John D., "The relation of strength of stimulus to rapidity of habit-formation." *Journal of Comparative Neurology and Psychology,* 18, 459-482, 1908.

Warr, P.B. "Decision latitude, job demands and employee well-being," *Work & Stress,* 4, 285-294. [ISI], 1990.

Warren, Rick. *The Purpose Driven Life.* Grand Rapids, MI: Zondervan, 2002.

2699734

Made in the USA